Understanding

Social

Divisions

Understanding Social Divisions

Shaun Best

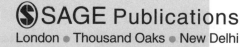

SAGE Publications
London • Thousand Oaks • New Delhi

First published 2005
Reprinted 2006

SAGE Publications Ltd
1 Oliver's Yard
55 City Road
London EC1Y 1SP

SAGE Publications Inc.
2455 Teller Road
Thousand Oaks, California 91320

SAGE Publications India Pvt Ltd
B-42, Panchsheel Enclave
Post Box 4109
New Delhi 110 017

British Library Cataloguing in Publication data

A catalogue record for this book is available
from the British Library

ISBN-10: 0-7619-4296-3   ISBN-13: 978-0-7619-4296-2
ISBN-10: 0-7619-4297-1 (pbk)   ISBN-13: 978-0-7619-4297-9 (pbk)

Library of Congress Control Number available

Typeset by C&M Digitals (P) Ltd., Chennai, India
Printed in Great Britain by The Cromwell Press Ltd, Trowbridge, Wiltshire

To Jane, Jessica and Jonny (again)

Contents

Introduction: Placing Myself in the Social Divisions

A boundary is not that at which something stops but, as the Greeks recognized, the boundary is that from which something begins its presencing.

Martin Heidegger, 'Building, Dwelling, Thinking' (1951)

Sociology is about the answer to one question: How is society possible? The question has been explored in a number of ways and from a number of competing perspectives. However, the question becomes doubly difficult when we take into account social division: How is society possible when that society is itself rife with boundaries, hostile groupings and any number of classifications and categories? This book is about attempting to understand and explain those social divisions.

Ideas about the nature of social division are used as resources in a process of self-definition that has come to be known as *subjectification*. One important element of social division is how individual people as agents within a social structure attempt to define themselves in relation to a range of powerful discourses. However, this concept of subjectification is not solely about self-definition; subjectification is only possible in relation to social division. For successful subjectification to take place, we need to create a category of the Other – a process that has become known as *alterity*. The social construction of alterity is directly related to both order and social division. The word 'alterity' is derived from the German word '*alter*' and means Otherness, in the sense of a systematised narrative for the construction of categories or social divisions rather than a distinction between the individual self and others based upon individual differences. In this process we institutionalise the cultural assumptions or prejudices that define who we are into our laws and customs. In other words, how 'I' came to define myself as part of 'We' and at the same time how this process of 'subjectification' allows us to view the Other not as part of 'We' but as part of a group of Others.

We also have to keep in mind that social division is not a static thing but reflects a dynamic set of processes; for example, over the last ten years or so there has been a great deal of interest in the notion of 'globalisation'. Both its critics and supporters assume that capitalism is the driving force behind a whole series of economic and cultural transformations. The impact of globalisation on social division has been less well investigated. Globalisation has demonstrated the arbitrary nature of social division. Globalisation has racialised our notions of citizenship and led us to question the validity of the nation state as a political entity; it has caused riots and 'ethnic cleansing' – all of this has been well explored.

Areas of social life such as gender divisions have also changed radically along with economic and cultural transformations. Second-wave feminists in the 1970s looked to the state to provide legal protection to women and to maintain their hard-won rights. The processes of globalisation have demonstrated, however, that nation states are arbitrary political groupings that appeal to blood and family as their basis. This appeal to blood and family can be seen in debates about citizenship and asylum across the globe. Nation states are highly traditional and patriarchal in nature and place the protection and control of women's sexuality at their core. The systematic detention and sexual abuse of women in Bosnia by the Serbian military during the Balkans conflict demonstrates the attempt to undermine a people's quest for nationhood by demonstrating its inability to protect its women. Many feminists would argue that global capitalism is a socially constructed process that relies upon conventional patriarchal meanings. Suzanne Bergeron has argued the case for a feminist discourse of globalisation: 'The only effective form of resistance to global capital is global sisterhood, which means shedding our no longer meaningful national and local identities in favour of global ones' (Bergeron 2001: 995).

We live in a world of meaning; we live in a world of communities. All of us have some link to a nation state, a class, a sexuality, a race, an ethnicity and any number of other categories. In addition, we define the 'totality' to which we belong: the nation state, the European Union, the global community; and whatever affinity we have towards that totality, there will be significant social divisions. Some social divisions are formal, often legally defined and policed, while others are informal and blurred. Why do we have such social divisions and why are they often so entrenched? One of the aims of the book is to explain how differences are constituted as relations of subordination.

What is the purpose of this project and why am I undertaking it? For a long time I assumed that social divisions apply to other people and not to me. After all, I am a white person, therefore I have no ethnicity; I am a heterosexual therefore I have no sexuality. In everyday life, and in much of our academic discourse, the 'person' as an abstract individual and as a generalised other that gazes upon us is assumed to be an able-bodied, adult, healthy, white, heterosexual male. 'Others' are excluded from being the abstract individual on the grounds that they are in some way less than human. Such 'others' must be divided, categorised and in some way examined and explained. We only accept the notion of a plurality of human beings and the differences between people when we accept that social division is morally and politically valid. In this book I want to undermine the notion of 'natural' and 'invisible' or 'non-problematic' categories of social division and demonstrate that all of us are involved in a process of social division. In other words, to borrow some terminology from Giddens, the process of social division is *instantiated* in people's life histories; social division is both a *medium* and an *outcome* of processes in which we all participate every day. We live in a world with social division because people like you and me invent, impose and regulate such divisions; people like you and me create the category of the Other – people whom we may fear, despise, patronise or criminalise. I want to identify the categorising processes that underpin social division.

The classification of people into groups on the basis of class, race and sexuality became markers of certainty; hence boundary crossing was seen as a violation of accepted social meaning, and in many cases would be classed as a 'crime'. This could be because individual people on one side of the division regard people on the other side as a batch of inferior people who are flawed because of a characteristic that they are perceived to share. Perceiving yourself to be on the right side of the division is the foundation for a legitimate claim for greater *resources*, in the widest possible sense of the term: income, wealth, housing, respect, dignity and status should all be included in our definition. The legitimate claim for resources involves distancing oneself from those whom we perceive to be inferior, but still keeping them in view. We are still part of the same society, but we regard ourselves as being superior within that society. This view need not manifest itself in terms of hostility, it can also take the form of offering help and assistance to those whom we perceive as less fortunate. The acceptance of such help is dependent upon the acceptance of inferior status. As a 12-year-old, my school friend Paul Dwyer came round to our house to play, it was the first time that Paul had been to my home. During his visit my mum gave him several pairs of my old trousers to try on for size. The trousers no longer fitted me, and Paul was of smaller stature. He accepted them politely and went home. The next day at school he was very cross with me: 'So do you think that I am a charity case?' he said several times with an increasingly angry tone.

We live in a world where there is a very wide range of resources. However, most people appear to assume that all resources are finite. Therefore, people have to bid for resources and this bidding process involves taking some aspect of yourself, a quality that you feel is something that others do not possess in great quantity, and using this as a foundation for making your claim. Many of us feel that we live in a bounded world in which there is a zero-sum conception of resource. If I gain some resource of status or prestige, then someone else must have lost some status.

Claims for resources are more effective if a person can make a division into the legitimate and illegitimate claimants. Legitimate claims for resources can be met by counter-claims that attempt to undermine the legitimacy of the initial claim. If I were to argue that black people or women were inferior and should not be awarded with promoted posts within the institution, this view would be met by a counter-claim that my view was not legitimate and was based upon racial hatred, sexism and bigotry. Moreover, it could be legitimately claimed that people who held such bigoted views should not be employed within the institution. This would undermine me as a racist and at the same time create the division between the bigoted and the unprejudiced, with the latter having the greater and more legitimate claim for resources.

The study of social divisions has dominated sociology since the creation of the discipline. Most of the early research work was about major issues of stratification: class, race, gender, and age although in more recent years issues such as sexuality, disability and exclusion have come to the fore. However, social divisions also exist on a micro-level and we experience a rich diversity of such divisions in our everyday lives which is less easy to describe and explain. It is interesting to think back to when you first became aware of social divisions. I can recall as a child explaining to my head teacher Sister Joseph that I could not join the choir at St Bridget's on a Sunday because I played football. Several hours after this conversation I was asked by my form teacher if I was a 'proper' Catholic. The teachers, like the children, made a distinction not only between Catholics and non-Catholics, but also between proper Catholics and non-proper Catholics. A week or so later my mum told me that she had been invited to the school by Sister Joseph and that I should leave the school on the grounds that I was not a proper Catholic, a view reinforced by the fact that my father was an Anglican, to which my mother replied that I was as much a Catholic as Sister Joseph was. When the other children found out that my dad was not a Catholic I was challenged on this issue: Rodney Eglin asked me if my dad was a pagan.

The background to my decision to decline the invitation to join the choir was on reflection an interesting one. I did play football and yes I would have missed it, but more importantly, by the age of ten I had recognised that my class was the lower stream of two general ability bands in the school. In addition, only people from the lower-stream classes were invited to join the St Bridget's choir. St Bridget's was a local girls' secondary modern school and mass was held there on Sunday morning in the school hall. Children from the higher stream were invited to join the choir in St Patrick's Church. The invitation given to me was viewed as a second-best alternative. In a similar fashion, when we had a school play, children from the higher stream were invited to give their performances to the public in the Church Hall, whereas children from the lower stream were invited to give their performances in the School Hall with no parents or members of the public present.

During my time at St Charles I also became aware of wider forms of stratification in relation to class, race and gender. Like all other Roman Catholic children educated in the late 1960s, I was invited to 'give some money to the black babies', in other words, to make a financial donation towards helping the plight of children in the underdeveloped world. I also remember a series of incidents in which a child, who from his appearance was not from a well-off family, was asked very aggressively in the class about why he had not paid his dinner money for several weeks. To every request for information he answered 'Yes Sister' in a polite manner. 'You say "yes Sister", but nothing happens, you are paying for meals that you had weeks ago.' I can also remember Mr Walsh in the last year before he retired giving Helena Ritker and myself the cane and explained to Helena that this was the first time he had had to give a girl the cane. I left St Charles with the idea that there are social divisions and that on the basis of these divisions, people are treated differently. I never saw Helena again and in the late 1970s she lost her life at the hands of the Yorkshire Ripper. I recall at the time questioning the distinction that the newspapers were making between the *innocent* victims and the prostitutes, such as Helena. There could have been no more innocent a victim than Helena.

It was not until I went to secondary school that these divisions were put into sharper focus. I had 'failed' my 11+ exam – although, strictly speaking, children did not pass or fail this exam, there were merely allocated to the most appropriate school on the basis of their aptitude and ability. On the basis of the test, I was sent to St Kevin's Roman Catholic secondary modern school because I was said to deal more easily with concrete objects than with abstract ideas. Secondary modern schools were seen by all as schools for failures and St Kevin's was no exception.

I recall on my first day at school, I was walking to catch the bus when Anthony Hines's mum came out to speak to me. She stood in front of me and looked at my school uniform from head to foot. She rubbed the label of my blazer between her index finger and thumb and said that I looked very smart 'as if you're going to a proper school'. This comment made me feel like Scarlet O'Hara throwing the carrot to the ground that she had just pulled from the earth, with the words 'As God is my witness, I'll never be hungry again' or perhaps Arnold Schwarzenegger in a range of films: 'I'll be back'. Over the coming years I was to hear accounts of how Anthony wanted to be a doctor, how he was going to have a successful career. My mum reinforced my feeling of failure by finding examples of people who had been to grammar school and had been unsuccessful in the labour market.

The memory of my first day at St Kevin's has stayed with me to this day. I recollect the feeling of seeing some 500 children together and thinking how we were 500 failures together. During the first two weeks at the school, the new intake of pupils were given a number of tests in various subjects, the results of which were to be used as the basis for streaming the children into two general ability bands. These were named E classes and T classes. The E classes were people who were going to be eventually allowed to enter for CSE exams, whilst T class children were expected to leave school at the earliest opportunity without attempting public examinations. At the end of the year, children would take informal class exams and students would be ranked against all the other children in their class. It is interesting to reflect for one moment on what the self-respect of a person who came bottom in one of the T classes would be like; a person who came bottom of the class in the lowest ability band for the school for failures.

I lost my friends from primary school and made new ones at St Kevin's. I also made new friends outside of school, one being Shaun Wilson, whom I met through the football team that I played for on Sundays. One day, very much out of the blue, Shaun said to me that although he was my friend, this did not mean that he wanted to go to my school. The words may have come out of his mouth, but it was his mum's voice that I could hear, she was the author of this message. When I later went on to a different school to do my A levels, a young girl who lived on the opposite side of the road to Shaun spoke to me at school. I very much got the impression that Shaun's mum was checking to see if the account of my doing A levels was correct. I enjoyed my time at Corpus Christi studying Sociology, Economics and Social and Economic History, although I was always conscious of the fact that I was an outsider, a person who had joined the sixth form from another school rather than a person who had graduated from Corpus Christi. I was successful at A level and went on to University to read Sociology and Politics. Anthony Hines found A level work much more demanding, and at one point it looked as if I would graduate from University before Anthony had completed his resit A level course. I fantasised about applying for a teaching job at Park Lane College where Anthony was retaking, amongst other subjects, A level Sociology. What pleasure I would have got teaching Anthony, marking his homework and discussing his progress with his parents. Sadly, this did not happen.

My personal account demonstrates that from an early age we are all introduced to a range of social divisions. I am sure that you, the reader, could have outlined a similar set. What is significant is the way in which they were presented as both neutral and natural. In summary, as a child I was introduced to a number of social divisions: males and females; Catholics and Pagans; the educationally successful and the educational failures; the Irish and the English; home owners and council tenants.

Social Divisions

What is the nature of social division? What are social divisions and where do they come from? Chapter 1 will provide an outline and evaluation of the theories and research into the ways in which people have been classified into different types over a long historical period. A starting point for the discussion will be sociological in nature, for example, Foucault on classification and dividing practices; Bauman on the gardening state.

In *The Order of Things*, Foucault identifies the arbitrary nature of systems of classification that users may believe to be both valid and 'natural'. He opens the book with an example from a Chinese encyclopaedia which divides animals into the following categories:

> (a) belonging to the Emperor, (b) embalmed, (c) tame, (d) suckling pigs, (e) sirens, (f) fabulous, (g) stray dogs, (h) included in the present classification, (i) frenzied, (j) innumerable, (k) drawn with a very fine camelhair brush, (l) *et cetera* (m) having just broken the water pitcher, (n) that from a long way off look like flies. (Foucault 1970: xv)

For Foucault, phases of history are organised around their own distinct *episteme* or set of organising principles, which enable us to categorise whatever we come into contact with. Epistemes generate 'orders of discourse' or 'discursive formations' which inform us how we should construct our view of the world. *Discourse* is a system of representation that regulates meaning so that certain ways of thinking, speaking and behaving become 'natural'. Discourse is made up of statements, and one of the central purposes of the discourse is to establish relationships between statements so that we can make sense of what is being said to us. From the initial analysis of classification, in his later books Foucault develops his *genealogical analysis* to examine the history of how groups of ideas come to be associated with normal sexuality. One of the central themes of Foucault's work is how discursive power works on bodies and this is seen most clearly in his *The History of Sexuality* (1978). In this way discursive formations allow us to allocate people within a network of categories: in other words, to describe people as 'types': hetro/homo, etc. In his discussion of discipline in *Discipline and Punish*, Foucault described the spreading notion of what constituted 'normal' through society as the 'carceral continuum'. All of us become self-regulated subjects, written on by institutions such as the family, educational institutions and employers.

Foucault's work is important in understanding how certain aspects of sexuality have become 'normal'. Indeed, his work has a significant impact on understanding and politicising such diverse issues as: the nature of 'the closet'; why sexual intercourse is equated with closeness and intimacy; and why the attainment of orgasm-via-penetration is regarded as the aim and measure of successful sex.

However, we can also draw upon a range of social, psychological, political and medical research into the nature of stigma and its role in defining people as insiders or outsiders. The approach will be along the lines of: Who introduced us to the 'generalised Other' and why does it have such an influence upon us? Who provided 'the looking glass' and why might we be alarmed by what we see? The point of reference from this range of disciplines will be how they theorise the categories that are used to divide people, what the origins of such categories are, and how these categories are maintained, in relation to such divisions as:

- The affluent and the poor
- The citizen and the non-citizen

- The feminine and the masculine
- The gay and the straight
- The migrants and the hosts
- The globals and the locals
- The beautiful and the ugly
- The obese and the anorexic
- The criminal and the law-abiding
- The diseased and the healthy
- The insane and the sane
- The religious and the secular
- The logoed and the non-logoed
- The young and the old
- The celebrity and the unknown
- The perverse and the well-behaved
- The fundamentalist and the moderate
- The terrorist and the terrorised
- The educated and the ignorant
- The urban and the rural
- The intoxicated and the abstemious.

Social divisions are sets of categories. Social categories are not simply given, they have to be established and maintained and the process through which they appear is known as *social division*. However, as Anne McClintock (1995) argues, such categories are not separate areas of experience for people, rather each category comes into existence in and through relations with other categories. McClintock describes class, race and gender as 'articulated categories'; in other words, they are categories that are not reducible to, or identical with other categories but exist in mutual and at the same time opposing relations. She gives the following example:

> Islamic fundamentalism continues to legitimise woman's barred access to the corridors of political and economic power, the persistent educational disadvantage, the domestic double workday, unequal childcare, gendered malnutrition, sexual violence, genital mutilation and domestic battery. (McClintock 1995: 14)

'Scarcity' is an issue between all individuals and within all social groups. Individual people have to draw upon the belief that such categories are both right and just in an effort to successfully take resources that might otherwise be directed elsewhere. In addition, resource allocation on an equal basis is difficult to achieve even under socialism, where it was one of the primary aims of the social formation. People differ in many ways; many differences take on a *relational form* where we differentiate ourselves from others who are thought to share a common feature that makes them superior or inferior. Differences of this kind are social divisions and they share a number of common features:

- They are found in all social, historical and cultural settings
- They are significant for the lives of individuals
- They can be institutionalised and well established by legal codes
- They are often connected with inequality and injustice
- They are connected with processes of social change
- They can be material, cultural and social in nature, but form the basis for the allocation of *resource* in its widest sense of the term, including the scarce resources of prestige, admiration and respect.

ACTIVITY

Read the quote below from Anne McClintock (1995) and answer the questions beneath.

No social category exists in privileged isolation, each comes into being in social relation to other categories, if in uneven and contradictory ways. (McClintock 1995: 9)

Questions:

➢ Do you accept or reject McClintock's premise? Give the reasons for your answer.

➢ Is one social division – be it class, race, gender, disability or whatever – more important than the others?

Individual people have a need for resources in order to survive; such resources include food, clothing and shelter. In order to get such resources, individual people have to make a legitimate claim to them. In addition, the greater the amount of resource acquired, the greater the level of comfort, security or whatever you desire the most, which could be anything: more living space, a better car, exotic food, designer clothes – the choice is yours. We live in a world where claims for resources are successfully made by positioning oneself in the most advantageous places in the marketplace for resources. Convincing oneself and others that you deserve more of the available resource because your claim is greater is the most effective tool for gaining additional advantage. Such claims include arguments such as:

- 'I deserve more pay because I have greater skill.'
- 'I deserve more pay because I have better qualifications.'
- 'I deserve more pay because I have greater commitment to the job.'
- 'I deserve more pay because I work longer hours.'
- 'I deserve more pay because other people I work with are lazy.'

In addition, it is possible to substitute any desired resource for the word 'pay' and similar arguments can be used, for example: 'I deserve more respect because I have greater skill'; 'I deserve longer holidays because I have greater skill'; 'I deserve more opportunities for promotion because I have greater skill.'

There is an interface between our need for physical survival and the social world, with its marketplace for resources. Moreover, even though we may be lucky enough to feel secure for the moment, we can never stop questioning whether *all* of our material and emotional needs are being met and will continue to be met. Marketplaces are dominated by feelings of scarcity, choice and competition. The positions that we occupy in the social world are constantly in need of additional resourcing.

The nature of our *needs* is difficult to understand, even thought we all experience needs, wants and desires. However, in the marketplace of scarcity and choice, making legitimate claims for resource involves not only advancing oneself through a process of cultural promotion, but also identifying differences between other people, placing people into categories, and attempting to claim legitimately that individuals who inhabit such categories have less of a legitimate claim for the scarce resource. Such categories are always arbitrary, but if successfully used as a basis for legitimately denying a resource, they gain acceptance on the basis of convention. Over the centuries, race, gender, class, age, religion, nationality, language, body weight, disability, hair loss, language, accent, taste, sexual preference, sexuality, style of dress, and any number of arbitrary classifications have been used legitimately to deny individuals access to scarce resources. This is a case not only of having self-worth or of showing oneself off in the best possible light, but of making competing choices that attempt to set parameters of social differentiation, to satisfy one's own need for prestige, and to undermine the prestige of others by making them feel that they have made an inferior choice.

There is a peer group or social category group form of socialisation into the correct preferences that can be used as a resource for the narcissistic cohesion of a category. People exclude others by developing the ability to relate themselves to self-selected desirable objects and claiming that others are not worthy of holding such objects. It is for this reason that advertising is much more than the personal appeal to an individual to 'Consume this, it is nice'. Advertising always moves beyond the personal to appeal to a category and say 'This product is for people like you and can be used to demonstrate your obvious superiority over the Other.' For successful subjectification to take place, we need to successfully create a category of the Other – the process of social division.

References

Bergeron, Suzanne (2001) 'Political Economy Discourses of Globalization and Feminist Politics', *Signs: Journal of Women in Culture and Society*, 26(4): 983–1006.

Carling, Alan (1991) *Social Division*, Verso, London.

Foucault, Michel (1970) *The Order of Things*, trans. A. Sheridan, Tavistock, London and Pantheon, New York. First published in French as *Les mots et les choses* in 1966.

Foucault, Michel (1977) *Discipline and Punish*, trans. A. Sheridan, Tavistock, London and Pantheon, New York. First published in French as *Surveiller et punir* in 1975.

Foucault, Michel (1978) *The History of Sexuality*, trans. R. Hurley, Pantheon, New York. First published in French as *La volonté de savoir* in 1976.

McClintock, Anne (1995) *Imperial Leather. Race, Gender and Sexuality in the Colonial Context*, Routledge, London.

One

Chapter Outline

By the end of this chapter you should have a critical understanding of the major contributions to class analysis including:

- The Marxian analysis of class

- The Weberian analysis: class, status and party

- Nietzsche on the *will to power* and the *will to truth*

- The functionalists conception of class: Talcott Parsons; Davis and Moore

- The rise of meritocracy: Michael Young, Peter Saunders

- The rise of the underclass and the *culture of poverty*: Oscar Lewis, Charles Murray and Loic Wacquant

- Harry Braverman's *Labour Process Theory*

- Class structuration: Anthony Giddens

- Later Marxists on class: John Roemer; Erik Olin Wright; Guglielmo Carchedi; Nicos Poulantzas

- The Regulation School: Michel Aglietta, Bob Jessop, Alain Lipietz

- The neo-Gramscian turn in class analysis: Stuart Hall, Ernesto Laclau and Chantal Mouffe

- The linguistic turn in class analysis: Patrick Joyce, William Sewell Jr and Richard Price

- Postmodernity and social frameworks: Malcolm Waters, David Ashley and Daniel Bell

- The move away from Marxian orthodoxy: Jean Baudrillard and Fredrick Jameson

- Zygmunt Bauman and the concept of stratification.

Class Division

Introduction

All societies appear to have some form of inequality between people in terms of income, wealth and prestige. Inequality may be real, but class analysis is a set of concepts. One cannot point to inequality in the world and assume that this is a sufficient justification for accepting class analysis. *Class analysis* is a range of possible explanations for these persistent inequalities. In addition, explanations for the persistence of such inequalities change over time. In the nineteenth century Marx argued that ownership/non-ownership of the means of production was the central element in class division. In Marx's abstract model of class – the model found in his most influential book *Capital* (1867) – differences in income and status were essentially irrelevant. Conversely, for most of the twentieth century, inequality in income and wealth was synonymous with class analysis. Sociological explanations of class took their starting point from either Marx or Weber, and both approaches shared the assumption that classes were real and had a significant impact on people's life chances. Nevertheless, even in the early twentieth century, some theorists challenged the assumption that inequality was synonymous with class analysis: elite theorists, for example, attempted to explain inequality without reference to class. In the latter years of the twentieth century, class became increasingly irrelevant in academic analysis with concepts such as *cultural identity* – particularly in relation to gender, race, disability and sexuality, all of which will be fully explained in later chapters – having a more significant impact upon our chosen styles of living.

In this chapter the main forms of class analysis will be outlined and evaluated. The emphasis will be on the *processes of class formation*. In other words, the central questions will be:

- What is class?
- What are the factors that bring about the process of social division for each of the class theorists?

Marx on Class

The Marxian analysis revolves around the concept of class and Marx's great insight was to see the exploitation of the working class by the factory owners as the determining factor in social division. In the Marxist analysis of class, the forces and relations of production are the determining factors to bring about social change. Although Marx paid little attention to formal definitions of class boundaries, from the Marxian perspective if a group owns the means of production, they wield not only economic power but also political power. People's behaviour is determined by the class grouping in which they find themselves. In other words, class membership mediates people's agency; furthermore our ability to make perceptions of the world and act on the basis of those perceptions is class determined.

According to Marxian analysis, the state is viewed as an institution that helps to organise capitalist society in the best interests of the bourgeoisie. The legitimacy of the capitalist system is maintained by ideology; working-class people are victims of a *false consciousness*. In other words, working-class people are said to hold values, ideas and beliefs about the nature of inequality that are not in their own economic interests to hold. Working-class people have their ideas manipulated, by the media, schools and religion for example, and regard economic inequality as fair and just.

MARX AND CLASS DIVISIONS

In the nineteenth century Marx singled out class divisions as the engine of history. In particular he drew a sharp distinction between:

- **The bourgeoisie:** the class that owned the factories, shops and offices (i.e. the *means of production*) and
- **The proletariat:** the class of people who did not own the means of production, but who provided the labour.

In the Marxian analysis, the bourgeoisie exploit the proletariat by not paying them the full value of their labour power.

In *Capital*, Marx outlines his *abstract* model of class, which is essentially a two-class model. There are other classes in capitalist society but they are disappearing and in any case are largely irrelevant to the essential dynamic of capitalist society. The key distinction is ownership/non-ownership of the means of production; for Marx, it is this division that separates the classes. The bourgeoisie own the means of production (factories, shops and offices) and the proletariat do not own the means of production. The relationship between the bourgeoisie and the proletariat is an exploitative one; the bourgeoisie exploit the proletariat.

The exploitative relationship between the bourgeoisie and the proletariat is explained by the Labour Theory of Value, which Marx derived from David Ricardo. Marx begins *Capital* with a discussion of the commodity. A commodity is anything that is manufactured, has a value and can be sold. There are two forms of value for Marx, firstly there is *use value*, which reflects the intrinsic value or personal value that a person gets from having or consuming a commodity. Marx has little interest in the value, desire or pleasure that you or I can enjoy from consumption. Marx is interested in the second type of value, which he terms *exchange value*, or the value in monetary terms that a commodity can fetch in the marketplace. For Marx, the exchange value of a commodity reflects the amount of labour power that went into the production of a commodity.

What is labour power? Each worker has muscles, limbs and brains that they can use to make things. In other words, each person carries with them a potential stock or fund of labour – each person has a potential capacity to make products. Although each person has different skills, abilities and levels of intelligence, Marx argues that such differences can be subsumed under the abstract concept of a unit of labour power. It is the number of such abstract units present within a commodity that determines its exchange value. However, Marx argues that labour power is also a commodity, and the value of labour power reflects the amount of labour power that went into the reproduction of labour power itself.

Marx argues that workers have to be paid enough to feed themselves and clothe themselves and also be paid a little bit extra to produce, clothe and feed the next generation of workers. In other words, workers have to be paid enough to reproduce their own labour power. In terms of the length of the working day, Marx argues that the first part of the working day is *socially necessary labour time*, in which the workers are paid the full value of their labour power. However, any time that the workers work beyond socially necessary labour time is what Marx terms *surplus value labour time* in which the worker is not paid for the value of their labour power, but rather is creating surplus value for the bourgeoisie. People working for the bourgeoisie after they have completed socially necessary labour time is what Marx regards as *exploitation*. In addition, there is pressure on the bourgeoisie to extend surplus value labour time and pay workers only enough to reproduce their own labour power and little else. It is only by the bourgeoisie behaving in this exploitative manner that the profitability of individual capitalistic enterprises can be maintained. Hence Marx argues that workers will go through a period of getting poorer (*Verelendung*), a process of *immiserisation*.

MARX AND THE MODE OF PRODUCTION

Marx viewed society as a *mode of production*, and history is the change from one mode of production to the next. Initially people lived in a form of society that he termed *Primitive Communism*: a mode of production in which there was no private ownership, no class system, no family and no incest taboo. With the development of private ownership came institutions, such as the state and the family, which play a central role in modern capitalism.

The mode of production is made up of two parts: firstly the *economic base*, which contains the *forces of production* and the *relations of production*. The forces of production are all the things that we need to produce commodities such as raw materials and technology. The relations of production are the class relations; in capitalism this would be the relationship between the bourgeoisie and the proletariat.

Secondly, above the economic base there is the *superstructure*, this is the realm of culture, politics, ideas and ideology. In the Marxian analysis, the economic base determines culture and ideas within a society.

ACTIVITY

The Labour Theory of Value has come under some considerable critique, as Savage (2000) suggests:

A herb, for instance, which is found to be the cure for an illness may suddenly increase in exchange value despite the fact that no more labour is embodied in producing it (picking or growing it) than before. One Marxist response is to recognise the 'transformation problem' which emphasizes the distinction between price and value, and accepts that the price (though not the value) may change according to contingencies such as these. However, in this case the point of distinguishing the 'value' of a product becomes unclear. (Savage 2000: 11)

Questions:

➢ In your own words explain the critical point that Savage is making about the Labour Theory of Value.

➢ What do you understand by the 'transformation problem'?

In summary, for Marx, the human being is the sole source of value in production. The ratio of constant capital to variable capital is known by Marxists as the *organic composition of capital*. If less labour is employed, or more constant capital is employed in the production process, the organic composition of capital is said to rise. Marx argued that this rising organic composition will cause the rate of profit to fall over time. However, a central problem is the *transformation problem*. The transformation problem is concerned with how to transform labour values into the system of prices.

In the Marxian analysis, the formation of the working class is a process of proletarianisation. Working-class people have lost both the ownership and control of the means of production and have become a homogeneous group of wage-earners. The driving force behind this process of proletarianisation is 'material' in nature, as Marx made clear in his Preface to 'A Contribution to the Critique of Political Economy':

> In the social production of their life, men enter into definite relations that are indispensable and independent of their will, *relations of production* which correspond to a definite stage of development of their material productive *forces*. The sum total of these relations of production constitutes the economic structure of society, the real foundation, on which rises a legal and political superstructure and to which correspond definite forms of social consciousness. The mode of material life conditions the social, political and intellectual life in general. It is not the consciousness of men that determines their being, but on the contrary, their social being that determines their consciousness. (Marx 1968: 182)

ACTIVITY

Rewrite the above quote from Marx in your own words. Return to this activity after you have finished reading the chapter and ask yourself if you agree or disagree with the points that Marx is making. Give some reasons for your answer.

Max Weber on Class

For Weber, society is stratified in three distinct ways on the bases of: class, status groups and parties. However, all three of these forms of stratification are concerned with the distribution of power within a community. At its core, the Weberian analysis comprises:

- **Class:** concerned with stratification of the economic order
- **Status:** concerned with stratification of the social order
- **Party:** concerned with stratification of the political order.

A social class is made up of all the people who share the same market-class position in terms of common economic interests, a similar degree of control over consumer goods, assets and resources, and a similar level of marketable skill. Later Weberians have identified two components of the class position:

- **Market situation:** which reflects the amount of money a person receives
- **Work situation:** which reflects the conditions of service that a person enjoys.

From a Weberian perspective, classes then are formed in the marketplace according to the laws of demand and supply. If a person has marketable skills that are high in demand and in relatively short supply, then that person will be in a high social class position. In contrast, if a person has few marketable skills and/or there is little demand for those skills, then that person will be in a low social class position. A person's class situation reflects their ability to buy goods, gain a position in life and 'find inner satisfaction' (Weber 1978: 302). Weber discusses class relations under three headings:

- **The property class:** which reflects the amount of property that a person holds
- **The commercial class:** which reflects the marketability of goods and services
- **The social class:** which reflects the broad range of class situations.

WEBER AND CLASS SITUATION

The basis of class, Weber argues, is found in social action – any action that has an intention behind it. What is class situation? According to Weber, it is possible to speak of class in the following instances:

- When a number of people have in common a specific economic component of their life chances
- When economic interests have a central role to play in the possession of goods and opportunities for income
- When individuals can be linked in terms of the price that they can command for their skills within the labour market.

Ownership of property is one of the basic factors that Weber identified as giving certain individuals a distinct advantage in furthering their life chances. Weber uses the term *property* to cover a wide range of assets: 'ownership of mines, cattle, men (slaves), disposition over mobile instruments of production, or capital goods ... money' (ibid.: 928). Power over property in the market, therefore, is one of the key factors in the process of class formation for Weber. However, Weber is very keen to explain that classes are not groups created by their own internal dynamic. He argues that class situation is not created by people within the same class interacting with one another. More accurately, in the case of the entrepreneurs and the working class, class situation comes about because of the actions of people in different classes, for example, entrepreneurs' actions in areas such as the labour market, the commodities market and in the protection of their capitalist enterprises. The middle class, who may have little or no property from which they can derive an income, are differentiated by Weber on the basis of the skills that they possess; such skills form the basis of their market situation.

The Weberian class structure is economically determined and the classes are divided along the following lines:

- **The 'positively privileged' property classes:** these are the *rentiers* who derive their income from ownership of: men (in the case of slave owners); land; mines; factories and capital equipment; ships; creditors (of livestock, grain or money); securities
- **The 'positively privileged' commercial classes:** this group is made up of entrepreneurs, merchants, shipowners, industrial entrepreneurs, agricultural entrepreneurs, bankers, financiers and some top professionals with a high level of expertise, such as lawyers and doctors
- **The middle classes:** some middle-class people make a living from property, some may be small entrepreneurs, but often their income is derived from their acquired skills. This group comprises: self-employed farmers; self-employed craftsmen; public and private officials; the working class; the petty bourgeoisie; the non-propertied intelligentsia (including a range of white-collar occupations, technicians and civil servants with few qualifications and/or marketable skills)
- **The 'negatively privileged':** this comprises labourers; the 'unfree'; the declassed; debtors; and paupers.

The 'positively privileged' are involved in a process of wealth accumulation out of unconsumed surpluses and capital formation out of savings. They control loan capital and are the people who hold top executive positions in business. Finally, they are the people who consume most of the high-priced goods.

For Weber then, there are lots of different classes, and even quite small changes in market situation bring about changes in supply and demand for goods or services, which is enough to effect mobility from one class to another. This has raised the issue of the *boundary problem* in relation to Weberian conceptions of class: Where does one class begin and another class end? If income is used as the indicator of class division, then class barriers do not represent any real or significant division between one class and another.

Status

Status is the social estimation of honour and is not reducible to class and party. Status is about distance and exclusiveness in terms of our chosen lifestyle and the circle of people with whom we choose to associate. Status can be difficult to measure, but it is related to submission to fashion. Moreover status has the ability, when used effectively, to be a significant tool of social exclusion and may restrict our interaction with others. Status is associated with our sense of belonging, as Weber explains in a discussion of distinguished families. The First Families of Virginia or the descendants of Pocahontas, the Pilgrim Fathers or the Knickerbockers all derived a sense of dignity and excellence from belonging to 'society'. Our choice of marriage partner is status related, argues Weber. But what is the basis of status formation for Weber? He explains that status formation is: 'purely conventional and rests largely on usurpation' (Weber 1978: 933). The class structure may be economically determined, but status order is not. In fact, Weber claims that the workings of the economy are often hindered by the status groups in terms of people being made to feel uncomfortable by the worst excesses of conspicuous consumption. Weber defines status in the following terms: 'every typical component of the life of men that is determined by specific, positive or negative social estimation of *honor*' (ibid.: 932, italics in original).

Weber is interested in the relationship between race and status. He argues that 'poor white trash' in the Southern United States were always much keener on maintaining the racial division between themselves and the black American population than were the white plantation owners. This form of ethnic segregation was viewed by Weber as a status distinction which takes the form of a 'closed caste', guaranteed by conventions, laws and religious sanction; a form of stigma which draws upon ideas of ritualistic impurity. Social relationships between such status groups are restricted to the degree that Weber describes the situation as a 'diaspora strictly segregated' (ibid.: 934).

Rosemary Crompton (1993) has argued that Weber used the concept of status in three distinct ways:

- **Prestige grouping or consciousness community:** a group who share a common culture to exclude others; Crompton gives the example of the British ruling class forming networks around private clubs, the season and the tour. In this sense, status has an important role to play in class formation
- **Lifestyle or social standing:** here status refers to the formation of cultural practices that exclude others who do not share the right forms of dress, speech, and view of the world
- **Non-market-based claims to material entitlements or life chances:** these are groupings often made up of people who share the same professional occupation, such as doctors, who for the benefit of the community do not exploit their market advantage to the full.

As we can see, status and class are very closely linked. As a result of their privileged economic standing, some individuals are in a position to draw upon cultural resources that not only give them a social estimation of honour within a community, but also allow them – through shared accent, forms of dress, etc. – to participate in networks of social connections that exclude others from having the same life chances.

Party

For Weber, the people who hold political power do not necessarily hold economic power or have high status. Parties themselves, claims Weber, have an associational character, a rational order and a staff. The aim of the party is to win power. However, the routes to power are many and varied, from the naked use of violence to canvassing the voter by force of argument, truth claims, lies and deception. Even if a party cannot gain a monopoly of power within the structure of domination, the aim of the party is that of influence. For Weber, coercion was regarded as a non-legitimate use of power, in contrast to the three forms of legitimate rule which he outlines in his political sociology. Weber's discussion of party as form of stratification has an element of Nietzsche about it.

Friedrich Nietzsche attempted to undermine the foundations of truth, morality, science, identity and religion. Truth, in Nietzsche's view, was nothing more than a mobile host of metaphors and illusions, and in the last analysis the 'will to truth' is a manifestation of 'the will to power'. In other words, for Nietzsche, truth like everything else is a function of power. Nietzsche's 'project' was the transvaluation of all values, in which the *will to truth* would be seen for what it is, the social theorists attempting to impose their will or prejudices upon others, whilst presenting their ideas as truth. Above all, Nietzsche argued that all people attempted to impose their thoughts, ideas and morality on others, by all possible means including danger, pain, lies and deception, which he termed the *will to power*. When people say morals are necessary, what they mean is 'I don't like how you are behaving'. Hence for Nietzsche the police are always necessary to impose morality.

In *Beyond Good and Evil* (1886), Nietzsche makes a distinction between *master morality* and *servant morality*, and argues that the traditional ideals of Christian morality are based upon self-deception, as they were built upon the will to power. The concept of the slave morality was taken up by Nietzsche in his later works such as *The Antichrist, Curse on Christianity* (1888), where he argues that Christianity is a religion for weak and unhealthy people and that its central ideas, such as compassion for the less fortunate, have undermined Western culture in that people are made to feel guilty for attempting to fulfil their desires and that this undermines their happiness.

In *Thus Spake Zarathustra* (1883–85), Zarathustra informs the people that God is dead and that with an understanding of the eternal return, we need no longer be seduced by notions of good and evil or threats of hell and hopes of paradise. Moreover, because we have no soul that survives the death of the body, and no recollection of living our lives over and over again, escape is impossible. However, the concept of the eternal return is Zarathustra's gift to human kind. Armed with the knowledge of the eternal return, it is possible for a person to become an *Übermensch* (literally 'overman', or superman including people such as Caesar, Napoleon, Goethe, Dostoevski and Thucydides) and become involved in a process of self-overcoming. In this way people may liberate themselves from the arbitrary constraints of truth and morality imposed upon them, and become whatever they desire, and thereby achieve personal satisfaction. For Nietzsche, you are what you do. In other words, the person is constituted by practice, hence there is no 'being' behind doing, effecting, becoming; 'the doer' is merely a fiction added to the deed – the deed is everything. The *Übermensch* is a person with qualities beyond those of an ordinary person. As described by Nietzsche, the *Übermensch* was a self-created person who was emotionally 'tougher' than most people, because of having created a personality drawn from many contradictory dimensions.

WEBER'S THREE IDEAL TYPES OF LEGITIMATE RULE

- **Charismatic authority:** Weber is interested here in how a political system can be upheld by the strength of a leader's character. Often charismatic leaders are believed to have almost supernatural qualities
- **Traditional authority:** this is a political system that is upheld by continual reference to customs and traditions
- **Rational legal authority:** this is a political system that is regarded as legitimate in the eyes of the population because it is thought to be 'legal' and built upon rational processes; the ideal type discussed by Weber is the bureaucracy.

In his political sociology, Weber appeared to have some sympathy with the classical elite theories who rejected democracy and assumed that in any political system a few will lead the majority. In other words, there will always be a small, self-conscious elite with power and a large mass that has very little power.

All societies generally have a social structure, where oligarchy (the rule of the few) is inescapable. In addition, most classical elite theorists assume that the masses are psychologically inadequate and therefore unable to hold power. In addition, the masses also have an instinctual need to be dominated. Only the elite can satisfy that need; Robert Michels, who was a graduate student of Weber's, termed this 'The Iron Law of Oligarchy'.

Summary – Marx and Weber

Before we move on to examine the work of theorists and researchers who have been influenced by the work of Marx and Weber, let us take stock of the argument so far. The foundation of class analysis is found in the work of Marx and Weber. In the nineteenth century, Marx singled out class divisions as the motor of history – the factor that pushed history forwards. In particular he identified:

- **The bourgeoisie:** the class that owns the factories, shops and offices
- **The proletariat:** the class of people who do not own the factories, shops and offices.

In the Marxian analysis, the bourgeoisie exploit the proletariat by not paying them the full value of their labour power. Working-class people have their ideas manipulated, by the media, schools and religion, for example, and regard economic inequality as fair and just. Marxists refer to this manipulation of the ideas of the working class as ideological – working-class people are said to be victims of a false consciousness.

Marx also recognised the inventiveness that flourished under capitalism: the railway, the electric telegraph, the application of chemistry to both industry and agriculture, and steam navigation were all discussed by Marx in positive terms. It was upon this premise that Marx developed the Labour Theory of Value. In addition, for Marx, individual people are essentially creative beings: making things is the key element of our *species being*, Marx argued.

In contrast to Marx, at the turn of the twentieth century a sociologist named Max Weber argued for an alternative view of class. For Weber, a social class is a group of people who share the same class (market) position. According to Weber, in addition to the bourgeoisie, the people who own large amounts of land – whom he named the *rentier class* – also had significant power. Outside of these groups, class was determined by:

- **Market situation:** people in the same class earn a similar amount of money
- **Work situation:** people in the same class have similar conditions of service at work.

If a skill is in short supply, if only a few people have a particular ability and there is a big demand for that skill or ability, then such people will be in a position to demand high financial rewards. In a similar fashion, if people have few skills, or skills that are easily acquired, then such people are not in a position to demand high financial rewards. However, for Weber, social class is only one aspect of a person's *stratification position*: other aspects of how people are divided into strata are:

- **Status:** which Weber defined as the social estimation of honour
- **Party:** which Weber believed determined the amount of political power that a person or group enjoys.

Weber argued that status was independent of both social class and party. In other words, a person may have a high social class position but this does not guarantee that they will have a high status position. Similarly, a person may have low social class position but high status. Moreover, in contrast to Marx, the people who hold political power can come from any social class and may or may not have a high status.

Talcott Parsons on Stratification and Class

Talcott Parsons was a functionalist and he argued that there are two essential reference points for his analysis of stratification within any social system:

- The role of stratification in terms of the functional requirements of a social system
- The place of stratification inside the cybernetic hierarchy within a social system – in other words, an analysis of the processes of control within the social system.

In his 1940 paper 'An Analytical Approach to the Theory of Social Stratification', Parsons appears to collapse the three Weberian categories of class, status and party into one grouping which he refers to as *social stratification* – the differential ranking of individuals and their treatment as superior and inferior relative to one another in 'value' terms. As with Weber, Parsons views stratification as rooted in social action, that is, individuals apply a moral evaluation to others as moral units worthy of 'respect' or 'indignation'. Moreover, although the standards and criteria for ranking individuals may differ from one social system to the next, stratification is always a central element of any social system because of its focus on the 'structuralization of action' (Parsons [1940] 1996: 125). Parsons believed stratification to be important because it is built from ideas of moral worth into a tangible and durable structure of reward which is material in nature. Stratification for Parsons is both functional and inevitable in all social systems. Individual social actors use the value system as an action frame of reference, as a resource that they can draw upon to provide a justification for legitimately ranking others as superior or inferior and rewarding them with both status and income accordingly. For Parsons, this ordering of relationships on the basis of social stratification is important to the integration of the social system and is necessary for providing stability.

Parsons: The Active Frame of Reference:

Read the passage below and write a short paragraph in which you explain what Parsons understood by the action frame of reference and what the relationship between the action frame of reference and the system of social stratification is.

For Talcott Parsons there are two essential reference points for his analysis of social systems:

1 The categorising of functional requirements of a social system.
2 The categorising of the cybernetic hierarchy within a social system – in other words, an analysis of the processes of control within the social system.

The starting point for this analysis is the action frame of reference; the social actions and interactions of individual people that make up the social system. Parsons argued that action is not simply an ad hoc reply or response to a stimulus. Individual people develop a strategy of responses based upon a range of possible expectations about a given situation. This range of expectations is often based upon the needs of the person and a prediction of the possible gains and losses to the person from various responses to action. This form of interaction is possible because there is a system of shared cultural symbols which are understood within a community. Parsons's definition of a social system then is thus:

> [A] social system consists in a plurality of individual actors interacting with each other in a situation which has at least a physical or environmental aspect, actors who are motivated in terms of a tendency to the 'optimization of gratification' and whose relation to their situations, including each other is defined and mediated in terms of a system of culturally structured and shared symbols.' (Parsons 1951: 6)

For a fuller account of Talcott Parsons and the functionalist analysis see Best (2003: 16–45).

Parsons identifies six bases of differential valuation:

1 **Membership of a kinship group:** family members share the same status and position in the hierarchy, which is beyond the status achieved through a person's occupation.
2 **Personal qualities:** qualities such as sex, age, personal beauty, intelligence, strength or any other quality that is not based upon 'personal effort'.
3 **Achievements:** Parsons defines achievements as the 'valued results of the actions of individuals' (Parsons [1940] 1996: 129). The greater the contribution that a person makes to an organisation, the greater their status valuation should be.

4 **Possessions:** these need not be material objects, they can also include non-material things. What is important is that the possession is seen to belong to an individual and is valued by others.
5 **Authority:** the institutional right to influence others becomes a source of differentiation. Authority over a person means superiority over that person.
6 **Power:** people who have the ability to influence others and acquire possessions without the support of any institutional sanction; without claiming the right to do so from an organisational institution.

Parsons explains the significance of these bases for valuation as follows: 'The status of any given individual in the system of stratification in a society may be regarded as a resultant of the common valuation underlying the attribution of status to him in each of these six respects' (Parsons [1940] 1996: 130).

Status can then be *ascribed* – a form of caste-like system in which a person's rank is fixed at birth (e.g. the status of children within the family) or *achieved* – where status is determined on the basis of achievement within an occupational system and founded on universal criteria of performance, under conditions of equality of opportunity: 'The measures of achievement are technical and specific for each particular field' (ibid.: 136); although there is a tentative measure on the basis of income.

In a later paper, 'Social Classes and Class Conflict in the Light of Recent Sociological Theory' (1949), Parsons argues that the social system is hierarchical on the basis of two forms of differentiation which form 'the instrumental complex':

1 The level of skill and competence involved in a person's performance of their social roles.
2 The ability to exercise leadership and authority, the ability to coordinate the actions of others.

These two factors allow us to rank individuals within a general social hierarchy. However, most of our ranking is related to the world of work, because it is at work that we find the highest degree of specialisation in terms of roles. We also have ranking in terms of ownership of property. In this latter paper, Parsons reinforces the essentially moral nature of the classification of people within the stratification system: 'As with all other major structural elements of the social system, the norms governing its stratification tend to become institutionalised' (ibid.: 325).

In 1953 Parsons returned to the issue of stratification in his paper, 'A Revised Analytical Approach to the Theory of Social Stratification'. In this revision Parsons reaffirmed that stratification is the ranking of *units* – which could be individuals or families – in accordance with the standards of the common value system. However, Parsons is much more specific in this paper on the links between the action frame of reference and the stratification system. Parsons argues that a property that we rank highly, such as good performance at work or a possession such as intelligence, is linked to the stratification system by our personal judgement or *agency* (Parsons [1953] 1996: 144). All such judgements about people and where to rank them in a stratification system are based upon a judgement concerning the starting point for their acquired possession or acquired skills, which Parsons terms the 'ascriptive base of a social status.' (Ibid.: 144). In other words, we consider where a person or family started from when we rank then in terms of honour, income, skill, status or prestige, and then we make a judgement on how well they have performed over a period of time. The ability to climb up a stratification system, achieve goals, command respect, control possessions, etc. is referred to by Parsons as the ability to actualise one's interests, and it is directly related to a unit's capacity to exercise power.

What Parsons is moving towards in the 1953 paper is a theory of class structuration, in which individuals or families (units) attempt to draw upon resources and exercise power – which for Parsons, following Weber, is the ability to make somebody do something that you want them to do – in an effort to gain a higher position with a stratification system. Other human agents observe the performance of such units and make a judgement, on the basis of ascertainable qualities, about ranking that unit as superior or inferior in relation to others: 'relative to an integrated common value-system' (ibid.: 145).

Parsons outlines four forms of evaluation in relation to status qualities:

- Universalistic values in relation to the efficiency of achieving a goal (a goal attainment criterion)
- Action processes often defined as *performance* or *achievement* (a pattern maintenance criterion)
- The quality of the attitude – when a personal or similar particularistic value satisfies an integrative need of the social system (an integrative criterion)
- Maintaining the *base* of the action frame of reference – from which all other status-defining qualities take their point of departure (an adaptive criterion).

The human agent uses the general categories that are employed to identify the problems and solutions that social systems in general face when judging the status ranking or stratification position of other agents. Both sets of categories are categories of meaning, which overlap because each judges what is important for a social system in general and what individuals should be doing specifically to maintain that system for the good of all. The criteria that we use in defining who goes where in a stratification system are essentially utilitarian in nature – whatever actions, achieved goals or performances give the greatest good to the greatest number will be rewarded with higher status and rewards.

However, Parsons did recognise that lack of equality of opportunity would clearly have an impact on an individual's opportunity to make a contribution to the organisation or the wider social system. In a discussion of sex roles in 1953, Parsons argued that:

> Obviously the whole situation, however, produces another fundamental limitation on full 'equality of opportunity', in that women, regardless of their performance capacities, tend to be relegated to a narrower range of functions than men, and excluded, at least relatively, from some of the highest prestige statuses. (Ibid.: 171)

In 1970 Parsons attempted to broaden his discussion of class by looking specifically at the processes of class formation. He maintained that the institutionalisation of stratification – in other words, the legitimation of inequality – was a central aspect in the solution to the problem of order within social systems. In this discussion Parsons draws upon arguments which in 1976 were to emerge in Anthony Giddens's work as the process of mediate structuration (see below). Parsons outlined the ways in which parents, often as an unforeseen consequence of loving their children, help to give their children the skills, abilities and attributes which will enable them to find an occupational status at least equal to that of their parents. As Parsons explained:

> [T]he children of higher status parents derive special competitive advantages from their socialization, precisely in the form of capacities for more independent and more responsible action, so that their chances of maintaining or improving the parental level of status are actually improved, relative to children of less 'advantaged' homes ... Hence the seeming paradox arises, that the ascription of children by birth to the families established by parental marriage, accentuates the child's competitive advantage in the institutions governed by the value of equality of opportunity, rather than compensating for status disadvantages. (Parsons [1970] 1996: 194)

Parsons argues that in the United States there are three broad stratification bands: the upper class, the middle class and the working class. Individual people within the social system place people in one of these three bands based on their evaluation of the contribution that the person makes to the overall running of the social system; the greater the contribution to the social system, the higher the ranking. However, as Curt Tausky ([1953] 1965) pointed out, there are problems with the Parsonian concept of 'functional importance'. Doctors and street cleaners may make an equal contribution to the social system in that they both reduce the possibility of people contracting disease. However, doctors are ranked higher in the stratification ladder because they have higher prestige, but the prestige of the occupational role is not based upon the contribution to the social system. In the last analysis, Parsons seems to suggest that income is the main determinant of class status. This position was made explicit by fellow functionalists Davis and Moore who argued that: 'The amount of the economic return therefore becomes one of the main indices of social status' (Davis and Moore [1945] 1996: 266).

Davis and Moore

For Davis and Moore, stratification is a functional necessity for any social system. All social systems have to legitimately place individuals within a social structure and motivate them to play their social roles. Stratification is necessary in order to recruit people with the right talents into the right social roles. In order to do this effectively, the social system must ensure that people who have ability are prepared to go through often extensive periods of training in order to gain qualifications. Hence, stratification is universal, it is found within all social systems:

> Social inequality is thus an unconsciously evolved device by which societies insure that the most important positions are conscientiously filled by the most qualified persons. Hence every society, no matter how simple or complex, must differentiate persons in terms of both prestige and esteem, and must therefore possess a certain amount of institutionalised inequality. (Davis and Moore [1945] 1996: 261)

Differentiation is on the basis of two criteria. People will be given the greatest reward if they

- Perform roles that have the greatest importance for the social system
- Perform social roles that require greater levels of training and/or talent.

Melvin Tumin has challenged the assumptions upon which Davis and Moore build their analysis. He argues that within any stratification system, people have a vested interest in restricting the opportunities of others and enhancing the opportunities for their loved ones, which they can do because of their differential access to resources. In addition, Tumin challenges the notion of 'sacrifice' in terms of hard work and studying, which well-rewarded people have to go through before they can attain the most important social roles. Tumin views this argument as an apology for inequality and argues that the notion of 'sacrifice' is unsupported by any real evidence. Finally, Tumin challenges the notion of 'functionally important' social roles as the basis for differential rewards. He argues that 'functionally important' is viewed in terms of the 'survival value' of a role for a social system. In other words, roles that help to maintain the social system's survival are highly valued and should be highly rewarded.

In response to Tumin's critique, Wilbert Moore argued that Tumin had 'made the major mistake of not explicitly defining social stratification, which in turn led him to assume that differential rewards and inequality of opportunity are the same thing' (Moore [1953] 1996: 397). Differential rewards and inequality of opportunity are one and the same thing. It is often the case that differential rewards are based upon restricting the equality of opportunity of others; an idea that was understood by Parsons and an idea that was to form the basis of Giddens's notion of *mediate structuration*.

In Kingsley Davis's (1953) reply to Tumin, he argues that he and Moore recognised that ranking in a stratification system was not based upon functional importance alone, but was also based upon 'the scarcity of qualified personnel' (Davis [1953] 1996: 285). On Tumin's point that stratification systems often prevent talented people from gaining important social roles, Davis argues that their argument: 'is a theory explaining the differential prestige of *positions* rather than individuals.' (ibid.: 285, emphasis in original). Davis also argues that there is some confusion about how both they and Tumin use the term 'stratification': 'On the one hand it is used by us to designate the institutionalised inequality of rewards as between broad strata. On the other hand, it is used (as Tumin does implicitly) to mean the inheritance of class status' (ibid.: 286).

This reply raises an important issue: What is the relationship between the 'class position' and the person who occupies the class position? As a reader of class analysis you have to decide where you stand on this issue. Does stratification of 'class' exist independently of the activities of people? Class is a concept that has been devised by social scientists to explain the inequality that can be discerned between people. If we take people out of the equation, what are we left with? Davis and Moore are guilty of *reification*; in other words, they are guilty of believing that concepts are real things that exist in the outside world independently of the people whose behaviour they were invented to explain. Concepts do not have a life of their own and Davis and Moore undervalue the role of the human agent in class analysis.

In contrast to Tumin's arguments, Davis and Moore never claimed that everybody would occupy a position that was compatible with their talents and abilities. Moreover, in his book *Human Societies* (1949), Kingsley Davis accepted the argument that middle-class and professional families could secure advantages for their children at the expense of people lower down the class ladder.

However, an important question for Davis and Moore is this: What are the processes that underpin or drive the social division of inequality? Their answer has a neo-Darwinian feel to it: 'Social inequality is thus an unconsciously evolved device' (Davis and Moore [1945] 1996: 261). The problem with this reasoning and with their argument of 'functionally important' social roles as the basis for differential rewards is that there are socially useless positions that are very well rewarded. For example, people who devise successful advertising campaigns for tobacco companies are well rewarded, as are Premier League footballers, television personalities and game-show hosts, yet the role of parent is financially unrewarded and financially costly. Why have such socially useless positions not been eradicated from the social system via the process of adaptation?

Parsons, in contrast, has no such problem explaining the existence of socially useless positions, because his analysis puts the emphasis on the individual human agent to make the valuation of the worth of individual social roles. If sufficient individual human agents believe that a social role is worthy of high reward, then irrespective of the content of that role, the role will be highly rewarded.

What is the nature of social division for Davis and Moore? Dennis Wrong ([1959] 1996) argued that Davis and Moore did not formulate their theory in a way that focused attention on the power aspect of stratification. In contrast to this view, we could argue that in the last analysis, Davis and Moore by making the comment 'Social inequality is thus an unconsciously evolved device' ([1945] 1996: 261) assume that people have a psychological and unconscious need or desire for inequality, which in many respects is the Nietzschean concept of the *will to power* that we found in Weber's conception of domination.

As we saw above, for Nietzsche, morality, including ideas of what is right and just, is imposed upon us by people who have the *will to power*. The powerful invent ideas of moral superiority to control the behaviour of others. Nietzsche's philosophy is a philosophy of 'becoming' in which the person should be free to lead their life as they wish and 'become' whatever they wish. Nietzsche allows us to think beyond the limits of moral obligation and what he would see as the fictitious demands of an imaginary god.

In 'Social Stratification and the Functional Theory of Social Differentiation' ([1958] 1996), Walter Buckley makes a number of informed points which can be used to reinforce the Nietzschean element of Davis and Moore's argument. Buckley argues that when Davis and Moore point to the close correlation between superior capacities, importance of position, and high rewards, they inevitably have to concern themselves with the characteristics of individual people. In other words, they postulate that individuals have superior positions because of their superior qualities. However, it is unstated in Davis and Moore's argument as to why they perceive functional differentiation of role as a relationship of superiority and inferiority. Unless, as we have suggested, they are looking at the world through the eyes of Nietzsche.

ACTIVITY

Do Authority Relationships Need to be Stratified?

Read the passage below and outline in your own words the critique of Davis and Moore that it contains.

Dennis Wrong argues that:

> Davis and Moore seem to perceive the functional inevitability and stratifying role of authority relationships. ... For example, when they discuss 'government' they say that 'stratification is inherent in the nature of political relationships.' ... In consequence, it may be said that if there is any functional necessity for stratification, it is the necessary of stratification according to the criterion of authority and not according to the criterion of material advantage or prestige. Nor does the necessity of stratification derive from the need to induce people for acquirement of qualifications, but from the very fact that humans live collectively. (Wrong [1959] 1996: 349)

Question:

➤ Do you accept or reject the points that Dennis Wrong is making in this passage?

In summary, the functionalist theory of stratification rests on the link between the unit (which could be an individual or family) and the relationship between common values and evaluation. In addition, the theory is universal in that it applies to all societies and at all periods of time. For the functionalist, whenever we have society we have stratification, because stratification is functionally necessary for the smooth running of the social system. Functionalists also assume that human motivation is universal and unchanging, as we all have a need for resources, self-respect and the good things in life.

The Tumin critique had a significant impact on class analysis and wider social policy. The idea that people should not be exploited or economically disadvantaged irrespective of whether they do or do not have talent or ability became widely accepted, and in 1958 the term *meritocracy* was coined by Michael Young to capture the sentiment.

Young and Saunders on the Rise of the Meritocracy

The Britain of the elite is over. The new Britain is a meritocracy where we break down the barriers of class, religion, race and culture. (Tony Blair, *Daily Telegraph*, 25 October 1997)

The term 'meritocracy' was originally coined in 1958 by Michael Young, however, the concept is clearly based upon the 'merit principle' which underpins the Davis and Moore class schema, in that 'meritocracy' stands for a society where achievement in the occupational class system depends exclusively on individuals' ability and motivation. Young invented the formula:

$$I + E = M$$
(Intelligence plus Effort equals Merit)

This means that in a meritocratic society, the social class that an individual is born into will have no significant impact on that person's future achievements in life. As Peter Saunders explains, 'If they are equally bright, and equally hard-working, the child of a road sweeper will do just as well as the child of a merchant banker' (Saunders 2000: 27).

In an effort to evaluate whether Britain is a meritocratic society or not, Peter Saunders tested two hypotheses:

- **The SAD hypothesis:** that social advantages and disadvantages determine where people end up in the class system
- **The meritocracy hypothesis:** that individual ability and effort are the key determinants of occupational success or failure.

Saunders drew upon data from The National Child Development Study (NCDS) – a well-respected longitudinal study which has followed all the children born in the first week of March 1958 through their school and work careers. Since 1958 the NCDS has recorded information on:

- The occupations of the parents of panel members
- These parents' behaviour and attitudes in relation to their children as they were raising them
- The housing conditions in which the children were raised
- Their schooling and examination records; their measured ability at 7, 11 and 16
- The employment histories of the panel members since leaving school
- Their attitudes to work and employment
- Their aspirations through childhood and adulthood.

In other words, the NCDS data should give a clear indication of the role of both ability and individual effort on a person's performance in the class hierarchy. In addition, the data should also help to resolve the central issue that Melvin Tumin raises against the Davis and Moore 'merit principle' argument.

Saunders's central conclusion was that there was an 'extraordinarily high degree of fit between Goldthorpe's findings and a model of perfect meritocracy' (Saunders 2000: 29). In a comparison of actual rates of social mobility with the rates predicted by a model of perfect meritocracy, Saunders tabulated the following:

Table 1   *Actual rates of social mobility with the rates predicted by a model of perfect meritocracy*

Mobility Pattern	Predicted %	Actual %
Middle class > middle class	59	59
Middle class > working class	21	15
Working class > middle class	18	16
Working class > working class	58	57

Source: Saunders 2000

As Saunders posited, 'Clearly, the meritocratic thesis proves much stronger than the SAD thesis in explaining why some individuals succeed while others from comparable social backgrounds do not.' He further concluded that:

- Class destinations reflect individual merit (ability and motivation) much more than class background
- Private schooling, parental contact with schools, material conditions in the home, the 'cultural capital' passed on by middle-class parents to their children, and even gender bias in the school or the workplace exert only relatively minor effects on people's class destinies

- By contrast, the factors that sociologists have so often ignored, or even dismissed as self-evidently absurd or unimportant – factors having to do with the intellectual capacities of individuals – turn out to be much more important.

> Summarising all of this, we may say that, in predicting where people are likely to end up in the occupational class system at age 33, their ability alone is well over twice as important as their class origins, three times more powerful than the degree of interest their parents showed in their schooling, and is five times more powerful than their parents' level of education or the aspirations which their parents harboured for them while they were growing up. (Saunders 2000)

There are, however, a number of methodological issues in relation to Saunders's use of the NCDS data, as he explained:

- A number of people were omitted from the analysis because they could not be allocated to a particular social class position on the basis of their own current occupation
- Panel 'wastage' 'reduced the total size of the sample substantially, and proportionately more individuals from lower-class origins have dropped out, thereby skewing the sample towards the middle class both in terms of class origins and class destinations'
- Panel members not in *full-time* employment were omitted from the analysis because they could not be allocated to a particular social class position on the basis of their own current occupation. This included:

  — part-time employees (45 percent)
  — 'housewives' (37 percent)
  — unemployed (10 percent)

- The sample consisted of 6,795 individuals, 85 percent of whom were employees and 15 percent self-employed
- More women than men are to be found in part-time employment or in full-time housework
- 'A disproportionate number of women have been dropped from the analysis'
- The final sample consisted of 70 percent males and 30 percent females.

As we shall explore more fully in the chapter on gender divisions, there are serious implications for any study of social mobility if women are excluded or largely excluded from the analysis. There is a great deal of evidence to suggest that gender has a significant impact on the mobility chances of both men and women. The Essex Mobility Study conducted by Marshall (1988) found that when women entered the labour market for the first time, they were likely to be downwardly mobile compared with their father's occupation. However, over the course of their working life, single women and women without children did experience upward mobility. The key point in a woman's journey through the labour market came when she decided to have children: women with children are on average almost certain to experience downward mobility and most return to work with a significantly diminished market and work situation. The majority of women returning to work have lower pay and poorer conditions of service than they had when they first entered the labour market, very often as part-time employees. The problem with Saunders's analysis is that the relative upward mobility chances of men are enhanced – making the occupational class system appear open and meritocratic only because women with children are dominating the lower end of the occupational class ladder. (We shall look in detail at the debates about gender, class and social mobility in the chapter on gender division.)

As you might reasonably expect given their vision of the class structure, Marxists have had little to say about social mobility between occupational classes. However, in 1974 Harry Braverman, writing from within a Marxian perspective, did discuss the notion of *proletarianisation* which we should be aware of before we look at Anthony Giddens's work on class structuration and the work of later Marxian analyses of class.

The Culture of Poverty

Just as the notion of meritocracy is underpinned by the merit principle, the notion of the underclass is underpinned by a person's relationship to the same individualistic-achievement oriented discourse. Both the notion of meritocracy and the right-wing notion of underclass place a strong emphasis on moral calibre. Similarly, both concepts contain the same presuppositional bias that equality of opportunity is sufficient in itself to legitimise a significant degree of inequality. This is because applying your effort and achievement to market forces is in itself sufficient to bring about an egalitarian effect. The term *culture of poverty* was first used by Oscar Lewis.

Oscar Lewis, The Children of Sanchez

Oscar Lewis's study *The Children of Sanchez* (1961) is a 'biography' – an in-depth psychological study of Jesus Sanchez and his four adult children. This Mexican family lived in a one-room *vecindad* in the Casa Grande area, a ten-minute walk from Mexico City's great Cathedral, Presidential Palace and main plaza. The *vecindads* are largely self-contained areas of slum housing, usually brick-built tenement buildings surrounding a courtyard. They are found in or near city centres and are notorious for chronic water shortages and very poor sanitary facilities. Casa Grande was home to 700 people and contained a market, public baths and food stores. According to Lewis, many of the tenants seldom left the *vecindad*.

The Sanchez family were selected at random, but Lewis claims that they typified many of the social and psychological problems experienced by lower-class Mexican families. The book is organised as a series of – often moving – individual life histories as people give accounts of their experiences, goals and life choices.

Lewis defines culture as 'a design for living which is passed down from generation to generation' (Lewis 1961: xxiv). He argues that poverty is not simply a state of economic deprivation:

> It is also something positive in the sense that it has a structure, a rationale, and defence mechanisms without which the poor could hardly carry on. In short, it is a way of life, remarkably stable and persistent, passed down from generation to generation along family lines. The culture of poverty has its own modalities and distinctive social and psychological consequences for its members. (Ibid.: xxiv)

The *culture* within the culture of poverty is provincial and local in nature, with a strong emphasis on finding local solutions to problems. This culture is shared by people at the very bottom of the class ladder whom Lewis describes as the *lumpenproletariat*. Although Lewis conducted most of his research in Central America, he argues that the culture of poverty can equally be found in most large cities with poor populations: London, Glasgow and Harlem as well as Mexico City. The culture of poverty is a culture of marginal people who are not integrated into national institutions – including such diverse bodies as schools, political parties, trade unions, banks, hospitals, museums, department stores, art galleries and many more. The rejection of these institutions is partly because poor people do not trust them, but also because they are often ineligible to join or cannot afford to use them. The people who share the culture of poverty share a set of social and psychological characteristics that include:

- Living in crowded quarters
- Lack of privacy
- Gregariousness
- High incidence of alcoholism
- Frequent resort to violence in the settlement of quarrels
- Frequent use of physical violence in the training of children
- Wife beating
- Early initiation into sex
- Free unions or consensual marriages
- High incidence of the abandonment of mothers and children
- A tendency towards mother-centred families
- A strong predisposition to authoritarianism
- Strong present-time orientation – little ability to defer gratification
- Little planning for the future
- A sense of resignation and fatalism
- A belief in male superiority – *machismo* – the cult of masculinity
- Corresponding martyr complex amongst women
- A high tolerance for psychological pathology.

Contrary to the common perception of Lewis's work, he did not regard Jesus Sanchez or his children as lazy people. What comes across very clearly from the accounts that Lewis presents is that in Central America at the time that he was doing his research, unemployment was not an option for people. The people in Central America were living in a society without a social security system and the choices for poorer people were between different degrees of underemployment. Jesus Sanchez's own story is one of very hard work for very low wages from the age of ten. At the time Lewis interviewed him, Jesus had been employed in the same restaurant for 30 years. It was only in the 1980s with the work of Charles Murray that the culture of poverty became associated with lazy people who rely upon cash income from the state to fund a deprived and amoral lifestyle. In contrast, what Lewis is arguing is that irrespective of how hard-working poor people may be, the culture of poverty – the style of living into which they are socialised by parents, a wider set of kin and tight-knit communities – prevents them from rising above their poor condition.

Oscar Lewis's work has been subject to severe critique. Peter Townsend argues that Lewis's methodology is 'individual-oriented and uncontrolled ... vivid reportage about the lives of individuals belonging to a single extended family' (Townsend 1979: 66–7). Townsend argues that Lewis makes use of unstructured individual self-histories: Lewis is unclear in terms of his unit of analysis and is unrepresentative in his choice of families. Lewis's work is characterised by unconscious and conscious bias, in that many of the criteria used to distinguish the culture of poverty from the wider culture are formulated in terms of middle-class values. Townsend maintains that Lewis's key terms suffer from ambiguity: 'All the criteria used to distinguish the sub-culture of poverty were inexact. The boundaries of the sub-culture were not specific, still less quantified' (ibid.: 67). This means, argues Townsend, that the thesis is not in a form that can be tested and much of the evidence that Lewis presents is inconclusive. On the one hand, claims Townsend: 'Lewis seems to be resurrecting the Victorian notion of the "undeserving poor"' (ibid.: 69). However, at the same time Lewis is unable to adequately distinguish between working-class culture and the culture of poverty.

Charles Murray

According to Charles Murray, the American underclass is predominantly urban and black and essentially this group shares a poverty of the spirit:

> Underclass is not a synonym for poor or even for disadvantaged. By underclass, I mean a population cut off from mainstream American life; not cut off from its trappings (television and consumer goods penetrate everywhere), but living a life in which the elemental building blocks of a life; productive work, family, community; exist in fragmented and corrupted forms. Most members of the underclass have low incomes, but its distinguishing characteristics are not poverty and unmet physical needs, but social disorganization, a poverty of social networks and valued roles, and a Hobbesian kind of individualism in which trust and cooperation are hard to come by and isolation is common. (Murray 1999: 1)

Murray makes use of three indicators to identify the underclass:

- Illegitimacy among low-income young women
- Criminality
- Voluntarily dropping out of the labour force by low-income young males.

In Murray's opinion the destigmatisation of illegitimacy in the twentieth century is a bad thing in itself. However, a large proportion of male children who grow up without fathers, tend to grow up unsocialised, 'unready to take on the responsibilities of work and family, often criminal, often violent. The effects of absent fathers are compounded by the correlations of illegitimacy with intellectual, emotional, and financial deficits among the mothers that in turn show correlations with bad parenting practices' (1999: 1). In addition, young males can become socialised into the role of the *unconnected male;* a person who defines a successful life by the number of sexual conquests and who views parental responsibility as 'a trap for chumps'.

The habitual criminal is the classic member of an underclass; such criminality creates an environment in which law-abiding people are literally *demoralised* as the predatory ethic of the underclass spreads beyond the criminals. For Murray it is violent crime that is the most directly symptomatic of an emerging underclass:

> Public order deteriorated. I refer here not to the homeless or to crime, though both of those represent a deterioration of public order, but to an in-between category. Graffiti is the classic example. It seems a trivial thing in itself but recall how omnipresent it used to be, covering subway cars, urban buildings, highway underpasses, billboards, bus shelters, and the pavilion in the park. It was ugly and scary. The squeegee men were another form of this deterioration, as were knots of menacing teenagers and prostitutes working the streets in what were otherwise 'nice' parts of town. (Ibid.: 15)

One of the basic elements of the social contract is that healthy young men go to work; the economic and social institutions of mainstream society depend on it. To work is morally superior to not working for Murray because 'Jobs provide regularity, structure, and dignity to family life' (ibid.: 11). In the last analysis, Murray argues that 'a large number of Americans are not just cash-poor, but enmeshed in patterns of behavior that assure continued poverty of many kinds, economic and moral alike' (ibid.: 2).

In summary, Murray argues that teenagers from lower-working-class neighbourhoods in both the United States and to a growing extent in the United Kingdom 'lack good parents' and are growing up in a 'underclass culture' (Murray 1990: 33), in which the community does little to reward responsibility and refuses to stigmatise irresponsibility.

What is to be done? For Murray the key to breaking the underclass culture is to have authentic self-government, which allows people who value two-parent families to live with like-minded people in neighbourhoods where public expenditure on social security is decentralised from national to local level. In this sense, local neighbours could reward their unemployed neighbours as they see fit: 'Even if the underclass is out there and still growing, it needn't bother us too much as long as it stays in its own part of town.' (1990: 35).

Urban Underclass Spillover

Read the following passage by Murray on the urban black underclass culture, and then answer the question below.

> American underclass has been predominantly urban and black. Urban black culture has been spilling over into mainstream American culture for more than a century now, historically to its great advantage. Urban black culture continues to spill over as much as ever, but during the last three decades it has increasingly been infiltrated by an underclass subculture that celebrates a bastardized code duello, predatory sex, and 'getting paid'. The violence and misogyny that pervade certain forms of popular music are coordinate with these values. So is the hooker look in fashion and the flaunting of obscenity and vulgarity in comedy. Perhaps most disturbing is the widening expression, often approving, of underclass ethics: Take what you want. Respond violently to anyone who antagonizes you. Despise courtesy as weakness. Take pride in cheating (stealing, lying, exploiting) successfully. I do not know how to measure how broadly such principles have spread, but that they are more openly espoused in television, films, and recordings than they used to be is hard to deny. I am suggesting that among the many complicated explanations for this deterioration, cultural spillover from the underclass is implicated. (Murray 1999: 17)

Question:

> ➤ To what extent do Peter Townsend's criticisms of Oscar Lewis's work apply to Charles Murray's analysis?

The three factors associated with the growth of the underclass for Murray – illegitimacy among low-income young women; criminality; and dropout from the labour force among low-income young males – are not specifically identified as factors that are *causing* the expansion of the underclass. As Morris (1994) points out, a problem with all 'culture of poverty' accounts is that they are tautological in nature: values are inferred from behaviour – welfare dependency, illegality, lack of self-discipline, increased lone parenting amongst young black women and young black men are dropping out of the labour market – and behaviour is explained by the assumed subcultural value system.

Morris argues that 'culture of poverty' accounts place scant emphasis on the economic structure or domination in the process of underclass formation. The damaging economic and political transformations of the late twentieth century significantly refashioned the working-class black culture. In the United States, social change in the 1980s and 1990s saw an outward migration of non-poor black people out of the inner city, leaving behind an increasingly isolated and increasingly spatially concentrated group of people who were having to cope with the falling demand for manual and low-skilled occupations in the labour market. This argument was reinforced by the work of Loic Wacquant (1996), which is discussed below.

Finally, in contrast to Murray, Jencks pointed out that in the United States:

> Teenage boys have never earned enough to support a family, even when they had jobs, and they seldom married even in the 1950s ... in 1960 less that 4 percent [of 16–19-year-old] black men who worked throughout the year were married." ... Furthermore, blacks constitute a declining proportion of welfare recipients, falling from 45 percent in 1969 to 40 percent in 1987. (Jencks 1992: 158, 170)

Nick Buck (1996) argues that the culture of poverty accounts tend to blame the victims for their own poverty – if only people would choose to do something about their pathological behaviour, then poverty would largely disappear. In addition, by using the term *underclass*, the problems that poor people have appear to be unique to them, whereas in reality the underclass share many problems with the working class in general.

Heath (1992) and many other similar studies found that data from the British Social Attitudes Survey suggested that people who were in receipt of benefit were no different in terms of their *culture* than other working-class people.

The *New* Urban Poor

Loic Wacquant (1996) argues that urban poverty in Europe is becoming increasingly 'Americanised'. In his comparative ethnographic study of the structures of the 'new urban poverty' in Paris and Chicago, Wacquant observes that urban poverty has a number of common characteristics: multiple deprivations; insecure occupational attachment; withdrawal of people from wider social networks; and the open increase of 'street persons'. Wacquant argues that two interconnected trends have shaped these factors: socio-economic marginality that has a spatial segregation element to it and xenophobic or racial ideologies.

Wacquant found that in both the *Black Belt* of Chicago and the *Red Belt* of Paris the poor live in a bounded and segregated space which had a powerful stigma attached to it:

> To dwell in a Red Belt low-income estate means to be confined to a branded space, to a blemished setting experienced as a 'trap' ... The verbal violence of [the] youths, as well as the vandalism and symbolic violence they feel subjected to by being thus relegated in a defamed place. Not surprisingly, there is a great distrust and bitterness among them about the ability of political institutions and the willingness of local leaders to rectify the problem. (Wacquant 1996: 238–9)

To live in such an area is a sign of moral and cultural depravity. As such, 'territorial stigmatisation' has an influence on how the residents are treated by potential employers elsewhere in the city, the perception of the police and courts, as well as access to banks and other financial institutions. All this reinforces both the poverty and spatial segregation of the people who live there. The overall effect upon the residents is one of demoralisation. The coping strategies in both communities were very similar; the residents of both areas were involved in a process of 'stigma management' that included two major factors:

- The elaboration of difference between people who lived within the area, the formation of rigid micro-hierarchies
- The identification of scapegoats, such as lone parents, drug dealers, problem families and foreigners.

The areas become divided within themselves, which manifests itself as open conflict (a culture of terror) or mutual avoidance; in any event the residents have no sense of community and no collective will to campaign for change.

In a similar fashion to Loic Wacquant, Francesca Zajczyk (1996) discovered in her study of the *new urban poor* in Milan that poor people were found in several areas across the city. She identified several common factors that contributed to the creation of slum areas:

- Areas with a high proportion of elderly residents
- Areas that contained significant numbers of 'highly discriminated groups' – such as gypsies and immigrants
- Poor socio-economic context – such as poor job chances.

Enrica Morlicchio (1996) who also researched the new urban poor in Naples, found that the processes associated with the de-industrialisation of the city were key contributory factors. Impoverishment affected the whole of the city, but some social groups were hit harder that others – such as the homeless, people with large families, and young black people. In other words, the new urban poor were largely made up of people who had traditionally fared badly in the labour market.

Debates about the underclass have tended to ignore the processes that bring about the underclass. Norman Fainstein (1996) argues that the processes of underclass formation are a product of the wider economic polarisation that dictates world capitalism. Both in the United States and Europe, poverty is a process and not a condition – the poor are not excluded from global capitalism, they are the most exploited part of its labour force. The marginal existence of the poor is maintained by capitalism to keep down the cost of labour. However, most arguments about underclass formation are bound up with wider issues of race and gender. (In the later chapters on race and gender we shall return to the important issue of class formation at the very bottom end of the class structure.)

ACTIVITY

Underclass Formation

Below is a list of possible causes of underclass formation:

- Attempts to liberalise the operation of the labour market
- A decline in morality
- A denial of the work ethic
- A rise in psychological incapacity and welfare dependency
- The decline in full-time employment for men
- The decline of the traditional nuclear family
- The rise in single motherhood
- The withdrawal of the state from providing comprehensive social security.

Question:

➤ Which of the above causes for underclass formation do you find the most convincing and why?

Harry Braverman on Proletarianisation

Braverman's Labour Process Theory is derived from Marx. In a nutshell, *labour process* is any organised system of activity whereby the human capacity to produce results in a useful article or service. Braverman attempted to bring Marx's analysis up to date and argued that in the twentieth century, large-scale industrial organisation led to monopoly capitalism and increased degradation at work.

The main tenets of his arguments were as follows:

- The real subordination of labour was only completed in the twentieth century
- The main symptoms were a loss of skill, loss of creativity and loss of control

- A further symptom was the increasingly sophisticated science and technology of management
- The above results in a process of 'deskilling'
- Possibilities for personal initiative, direction and control of the work process have been gradually taken from workers and given to machines and managers
- This results in proletarianisation and homogenisation.

In the literature there are three forms of proletarianisation:

1 **Proletarianisation of places in the class structure:** where whole occupational classes become downwardly mobile
2 **Proletarianisation of people:** where individual skills are no longer valued or rewarded
3 **Socio-political proletarianisation:** where middle-class people adopt the consciousness of the proletariat.

For Braverman a key element in the processes of proletarianisation was the invention and application of Scientific Management, invented by Fredrick Taylor in his book *The Principles of Scientific Management* (1911). The key elements of Taylorism were:

- A science of the management of others' work under capitalism
- Workers were made to work at their 'optimum'
- All aspects of the labour process must pass into the hands of management
- Ordinary management was inadequate because management were ignorant of what constitutes a proper day's work
- This was the starting point for Scientific Management
- Taylor's original fieldwork was a series of experiments at the Midvale Steel Company which lasted for 26 years
- Machinists were required to work in accordance with instructions derived from Taylor's experiments
- Machinists were not allowed to use their own knowledge or experience.

TAYLOR'S THREE PRINCIPLES OF SCIENTIFIC MANAGEMENT

1 Dissociation of the labour process from the skills of the workers.
2 All brain work to be removed from the shop floor.
3 Control by management of all aspects of the labour process and its mode of execution.

Management were expected to select the best person for the job, instruct them in efficient methods of work and provide cash incentives.

There have been several critiques of the proletarianisation thesis:

- **The 'upgrading thesis':** labour may have enhanced its skills
- **'Social constructionist' view of skill:** skill labels are a tool of management
- **Existence of 'internal labour markets':** rewards used to segment workers
- **Misdefinition of gendered skills:** many women workers use 'skills' which are not defined as 'skills', for example, keyboard skills, cooking and preparing food, mending and sewing clothes, child care.

Anthony Giddens on Class Structuration

In 1973 Anthony Giddens put forward an alternative view of what he termed *class structuration*. Unlike the models of class suggested by Marx and Weber, Giddens argued that individual people create social class through a process of structuration. For Giddens there are two forms of class structuration, *mediate structuration* and *proximate structuration*.

Mediate structuration is concerned with the ways in which class advantages are passed on from one generation to the next. Parents love their children and want them to be successful in life. In this way children from professional middle-class families are given greater access to additional skills, abilities and resources. Middle-class children may be informally taught to be more articulate by their parents. The additional language skills can be used as a resource by children in schools, helping them to gain qualifications and get professional middle-class occupations.

Proximate structuration has three elements to it:

1 **Division of labour:** there are some occupations that we look up to, such as traditional occupations like doctors, barristers and solicitors or high-profile celebrities such as professional footballers or pop stars. Similarly, there are occupations that we look down upon, such as refuse collectors or shop assistants. If our estimations are commonly shared and accepted by the people in those occupations, this helps to reproduce a hierarchy of occupations, or social class hierarchy.
2 **Authority:** in any place of work there are people who give orders and people who do as they are told. If you are given an instruction at your place of work and carry it out because you believe that the person giving you the instruction has a right to do so, again this helps to reinforce the social class hierarchy.
3 **Distributive groupings:** unlike Marx and Weber, for Giddens 'consumption' also has a role to play in the process of structuration. The type of house you live in, the area of the town or city where it is located, where you shop, what car you drive, the clothes you wear and the logos you display are all significant. If others see your patterns of consumption as 'better', then this helps to reinforce the class hierarchy.

However, in the 1990s Giddens changed his mind about class and argued that class divisions were no longer significant in determining people's life chances. In *Beyond Right and Left* (1994) he argued that:

- Class is no longer experienced as 'class', but as a series of individual constraints and opportunities
- Some professional people and other high-income earners attempt to exclude themselves from the wider society by not making use of the NHS or state schools and living in houses or apartments that are patrolled by guards
- Lifestyle and taste have become significant as markers of social differentiation
- The 'generational transmission belt' of class is broken; parents have much less importance in determining the life chances of their children
- Class is no longer a 'lifetime experience' because of 'global influences upon the economy, movements up and down the class ladder affect everybody.

The only significant 'class' division within the population is between the people who are employed and the new poor who have become excluded from the labour market.

Later Marxian Class Analysis

As Joyce (1995b) argues, in the nineteenth century there was an uneven expansion in technological development and a variety of different forms of social division. Rather than the wholesale deskilling of what was to become the proletariat, there was a significant degree of cohabitation between feudal fiefdom and capitalist class relations, often with capitalists drawing upon the extra-economic forms of compulsion in order to generate profit.

John Roemer on Class

John Roemer attempts to construct a Marxian theory of exploitation without drawing upon the Labour Theory of Value, because he argues: 'The labor theory of value claims that market prices should be proportional to the labor time required to produce commodities, but this is simply not the case' (Roemer 1988: 2).

In contrast to the traditional Marxian view, Roemer argues that differential property relations rather than the labour market should be the focus of attention. It is property relations rather than the extraction of surplus value from workers that is the basis of real exploitation. Classes are social divisions based upon 'a group of people who relate to the labor process in a similar way' (ibid.: 5). All the people who sell their labour power are in one class; all the people who buy that labour power are in a different class; with people who work for themselves forming a third class. Moreover there is a constant struggle between employers and employees. Capitalists take 'unfair advantage of workers' and that is 'ethically indefensible' (ibid.: 14). Roemer argues that if people are expected to work for longer than the hours that they need to work to purchase all the things they require without being rewarded for that additional time, then those people are being exploited. This is because the bundle of things they consume contains less labour than the worker expended. Hence capitalists 'live off' the labour of workers not because the capitalists are cheating or using coercion, but because those capitalists have possession of capital. Roemer argues: 'Thus, there are three essential consequences of the differential ownership of the capital stock: the emergence of exploitation, class, and accumulation' (ibid.: 27). Roemer further claims that 'If one had to name the one site that accounts for the inequality Marxists call exploitation, one should choose neither the labour process nor the capital market, but the initial determination of unequal capital stocks' (ibid.: 103).

The fact that some workers are paid less than they expend and the bundle of things they consume contains less labour than they have used up is important for Roemer only because it reflects the underlying inequality of capital distribution. Exploitation status and class position are systematically linked and ethically unacceptable.

In Roemer's view a person is *'capitalistically exploited* if he would gain by virtue of an egalitarian redistribution of society's alienable means of production, and a person as *capitalistically exploiting* if he would lose by such a redistribution' (ibid.: 135; italics in original). In an earlier text entitled 'A General Theory of Exploitation and Class' (1982), Roemer refers to this form of exploitation as the Class Exploitation Correspondence Principle, which states that 'every producer who must hire labour power to optimize is an exploiter, and every producer who must sell labor power to optimise is exploited' (Roemer 1982: 15). He further argues that a person is exploited if they 'cannot possibly purchase a bundle of goods which embodies as much labour as he in fact worked' (ibid.: 17).

Exploitation is 'unethical' for Roemer only if the initial distribution of wealth could be said to have come about by immoral means. Roemer's approach is based upon an assumption that egalitarian property entitlement is ethical and that barriers to such equality are unethical. The reasoning behind this is that 'exploitation must involve some coalition's benefiting at another coalition's expense – rather than benefits or expenses accruing from a purely natural or technological phenomenon, such as scale economies' (ibid.: 199).

But why does Roemer reject the traditional Marxian Labour Theory of Value? In the 1982 text he argues that in contrast to the traditional Marxian view, the value of labour is dependent upon the market (ibid.: 19). In addition, traditional Marxian approaches fail to take into account *differential labour endowments*, in other words some individuals work harder, have a higher level of skill and ability and/or more strength. The Labour Theory of Value will not work if an assumption of homogeneous labour – the assumption that all workers are equally endowed with skill, ability and strength – is dropped.

The impact of John Roemer's work can be seen most clearly in the writing of Erik Olin Wright on class.

Erik Olin Wright on *Classes*

Wright is attempting to rethink systematically the structural categories of class. The objective of Wright's (1985) model of class was to demonstrate the continued usefulness of Marx's conception of class to life in the United States at the end of the twentieth century. Class relations are: 'intrinsically relations of objectively opposed interests' (Wright 1985: 283). Wright's classes are embedded within three forms of exploitation relating to capital assets, organisation and skill. For Wright, classes are not income groups but rather underlying elations of production. Wright begins with the classical Marxian abstract model of class:

- **The bourgeoisie:** who own the means of production
- **The proletariat:** who own only their labour power.

However, Wright argues that no capitalist society exhibits complete polarisation of class. Other classes exist which are neither bourgeoisie nor proletariat, but often demonstrate defining elements from both classes. Managers as a group are said by Wright to have a *contradictory class location*, in that they are employees who sell their labour power and do not own the means of production, however they are also responsible for controlling the means of production and managing exploitation of the proletariat. In addition, Wright argues that no society has a pure capitalist mode of production: for example, the *petty bourgeoisie*, a group made up of subgroups such as small shop keepers and small farmers, are seen by Wright as a hangover from feudal times. Wright also describes a group whom he refers to as *semi-autonomous workers*, professionals who exploit their own skills and abilities and who have had a foothold in both the feudal mode of production and the capitalist mode of production.

WRIGHT'S CLASS MODEL

- Bourgeoisie
- Small employers
- Petty bourgeoisie
- Managers and supervisors
- Semi-autonomous workers

The proletariat (working class) is the largest class and has the greatest number of people in exploitative locations within the class structure. The middle class is made up of both exploiters and exploited.

Wright makes a distinction between *class structure* and *class formation*: 'Class structure refers to the structure of social relations into which individuals (or in some cases families) enter which determine their class interests' (1985: 9). A class structure is, for Wright, an objective set of empty places which are filled by people. This class structure exists independently of the people who occupy the positions within the class structure. In contrast, class formation is strongly mediated by subjective factors such as politics and ideology and 'refers to the formation of organized collectivities within that class structure on the basis of interests shaped by that class structure. Class formation is a variable' (ibid.: 9).

- **Class structure:** social relations *between* classes
- **Class formation:** social relations *within* classes.

Wright's (mark II) analysis involves a shift from exploitation, in the traditional Marxian sense and based upon the Labour Theory of Value, to domination, in the Weberian sense of the ability of people to make others do what they want them to do. In particular, domination at the point of production is the factor that gives effective control within labour–capital relations. As Wright explains, forms of domination 'play an important role in explaining the forms of class organization and class conflict' (ibid.: 72).

Wright's Concept of Domination

Read the quote below.

> The essential argument is that the concept of contradictory locations, like much neo-Marxist class analysis, has effectively displaced the concept of 'exploitation' from the core of the concept of class structure, replacing it with the concept of 'domination'. (Wright 1985: 15)

Question:

> ➢ To what extent does Wright's argument differ from the traditional Marxian view of 'exploitation'?

For Wright there are three interrelated but distinct domination/exploitation processes at work:

1 The principal form of exploitation, based upon ownership of the means of production
2 Skill exploitation.
3 Exploitation of organisational assets – control of the assets around which exploitation takes place.

Wright also makes a distinction between 'economic oppression' and 'exploitation'. The notion of 'economic oppression' defines a set of objective material interests in that people with disabilities, the unemployed and the children of workers could be better off under counterfactual conditions and are therefore 'economically oppressed'. With 'exploitation', according to Wright, 'the welfare of the exploiting class depends upon the work of the exploited class' (ibid.: 75). The exploiting class has a vested interest in defending their assets which they need as the basis for their style of living: 'To appropriate the fruits of someone else's labour is equivalent to saying that a person consumes more than they produce' (ibid.: 75).

Organisation, for Wright is 'the condition of coordinated cooperation among producers in a complex division of labour – [it] is a productive resource in its own right' (ibid.: 79). In capitalist societies organisational assets are either effectively controlled by managers under constraints imposed upon them by capitalists or they are directly owned and controlled by the capitalists themselves. Exploitation is said to take place in relation to the control of assets because such assets are not distributed equally; by controlling such assets, managers are better off and non-managers worse off as a consequence. However, again by deploying such arguments, Wright moves away from the traditional Marxian perspective and towards a Weberian conception of domination. As Wright himself makes clear, 'The notion of organizational assets bears a close relation to the problem of authority and hierarchy' (1985: 80).

Finally, Wright discusses *skill exploitation* by arguing that 'Experts control their own skills or knowledge within production, and by virtue of such control are able to appropriate some of the surplus from production' (ibid.: 85). Again Wright is making use of Marxian-sounding conceptions but with a radically different meaning from what Marx intended. Also it is clear from Wright's text that he has some doubts about the role of skill exploitation in the process of class formation, probably because the valuation of skill in the marketplace is a key Weberian argument in his discussion of social class. To quote Wright, 'while skills or credentials may be a basis for exploitation, this asset is not really the basis of a class relation' (ibid.: 85).

In 2001 Wright gave a wide-ranging interview to Mark Kirby in which he explained his position. In 1981, during his deliberations with the Analytical Marxism group, Wright became convinced that

> the technical apparatus of the Labor Theory of Value was unsatisfactory, it simply could not do the theoretical work it was intended to do. But we also came to realize that for the elaboration of a coherent concept of exploitation and its linkage to class analysis, the Labor Theory of Value was also not necessary. (Wright 2001: 12–13)

In a nutshell, Wright describes Marx's Labour Theory of Value as both incorrect and unsatisfactory.

Rather than defending or developing the analysis of Marx, Wright developed a 'normatively-driven analysis' (ibid.: 34) or 'an egalitarian normative critique of capitalism' (ibid.: 13). Exploitation was to remain as a central analytical concept for Wright, but it was to be deployed normatively:

> Normatively, it matters not simply that some people have more assets than others, but that they use those assets to take advantage of the vulnerability of others. Exploitation is the way we talk about this specific way of using one's resources. Sociologically, exploitation describes a particularly explosive form of interdependency between people, an interdependency in which one group (exploiters) simultaneously depend upon another (the exploited) for their own material well-being and impose harms on the well-being of the group on whom they depend. This defines a distinctive kind of social relation which is not captured just by talking about unequal endowments of assets. (Ibid.: 14)

As Mark Kirby rightly indicates, Wright's analysis 'leaves us with nothing to judge the value of things other than price, and therefore no basis for a critique of the market. Is this not a weak basis for Marxism?' (Wright 2001: 24). In response to this criticism Wright states that:

> There are masses of criticisms of the market in general, and capitalist markets in particular, that do not depend upon the Labor Theory of Value:

- Capitalist markets generate socially destructive inequalities.
- Capitalist markets generate exploitation (this does not depend upon the Labor Theory of Value).
- Capitalist markets lead to concentrations of power which undermine democracy.
- Capitalist markets produce ecological devastation by biasing production towards underpricing negative environmental externalities.
- Capitalist markets generate a culture of consumerism.
- Capitalist markets threaten communities and the values of community (solidarities, altruism).

None of these points depend upon the specific thesis that in a competitive equilibrium the rates of exchange of commodities will be determined by the relative amounts of abstract labor which they contain. (Ibid.: 25)

You do not need to be a Marxist to agree with these points; however, you do need to accept a Weberian notion of domination to accept many, and a moral conscience to accept the rest. The reader is left wondering why Wright continues to use the label 'Marxist' to describe his own work.

In addition to rejecting the Labour Theory of Value and the traditional Marxian conceptions of class and exploitation, Wright also rejects the traditional Marxian conception of constraint, in favour of a form of constraint which shares many of the qualities of Giddens's notion of structuration:

Like Ulysses and the Sirens, one can choose one's constraints, so to speak. And, among the things which one can deliberately choose, none is probably more important than the community-of-dialogue in which one is embedded. Most scholars, I believe, don't think much about this. (Ibid.: 2)

ACTIVITY

Wright's 'Choice of Constraints'

Wright justified the comment above by arguing:

I suppose the proper way to have made my earlier point would be to say that, 'within broad constraints one can choose narrower constraints.' I believe choices are real: we are not robots following scripts, and sometimes our choices matter quite a lot. One of the ways choices matter is in shaping some aspects of the constraints one faces for future choices. Knowing that since humans are pretty smart, we can make choices in the present with the intention of affecting future choices, and thus we in a sense 'choose our constraints'. But even these constraint-making choices occur within a social context that defines obstacles and possibilities for action. 'People make history but not just as they choose'. 'Making history' means creating constraints which operate in the future, not just the present; not just as they choose means that even this takes place under constraints. This doesn't undermine the notion of structure at all. It explains how structure works in a world of conscious agents. (Wright 2001: 34)

(Continued)

(Continued)

Questions:

> ➤ In the traditional Marxian conception of class, can people *choose* to opt out of exploitative class relationships?
> ➤ In Wright's re-conceptualisation of exploitation, by reference to game theory, can people opt out of exploitative class relationships?
> ➤ Do you feel that Erik Olin Wright can legitimately describe his analysis as 'Marxist'?

In contrast to Roemer and Wright, Ken Post (1996) argues that the extraction of surplus value is central to any Marxian understanding of class and exploitation and that those endowments – either intrinsic or extrinsic – are determined by the class system. For Post, Roemer's argument is a 'truly petty bourgeois perspective' (Post 1996: 177–8) because exploitation is a basic ontological issue, exploitation is the uncompensated personal expenditure or loss of labour power. The bourgeoisie gain, the proletariat lose: 'Moreover, what is being lost is not some just and equal place in a system of "the distribution of productive assets and resources" which is Roemer's proposed substitute' (ibid.: 281).

Guglielmo Carchedi (1991) argues that in Roemer's class analysis there are no objective criteria to identify if a person is being exploited or not. Carchedi takes exception to phrases used by Roemer in his discussion of exploitation such as *hypothetically feasible alternative*, describing such criteria as 'purely arbitrary'. In addition, different people can think up different hypothetically feasible alternatives to the situation that the working class are in and thus adopt different conceptions of exploitation. Carchedi argues that Roemer does not place the theory of exploitation on a more rigorous basis as he claimed to do.

Carchedi (1986) is also highly critical of Wright's class analysis and in particular of Wright's conception of 'exploitation'. He argues that Wright's unit of analysis is 'the individual' rather than 'class'. Although Carchedi recognises that individuals exist and make a difference in the world, he maintains that the individual should not be placed at the centre of any Marxian analysis because the individual 'is unsuitable to explain historical trajectories and choice' (Carchedi 1986: 196).

For Wright, class locations structure the objective interests of the individuals within each class. There are two *objective* interests that Wright identifies:

- People have an interest in reducing the hours of work necessary to attain the level of consumption that they desire
- People have an interest in increasing their capacity to do the things they desire.

For Wright, exploitation is related to these two objective interests. In Wright's view, if one of the classes were to disappear and this were to allow more consumption and/or less work to be done, then there is evidence of exploitation having taken place. What Carchedi takes exception to here is that Wright defines exploitation without reference to production and his argument is more concerned with the distribution of consumption. Carchedi explains that classes for Wright are distributional groups which are essentially occupational groups, therefore Wright's analysis shares a great deal in common with Weber's analysis of class.

Rigby (1998) is also critical of Roemer's position. Roemer regards 'unequal exchange' as 'exploitation' because if in a society (N) there is a coalition of agents (S) and a number of people who are part of society, but who are not part of the coalition of agents, who are labelled (T), the coalition 'S' is said to be exploited if *there is an alternative* which we can conceive of as hypothetically feasible, in which 'S' would be better off than in their present situation and where 'T' would be worse off. Moreover, 'T' must be in a position of power over 'S' and able to prevent 'S' from realising the alternative. When we argue that workers are exploited under capitalism, we are arguing that there is an alternative form of society where the provision of resources and the rest needed to produce commodities could be provided without the bourgeoisie and where the proletariat would be better off – what Roemer would describe as *hypothetically feasible*. However, for Roemer 'coercion' is not 'exploitation' if the proletariat are gaining their maximum benefits. As Rigby points out, 'everyone being forced to drive on the left-hand side of the road is thus a restriction but not an oppression' (Rigby 1998: 211) but 'better off' and 'hypothetically feasible' are terms based upon subjective moral criteria. In addition, there has to be agreement on what constitutes a 'practical alternative'. Socialism may be a 'practical alternative' for socialists, but may be less appealing to the rest of the population.

Probably the last theorists to draw upon the Labour Theory of Value were Poulantzas (1975) and Carchedi (1977). However, when it comes to explaining the boundaries of social division, both Poulantzas and Carchedi move away from the traditional Marxist stance by placing a great deal of emphasis on the role of *authority* in defining the division between the working class and the new middle class.

Poulantzas on Class

At first sight, Poulantzas's analysis looks like a traditional Marxian conception of class:

> In the capitalist mode of production, productive labour is that which directly produces surplus-value, which valorises capital and is exchanged against capital. [...] We shall say that productive labour, in the capitalist mode of production, is labour that produces

surplus-value while *directly reproducing the material elements that serve as the substratum of the relations of exploitation: labour that is directly involved in material production by producing use-values that increase material wealth.* (Poulantzas 1975: 211, 216; italics in original)

Poulantzas argues that as a mode of production, capitalism can only exist if its class relations are reproduced, because class struggle is the motor of history. In addition he defines class relations as relations of exploitation and moreover, that within capitalism there is 'intensive exploitation of labour (relative surplus value)' (ibid.: 141). He also argues that the falling rate of profit within capitalism is a sign of working-class resistance against their exploitation. In addition, a key element in this process of reproduction is the reproduction of the political and ideological elements of class relationships. However, Poulantzas argues that people other than manual workers can create surplus value and he makes a similar distinction to Carchedi (1977) between the working class and the new petty bourgeoisie or the new middle class. He outlines three criteria for differentiating the working class from the new middle class:

1 **The economic criterion:** in which class is defined by the distinction between productive and unproductive labour
2 **Political and ideological relations:** which secure the reproduction of the dominant mode of exploitation, accomplished through the relations of supervision and authority
3 **The division between mental and manual labour:** which reinforces the subordination of workers to capital by excluding them from the secret knowledge of production.

Managers and supervisors are in an antagonistic relation to the working class because of the role they play in the reproduction of capitalism at an ideological level.

In addition, Poulantzas accepts an empiricist conception of classes as the sum total of individuals who together constitute a class. Classes are not viewed as objective places in a class structure or framework, but as concrete individuals who are found within classes. This definition of class is very much along the lines suggested by Weber, that a social class is made up of all the people who share the same class position. Finally, Poulantzas also gives a much greater role to political factors in the process of class formation than one would find in a traditional Marxian class analysis. For Poulantzas, the state apparatuses and the ideological state apparatuses have a decisive role to play in the reproduction of class.

Carchedi on Class

Guglielmo Carchedi (1977) divides the working population into two groups: a wage-earning working class and a revenue-earning new middle class. Workers and the new middle class are similar in that they do not own the means of production. The working class is involved in the production of use-values within a complex and differentiated labour process, which Carchedi refers to as the *function of the collective worker*. The new middle class, on the other hand, are not involved in the production of use-values but instead are involved in the control and surveillance of the labour process; what Carchedi refers to as the *global function of capital*. The exercise of supervisory authority by the new middle class is fundamental to the expropriation of surplus value.

Carchedi's broad theoretical framework is drawn from Marx. Carchedi explains that there are two abstract levels to his analysis, namely the pure capitalist level and the socio-economic system. At the pure capitalist level, use-values are produced only as a means to produce exchange values. A key element of this process is the relationship between the 'production agents' of the capitalist system; the capitalists and the working class. However, at the socio-economic level, both the 'old' and the 'new' middle class also have a role to play in terms of their control function for capital. The economic base is always determinant, argues Carchedi; moreover the superstructure is always determined and the limits of any variation of the superstructure are always determined by the economic base. The rise of the new middle class is a consequence of the rise of monopoly capitalism and for Carchedi, this is no justification for a departure from the traditional Marxian class analysis.

CARCHEDI'S DEFINITION OF CLASSES

Classes are defined by Carchedi as large groups of agents differing from each other by:

1   The place they occupy in a historically determined system of social production;
2   Their relation (in most cases fixed and formulated in law) to the means of production;
3   Their role in the social organisation of labour; and
4   Consequently, (a) by the share of social wealth going to a class, (b) by the mode of acquiring this wealth, and (c) by the wealth's origin. (Carchedi 1977: 3)

This new middle class live off the surplus value produced by the proletariat. They are a hybrid class; a mixture of the two 'pure' classes – the bourgeoisie and the proletariat. The new middle class perform a balance between the function of labour and the function of capital. Under the changed conditions of monopoly capitalism, individual capitalists are simply unable to control and supervise large groups of workers – whom Carchedi refers to as the *collective labourer*. The middle class have a control and surveillance role to play in the extraction of surplus value from the proletariat. Carchedi refers to this essential role for the new middle class as the *global function of capital*. The middle class is viewed by Carchedi as a 'large number of agents hierarchically and bureaucratically organised in a complex structure … performing the global function of capital' (Carchedi 1977: 7).

The new middle class are 'unproductive' in the traditional Marxian sense, and as such they are not exploited in terms of the Labour Theory of Value. However, although the new middle class do not have surplus value appropriated from them, they do provide surplus labour, and according to Carchedi, they are economically oppressed. The difference between *exploitation* and *oppression* is that exploitation is economic in nature, whilst oppression is a form of domination, similar to political domination. Carchedi argues that the wages of the proletariat are determined by the value of labour power. However, the new middle class are not paid wages in the Marxian sense but rather derive revenue from the capitalist as a reward for their services. In addition, because the control and surveillance of labour is a skilled occupation, Carchedi argues that:

> in order to perform the work of control and surveillance, [the new middle class] *must be hierarchically higher than the labour* [*they*] *control*. Thus the political and ideological components are a *constant feature* of the revenues but not of wages. (Ibid.: 13; italics in original)

In a later book on the European Union, *For Another Europe: A Class Analysis of European Economic Integration* (2001), Carchedi develops this class analysis by looking at the role of supranational organisations in class exploitation. Class analysis, argues Carchedi, has been 'expelled' from academic discourse for ideological reasons. In a similar Marxian vein to his work in the 1970s, Carchedi argues that the structure or base of society is its class relations under capitalism, which are *contradictory* and *functional* in their content. In order for class relations to be reproduced, they need to be interrelated with institutions. Class determines the shape and form of all social relations and the institutions are viewed by Carchedi as the *concrete form* of appearance of class relations. In other words, contradictory class relations give rise to a series of institutions, notably nation states and supranational institutions. In particular, the European Union is seen as one of the 'concretisations of the interests of (perhaps nascent) social classes, or fractions of classes, or interclass social groups' (Carchedi 2001: 8).

It is the need for capitalists to generate the highest possible profits which underpins the process of EU integration and expansion. Carchedi argues that European oligopolies and oligopolistic competition are the key factors which have defined EU competition policy, which is evident in the way that EU competition policy favours Europe's oligopolies. The European Monetary Union is described by Carchedi as having the central theme of 'the appropriation of value through international seignorage' (ibid.: 4).

Carchedi's Inner Dynamics of Capitalist Economics

Read the passage from Carchedi below and address the questions that follow.

the production and appropriation of (surplus) value ... is the hub of capitalist economics and [capitalists and labourers] are its fundamental classes. However, it is clear that the
class structure of any capitalist society is articulated in more than these two classes. Even
at the level of capitalist production, one can theorize both old and new middle classes.
Moreover, while the capitalist production relations are the fundamental ones, a capitalist system encompasses also other production relations, such as those defining producers and peasants. Finally, if political and ideological factors are considered, both fractions
of classes and social groups cutting across classes emerge. This more detailed class
analysis, irreplaceable in a different context, is omitted here since focus on the two fundamental classes is sufficient for the purpose of this work, which is that of revealing the
inner dynamics of capitalism and thus of the European Union. (Carchedi 2001: 78)

Questions:

➢ Do you accept or reject the view expressed by Carchedi that production and appropriation of (surplus) value by capitalists and labourers is the hub of capitalist economics?

➢ Can we ignore the old and the new middle classes if we are attempting to reveal the
   inner dynamics of capitalism?

What is significant about Carchedi's work in the late 1970s and in 2001 is that the
Marxian analysis is only used to explain social division, while one aspect of the
class system – the growing middle classes and the process division that they are
part of – is explained by concepts and ideas that have a much more Weberian feel
to them.

The Regulation School on Class

Another group writing within a Marxian tradition who discuss class without
reference to the Labour Theory of Value is the Regulation School. These writers
explore a range of *modes of articulation*, which are mainly political strategies developed by the state to control societal forces and help stabilise capitalism. In

particular, the Regulation theorists are associated with ideas of Fordism and Post-Fordism, 'Bloody Taylorism' and the emergence of a 'global Fordism', where the problems of falling profitability are dealt with by shifting labour-intensive work processes to newly developing countries; a relocation in search of lower wages. However, Bob Jessop (1990) argues that the Regulation School is not a single school with a fixed and coherent set of theoretical constructs although regulation theorists do share a common Marxian heritage, realist ontology and epistemology.

The Parisian School of Regulation theorists, starting with the work of Michel Aglietta, work within three key concepts: *the regime of accumulation, the mode of growth* and *the mode of regulation*. Over-accumulation is a problem for capitalism, as it helps to explain falling profits because the development of productive forces is blocked by the current relations of production. But what is to be regulated? Changes have to be made in the relationship of wages to accumulation and in competition between capitalists in an effort to create stability and better conditions for profitability. As Jessop explains:

> An accumulation regime comprises a particular pattern of production and consumption considered in abstraction from the existence of national economies which can be reproduced over time despite its conflictual tendencies ... A mode of regulation refers to an institutional ensemble and complex of norms which can secure capitalist reproduction *pro tempore* despite the conflictual and antagonistic character of capitalist social relations. (Jessop 1990: 174)

Such forms of regulation are political and institutional forms of class compromise, resulting in 'politics' rather than labour power as the key element in the reproduction of capitalism.

Michel Aglietta starts his influential analysis with a number of Marxian sounding phrases: 'Capital depends on the commodity' (Aglietta 1987: 37). In addition he postulates that within capitalism there is a uniform process of *valorisation* that produces and reproduces the relations of production. Aglietta argues that accumulation reproduces the relations of production via a *regime of accumulation* in which there will be:

- Wage-earners with legally defined hours of work
- Procedures for negotiation of pay and conditions of service
- Standardised insecurity and risk in which compulsory and contractual systems of insurance exist, notably unemployment benefit.

There is state control over the 'social wage': health services, education services etc. largely free at the point of delivery. Within these Fordist arrangements, the rate of surplus value is maintained by developing a set of social relations that attempt to link the labour process with a 'social consumption norm'. The creation of a consumer society in which there emerged the continual demand for commodities, fed by newer and more effective advertising techniques, helped to resolve the crises within capitalism. In other words, Aglietta is arguing that the labour process shaped the mode of consumption.

Alain Lipietz argues that 'the term *regime of accumulation* refers to a systematic and long-term allocation of the product in such a way as to ensure a certain adequation between transformation of conditions of production and transformation of conditions of consumption' (Lipietz 1987: 32). A central element of this relationship between the transformation of conditions of production and transformation of conditions of consumption is the *schema of reproduction*, which describes how labour is to be allocated and the allocation of products to different groups. In other words, by regulating wages by binding collective agreements, state minimum wage legislation, financial regulation and regulation of the market, potential crises of over-production and/or under-consumption are managed to allow profits to remain stable and allow capital accumulation to continue.

ACTIVITY

The System of Regulation

Read the passage below from Robert Boyer and explain in your own words the points that you think he is making:

> We will use the term 'regulation' to designate the set of mechanisms involved in the overall reproduction of the system, given the state of the economic structures and social forms. This system of regulation lies at the origin of the short- and medium-term dynamics of the economy ... Its long-run dynamics, for their part, do not simply result from the succession of these fluctuations and cycles. A crucial role is also played by political and social struggles which, while partially determined by the dynamics of accumulation, cannot be reduced to it. (Boyer 1990: 119)

Question:

For the Regulation theorists, is the Marxian Labour Theory of Value necessary for the construction of their concepts of *accumulation* and *regulation*?

In summary, the Regulation theorists attempt to identify 'regimes of accumulation' within capitalism – social forces used by the state to stabilise the reproduction of the capitalist system. Examples of such regimes range from Fordism to Post-Fordism. However, the Regulation theorists' analysis is rooted in the key role of *governance* in the process of accumulation.

The Neo-Gramscian Turn and Class

The *neo-Gramscian turn* in class analysis is represented by the work of Stuart Hall (1980), Ernesto Laclau and Chantal Mouffe (1985, 2001), and Patrick Joyce (1990, 1993, 1995b). These writers reject the economic determinism of Marx and disregard the labour theory of values; instead they place a great deal of emphasis on the role of *discourse* in the process of social division.

Nicos Poulantzas (1975) argues that the class background of individuals in top state positions is unimportant. The structure of society is capitalist, and the role of the state is to maintain that structure. The state must have a high degree of autonomy, or independence, from individual capitalists in order to choose effectively between the competing demands for state action by different capitalists. In other words, the state is always functional to the needs of capital, even though individual members of top state institutions are not from a top-class background. As Poulantzas explains:

> Let us concentrate for a moment on the heads of these apparatuses. These generally belong to the bourgeois class, not by virtue of their interpersonal relationships with members of capital itself, but chiefly because, in a capitalist state, they manage the state functions in the service of capital. (Poulantzas 1975: 187)

Antonio Gramsci (1957) rejected the economic determinism contained in the type of argument that Poulantzas is putting forward. Writing from the prison cell he was placed in by Mussolini in the 1930s, Gramsci made a distinction between two parts of the state:

1 **Political society:** which contains all the repressive state institutions, such as the police and the army
2 **Civil society:** which contains all the institutions, such as the mass media, that attempt to manipulate our ideas.

The state rules by consent although it has the ability to use force if necessary. However, the state would always prefer to use negotiating skills to produce a compromise. The state attempts to form a *historic bloc*, which involves making compromises with different groups, in an effort to maintain solidarity. Consent is maintained by *hegemony*, a body of ideas that becomes part of our consciousness and which we accept as right. Capitalism can only be overthrown by challenging and reformulating hegemony and establishing a new historic bloc.

Ernesto Laclau and Chantal Mouffe (2001) argue that the notion of hegemony involves the: 'privileging of the political moment in the structuration of society' (Laclau and Mouffe 2001: xii). In other words, using the notion of hegemony is to acknowledge that the political is independent of any significant determining economic factors. They argue that social democracy – including the third way or life politics of Beck and Giddens – is an 'attempt at addressing the autonomous political intervention which was made possible by the structural dislocation between actors and democratic tasks that resulted from the development of capitalism' (2001: xii). Social division is the product of democratic politics: 'Politics, we argue, does not consist in simply registering already existing interests, but plays a crucial role in shaping political subjects' (ibid.: xvii).

Laclau and Mouffe are highly critical of Erik Olin Wright and Nicos Poulantzas's attempts to redefine the working class within new boundaries:

> The reason for this Diogenes-like search for the 'true' working class is, of course, political: the object is to determine that category of workers whose *economic* interests link them directly to a socialist perspective, and who are therefore destined to lead the anti-capitalist struggle. The problem, however, with these approaches which start from a restricted definition of the working class, is that they are still based on the concept of 'objective interest' – a concept which lacks any theoretical basis whatsoever, and involves little more than an arbitrary attribution of interests, by the analyst, to a certain category of social agents. (Ibid.: 83)

In her book *The Democratic Paradox* (2000), Mouffe develops this argument on the nature of social division. One of the central themes is a critique of the assertion that in democratic societies there is always a division between 'us' and 'them' – between the people who belong (the citizens) and the people who do not belong (the non-citizens). Moreover, she argues that all democratic societies set clear limits on popular sovereignty in the name of liberty. In addition, Mouffe was highly critical of the new centre-left, characterised by Blair in the UK, Schroder in Germany and Clinton in the USA. These politicians championed a form of politics which is *beyond right and left*, in other words which attempts to get rid of the old political divisions by making legitimate a 'Third Way'.

However, in contrast to the traditional Marxian division between bourgeoisie and proletariat, Mouffe's argument is that 'them' is not a simple reversal of 'us'. Drawing upon Derrida's conception of the 'constitutive outside', Mouffe argues that people who are classed as being on the outside are regarded as incommensurable with us, the insiders. This provides the essential condition for the emergence of an antagonism that becomes political in nature, as people are given collective identities which locate them on either side of a political divide. As Mouffe explains:

> This implies that we should not conceptualise power as an *external* relation taking place between two pre-constituted identities, but rather as constituting the identities themselves. This point of confluence between objectivity and power is what we have called 'hegemony'. (Ibid.: 21; italics in original)

ACTIVITY

Poulanzas's Economic Analysis

In the last section I assumed that Poulantzas's analysis is deterministic in nature. In other words, I have assumed that for Poulantzas the economic base determines the nature and content of the superstructure. Is this a fair reading of Poulantzas? Read the quotation below and write a paragraph in which you state whether you believe Poulantzas's analysis to be economically deterministic, or can ideas, politics and ideology be independent of the economic base?

> The principal role of the state apparatuses is to maintain the unity and cohesion of a social formation by concentrating and sanctioning class domination. Political and ideological relations are materialised and embodied, as material practices, in the state [...] [However] State apparatuses do not possess a 'power' of their own, but materialize and concentrate class relations, which are precisely what is embraced by the concept of 'power'. [...] Nevertheless, in the relationship between the class struggle and the apparatuses, it is the class struggle which is fundamental [...] [T]he state apparatuses, and the ideological state apparatuses, have a decisive role in the reproduction of social class. (Poulantzas 1975: 24–8)

Questions:

➢ What is the significance of Poulantzas's use of the term *class domination* rather than *class exploitation*?

➢ What do you believe Poulantzas understands by the term *power*?

Patrick Joyce and Lynette Finch: The Linguistic Turn in Class Analysis

Joyce is highly critical of the realist approach of social historians in the field of class analysis. He argues that historians should adopt postmodern concepts and view class in terms of *discourse* rather than as a product of determining material factors outside of the control of individual people.

Taking his starting point from Foucault's notion of 'governmentality', Joyce argues that in the same way that gender 'cannot be determined from an external referent, the same follows for class' (Joyce 1995a: 82). In other words, class should not be seen as a concept that has a foundation or cause outside of the individual. The reason for this view is that for Joyce the social is a discourse or a product of history:

> 'Class' is indeed regularly stacked up with other similarly stable identities (race, nation, gender and so on). Out of these rough-hewn blocks sociologies and histories continue to be made. Perhaps it is time for a more credible notion of identity, one which considers the systems by which relations of difference work, including those means by which differences are composed into unities, however conditional these unities may sometimes be. (Ibid.: 82)

For Foucault, human subjectivity as expressed in the idea of the 'individual' is itself a historical creation dating from the eighteenth century with the emergence of 'man', who was constructed as an 'individual' in relation to 'the social'. Individual rights, duties and responsibilities, together with ideas of 'normality' in areas as diverse as sexuality, mental health and crime, were defined in relation to threats to the public sphere or civil society. In this case both the *public sphere* and *civil society* are simply other names for the social. From the eighteenth century the 'social' began to be seen as having a life of its own, becoming an object or 'thing' in the minds of people, in other words a 'foundational' concept. The source of class as a foundational concept should be seen within the same processes of political and moral legitimation, argues Joyce. However, contrary to its use by social historians, 'class' is a collection of individuals who are defined as such against the backcloth of the 'social'. However, the 'social' is not an objective entity, it is defined by discourses of power. Consequently, 'class' for Joyce is: 'part of a normative, historically situated project' (ibid.: 84). In other words, no set of social variables – for example, class, occupation, income – lies objectively outside of the agent or observer:

> From a 'languages of class' perspective, one could view the discourse and practice of the public sphere and civil society as that which enabled people to view themselves as 'bourgeois' in the first place (rather than in a bourgeois class creating the public sphere). (Ibid.: 86)

The notion of *discourse* having a central – but largely unseen – role in the Marxian analysis of class was initially taken up by William H. Sewell Jnr. In his 1993 study Sewell takes issue with the 'materiality' of the economy, as distinct from the non-material 'social' in Marxian analysis. For Marxists, the key element in the capitalist mode of production is 'the economic base' which contains the forces of production and the relations of production. The forces of production include all the elements from nature that we need to produce commodities. This 'material' set of factors has a determining influence on the shape and form of class relations – which Marx names as the 'relations of production'. Sewell looks at the history of 'the material' in Marxian analysis and attempts to trace the origins of this insight in Marxian theorising. Before the pioneering work of Charles Darwin in the nineteenth century, the 'material' or 'nature' was seen to be something that was disordered and morally improper. What Darwin did was to make nature ordered and so the forces of nature could determine key elements of human activity. As Joyce argues: 'nature became the stuff of laws and science' (Joyce 1995a: 77).

Likewise Marx, a contemporary of Darwin, viewed the 'material' as something that imposed order upon the social.

Sewell argues that this split between the material economy and the non-material social emerged out of traditional Christian and aristocratic discourse:

> Marxists proudly proclaim their radicalism by employing an arbitrary identification of the economy as material, never realizing that they have inherited the idea intact and uncriticized from traditional Christian and aristocratic discourses. Would-be friends of the proletariat hence believe they are being progressive when they denounce as 'idealists' historians who actually take seriously what past proletarians thought. The claims that the economy is uniquely 'material' always was arbitrary, misleading and tendentious: that it continues to be clung to by purportedly leftist scholars is an embarrassing anachronism. (Sewell 1993: 22–3)

The central idea that underpins the notion of *discourse* in the social sciences is summed up by Joyce: 'The human capacity to imagine order is seen to be at the foundation of society itself' (Joyce 2002: 5).

Lynette Finch

In the middle of the nineteenth century a number of social commentators were concerned that they knew so little about the lifestyles of poorer people. Drawing upon the language of exclusion, William Booth (1890) in his book *Darkest England and the Way Out* used 'black Africa' as a simile for 'dark England' and described the poor as 'tribes of savages'. In a similar vein, George Sims in his book *How the Poor Live*, describes a 'dark continent that is within easy walking distance of the General Post Office ... the wild races who inhabit it will, I trust, gain public sympathy as easily as [other] savage tribes' (Sims 1883: 64–5). Henry Mayhew in *London Labour and London Poor* (1861) similarly described the poor as London's 'wandering tribes of bushmen'.

However, it was Seebohm Rowntree in 1901 who conducted the first systematic study of poverty of poor people in the city of York. Based upon scientific evidence from researchers such as Dr Dunlop, who had carried out research on prisoners in Scotland to find the minimum nutritional requirement for a person to live; Rowntree identified the amount of money needed to satisfy their basic food, clothing and housing needs. A family was said to be in poverty if its income fell below this level.

Rowntree made a distinction between:

- **Primary poverty:** when income fell below the minimum required because of:
  - death of the chief wage-earner
  - incapacity of chief wage-earner, because of accident, illness or old age

— chief wage-earner out of work
— chronic irregularity of work
— largeness of family
— lowness of wage

- **Secondary poverty:** when people were unable to meet their minimum requirements because of: 'drink, betting and gambling. Ignorant or careless housekeeping, and other improvident expenditure, the latter often induced by irregularity of income' (Rowntree 1901: 141–2).

In other words, Rowntree made a distinction between the *deserving* and the *undeserving* poor, which has had a lasting impact upon social policy to this day. The Beveridge Report (1942) was based upon Rowntree's research, and the Beveridge Plan was the foundation for the post-1945 Welfare State. The Beveridge Plan aimed to create a comprehensive and universal welfare state that would address the five giant problems of disease, ignorance, squalor, idleness and want.

Drawing upon a range of nineteenth-century documents from Europe and Australia, Lynette Finch (1993) argues that the middle classes used the information from Booth, Rowntree and others to construct a set of moral categories within which to place poorer people. As we have seen in the case of Rowntree, nineteenth-century researchers divided poorer people into one of two categories: those who were moral and respectable and those who were not. To differentiate between the two, Rowntree and others asked a few simple questions that were to form the basis of a middle-class psychological scrutiny: Did the poor person drink? In the case of poor men, did their level of drinking damage their ability to reason? In the case of poor women, did their level of drinking render them more promiscuous? Secondly, Rowntree asked questions about overcrowding: Did poor people live in overcrowded conditions by choice, or was it brought about by factors outside of their control? Some poorer people were poor because of moral failings, they had urges that they could not control and this lack of control was the cause of their poverty.

The discourse of morality and class was common not only amongst liberal reformers of the nineteenth century; Marx and Engels also employed the same moral discourse to divide the working class. In the *Communist Manifesto* Marx and Engels refer to the *lumpenproletariat* – a class beneath the respectable proletariat – as thieves, vagabonds and prostitutes, the rotting scum thrown off from the remains of the old society. In a similar fashion in the *Eighteenth Brumaire of Louis Bonaparte* the *lumpenproletariat* are described as a 'dangerous class', including 'vagabonds, discharged soldiers, discharged jailbirds, escaped galley slaves, mountebanks, *lazzaroni*, pickpockets, tricksters, gamblers, maquereaus, brothel keepers, porters, *literati*, organ-grinders, rag-pickers, knife grinders, tinkers, beggars' (Marx and Engels 1977: 136–7).

The 'working class' is then a discursive category, formed in the latter years of the nineteenth century and constructed out of moral conceptions of drink and pathological sexual disorders. In the early to mid-nineteenth century the term 'working class' was not widely used, instead a range of descriptions were used such as the lower orders, etc.

It is never possible to know the *real* outside of the definitions of the real. In other words, we can never experience the real; we are only ever aware of discourse about the real.

For Finch (1993) the group that were labelled as 'the working class' could have been described in a number of other ways, within a different category and subject to alternative definitions. Class then is constructed through discourse rather than determined by economic factors.

Many of the critiques of the linguistic turn in the class analysis of social historians have been ill informed and never really get above the level of name calling. Richard Price (1997) attempts to make the argument that postmodernism is one and the same as Thatcherism:

> As an ideology of late capitalism – the capitalism shaped politically by Ronald Reagan and Margaret Thatcher – it is hardly surprising that postmodernism has strong affinities with conservative politics. It was, after all, Margaret Thatcher who first brought to public attention Baudrillard's claim that there was no such thing as society. The dismantling of the political economy that supported labour rights was the most obvious expression of this philosophy and, indeed, a generally contemptuous attitude towards the popular classes and their politics is increasingly characteristic of Baudrillard's pronouncements. We should not be surprised, then, to find powerful affinities between traditional conservative approaches to history and those who swim in postmodernist streams. (Price 1997: 26)

This is a common critique, but as in the case of Richard Price, no evidence or arguments are presented in support of the Thatcherite nature of postmodern arguments. A much more interesting point is made by Richard Price later in his critique:

> [A]rbitrariness is not the way words actually attain meaning; they gain meaning because they explain a recognizable context and the more reasonable they seem within that context, the more they will be accepted. Once we accept this, the way is open not only for an external reality to exist, but also for concepts like 'class' or 'the state' to endure outside of our particular naming of them. (Ibid.: 32)

What is interesting about this point is that it is not a critique of the reasoning behind Joyce's or Finch's contributions to the linguistic turn. What Price is saying here is that if words have a personal feel of validity for him and accurately describe the external world for him, then such a *strong discourse* can provide the basis or foundation for concepts such as 'class' or 'the state' to appear to exist for him independently of discourse. The problem for Price is that foundational concepts always take the form of strong discourse, but as Foucault clearly demonstrated, such strong discourse should still be seen within the same processes of political and moral legitimation. Simply finding a concept more convincing does not in itself mean that we should privilege that concept or ignore how and why it has such a convincing feel to it.

Postmodern Stratification

Within modernity, life had a secure and logical feel to it. In contrast, postmodernity is the form of society we are left with when the processes of modernisation are complete and human behaviour has little or no direct dealing with nature. We live in a fashioned or manufactured environment. In the postmodern condition, the world has an abandoned, relative and unprotected feel about it for the individual human agent.

According to Zygmunt Bauman (1996), identity was a modern innovation. In the modern world, the problem was how to construct and maintain one's identity in an effort to secure one's place in the world and avoid uncertainty. The creation of modern identity was seen as a pilgrimage. Without our pilgrimage to a secure identity, we might have become lost in the desert. In the first instance, on our journey to a fixed identity, we need a place to walk to. This was our life project, which ideally should be established early in life and be used to make sense of the various uncertainties, fragments and divisions of experience that make up the post-traditional world. In other words, by creating a fixed and secure identity, we attempt to make the world more ordered and more predictable for ourselves.

In contrast, in the postmodern world the problem of identity is one of avoiding a fixed identity and keeping our options open, avoiding long-term commitments, consistency and devotion. In place of a life project established as early as possible to which we loyally adhere, postmodern people choose to have a series of short projects that are not fixed. The world has a feel to it of being in a continuous present; it is no longer agreeable to pilgrims. In place of the pilgrim there are a number of other lifestyles that emerge: the stroller or flâneur, the vagabond, the tourist and the player. These lifestyles are not new to the postmodern world, but whereas in previous times marginal people in marginal situations practised these lifestyles, they are now common to the majority of people in many situations.

In the postmodern world we are all cast into the role of consumers. However, not all of us have the resources to be effective consumers. Some of us are 'tourists' and our choices are 'global'; others are 'vagabonds' cast in the role of 'flawed consumers' who are forced to live as 'locals':

> [In] the world of the globally mobile, the space has lost its constraining quality and is easily traversed in both its 'real' and 'virtual' renditions. ... [In] the world of the 'locally tied', of those barred from moving and thus bound to bear passively whatever change may be visited on the locality they are tied to, the real space is fast closing up. (Bauman 1998: 88)

Malcolm Waters (1997) argued that the stratification system is moving from a *class-based economic system* to a *culturalist or status-conventional phase*. This social transformation is part of the movement from modernity to postmodernity. The status-conventional form of stratification is built upon four concepts, which Waters identifies as:

1 **Culturalism:** lifestyle choices, aesthetic preferences and value-commitments
2 **Fragmentation:** shifting and unstable associations
3 **Autonomisation:** in contrast to the concept of the 'rational consumer', the ordered nature of such preferences has given way to market seduction
4 **Resignification:** the constant change of subject interest, choice and emotion, which constantly regenerates people's feelings and fears of distress, abuse and desire.

What is significant about these changes that Waters outlines is that 'occupation' is now only significant as a 'badge' of status, which says something about a person's ability to make use of the nice things in the world. Occupation is no more important than our 'consumption status', our ability to demonstrate to others that we can fully appreciate nice things.

David Ashley (1997) argues that most postmodern theories of stratification take their starting point from Daniel Bell's notion of the post-industrial society – a society in which cultural experts and other professionals who manipulate, manufacture and disseminate knowledge are the major class. However, Ashley argues that postmodernists over-emphasise simulations, culture and sign values at the expense of exploitation. As Bell posits, 'The concept of a post-industrial society is not a picture of a complete social order; it is an attempt to describe and explain an axial change in the social structure of the society' (Bell 1973: 119).

In Bell's analysis, 'social frameworks' are conceptual schemata that are built upon an axial principle and axial structure which provide an organisational frame. This allows Bell to suggest answers to key questions such as: How does a society hang together? (ibid.: 10). In Bell's analysis, social frameworks do not determine, rather they suggest questions and pose management problems. 'The major class within the post-industrial society is a professional class, who have knowledge rather than property' (Bell 1973: 22).

Ashley acknowledges that classes are changing, that classes are less well-defined, class boundaries may be more difficult to identify and individuals are less sure of their class identity. However, he maintains that this does not mean that the *service class* of cultural experts has displaced the bourgeoisie or has taken over as the dominant class within capitalism. Ashley makes the strong point that although there has been a significant decline in production within the West, from a global viewpoint production has not declined. Production is taking place in what were once described as third world societies. Moreover, as Ashley makes clear:

I also think that the *inability* to recognize systematized exploitation in the world is strongly associated with the widespread misconception that postmodernity is far too dizzying to be grasped as a whole ... I cannot accept that under postmodernization 'action is *divorced* from underlying material constraints (or rather these constraints disappear) and enters the voluntaristic realm of taste, choice and preference.' (Ashley 1997: 145)

From this starting point one would expect Ashley to make the case for the continued relevance of the Labour Theory of Value, but he does not. Rather, as with other Marxists we have reviewed in this chapter, he substitutes *domination* for *exploitation* and stresses the importance of the legal ownership of assets within capitalist relations of production:

Because class relations can subdivide humans as well as societies, they do not merely separate groups that are wholly exploitative from groups that are wholly nonexploitative. On the contrary, class relations typically organize extremely complex social relations among groups and individuals whereby quite different media (e.g. money, power, expertise, value commitments) can help sustain an overarching system of class domination that perpetuates or widens structures of inequality ... A mode of class domination (which can combine markets, power, ideology, etc., in any regulatory combination) generates particular and historically variable class relations (property relations) ... The corporate managerial elite, for its part, downsizes and downbenefits the workforce and manages the new relations of production that in recent years have transferred massive amounts of wealth from average wage earners to the holders of capital assets. (Ashley 1997: 148–9)

The process of class formation in Ashley's analysis is built around non-Labour Theory of Value factors, notably 'domination' that is possible because of the 'holding' of assets. This raises the important question: What is wrong with the Labour Theory of Value? To answer this question, we need to look at the work of two 'Marxists' who moved away from the traditional Marxian orthodoxy, Jean Baudrillard and Fredric Jameson.

In his *Mirror of Production* (1975), Jean Baudrillard casts doubt upon the Marxian distinction, outlined above, between use-value and exchange-value. In Baudrillard's opinion, *use value* is seen by Marxists as based upon genuine need, whereas *exchange value* is brought about by capitalists distorting the consciousness of the population by ideology and alienation. By *alienation*, Marx means that individual people who are essentially creative in nature are obliged within capitalism to perform work that is dull and boring to such a degree that they are unable to express their creativity. In contrast, in a socialist society, people would work for the common good. Making use of the Marxian concepts outlined above, we could say that a socialist society is based upon the principle of 'From each according to his ability, to each according to his needs'. In other words, solely taking care of our 'use values' would satisfy all our needs. For the Marxist, the concepts of 'value' and 'labour' are non-negotiable concepts, they cannot be questioned, and they are essential for any analysis of the world. In contrast, for Baudrillard, genuine need is impossible to identify, without taking into account how our needs are manipulated, explained and even created by the mass media.

For Fredric Jameson postmodernity is at the end of the process of modernisation. Postmodernism is a 'systemic modification of capitalism itself' (Jameson 1991: xii). Unlike most postmodern writers who reject Marxism, Fredric Jameson has attempted to absorb postmodern insights into the Marxian analysis. Jameson sees post-modernity as the third great stage in the global expansion of capitalism.

For Jameson, postmodern culture has a high level of class content. Jameson's account of this new stage of capitalism is a completely new world economic system. Moreover, for Jameson it is still possible to view the world in terms of class struggle, but individuals are unable to place themselves within the network of classes that make up capitalism. Radical politics is about cognitive mapping, where people are able to define their place in the world. Novels could provide such cognitive maps, helping people to define their place in the world and for-mulating political demands. Radical politics is no longer about the proletariat but about finding commonality and building alliances between groups who have experienced oppression within capitalism: women, ethnic minorities, gays and lesbians etc.

In Jameson's view, 'value' emerges as something independent of the labour power that went into making it. The significance of this is that Jameson has col-lapsed the economic base into the superstructure, and suggested that we can only make sense of the world in cultural terms. The economic base, including the rela-tions of production, is irrelevant in the postmodern condition. The economic base is no longer the force that moves history forward; rather it is culture and ideas which generate social change.

It can be noted then that although Jameson does not reject the Labour Theory of Value, he rejects its traditional form, and redefines it as a cultural or super-structural thing. We could argue that he places the Labour Theory of Value outside of the traditional Marxian analysis.

Zygmunt Bauman on Stratification and Underclass

The opposition between the tourists and the vagabonds is the major, principal division of the postmodern society. We are all plotted on a continuum stretched between the poles of the 'perfect tourist' and the 'vagabond beyond remedy' ... The more freedom of choice one has, the higher is one's rank in the postmodern social hierarchy. (Bauman 1997: 93)

Irrespective of how many people are without work across Europe and North America, full employment is seen as a feature of a normal society. Being in paid employment is the norm that the state of 'being out of work' transgresses. It is universal to assume that all males of working age will be gainfully employed; paid work is both a duty and a responsibility. It is central element of the work ethic that gainful employment is morally superior to all the alternative lifestyle options. As Bauman makes clear, the work ethic defines what is normal, but also defines what is abnormal – and it is an abnormal moral failure not to work.

In the past under the Fordism outlined by the Regulation School, industry provided for the needs of workers and their families and the welfare state filled any gaps. If a person was 'out of work', it was assumed that this was a temporary thing and the role of the welfare state was to maintain the body, mind and skills of the person in order for them to be gainfully employed again at the earliest opportunity. The unemployed were seen as a 'reserve army of labour power'. Unemployment was seen as a *collective problem* caused by factors that were largely outside the individual person's control, for example, a shift in the market which could be rectified by a *collective response* to the welfare state. However, this is no longer the case; industry has been down-sized and deregulated, and so has the fate of the people who work within it. People without work are now an underclass, not a 'reserve army of labour power' but 'fully and truly the redundant population' (Bauman 1997: 43). Or as he articulated even more forcefully, they are 'that huge and growing warehouse where the failures and the rejects of consumer society are stored' (ibid.: 93).

In Marxian terms, the unemployed labour has ceased to be a commodity. Employers have no need for well-educated, confident and highly skilled workers. In the deregulated capitalist enterprise, people are expected to work under conditions of *flexploitation*, a term invented by Bourdieu to describe the uncertain and irrational nature of labour markets which have to respond quickly to a consumer society that is itself built upon the irrationality of individual consumers attempting to fulfil their constantly changing desires.

The state of being without gainful employment is seen as an individual moral failing while becoming poor is viewed as the product of criminal predispositions or intentions, such as drug or alcohol abuse, gambling or truancy. The poor are vagabonds who do not deserve our protection or support, but rather our revulsion and disapproval.

For his book, *The Jail: Managing the Underclass in American Society* (1985), John Irwin interviewed a randomly selected sample of 200 people in the San Francisco jail system. Irwin addresses the question: 'What is the purpose of the American jail?' and concluded that the United States uses its jails to manage and keep the poor and destitute apart from the rest of society, because the poor behave in ways that affluent people find threatening. In a nutshell, the poor are jailed not because of the seriousness of the crimes they commit but because of the offensiveness of their behaviour to middle-class sensibilities.

In a similar vein, Bauman quotes Richard Freeman, a Harvard economist, as saying: 'If the long-term unemployed in Europe are paid compensation – in the USA we put them in prisons' (Bauman 1997: 43). For Bauman we live in a world where the unemployed are no longer seen as a reserve pool of labour power, a potential resource for the future generation of wealth, but instead as a serious social problem.

Taking his starting point from Jeremy Seabrook's comment that the poor do not inhabit a different culture from the rich, they simply have to live in a world that has been created for the benefit of people with money, in *Globalization: The Human Consequences* (1998) Zygmunt Bauman argues that we live in a consumer society. We may all desire to be consumers but not all of us can be consumers, and desire in itself is not enough. To lead a 'normal life' is to be a consumer, and people who do not work cannot consume to the same degree; in a consumer society such people are defined 'first and foremost as blemished, defective, faulty and deficient – in other words, inadequate consumers ... In a society of consumers, it is above all the inadequacy of the person as a consumer that leads to social degradation and "internal exile"' (Bauman 1998: 38). In other words, like all other societies, the postmodern consumer society is a stratified one. The processes of division within the consumer society are found within access to global mobility. The postmodern city contains a rigid form of apartheid – 'a caste-bound experience' (ibid.: 101) – between *the globals*, who are the consumers, and *the locals*, who are the flawed consumers. The globals get pleasure from the postmodern freedom to travel and are welcomed with open arms. The locals, by contrast, are moved on and get no pleasure from a form of postmodern slavery – the status of the modern-day nomadic vagabond or 'involuntary tourist'. The movement of the 'locals' is restricted by the people they are intent on moving towards, forcing the 'locals' to move surreptitiously and/or illegally; if found on the move, the 'locals' will be deported. For Bauman, the consumer society is one in which the lifestyle of poorer people has become increasingly criminalised while the 'globals' dream above all else of a world free of such vagabonds.

In *Community: Seeking Safety in an Insecure World* (2001), Bauman developed this theme. He argued that the poor are subjected to spatial segregation and immobilisation, because such processes are seen as mechanisms of segregation and exclusion that are necessary for the safety of decent people. Bauman quotes Loic Wacquant:

> [T]o be poor in a rich society entails having the status of a social anomaly and being deprived of control over one's collective representation and identity; the analysis of public taint in the American ghetto and the French urban periphery [shows] the *symbolic dispossession* that turns their inhabitants into veritable social outcasts. (Wacquant 1999, cited in Bauman 2001: 119; italics in original)

Ghettoisation and in particular tying people to the ground – keeping them in one locality – is a key element in the criminalisation of the lives of poorer people, as Bauman explains:

> In a world in which mobility and the facility to be on the move have become principal factors of social stratification, this is (both physically and symbolically) a weapon of ultimate exclusion and degradation, of the recycling of the 'lower classes' and the poor in general into an 'underclass' – a category that has been cast outside the class or any other social system of functional significance and utility and defined from the start by reference to its endemically criminal proclivities. (Bauman 2001: 120)

Consumption, the acceptance of market seduction and being seen to act on our desires, have become the measure of a successful life; and the poor are seen as 'depraved rather than deprived' (ibid.: 117).

ACTIVITY

The Differences between the Classic Marxist and Weberian Theories of Class

Read the passage below and answer the subsequent question, drawing on the preceding discussions.

The five most important distinctions between the classical Marxist and Weberian theories of class:

1   Marx conceptualizes class as an objective *structure* of social positions, whereas Weber's analysis of class is constructed In the form of a theory of social *action*.
2   Marx holds to a *unidimensional* conception of social stratification and cleavage, with class relations being paramount, whereas Weber holds to a *multidimensional* view in which class relations intersect with and are often outweighed by other (non-class) bases of association, notably status and party.
3   In Marx's theory, the essential logic of class relations and class conflict is one of *exploitation*, where political and ideological domination are interpreted as merely the means by which exploitation is secured, whereas for Weber *domination* is conceived as an end in itself, with its own independent force and logic.
4   For Marx, classes are an expression of the social relations of *production*, whereas Weber conceptualizes classes as common positions within the *market*.
5   Economic conflicts between classes are seen by Weber as merely one instance of the more general phenomenon of political struggles between dominant (privileged) and subordinate (disprivileged) collectivities (Burris 1987).

Question:

➤   Has the Marxist analysis of class division changed significantly from the way it is presented in the above quote from Val Burris? Give reasons for your answer.

Conclusion

This chapter opened with the statement: 'Inequality may be real, but class analysis is a set of concepts.' One cannot point to inequality in the world and assume that this is a sufficient justification for accepting class analysis.

Inequality between people on the basis of income, wealth and prestige can be clearly seen in most societies. However, is class analysis the best explanation for these persistent inequalities? As we have seen, class-based explanations have changed over time: In the nineteenth century Marx argued that *exploitation* – in terms of the extraction of surplus value from the working class by the owners of capital – was the basis for explaining class division. However, by the 1980s this view had been roundly rejected by most researchers, including most Marxists, as it became increasingly unclear – even in the Marxist analysis – what the significance of ownership of the means of production was in the process of class division.

Researchers turned increasingly to Weberian concepts in relation to domination and status to explain class division. Income and conditions of service were seen as key elements in determining the life chances of people in capitalist societies. Yet as we have seen, the classes in Weber's analysis are groups that have little or no internal coherence. Weberian classes are merely sets of people arbitrarily grouped together by social scientists on the basis of market situation (the amount of money they earn) and work situation (their conditions of service). Small changes in either the supply or the demand for a service or skill will change the class position of a person. This suggests that there are many classes in Weberian class analysis, but the boundaries between them are unclear and constantly moving. The other stratification concepts of *status* and *party* also add little to our understanding of class division. However, although there are problems with Weberian analysis, the assumption that Marx made in his abstract model of class difference that income and status were essentially irrelevant was no longer accepted. For most of the twentieth century, inequality of income and wealth was synonymous with class analysis.

In this chapter the main forms of class analysis have been outlined and evaluated, but what have we found?

- There is no agreement on what constitutes class
- There is no agreement on what constitutes the processes of class formation.

Most sociological explanations of class took their starting point from either Marx or Weber. Both these approaches shared the assumption that classes were real and had a significant impact on people's life chances. In the latter years of the twentieth century, class analysis became increasingly irrelevant in academic analysis with concepts such as cultural identity – particularly in relation to gender, race, disability and sexuality – having a more significant impact upon our chosen styles of living. It is to these areas that we now turn our attention.

References

Aglietta, M. (1987) *A Theory of Capitalist Regulation: The US Experience*, trans. David Fernbach, Verso, London.

Ashley, D. (1997) *History without a Subject*, Westview, Boulder, Col.

Baudrillard, J. (1995) *Mirror of Production*, Telos, St. Louis.

Bauman, Zygmunt (1997) *Postmodernity and its Discontents*, Cambridge, Polity Press.

Bauman, Zygmunt (1998) *Globalization: The Human Consequences*, Columbia University Press, New York.

Bauman, Zygmunt (2001) *Community: Seeking Safety in an Insecure World*, Polity, Cambridge.

Bauman, Zygmunt (2002) *Society Under Siege*, Polity, Cambridge.

Bell, D. (1973) *The Coming of Post-Industrial Society*, New York, Basic Books.

Best, S. (2003) *A Beginner's Guide to Social Theory*, London, Sage.

Bond, P. and Saunders, P. (1999) Routes of Success, *British Journal of Sociology*, 50.

Boyer, R. (1990) *The Regulation School: A Critical Introduction*, trans. Craig Charney, Columbia University Press, New York.

Braverman, H. (1974) *Labor and Monopoly Capital: The Degradation of Weberian Twentieth Century*, Monthly Review Press, London and New York.

Buck, N. (1996) 'Social and Economic Change in Contemporary Britain: the Emergence of an Urban Underclass?' in Minione, E. (ed.) *Urban Poverty and the Underclass*, Blackwell, Oxford.

Buckley, Walter [1958] (1966) 'Social Stratification and the Functional Theory of Social Differentiation' in Scott, John (ed.) *Class: Critical Debates*, Routledge, London.

Burris, Val (1987) 'The Neo-Marxist Synthesis of Marx and Weber on Class' in N. Wiley (ed.) *The Marx–Weber Debate*, Sage, Newbury Park, Cal.

Carchedi, Guglielmo (1977) *On the Economic Identification of Social Classes*, London, Routledge.

Carchedi, Guglielmo (2001) *For Another Europe: A Class Analysis of European Economic Integration*, Verso, London.

Crompton, Rosemary (1993) *Class and Stratification: Introduction to Current Debates*, Polity, Cambridge.

Davis, Kingsley [1953] (1996) 'Reply to Tumin' in Scott, John (ed.) *Class: Critical Debates*, Routledge, London.

Davis, Kingsley and Moore, Wilbert, E. [1945] (1996) 'Some Principles of Stratification' in Scott, John (ed.) *Class: Critical Debates*, Routledge, London.

Edgell, Stephen (1993) *Class*, Routledge, London.

Fainstein, Norman (1996) 'A Note on Interpreting American Poverty' in Minione, Enzo (ed.) *Urban Poverty and the Underclass*, Blackwell, Oxford.

Finch, Lynette (1993) *The Classing Gaze: Sexuality, Class and Surveillance*, Allen & Unwin, St Leonards, NSW.

Giddens, Anthony (1994) *Beyond Right and Left. The Future of Radical Politics*, Polity, Cambridge.

Hall, S. (1980) 'Teaching race', *Multiracial Education*, 9(1): 33–13.

Heath, A. (1992) 'The Attitudes of the Underclass' in Smith, D.J. (ed.) *Understanding the Underclass*, Policy Studies Institute, London.

Jameson, F. (1991) *Postmodernism, or the Cultural Logic of Late Capitalism*, Durham, Duke University Press.

Jencks, C. (1992) *Rethinking Social Policy*, Harvard University Press, Cambridge, Mass.

Jessop, B. (1990) 'Regulation Theories in Retrospect and Prospect', *Economy and Society*, 19(2): 154–216.

Joyce, Patrick (1990) 'Work', *The Cambridge Social History of Britain, 1750–1950*, Cambridge, Cambridge University Press.

Joyce, Patrick (1993) *Democratic Subjects: the Self and the Social in 19th-century England*, Cambridge, Cambridge University Press.

Joyce, Patrick (1995a) 'The End of Social History?', *Social History*, 20(1): 73–91.

Joyce, Patrick (1995b) 'Introduction' to Joyce, Patrick (ed.) *Class*, Oxford University Press, Oxford.

Joyce, Patrick (2002) 'Introduction' to Joyce, Patrick (ed.) *The Social in Question: New Bearings in History and the Social Sciences*, London, Routledge.

Kirby, M. (2001) *An interview with Erik Olin Wright*. Found at http://www.theglobalsite.ac.uk/press/105wright.htm

Laclau, E. and Mouffe, C. (1985) *Hegemony and Socialist Strategy*, London, Verso.

Laclau, E. and Mouffe, C. (2001) *Hegemony and Socialist Strategy* (2nd edn), Verso, London.

Lewis, Oscar (1961) *The Children of Sanchez: Autobiography of a Mexican Family*, Penguin, Harmondsworth.

Lipietz, A. (1987) *Mirages and Miracles: The Crises of Global Fordism*, trans. Macey, Verso, London.

Marshall, G. (1988) *Social Class in Modern Britain*, London, Routledge.

Michels, R. [1911] (1962) *Political Parties*, Glencoe, The Free Press.

Marx, Karl (1968) 'A Contribution to the Critique of Political Economy' in *Marx and Engels: Selected Works*, Lawrence & Wishart, London.

Marx, Karl (1977) 'The Eighteenth Brumaire of Louis Bonaparte' in *Selected Works, Vol. 1 Karl Marx and Frederick Engels*, Progress Publishers, Moscow.

Moore, Wilbert E. [1953] (1996) 'Comment on Tumin' in Scott, John (ed.) *Class: Critical Debates*, Routledge, London.

Moricchio, E. (1996) 'Exclusion from Work and the Improvershment Processes in Naples' in Minione, Enzo (ed.) *Urban Poverty and the Underclass*, Blackwell, Oxford.

Morris, L. (1994) *Dangerous Classes: The Underclass and Social Citizenship*, Routledge, London.

Mouffe, Chantal (2000) *The Democratic Paradox*, Verso, London.

Murray, Charles (1990) *The Emerging British Underclass*, London IEA Health and Welfare Unit.

Murray, Charles (1999) 'The Underclass Revisited' published by The American Enterprise Institute for Public Policy Research at http://www.aei.org/ps/psmurray. htm

Nietzsche, F. [1888] (1968) *The Antichrist, Curse on Christianity*, trans. Walter Kaufmann, in Kaufmann, W. (ed.) *The Portable Nietzsche*, New York, Viking Press.

Nietzsche, F. [1886] (1966) *Beyond Good and Evil*, trans. Walter Kaufmann, New York, Random House.

Nietzsche, F. [1883, 1885] (1999) *Thus Spoke Zarathustra*, trans. Thomas Common, Mineola, Dover Publications.

Parsons, Talcott [1940] (1996) 'An Analytical Approach to the Theory of Social Stratification' in Scott, John (ed.) *Class: Critical Debates*, Routledge, London.

Parsons, Talcott (1949) 'Social Classes and Class Conflict in the Light of Recent Sociological Theory' in Parsons, T. (1954) *Essays in Sociological Theory*. New York, The Free Press.

Parsons, Talcott (1951) *The Social System*. London, Routledge and Kegan Paul.

Parsons, Talcott [1953] (1996) 'A Revised Analytical Approach to the Theory of Social Stratification' in Scott, John (ed.) *Class: Critical Debates*, Routledge, London.

Parsons, Talcott [1970] (1996) 'Equality and Inequality in Modern Society, or Social Stratification Revisited' in Scott, John (ed.) *Class: Critical Debates*, Routledge, London.

Post, Ken (1996) *Regaining Marxism*, Macmillan, Basingstoke.

Poulantzas, N. (1975) *Classes in Contemporary Capitalism*, trans. David Fernbach, NLB, London.

Price, Richard (1997) 'Postmodernism as Theory and History' in Belchem, John and Kirk, Neville (eds) *Languages of Labour*, Ashgate, Aldershot.

Rigby, S.H. (1998) *Marxism and History: A Critical Introduction*, Manchester University Press, Manchester.

Roemer, John (1982) *A General Theory of Exploitation and Class*, Harvard University Press, Cambridge, Mass.

Roemer, John (1988) *Free to Lose: An Introduction to Marxist Economic Philosophy*, Radius, London.

Rowntree, S. (1901) *Poverty: a Study of Town Life*. London, Macmillan.

Saunders, P. (1995) 'Could Britain be a Meritocracy?', *Sociology*, 29.

Saunders, P. (1996) *Unequal but Fair?*, Institute of Economic Affairs, London.

Saunders, P. (1997) 'Social Mobility in Britain: An Empirical Evaluation of Two Competing Explanations', *Sociology*, 31.

Saunders, P. (2000) 'Intelligence, Meritocracy and Class Differences'. Paper presented at the New South Wales Institute of Educational Research Forum, 17 May.

Savage, Mike (2000) *Class Analysis and Social Transformation*, Open University Press, Buckingham.

Sewell, William H., Jnr. (1993) 'Towards a Post-materialist Rhetoric for Labour History' in L.R. Berlanstein (ed.) *Rethinking Labor History: Essays on Discourse and Class Analysis*, Urbana University Press, Urbana, Ill.

Simpson, Richard L. [1956] (1996) 'A Modification of the Functionalist Theory of Social Stratification' in Scott, John (ed.) *Class: Critical Debates*, Routledge, London.

Tausky, Curt [1953] (1996) 'Parsons on Stratification: An Analysis and Critique', in Scott, John (ed.) *Class: Critical Debates*, Routledge, London.

Townsend, P. (1979), *Poverty in the United Kingdom*, London, Allen Lane.

Tumin, Melvin M. [1953] (1996) 'Some Principles of Stratification: A Critical Analysis' in Scott, John (ed.) *Class: Critical Debates*, Routledge, London.

Tumin, Melvin M. [1954] (1996) 'Rewards and Task-orientations' in Scott, John (ed.) *Class: Critical Debates*, Routledge, London.

Tumin, Melvin M. [1963] (1996) 'On Inequality' in Scott, John (ed.) *Class: Critical Debates*, Routledge, London.

Wacquant, Loic (1996) 'Red Belt, Black Belt: Racial Division, Class Inequality and the State in the French Urban Periphery and the American Ghetto' in Minione, Enzo (ed.) *Urban Poverty and the Underclass*, Blackwell, Oxford.

Waters, M. (1997) 'Inequality after Class' in Owen, David (ed.) *Sociology after Postmodernism*, Sage, London.

Weber, M. [1922] (1978) *Economy and Society: An Outline of Interpretive Sociology*. Edited by Roth, G. and Wittich, C. Berkeley Los Angeles, University of California Press.

Wesolowski, Wlodzimierz [1962] (1996) 'Some Notes on the Functionalist Theory of Stratification' in Scott, John (ed.) *Class: Critical Debates*, Routledge, London.

Wright, E. (1985) *Classes*, Verso, London.

Wright, E. (2001) 'Interview with Mark Kirby'. Found at www.theglobalsite.ac.uk/press/105wright/htm

Wrong, Dennis H. [1959] (1996) 'The Functional Theory of Stratification: Some Neglected Considerations' in Scott, John (ed.) *Class: Critical Debates*, Routledge, London.

Young, M. (1958) *The Rise of the Meritocracy: 1870–2033: An Essay on Education and Equality*. Harmondsworth, Penguin.

Zajczyk, F. (1996) 'The Social Morphology of the New Urban Poor in a Wealthy Italian City: the Case of Milan', in Minione, Enzo (ed.) *Urban Poverty and the Underclass*, Blackwell, Oxford.

Two

Disability and Mental Illness

Introduction

The disabled and the mentally ill are two of the most powerless groups in society. Traditionally, disability was defined in terms of pathology, which caused bodily impairments that predisposed people to functional limitations in their everyday lives. Disability was seen in terms of a person's inability to fully participate in various activities that the rest of us take for granted, such as washing yourself, cleaning the floor, walking and driving, shopping, preparation of food and generally looking after oneself. Severe disabilities are regarded as an important public health concern. However, as many disability rights organisations have pointed out, in an accessible environment disability can disappear.

According to Shlomo Deshan (1992), in recent times there has been a shifting awareness of the needs and rights of previously repressed people: ethnic minorities, women, lesbian and gay people of 'unusual physiology':

> Disability studies are one of the most recent of the new socio-anthropological specializations. The basic premise of disability studies is that physical conditions do not, by themselves, determine the roles and positions that disabled people fill in society. Rather, it is the culture of both able-bodied and disabled people in any given society that conceptualises and moulds conditions of disability. According to this view, disabled people fill roles in society that are the outcome of cultural mediation. (Deshan 1992: 1)

The social division of disability, Deshan argues, is based upon powerful impulses that the able-bodied have to segregate the 'disabled' and place them in particular social niches.

What is Disability?

World Health Organisation: International Classification of Functioning, Disability and Health

In May 2001 The World Health Organisation (WHO) formally changed the way in which it defines disability, moving away from the terms 'impairment', 'disability' and 'handicap' and instead adopting a new International Classification of Functioning, Disability and Health (ICF). The ICF has two domains:

1 **Body Functions and Structures:** this comprises two classifications, one for functions of body systems, and one for body structures. A person's functioning and disability are conceived as a dynamic interaction between health conditions (diseases, disorders, injuries, traumas, etc.) and contextual factors which include both personal and environmental factors.
2 **Activities and Participation:** the Activities and Participation component includes what the WHO believe to be a complete range of domains which indicate all aspects of bodily functioning from both an individual and a societal perspective.

As the WHO explain:

> Functioning is an umbrella term encompassing all body functions, activities and participation; similarly, disability serves as an umbrella term for impairments, activity limitations or participation restrictions. ICF also lists environmental factors that interact with all these constructs. In this way, it enables the user to record useful profiles of individuals' functioning, disability and health in various domains. (WHO 2001: 2)

THE ICF COMPONENTS

Definitions

In the context of health:

- **Body functions** are the physiological functions of body systems (including psychological functions)
- **Body structures** are anatomical parts of the body such as organs, limbs and their components
- **Impairments** are problems in body function or structure such as a significant deviation or loss
- **Activity** is the execution of a task or action by an individual
- **Participation** is involvement in a life situation
- **Activity limitations** are difficulties an individual may have in executing activities
- **Participation restrictions** are problems an individual may experience in involvement in life situations
- **Environmental factors** make up the physical, social and attitudinal environment in which people live and conduct their lives. (WHO 2001: 10)

Disability Anti-discrimination Legislation

In terms of individual nation states, the Americans with Disabilities Act 1990 provides the starting point for disability anti-discrimination legislation. Below is an outline of the key points in disability legislation across a number of countries: the US, New Zealand, the European Union, the UK, Australia and Canada.

The United States: Americans with Disabilities Act 1990 (ADA)

The ADA aims to establish a clear and comprehensive prohibition of discrimination in such areas as employment, education, health services, public and private sector housing, transport, communication, recreation, voting, and access to public services on the basis of disability. Disability is defined by the ADA in terms of individuals with a physical or mental impairment that substantially limits one or more of their major life activities. In 1990 it was estimated that some 43 million Americans had these recognised impairments and that the number was likely to increase with the ageing population. Before the ADA, Congress believed that discrimination against people with disabilities was a serious social problem. However, unlike individuals who were discriminated against on grounds of gender, race, or age for example, people with disabilities had no legal recourse to rectify such discrimination. ADA prohibits all state, territorial and local government; including school districts and AMTRAK, from discriminating against people on the basis of disability. Any public body with 50 or more employees must have a disability grievance procedure to resolve issues under the Act and, in addition, any public body with 50 or more employees must appoint an ADA coordinator. The Act prohibits direct and indirect employment discrimination. Telecommunications companies offering a telephone service must also provide services suitable for the deaf.

As the text of the ADA makes clear, the Americans with Disabilities Act 1990 aims:

- To provide a clear and comprehensive national mandate for the elimination of discrimination against individuals with disabilities
- To provide clear, strong, consistent, enforceable standards addressing discrimination against individuals with disabilities
- To ensure that the Federal Government plays a central role in enforcing the standards established in this Act on behalf of individuals with disabilities
- To invoke the sweep of Congressional authority, including the power to enforce the fourteenth amendment and to regulate commerce, in order to address the major areas of discrimination faced day-to-day by people with disabilities.

New Zealand Disability Strategy: Making a World of Difference: Whakanui Oranga

Making a World of Difference: Whakanui Oranga is a discussion document that was launched in January 2001 for implementation by June 2003. The underlying assumptions of the document represent a shift in the New Zealand Government's approach to disability issues; a shift from the 'medical model' of disability towards a 'social model' of disability, where people with physical or mental impairments are disadvantaged by social and environmental barriers which prevent full participation in the wider society. The New Zealand Government wants to remove such discriminatory barriers to participation. The aim of the Strategy is to create a non-disabling society: 'a fully inclusive society, where our capacity to contribute and participate in every aspect of life is continually being extended and enhanced'. To bring this about, the New Zealand Government wants to create a *meaningful partnership* of respect, equity and well-protected human rights, between people with disabilities, communities, support agencies and the Government.

The Strategy aims to:

- Encourage and educate for a non-disabling society
- Ensure rights for people experiencing disability
- Provide the best education
- Provide opportunities for employment and economic development
- Foster leading voices by people experiencing disability
- Foster an aware and responsive public service
- Improve services to people experiencing disability
- Improve access to quality information
- Promote participation of Maori experiencing disability
- Promote participation of Pacific people experiencing disability
- Enable children and youth experiencing disability to lead full and active lives
- Improve the quality of life for women experiencing disability
- Value families, *whanau* (the extended family within Maori culture) and carers.

(Source: www.nzds.govt.nz/nzds-toc.html)

European Union Programmes

The European Union's commitment to people with disabilities has changed significantly in recent years. From the Treaty of Rome 1957 until the Treaty of Amsterdam 1997, EU policy was constrained because social policy was left almost totally in the hands of member states. However, some of the most important programmes before 1997 are outlined below.

Helios Programme I (1988–1991)

The central objective of the Helios I was to carry out a range of actions to promote the economic and social integration through vocational training and rehabilitation, in an effort to promote independent lifestyles for people with disabilities. Its objectives were to:

- Develop a Community approach based on the best innovatory experiences in the member states
- Develop exchange and information activities which can make a useful contribution

- Contribute to the implementation of Recommendation 86/379/EEC and the Council Resolution of 21 December 1988
- Continue Community support for European cooperation between non-governmental organizations
- Give appropriate attention to the vocational and social needs of disabled women and to those people caring for the disabled at home.

(Source: http://europa.eu.int/scadplus/leg/en/cha/c11405c.htm)

Helios Programme II (1993–1996)

The central aim of Helios II was to promote equal opportunities and greater integration of disabled people through: 'the development of a community-level policy of cooperation with the Member States and non-governmental organisations directly involved in the fields of functional rehabilitation, educational integration and economic and social integration.' Its objectives were to:

- Develop and improve exchange and information activities with the member states and non-governmental organisations (NGOs) and to ensure that they are disseminated
- Coordinate and increase the effectiveness of actions carried out
- Promote the development of a policy of cooperation in respect of integration, based on the best experience and practice in the member states
- Continue cooperation with European and national NGOs, where the latter are representative and have expressed a desire to cooperate at Community level.

(Source: http://europa.eu.int/scadplus/leg/en/cha/c11405c.htm)

Horizon (1994–1999)

Horizon was an *Employment Community Initiative*, funded from the Economic and Social Fund. The disabled were identified as one of the target groups that faced specific problems in the employment market.

EQUAL (1994–1999)

According to Anna Diamantopoulou, the Commissioner responsible at the time for Employment and Social Affairs:

> The aim of EQUAL is to test new ways of tackling discrimination and inequality experienced by people in work or looking for a job. It will provide the scope to try out new ideas that could change future policy and practice in employment and training.
>
> EQUAL is the successor to Adapt and Employment, the ESF Community Initiatives that ran from 1994 to 1999, and it builds on the successes and results of those programmes. Features such as *partnership, innovation, thematic approach, empowerment, mainstreaming* and *trans-nationality* are the key principles of EQUAL.

(Source: http://europa.eu.int/comm/employment_social/news/2001/nov/233_en.html)

Promise (January 1997 – June 1998)

The Promise initiative was related to the wider EU Information Society Initiatives; the aim was the greater dissemination of best practice in Information Society

Applications for People with Disabilities and other groups, such as older people who were not given equal access to ICT in Europe. It was believed that greater inclusion would come about by exchanging experiences and examples of good practice.

The Treaty of Amsterdam 1997

Article 13 of the Amsterdam Treaty of 1997 committed the EU to tackle discrimination on the grounds of disability, gender, sexual orientation, ethnic origin, religion and age. The Treaty provided the legal structure for a Council of Ministers Directive in November 2000 that established a general framework for equal opportunity in relation to employment. Articles 1 and 2 of the Directive made direct or indirect discrimination on the grounds of disability illegal. In addition, the Council of Ministers agreed on a Community-wide action programme to counter discriminatory practices by public bodies such as the police, health services and education. In addition, it became illegal to restrict or deny access to goods and services to people with disabilities. Areas covered include: housing, transport, leisure (culture and sport). Finally, the Directive also attempts to enhance participation in decision-making by people with disabilities.

However, no specific definition of disability is contained within the Treaty, and the task of implementing the policy is in the hands of the member states, many of whom have chosen to adopt narrow, medically-oriented conceptions of disability, such as Germany which defines disability in terms of individuals who are not fully capable of performing their usual day-to-day activities because of ill-health or injury. This has severely restricted the Directive's impact.

Gudex and Lafortune (2000) conducted an analysis of the definitions of disability document submitted by member states to the OECD. They found that in France disability was defined as a limitation in usual activities such as school or work, whilst 'severe' disability was defined as people who were restricted to their homes or people living in institutions. In contrast, in the Netherlands, an ADL (activities of daily living) conception of disability is used which places greater emphasis on functional limitations.

United Kingdom

Disability Discrimination Act 1995

The 1995 Act made it illegal to discriminate against disabled persons in the areas of:

- Employment
- Access to goods, facilities and services
- Buying or renting land or property.

The Act defines disability in terms of impairment that can be either physical or mental in nature, but must involve a *substantial* and *long-term adverse effect* on a person's ability to carry out normal day-to-day activities.

In terms of employment, it is illegal for an employer to discriminate against a disabled person in any of the following ways:

- The arrangements that a potential employer makes for employment selection must not discriminate against a person with a disability, as this would constitute indirect discrimination
- The terms of employment offered to people must be the same, irrespective of a person's disability status
- Refusing to offer a person employment on grounds of disability is illegal
- It is illegal for an employer to discriminate against a disabled person employed by the organisation
- Opportunities for promotion, transfer, training or receiving any other benefit offered must be the same irrespective of a person's disability status
- Dismissing a person on the grounds of disability, or subjecting a disabled person to any other detriment is illegal.

In terms of access to goods, facilities and services, the Act made it illegal for a public sector or private sector provider to discriminate against a disabled person, for example, by refusing to provide to a disabled person any service normally provided, or that the service provider is prepared to provide, to able-bodied members of the public.

In terms of buying or renting property, it is illegal for people arranging to sell or rent property to discriminate against a disabled person. The terms on which property is offered for sale or rent must be the same irrespective of a person's disability status. Similarly it is illegal to refuse to sell or rent property to a person because they have a disability. Since 1999 the Act has been policed by the Disability Rights Commission, which was established under the Disability Rights Commission Act 1999.

Disability Rights Commission Act 1999

The Commission has the following duties:

- To work towards the elimination of discrimination against disabled persons
- To promote the equalisation of opportunities for disabled persons
- To take such steps as it considers appropriate with a view to encouraging good practice in the treatment of disabled persons
- To keep under review the working of the Disability Discrimination Act 1995.

Special Educational Needs and Disability Act 2001

The Education Act 1996 enhanced the rights of the parents of children with disabilities. If the parents decide that their child would be more suited to an education in a mainstream school, then Local Education Authorities have a duty to educate children with special educational needs in mainstream schools in accordance with the wishes of the parents. In 2001 the United Kingdom Government brought these rights into line with the 1995 and 1999 Acts. It is illegal for the body responsible for a school to discriminate against a disabled pupil either in the school's admissions policy or by changing the terms on which the school is prepared to offer to admit a pupil to the school. It is also illegal for a school to refuse to consider an application for admission to the school from a disabled child.

Australia: Australian Disability Discrimination Act 1992

The Australian Disability Discrimination Act 1992 defined disability in terms of impairment and made it illegal to discriminate against people with disabilities in areas such as employment, education, housing and the provision of goods and services. In addition the activities of private bodies such as sports clubs were covered by the Act. Finally, harassment on the grounds of disability is also illegal under the Act. Discrimination is defined in terms of both direct and indirect discrimination, and a Disability Discrimination Commissioner was appointed to investigate complaints under the Act.

Canada: The Canadian Human Rights Act 1985

Every individual should have an equal opportunity with other individuals to make for himself or herself the life that he or she is able and wishes to have, consistent with his or her duties and obligations as a member of society.

(Source: The Canadian Human Rights Act 1985 Section 2
www.chrc-ccdp.ca/public/guidechra.pdf)

In Canada discrimination against disabled people comes under The Canadian Human Rights Act 1985. Under the Act, discrimination is understood to be *treating people differently, negatively or adversely without a good reason*. The Act makes it illegal for employers or service providers to discriminate against people on the grounds of:

- Race
- National or ethnic origin
- Colour
- Religion
- Age
- Sex (including pregnancy and childbirth)
- Marital status
- Family status
- Mental or physical disability (including previous or present drug or alcohol dependence)
- Pardoned conviction
- Sexual orientation.

Specific issues outlined in the Act include: employment; employment applications and advertisements; access to equal pay; access to employee organisations, such as trade unions; provision of goods and services; accommodation; discriminatory notices; hate messages; and harassment. Organisations covered by the Act include:

- Federal departments, agencies and Crown corporations
- Canada Post
- Chartered banks
- National airlines
- Interprovincial communications and telephone companies
- Interprovincial transportation companies
- Other federally regulated industries, such as certain mining operations.

All provinces and territories have similar laws forbidding discrimination in their areas of jurisdiction. The discriminatory practices specified in the act include:

- Differential treatment of an individual or a group of individuals based on a prohibited ground
- All forms of harassment
- Systemic discrimination – a seemingly neutral policy or practice which in fact is discriminatory.

(Source: www.chrc-ccdp.ca/public/guidechra.pdf)

The Medical Model of Disability

The medical model of disability has a long history, but as a sociological approach the model was developed by Talcott Parsons. The key assumption underpinning the model is that disability is a personal tragedy. The loss of a function that the rest of us take for granted or some other biological abnormality establishes the disabled person as having an inferior-stigmatised status. According to this model, the disabled are dependent, charity cases whom we should pity, although we should always be wary of possible violent tendencies, caused by the frustration they feel at having such medical and biological problems.

The notion of disability as personal tragedy is most clearly seen when parents have a child with disabilities. Having a child with a disability is assumed to be one of the most dreaded experiences for families. Kearney and Griffin (2001) argue that the literature on children with disabilities is dominated by an assumption of the negative impact that disability has on the lives of families. They argue that:

> Uncritical application of these theories in the interpretation of the behaviour of parents of children with disabilities has negative implications. Parents, for instance, can be labelled as responding pathologically. It is not unusual to hear professionals use expressions such as: 'They're not being realistic'; 'They won't accept the child'; 'They're shopping around, looking for someone who'll say there's nothing wrong.' When professionals

interpret parents' words and behaviours as denying reality, rather than demonstrating
the ideals of 'acceptance' and 'being realistic', the parents may be viewed as dysfunctional. (Kearney and Griffin 2001: 583)

The parents interviewed by Kearney and Griffin did not deny the diagnosis of
their children, but they did reject the professional's negative judgement, such as:
'They will be a vegetable'; 'They will do nothing'; and the advice to 'try for
another one'. Kearney and Griffin's conclusion is unequivocal: 'the parents in this
study were very clear – their children with disabilities are a great source of joy'
(ibid.: 588).

However, to return to my personal life history, the medical model did inform
my own perceptions of people with disabilities. As a child I recall in reception
class the teacher who brought in a bag of apples for the children to eat at play
time. I did not like the look of the apple I had been given and was suspicious of
any apple that did not come from a shop. So I put mine in the bin. The teacher
was a little cross to see the apple in the bin, with only one bite missing. She
pointed at me and asked if I had thrown it away. I looked around the class at all
the children staring at me, and as I looked around the following words came out
of my mouth: "It wasn't me Miss. I ate mine quickly, I think it was Mark Binney
who threw the apple away." Mark Binney was a child with Downes Syndrome. He
was so upset by my false accusation that he was unable to defend himself. The
teacher mistook his tears as a sign of guilt. Although as a child I had never heard
of Parsons or the medical model, I was familiar with the model's underlying
assumptions: I was in trouble, I was about to be told off by the teacher, but Mark
Binney had a disability and his wrongdoing would not be punished by the
teacher. The teacher had a duty of care, and had to give more care to people who
needed it most; hence she would exempt him from any sanction, because he had
a disability.

I was a child: perhaps I should be forgiven for this wrongdoing? However, as an
adult, I recall during my time as a lecturer in a Further Education College coming
out of the staff room on my way to teach an evening class. As I stepped into the
corridor, I noticed a young woman with learning difficulties leaning against the
wall, with her back to me, sobbing. My initial reaction was to move towards her
and ask if she needed assistance. However, because the day classes had ended and
the evening classes were yet to begin, the college was rather quiet and I was concerned that if somebody saw me with the young woman they might think that
she was crying because of something that I had done to her. Alternatively, she
may not hear me walking along the corridor and because she had her back to me,
I might frighten her, which could make matters worse; she might bite me! Again
the same assumptions about the inferiority of disabled people were at work
informing my actions.

The medical model is built upon such prejudices and assumptions. However,
from the late 1970s onwards, the social model of disability emerged to challenge

such assumptions about people with disabilities. The medical model effectively medicalised disability regardless of the specific nature of the impairment that the disabled person had.

THE MEDICAL MODEL VS. THE SOCIAL MODEL OF DISABILITY

Medical Model

'The main approach to understanding disability arises from the medical model – disabilities occur because of the physical impairments which have resulted from the underlying disease or disorder.' (Johnston 1996a: 205)

Social Model

Mike Oliver (1983) coined the term Social Model of Disability, which has the following characteristics:

- The model has a transformational aim – to remove barriers from disabled people's lives
- The model attempts to distance disability issues from 'biology'
- The model advocates *action* research, findings should be used to enhance the lives of people with disabilities
- '... discussions of disabled people's experiences, narratives and stories are couched firmly within an environmental and cultural setting that highlights the disabling consequences of a society organised around the needs of a mythical, affluent non-disabled majority.' (Barnes 2003: 10)

The Social Model of Disability

In contrast to the medical model, the social model of disability places a greater emphasis on needs rather than personal tragedy. Wider social forces beyond the immediate control of the person with disability are responsible for the problems disabled people face. Society generates forms of discrimination and exclusion that disabled people have to cope with. The problem is to be found in the *social constructions* of prejudice that surround disability and not in the bodies of disabled people. It is for this reason that the social model has become closely associated with New Social Movements and emancipatory forms of active research within Disability Studies. In addition, according to Stone and Priestly (1996) many advocates of the social model believe that able-bodied researchers on disability issues are *parasitic people* who treat disabled people as passive research subjects.

For Shakespeare and Watson (1997) the social model has a number of characteristics:

- The model advocates a social analysis of disability
- The model advocates a social construction view of disability
- The model *de-individualises* the relationship between medicine and disability by placing the doctor–patient relationship into a social context
- The model recognises that people manage their physical issues in various ways, but all disabled people recognise that physical and social barriers are, in the last analysis, rooted in prejudice and discrimination.

The philosophical origins of the social model are rooted in the work of Berger and Luckman, who argue that *reality* – which they define as 'a quality appertaining to phenomena that we recognize as having a being independent of our own volition' (Berger and Luckman 1966: 13) – is socially constructed. In other words, the world has its origins in our thoughts and ideas and is maintained by our thoughts and ideas. However, in our everyday lives, reality is simply taken for granted: we rarely question the construction of reality because it appears both 'normal' and 'self-evident'. This assumed acceptance of normality is what Berger and Luckman call *the natural attitude*; reality has a quality of *compelling facticity*:

> I apprehend the reality of everyday life as an ordered reality. Its phenomena are pre-arranged in patterns that seem to be independent of my apprehension of them and that impose themselves upon the latter. The reality of everyday life appears already objectified *as* objects before my appearance on the scene. (Ibid.: 35, italics in original)

We interpret the individual whom we encounter in everyday life by reference to a 'social stock of knowledge' made up of typifactory schemes that provide detailed information about the areas of everyday life within which we operate. We use the typifactory schemes within the stock of knowledge to classify individuals into types, such as: 'men', 'girls', 'Chinese', 'disabled', etc. Such typifications also inform us of the most appropriate way of dealing with these different types of people. In addition, we use language to place ourselves in what we consider to be an appropriate category, and we use the social stock of knowledge to define the situation we are in and the limits of our capabilities. The reason why humans involve themselves in these activities, claim Berger and Luckman, is because in the last analysis all social reality is uncertain and society is a construction to protect people from insecurity.

For Berger and Luckman, people also have a link with the environment through their biology, but they stress that:

> there is no human nature in the sense of a biologically fixed substratum determining the variability of socio-cultural formations ... The empirical relativity of these configurations, their immense variety and luxurious inventiveness, indicate that they are the product of man's own socio-cultural formations rather than of a biologically fixed human nature. (Ibid.: 67)

Berger and Luckman argue that the human organism is primarily characterised by its plasticity. However, the ways in which we define the limits and parameters of that plasticity 'cannot be adequately understood apart from the particular social context in which they were shaped' (1996: 68).

Berger and Luckman: The Relationship between Man and His Body

Read the passage below and give a brief outline of what you think is the central point that Berger and Luckman are trying to make:

> The common development of the human organism and the human self in a socially determined environment is related to the peculiarly human relationship between organism and self. This relationship is an eccentric one. On the one hand, man *is* a body, in the same way that this may be said of every other animal organism. On the other hand, man *has* a body. That is, man experiences himself as an entity that is not identical with his body, but that, on the contrary, has that body at its disposal. In other words, man's experience of himself always hovers in a balance between being and having a body, a balance that must be redressed again and again. This eccentricity of man's experience of his own body has certain consequences for the analysis of human activity as conduct in the material environment and as external-isation of subjective meanings. (Berger and Luckman 1966: 68; italics in original)

For Berger and Luckman, society is a human product that is experienced as an objective reality and the people within the world are also social products. The social world, and the ways in which people are classified within that social world, have no ontological status beyond the human activity that created it. Moreover, our individual biography and what we understand to be our personal identity are not wholly individual; they are based upon our subjective meanings acquired through the processes of socialisation. The potentially subjectively meaningful has to be made objectively available to us in order to become meaningful. What is subjectively meaningful to us can only be meaningful if those subjective ideas are interpreted against the typifications that are contained within the social stock of knowledge.

According to Berger and Luckman, when an individual performs a role, such as the role of a disabled person, then that role and the person who performs it are defined by the use of typifications. The role of the disabled person is typified by personal tragedy and loss, and although such roles can be internalised by the people who perform them and can become subjectively real to them, it is important to note that for Berger and Luckman this is not an irreversible process. The stock of knowledge, the typifications, the perception of roles and our subjective reflections and internalisations can all be redefined. We can redefine the unity between history and biography.

What Berger and Luckman bring to the surface is the link between disability and identity, which later disability researchers have developed. Nicholas Watson (1998) argues that the perception of disabled people is based upon stereotypical ideas about dependency and helplessness, which can often impact upon the disabled people's perceptions of themselves and their identities. Watson outlines a number of case studies of individual people with disabilities, and the anxiety that disabled people can feel because they do not conform to bodily cultural and social norms. One case is that of Joan (a 41-year-old married woman with two children) who had been diagnosed with multiple sclerosis 16 years previously. Joan did not see her life as worthwhile. Drawing upon the work of Charles Taylor on self, Watson tries to explain why many disabled people have these feelings of low self-worth.

Charles Taylor is concerned with the question: What is it to be a human agent? He explains: 'We talk about a human being as a "self" … meaning that they are beings of the requisite depth and complexity to have an identity' (Taylor 1989: 32). The self has a 'strategic capacity' and as such requires some form of reflective awareness. In addition, for Taylor, 'One is a self only among other selves. A self can never be described without reference to those who surround it' (ibid.: 35).

The notion of the self is peculiar to the modern world and would not be understood by individuals who lived in the distant past. Our modern self has a distinction between inside and outside: the inside contains our inner thoughts, desires and intentions, which requires a 'radical reflexivity'. Constantly reviewing *what* it does and thinks and *why* it does what it does and thinks what it thinks. The outside is the public domain, the image that we present to the outside world.

Taylor's work also falls within what sociologists call the 'linguistic turn' of sociology. For Taylor, we find sense in our lives by talking about it. In addition, Taylor introduces his notion of *moral frameworks*, which people make use of in order to create a self that they find acceptable. We define who we are from the position we speak from and whom we speak to. Our skill as speakers – Taylor uses the term 'interlocutors' – allows us to form relationships with others and to be involved in shared activities with others, which is essential to become an individual self: 'It's as though the dimension of interlocution were of significance only for the genesis of individuality' (ibid.: 36).

Moreover, as we shall see more clearly below, because disabled people are less likely to be employed in the media industries, it is able-bodied people who have control over the representation of the impaired body on television, film and literature. When it comes to the definition of the worth of people within *webs of interlocution*, it is the able-bodied who define and shape our perception of what it means to be disabled.

In the 1990s a number of critiques of the social model emerged. Shakespeare and Watson (1997) argue that the social model is atheoretical in nature and ignores the real and often painful medical problems that many disabled have to cope with. They argue that the notion of impairment was initially underplayed by advocates of the social model 'in order to develop a strong argument about social structure and social processes' (Shakespeare and Watson 1997: 298).

In the 1990s a debate emerged within Disability Studies on the status of 'impairment' and its role within the social model. Finkelstein (1996) argued that neither 'impairment' nor 'personal experience' should be included within the social model as they would dilute the effectiveness of the model. In contrast, Ruth Pinder (1997) argued that to separate impairment from disability is to gloss over the complexity of individual people's lives:

> [I]f we want to fully understand the ambiguities of lived experience, we need to come to grips with the many interlocking webs of significance in which impairment and disability are embedded. On their own neither tells the whole story. (Pinder 1997: 302)

Talcott Parsons: the Functionalist Perspective of Disability

Parsons was one of the key thinkers in the establishment of the medical model. According to Barnes, Parsons assumes that 'accredited impairment, whether physical, sensory or intellectual, is the primary cause of "disability" and therefore the difficulties; economic, political and cultural, encountered by people labelled "disabled"' (Barnes 2003: 4). Parsons argued that we should view disability in the same terms as *the sick role*: 'disablement [together with the sick role] ... constitute fundamental disturbances of the expectations by which men live' (Parsons 1951: 442).

In addition, disability is described by Parsons as 'a pathological condition' (ibid.: 443) in which the disabled person is 'often humiliated by his incapacity to function normally' (ibid.: 443). Disabled people are said to respond to their condition in one of two ways:

- Denial of their disability: refusal to give in to it
- Exaggerated self-pity: the need for 'incessant personal attention.' (Ibid.: 443)

For Parsons, disability operates in the same fashion as illness, it 'incapacitates for the effective performance of social roles' (ibid.: 430). Similarly, society has a *functional intent* to control and minimise illness to aid the smooth running of the social system. Like the sick role, disability is a 'negatively achieved role' (ibid.: 438). Disability is also regarded as a form of deviance and should be controlled by the same mechanisms of social control: 'both the sick role and that of the physician assume significance as mechanisms of social control' (ibid.: 477).

The role of the physician is to monitor the motivation of people who are attempting to remove themselves from their normal social role responsibilities by claiming to be sick or disabled. The sick or disabled person is a problem for the social system because they hinder its successful functioning. As Parsons explains:

> [I]llness is a state of disturbance in the 'normal' functioning of the total human individual, including both the state of the organism as a biological system and of his personal and social adjustments. It is thus partly biological and partly socially defined. (1951: 431)

> From the point of view of the stability of the social system, the sick role may be less dangerous than some of the alternatives ... [However] the motivational materials which enter into illness are continuous with those expressed in many other forms of deviance. (Ibid.: 478)

Parsons outlines four institutional expectations relative to the sick role:

- The sick person is exempted from normal social role responsibilities, as legitimised by a doctor
- The sick person cannot be expected to get better by an act of will – the person must be taken care of
- Being ill is undesirable and the sick person has an obligation to want to get well
- The sick person has an obligation to seek technically competent help and to cooperate with the doctor.

What constitutes disability is inherently universalistic in that there are generalised objective criteria that determine whether a person is disabled or not.

In the late 1970s Parsons returned to issues of illness and disability. In 1978 he argued that the sick role was 'rooted' in a context of Christian traditions concerned with maximising instrumental efficiency – in other words, illness and disability are rooted in cultural instrumentalism. The pattern variables that establish the cultural patterns within the social system also underpin medical knowledge and medical practice. Disability is viewed in terms of a *social cost* to the social system; disability prevents the efficient running of the social system because it seriously hinders the effective performance of social roles, hence there is a need for medical intervention.

Drawing upon Parsons (1978a, 1978b and 1978c), Chris Shilling (2002) argues that:

> Parsons perceived health not primarily as a quality of the body, but as the 'underlying capacity' of individuals; a capacity that society sought to manage via 'institutionised roles' incorporating 'valued tasks'. Parsons indeed, eventually defined health as the 'teleonomic capacity' to maintain a self-regulated state that is 'a prerequisite' for individuals undertaking 'successful goal-orientated behaviour' that improves the functional capacity of the social system. Illness, in contrast, constitutes a breakdown of such capacities, a 'disturbance in the normal functioning of the total human individual. (Shilling 2002: 624)

From these arguments we can conclude that from the perspective of the medical model in general – and for Parsons's specifically – people have a moral responsibility to regard bodily impairment as undesirable.

Shilling's focus is not on issues of disability but on how Parsons's arguments were a forerunner for later postmodern and poststructuralist argument on the body as a *project*. As Shilling points out, in the consumer society it is common-place to view the body as a project that we are responsible for constructing. We design our bodies; they are not to be regarded simply as a biological precondition for social action. The malleability of the body is central to the consumer society because there is a clear link between self-image and pleasure: 'In this context, the need to develop a healthy, adaptable and instrumentally efficient body has become an important variable in social success' (Shilling 2002: 627).

In summary, the medical model views impairment as disagreeable, a source of legit-imate stigma, a barrier to full participation in the consumer society and a problem for the social system. The consequences of exclusion from the consumer society are dire. As we saw in the section on stratification, Zygmunt Bauman argues we may all desire to be consumers but not all of us can be consumers. Consequently, the people who are excluded from consumer society are defined 'first and foremost as blemished, defective, faulty and deficient – in other words, inadequate consumers ... In a soci-ety of consumers, it is above all the inadequacy of the person as a consumer that leads to social degradation and "internal exile"' (Bauman 1998: 38).

The postmodern consumer society is stratified and the lifestyle of people who are excluded from consumerism has become increasingly criminalised.

> Consumption, the acceptance of market seduction and being seen to act on our desires, have become the measure of a successful life; and the poor are seen as 'depraved rather than deprived'. (Bauman 2001: 117)

As Parsons made clear, disability is deviance and disabled people have their functional significance and utility questioned, they are *flawed consumers* subjected to spatial segregation and immobilization:

> In a world in which mobility and the facility to be on the move have become principal factors of social stratification, this is (both physically and symbolically) a weapon of ulti-mate exclusion and degradation, of the recycling of the 'lower classes' and the poor in general into an 'underclass' – a category that has been cast outside the class or any other social system of functional significance and utility and defined from the start by reference to its endemically criminal proclivities. (Bauman 2001: 120)

The social model stresses the importance of stigma in the lives of impaired people, which is the next area we shall look at.

Stigma: Management of a Spoiled Identity

For Goffman (1963) stigma is explained in terms of the presentation of signs, and the ability of the normals to decode those signs. He is concerned with three different types of stigma:

1 **Abominations of the body:** the various physical deformities
2 **Blemishes of individual character:** perceived as weak will, domineering or unnatural passions, treacherous and rigid beliefs, and dishonesty, these being inferred from a known record of, for example, mental disorder, imprisonment, addiction, alcoholism, homosexuality, unemployment, suicidal attempts or radical political behaviour
3 **The tribal stigma of race, nation and religion:** these being stigma that can be transmitted through lineages and equally contaminate all members of a family. (Goffman 1963: 14)

For Goffman individual social actors with very different stigmas are all in a similar situation *vis-à-vis* the rest of the population. Moreover, stigmatised individuals, irrespective of the type of stigma they carry, respond to the wider population in a very similar fashion. We all have the capacity to play the role of *stigmatised* and *normal*. Both sets of social actors acknowledge that a stigma involves possessing shameful differences regarding identity. Goffman refers to this as the 'normal–stigmatized unity' (ibid.: 155). Normals regard stigmatised individuals as not fully human, and not only subject them to a variety of discriminations, but also construct an ideology to explain why the stigmatised are inferior and why they pose a threat, a process which Goffman defines as 'rationalising an animosity' (ibid.: 15). It is important to understand that the categories of *stigmatised* and *normal* are not concrete groups of people, but rather they are labels or perspectives. Almost all individual social actors carry with them some degree of stigma, but some individual social actors have life-long attributes which give them very high visibility causing them to be typecast as stigmatised in all social situations, continually in opposition to 'normals'.

So it is that a stigmatised person progresses along a socialisation path which Goffman calls a *moral career*; a process by which the stigmatised learns the normal point of view and that they are excluded from it. The rest of us, successfully on the whole, use a variety of techniques to restrict information about our minimal stigma. However, we live in constant fear that our stigma will be exposed. Goffman outlines examples of girls who examine themselves in the mirror after losing their virginity to see if their stigma shows, only slowly accepting that they look no different.

One such technique of information control, Goffman refers to as *covering*, this usually takes the form of not displaying the things about ourselves which we know are abnormal, if this is at all possible. Name-changing is one of the most often used covering techniques. Also, people with disabilities learn to behave in such a way as to minimise the obtrusiveness of their stigma.

However, as Olney and Brockelman (2003: 49) argue, 'feeling good about oneself because of rather than in spite of, one's disability is not presented as an option within the dominant culture'. This view is reflected in the medical model in general and Goffman's work in particular.

There are many similarities with Talcott Parsons; what constitutes disability is inherently universalistic, there are generalised objective criteria that determine whether a person is disabled or not based upon maximising instrumental efficiency. For both Goffman and for Parsons, illness and disability are rooted in cultural instrumentalism. Consider the following examples:

> It can be assumed that a necessary condition for social life is the sharing of a single set of normative expectations by all participants, the norms being sustained in part because of being incorporated. When a rule is broken restorative measures will occur; the damaging is terminated and the damage repaired, whether by control agencies or by the culprit himself.
> ... [I]n an important sense there is only one complete unblushing male in America: a young, married, white, urban, northern, heterosexual Prostestant father of college education, fully employed, of good complexion, weight and height and a recent record in sports. Every American male tends to look out upon the world from this perspective, this constituting one sense in which one can speak of a common value system in America. (Goffman 1963: 152)

There is however, a good deal of empirical research which casts doubt on Goffman's findings:

- **Cahill and Eggleston (1995)** argue that people with disabilities get a feel for specific situations in which they find themselves and change their mode of self-presentation accordingly. They might choose to embrace, discard, suppress or disclose their disability for reasons other than fear or shame
- **Glenn and Cunningham (2001)** argue that adults with 'mental retardation' rate themselves positively in terms of competence, social acceptance and self-concept
- **Antle (2000)** argues that children with disabilities do not differ in their measured self-worth from children without disabilities
- **Olney and Kim (2001)** argue that disabled people feel positive about having a disability even though they are aware of the negative evaluation of disability by the able-bodied. These people are rejecting the clinical labels that the able-bodied were attempting to apply and focusing instead on things other than their physical impairments
- **Rapley (1998)** argues that adults with 'mental retardation' often attempt to *pass* as nondisabled people. However, this was not out of fear or shame, rather individuals are attempting to secure an advantage from the way they present themselves
- **Frank (1988)** found, in a similar fashion, that people who choose not to wear prosthetic limbs, but rather to display their disability, are often attempting to manipulate the perceptions of others and enhance their opportunities in a given situation
- **Olney and Brockelman (2003)** found from their research with students that having hidden disabilities, disabled people attempt to control the conditions under which they disclose information about their disability to others. Individuals often share a great deal of information with people they are close to. However, perception management is much more complex than Goffman (1963) had suggested. Passing and covering techniques may not be couched in terms of fear and shame, but rather in terms of *self-determination* – in which the disabled person considers the benefits of sharing information with others:

> Self-disclosure is a contextual act that depends upon many factors, including situation, life stage, familiarity, and necessity. People with disabilities and other socially stigmatised

roles such as homosexuality employ a range of strategies to manage information about themselves such as sharing information on a 'need to know' basis, demonstrating their competence, or waiting until it feels safe to tell others about their difference. (Olney and Brockelman 2003: 36)

ACTIVITY

Can a Fat Woman Call Herself Disabled?

Charlotte Cooper (1997) raises the interesting question: 'Can a fat woman call herself disabled?' She argues that both the disabled and fat people are made invisible by the media, which is dominated by able-bodied, slender white bodies. Both disabled and fat people are subjected to stereotypes that generate feelings of shame and pity. In addition, fat people are regarded as legitimate targets for derision because they have brought their condition upon themselves. Cooper argues that: 'In my experience most people, even those of us who are fat, are rejecting of fat people' (Cooper 1997: 33).

In the same way that medicalisation became the dominant theoretical approach underpinning approaches to disability, so medical discourse that pathologises fat people is regarded as the only legitimate discourse for understanding fatness. Medicine imposes a 'judgmental attitude towards fat and disabled people which is similarly derogatory, identifying us as unworthy, pitiful or ugly, which is internalised by all' (ibid.: 37).

Cooper concludes by saying:

I consider the experience of being fat in a fat-hating culture to be disabling which, in addition to my impairment and the similarities I share with other disabled people, such as medicalisation and restricted civil rights, suggests to me that I am disabled. (Ibid.: 39)

Questions:

> Do you accept or reject Charlotte Cooper's argument?

> Do you accept the view that being overweight is a form of functional disability? Outline the reasons for your answers.

To be defined and labelled as a *fat person* is to be placed somewhere between ugly and disabled, however, it is important to note that there is a racial element to these issues. Tamara Beauboeuf-LaFontant (2003) argues that the weight that many black American women carry reflects the strong discourse that black American women are deviant and devalued as women, both within their own and the wider culture. She argues that the *Mammy* is a continuing controlling image of black womanhood and reflects her physical deviance, obesity and sexlessness. In American culture a sexual woman should be thin and white. Beauboeuf-LaFontant draws upon an example from Retha Powers's personal account of meeting a college counsellor to discuss her own compulsive eating and dieting. The counsellor explained to Retha Powers:

> You don't have to worry about feeling attractive or sexy because Black women aren't seen as sex objects, but as women ... Also fat is more acceptable in the Black community; that's another reason you don't have to worry about it. (Beauboeuf-LaFontant 2003: 113)

Marxian Analysis of Disability

There is no specific analysis of disability in the works of Marx or Engels. Mike Oliver, Paul Apperley, Viv Finkelstein and others have drawn upon Marxian concepts, such as ideology, hegemony and alienation but central Marxian concepts such as the Labour Theory of Value have not been used to explain the position of disabled people in contemporary society.

In his account of the lives of working-class people in Manchester, Engels did make a number of observations on the ways in which the processes of industrial capitalism damaged the bodies of the workers, in many cases turning them into 'cripples':

> a state of things which permits so many deformities and mutilations for the benefit of a single class, and plunges so many industrious working-people into want and starvation by reason of injuries undergone in the service and through the fault of the bourgeoisie. (Engels [1844] cited in Apperley 1998: 83)

Any Marxian analysis of disability is firmly rooted within the medical model; disability is seen as physical impairment. Moreover, disability is seen as a problem created by capitalism and is one of the things that will be abolished under socialism.

Later Marxian analysis takes up this theme and argues that within the capitalist system there is a contradiction between health and profit which generates impairment. Doyal and Pennell (1982) argue that:

- Commodities can be bad for health: there are known health risks associated with the consumption of red meat, sugar and alcohol
- Commodity production is bad for the health of the workers: shift work; deskilling; overtime and the use of dangerous chemicals are all potential causes of poor health
- Commodity production can also cause environmental health problems, because of pollution.

Taking a long historical perspective, which includes looking at smallpox and cholera epidemics and the incidence of TB in the nineteenth century, Doyal and Pennell argue that health is usually defined as the absence of incapacitating pathology. This involves looking at workers in 'functional terms'; the capitalist system views people primarily as producers and has no concern with pain, suffering or anxieties unless they damage profit margins. They argue that all ill health in the contemporary world can be traced to the capitalist mode of production, and the crisis in health care is caused by the contradictions within capitalism.

One of the key functions of the health care systems in capitalist societies is the reproduction of labour power. Organised health care helps to maintain the physical fitness of labour power. In Marxian terms, the health care system can make workers fitter so that the amount of surplus value extracted from the workers can be maintained at a high level.

The other major function of the health care systems within capitalist societies is ideological in nature. Health is defined in individualistic terms within capitalism; it is individuals who become sick often because of their own moral failings rather than socio-economic or environmental factors, which are possible causes of ill health. At the same time, the provision of a National Health Service in Britain allows the state to present a benevolent image of itself to the workers. Doyal and Pennel argue that the enactment of social legislation is the best strategy for stopping the spread of socialism. They quote Balfour, the Prime Minister in 1895: 'Social legislation is not merely to be distinguished from socialist legislation, but it is the most direct opposite and its most effective anti-dote.' Doyal and Pennel also attempt to show that scientific activity – such as medicine – reflects the dominant economic interests within the society that produced the science. Medical science reflects the dominant ideology within capitalism.

The Marxian approach to medicine is then 'functional' and 'teleological' in nature. The approach argues that the medical system is performing functions for the capitalist system as a whole and its purpose is explained in terms of future goals rather than prior causes. The reason why we have a health service is to support the future of capitalism and not because we have always had a problem of poor health in the population.

ACTIVITY

Is Capitalism Bad For Your Health?

Read the passage below, which derives from Best (2000) and answer the questions that follow:

According to Nikki Hart (1982) over the last two hundred years there has been an excellent improvement in human health: a significant fall in mortality and a momentous decline in infective and parasitic diseases. This can be seen in the expansion of the human lifespan and the general improvement in our physical welfare. Other improvements listed by Hart include:

- Extensive improvements in the sufficiency and the variety of our diet
- A sanitisation of human existence, brought about by the public control over the supply of clean water and disposal of sewage
- A transformation in average housing standards
- A revolution in the process of biological reproduction which has greatly extended human control over bodily processes with important implications for sexual freedom and gender equality
- Real progress in medical knowledge and technique – notably reducing the impact of physical congenital and non-congenital deformity and disability.

In contrast to Doyal and Pennel, Hart argues that capitalism has revolutionised human health and that Marxists cannot show in any conclusive way that the capitalist mode of production is the root cause of even one major degenerative disease today. Also in contrast to the Marxian view that human health would improve under socialism, Hart argues that if the capitalist mode of production were to disappear, then so may good health. In addition, Doyal and Pennel do not tell their readers how it is possible to bring about a socialist medical system. Finally, the points that Marxists make about the ideological nature of science and scientific activity are highly relativistic in nature. (Adapted from Best 2000)

Question:

> Is capitalism bad for your health? Draw up two lists: one of positive contributions that capitalism has made towards human health and one of negative effects that capitalism has had on human health.

Many researchers in the field of Disability Studies would agree that capitalism is bad for health and historically has been a major cause of physical impairment. Finkelstein (1980) discusses these issues in relation to an evolutionary materialist model, made up of three distinct historical phases:

1 **Feudalism**: where largely agrarian societies accommodate people with disabilities in the economic life of the community.
2 **Industrialisation**: which saw people with disabilities largely excluded from the wider society.
3 **Liberation from discrimination**: we are still only at the beginning of this phase of history, but this is a phase where disabled people working with medical and other professionals draw up technological advances to move beyond social restrictions.

However, as Paul Abberely (1998) has argued, there are objections to the Marxian argument that disability will disappear under socialism. First, it is not possible to reduce the level of disability to zero, as processes of industrial production do not cause all disabilities. Secondly, Marxists share a generally negative view of disability. Taking as his starting point Marx's 'Critique of the Gotha

Programme', in which Marx outlines how in a communist society 'labour is no longer just a means of keeping alive but has become a vital need' and that this will form the basis of a society based upon the principle of 'from each according to his abilities to each according to his needs' (Marx 1875 cited in Abberely 1998: 86), disabled people are deprived by their impaired biology that is inherently alienating in nature:

> Following Marxist theory thus understood, some impaired lives cannot then, in any possible society, be truly social, since the individual is deprived of the possibility of those satisfactions and that social membership to which her humanity entitles, and which only work can provide. (Ibid.: 87)

In the last analysis, claims Abberely, Marxists share the eugenic assumption that impaired bodies are undesirable and a problem.

Gleeson (1997) attempts to put together a *historically materialist* conception of disability, which remains true to the central assumptions of the Marxian analysis but which is liberating for disabled people. Gleeson argues that the way in which the basic material activities are organised under capitalism – notably work, transport, leisure and domestic activities – forms the basis for defining people with physical disabilities as *disabled*. Disability, for Gleeson, is something that is socially constructed through attitudes, discourse and symbolic representation that are 'themselves the product of the social practices which society undertakes in order to meet its material needs' (Gleeson 1997: 194).

Notions of disability are superstructural, or ideological, in nature and objectively emerge from the economic base in the same way that steam emerges from boiling water. As Gleeson makes clear, 'distinct social oppression, such as disability, arises from the concrete practices which define a mode of life' (ibid.: 196). There are a number of objections to this argument. Firstly, the Labour Theory of Value is Marx's theory of exploitation, and is used to explain the economic inequality experienced by the proletariat. The issue of oppression though gives rise to the more important question: 'What is to be done about the oppression experienced by people with disabilities?' Gleeson explains as follows:

> An obvious target for change is the social system through which the labour of individuals is valued (and devalued). This suggests that the commodity labour market must either be dispensed with or radically restructured so that the principle of competition is displaced from its control role in evaluating fitness for employment. The commodity labour market uses the lens of competition to distort and magnify the limitations of impaired people – a just society would seek to liberate the bodily capacities of all individuals. (Ibid.: 197)

The problem lies in defining people in terms of their 'bodily capacities' in the first instance. Defining people on the basis of biological characteristics is the basis for *disability*; it is the founding assumption which gives rise to all other forms of oppression that disabled people face. Social valuation, by competition in the labour market or otherwise, on the basis of 'bodily capacities', *is* disability.

The Disability Business: Rehabilitation in America

Drawing upon what he terms the *ecological model* in which the physical environment, cultural environment and biophysical factors come together to provide a social response to the problem of disability, Gary Albrecht (1992) argues that disability is a socially constructed problem. He goes on to explain that with the production of disability, there has been the development of a rehabilitation industry which is an institutional response to that perceived problem. In contrast to earlier times when disabled people were cared for by their families and profit was not a concern, today the rehabilitation industry aims to improve the economic position of people with disabilities so that they are fit for work. In the last analysis, the role of the rehabilitation industry is to generate profits. Disability is both a subjective problem for the people, in that people are made to feel that they are experiencing something that is undesirable, and in addition disability is an objective social problem in that it is seen as a potential threat to the well-being of society. Moreover, disability is often experienced by people who are already disadvantaged: people who are in poor health; ethnic minorities; women; people over 65 years of age; people with poor educational backgrounds and people who live alone.

However, in themselves the notions of disability and impairment have no meaning. The rehabilitation industry defines impairments as disability and therefore places disability issues within a context of medical problems and procedures. As Albrecht explains, 'The rehabilitation process effectively has been medicalized by physicians regardless of the nature of the specific impairment or the type of rehabilitation intervention' (Albrecht 1992: 128). In addition, the rehabilitation industry establishes a set of needs, stimulates a demand for a range of appropriate services, and identifies who is eligible for the services provided. The rehabilitation industry generates a series of symbols and meanings that we use to make sense of disability and how to respond appropriately to those issues. The Americans with Disabilities Act (ADA) (1990) established rehabilitation as an individual right, and made it illegal to prevent a person with a disability from entering the labour market.

Albrecht and Bury analysed the various stakeholder groups within the rehabilitation industry and found that the business was fuelled by the least powerful group in the system, namely the disabled:

> The vitality of this market is rapidly changing because in the United States, inpatient rehabilitation facilities depend upon Medicare for 70 percent of their revenues. As a consequence, hospitals and rehabilitation companies have merged to form chains such as the Continental Medical System group and the Allina System. To keep profits up, traditional medical rehabilitation providers are integrating vertically and horizontally, slashing costs, offering subacute care, providing niche marketing around problems such as wound care and HIV/AIDS, reorganizing therapy teams, and moving facilities into the community. (Albrecht and Bury 2001: 590)

A Sociology of Impairment

The disabled/impairment division and the relationship between 'disability' and ill health are problematic. If we allow impairment to be seen as the foundation upon which 'disability ' is based, then this opens the door to the medicalisation of the lives of disabled people. In recent years there has been a clear attempt to liberate impairment from medical discourse. However, there have been critical voices against this move. Susan Wendell has argued that the social constructionist view of disability ignores the fact that 'some unhealthy disabled people, as well as some healthy people with disabilities, experience physical or psychological burdens that no amount of social justice can eliminate' (Wendell 2001: 18).

Belinda Clayton argues that individuals and social facts – in the Durkheimian sense – are interwoven; this means that illness and disability are only meaningful within a given social, historical and/or linguistic context. Medical categories, she argues, are social codifications and this means that 'organic disruption does not constitute ill health prior to the social meaning it is given' (Clayton 2002: 839). Applying this argument to disability, we could argue that disability is not a *thing* unconnected from the social context. Disability has meaning because of the interrelationship between the concept and social reality. The individual person as a disabled person and disability are socially constructed.

Taking their point of departure from Foucault's (1979, 1980) work on discourse analysis, Hughes and Paterson (1997) argue that we need to construct an analysis of impairment that assumes that our somatic sensations are discursively constructed. This means that we should disregard the unhelpful distinction that the social model of disability makes between *body and culture* on the one hand, *impairment and disability* on the other. The Union of the Physically Impaired Against Segregation (UPIAS), who have argued for the development of the social model of disability, said in their initial statement that:

> 'Impairment' denotes a medically defined condition but 'disability' is something imposed on top of our impairments by the way we are unnecessarily isolated and excluded from participation in society. (UPIAS 1976: 14)

Hughes and Paterson argue that:

> In focusing on the ways in which disability is socially produced, the social model has succeeded in shifting debates about disability from biomedically dominated agendas to discourses about politics and citizenship. (Hughes and Paterson 1997: 325)

However, the social model places any discussion of *impairment* firmly within medical discourse. Lennard Davis, for example, describes the relationship between disability and impairment in exactly this way:

Disability is not so much the lack of a sense or the presence of a physical or mental impairment as it is the reception and construction of that difference. ... An impairment is a physical fact, but a disability is a social construction. For example, lack of mobility is an impairment, but an environment without ramps turns that impairment into a disability. ... a disability must be socially constructed; there must be an analysis of what it means to have or lack certain functions, appearance and so on. (Davis 2000 cited in Braddock and Parish 2001: 12)

For Hughes and Paterson, the impaired body should be viewed in the same way as the disabled body, as a product of history, culture and politics – not, as the medical model would have us believe, as a purely natural object. They share Donna Haraway's (1991) assumption that both our personal bodies and our social bodies are socially constructed and not natural.

ACTIVITY

What Is Discourse?

A 'discourse' for Foucault is a body of statements that is both organised and systematic, and is presented in the form of a set of rules. These 'rules of discourse' need, first, to be identified by the researcher and then described in terms of what they allow to be said and what they prevent from been said. The rules also allow space for new statements to be legitimately made. Discursive practices are used to present knowledge as 'true' and/or 'valid'.

Foucault's analysis of discourse is then historical, but it is a 'problem-centred' historical approach rather than a 'period-centred' approach. Foucault referred to his historical analysis of discourse as an 'archaeology' of knowledge (Foucault 1972), which he used to show the history of truth claims. Archaeology involves describing and analysing statements as they occur within the 'archive' and the 'archive' is 'the general system of the formation and transformation of statements' (Foucault 1972: 130).

For Foucault, a central concept in the history of any discourse is the *will to power* – a term initially used by Nietzsche to demonstrate that powerful people were in a position to have their views imposed upon others as right, just and truthful. Foucault's position is one of Pyrrhonian scepticism: we cannot know anything, including the assumption that 'we cannot know anything'. In other words, for Foucault, there is no objective viewpoint from which one could analyse discourse or society.

For Foucault, phases of history are organised around their own distinct 'episteme' or set of organising principles for categorising whatever we come into contact with. Epistemes generate 'orders of discourse' or 'discursive formations' which inform us as to how we should construct our view of the world. Discourse is a system of representation that regulates meaning, so that certain ways of thinking, speaking and behaving become 'natural'. Discourse is made up of statements, and one of the central purposes of the discourse is to establish relationships between statements so that we can make sense of what is being said to us.

(Continued)

(Continued)

From the initial analysis of classification, in his later books Foucault develops his *genealogical analysis* to examine the history of how groups of ideas come to be associated with normal sexuality. One of the central themes of Foucault's work is how discursive power works on bodies, and this is seen most clearly in his *History of Sexuality* ([1976] 1978). In this way, discursive formations allow us to allocate people within a network of categories, in other words to describe people as 'types': hetro/homo, normal/fairy, etc. In terms of his discussion of discipline, Foucault described the spreading notion of what constituted 'normal' through society as the 'carceral continuum'. All of us become self-regulated subjects, written on by institutions from the family, educational institutions and employers.

Question:

➢ From the passage above, write a short paragraph that explains what you understand by the term *discourse*.

In support of their argument, Hughes and Patterson (1997) give the example of *pain*. It is commonly assumed, and reinforced by medical discourse, that pain is a product of our anatomy and physiology. However, pain is both an experience and a discursive construction in that it has phenomenological parameters where our bodies meet with our minds and culture. It has to be defined and packaged as an unpleasant experience, and the people who get pleasure from experiencing pain are defined as having a mental health problem.

Hughes and Patterson question what is a normal body. In the same way that Foucault politicises sexuality and its role within the processes of self-formation, so Hughes and Patterson attempt to politicise impairment and show how discourse on impairment encodes and structures everyday life. Most of the theorists in the area of disability, including many who accept the social model, assume that impairment is a natural given. When impairment is couched in naturalistic language, it appears as a set of biological constraints that cannot be legitimately challenged without going against 'nature'. The medical model defined impairment as founded on a biological malfunction that was abnormal and essentially a medical *problem*. With the emergence of postmodernism in the 1990s and the Politics of Difference, new forms of gay and lesbian identity emerged that were *not* seen as deviations from the 'normal' heterosexual identity. Similarly, the social model of disability should look at impairment and the identity of the impaired person as something other than a deviation from the 'normal', able-bodied identity.

However, the problem with discursive postmodern perspectives on impairment and disability is that embodiment is more than conceptual. As Carol J. Gill has argued, bodies matter in Disability Studies: the experience of disability is an embodied experience, concerned with issues such as pain and unwanted physical limitations.

Learning Difficulties: Epistemes of Impairment

For Goodley, the 'turn to impairment' within Disability Studies has tended to ignore learning difficulties. The issue of learning difficulties remains an issue conceived as a biological problem and, as such, people with learning difficulties are categorised as the naturalised, irrational, Other. Goodley quotes Koegel:

> However, much we pay lip service to the influence of socio-cultural factors, we *do* primarily see mental retardation as a biomedical phenomenon and *do*, as a result, tend to attribute incompetent behaviour exclusively to physiological causes. (Koegel 1986, cited in Goodley 2001: 211; italics in original)

Goodley's argument is that learning difficulties should be seen in social, cultural, political and historical terms. The rationale for this thesis is that in the last analysis, learning difficulties are essentially discursive and relational in nature and not, as the medical model would have us believe, an element of an individual's natural impairment. Within the medical model, Goodley identifies three commonly held criteria for identifying a person with learning difficulties:

- Low intelligence
- Social incompetence
- Maladaptive functioning – or culturally abnormal behaviour.

It is assumed that factors indicate biological malfunctioning within an impaired individual. However, as has become well established with Disability Studies, our definition of what constitutes *normal* behaviour is social and cultural in origin. Oswin (1991) investigated the experiences of people with learning difficulties in relation to bereavement. Oswin found that emotional responses to the news of the death of a loved one were regarded by heath care professionals as 'challenging behaviour' whereas lack of an emotional response was regarded as evidence of 'retardation'. The idea that an emotional response to the news of the death of a loved one was perfectly normal behaviour was not considered. Goodley cites a comment from Martin Levine to support his argument:

> If someone else whispers a lot during the play, people might ignore it or get angry. If we whisper it is because we are retarded. It's like we have to be more normal than normal people. (Levine cited in Goodley 2001: 215)

Goodley's conclusion is that low intelligence, social incompetence and maladaptive functioning are not valid scientific categories. The definition of what constitutes learning difficulties is commonly assumed to be a value-free objective fact. However, the three categories are widely distributed amongst the population, amongst people who are not regarded as having learning difficulties. There is no compelling evidence that these categories are evidence of biological impairment; rather such categories are behavioural in nature – in other words, *epistemes* of *assumed* impairment: 'In the realm of signification, impairment becomes transformed into narratives about impairment' (Hughes and Paterson 1997: 335). The corporeal, personal and cultural collapse into one another: 'disability is embodied and impairment is social' (ibid.: 336).

This critique of the social model's conception of impairment is further developed by Bill Hughes, who argues that 'The connection between impairment and oppression is lost to the social model of disability because impairment is regarded as something that is constructed entirely in the domain of nature' (Hughes 1999: 168). Hughes argues that the social model has no critique of modernity, which is significant because modernity is particularly pervasive in its capacity to generate *strangers*. For Hughes, impairment is not discovered but constructed within a mode of perception which he terms the *non-disabled gaze*. The non-disabled gaze visualises and articulates people with impairments as strangers. The stranger is a deviant Other constructed at the very limits of tolerance and conformity and homogenised so as to be treated as a category of person, which in many cases can be reduced to a single word such as *spastic* – a word which is also a term of abuse in everyday life: 'The impaired body is rendered disorderly (and thus repulsive and detestable) by the "positive" observational practices that produce it' (ibid.: 158).

We read bodies through hierarchical categories. Observation is never a simple objective physical act. Our senses do not simply reflect the real world in an objective fashion, rather our senses are social constructed in themselves and are constructed to view impairment as a default from the normal able body. A central element in the non-disabled gaze is the medicalisation of impairment, which imposes a narrow regime of meaning onto the impaired body.

Hughes (2002) develops this argument by drawing upon Zygmunt Bauman's discussion of strangers. In *Modernity and the Holocaust* (1989) Bauman argues that within modernity there developed the 'gardening state', which separates wanted from unwanted elements within the society. For Bauman, nothing in itself is essentially 'clean' or 'dirty'. An omelette in a pan can be a thing of great beauty, but if I drop it on my trousers then it becomes dirty. The same is true of people; there is nothing essentially wrong with foreigners, asylum seekers or people with impairment, but they need to be moved to the appropriate place. If they cannot be moved to the appropriate place, we can attempt to assimilate them into our wider society. If we cannot assimilate them into the wider society, then we can divide them from the rest of us, by placing them in camps, ghettos or prisons. In the last analysis, what cannot be made clean must be dealt with by other means, because if the strangers are seen as dirt and less than human, we can destroy them.

Hughes reminds us that many thousands of disabled people perished in the Nazi concentration camps because modernity has great difficulty incorporating impairment. The impaired are seen as dirt and should be excluded from the wider society in the same way that the gardener excludes the weeds from the land. The weeds may be things of great beauty in themselves, but they are uninvited guests, in the wrong palace, cannot be assimilated and are regarded as dirt to be dealt with in the most efficient way possible. Modernity – any modern society – contains the elements needed to generate the mass destruction of people who are seen to be dirty. And as Hughes (2002) points out, the eugenic sterilisation enacted by the Nazis in 1933 was based upon a legal framework developed in California in the 1920s.

Burleigh (1994) argues that the Nazi policy towards psychiatric patients during the 1930s was based upon economic factors and the justification for the introduction of involuntary eugenic strategies was similar in kind, if not degree, to those pursued in a number of other countries:

> The decision to kill the mentally ill and physically disabled was taken by Hitler in order to clear the decks for war, and was justified with the aid of crude utilitarian arguments, as well as what limited evidence there was regarding popular attitudes on these issues. (Burleigh 1994: 213)

The role of the psychiatrist in this genocidal process was to identify potential victims, to sanction and certify their selection and in many cases to participate in their murder. Burleigh discusses how in 1920, the psychiatrist Alfred Hoche and the lawyer Karl Binding asked if the German nation could afford to maintain 'life unworthy of life' (ibid.: 215). One of the main targets for their arguments were people they labelled as 'mental defectives' and 'idiots'. Binding and Hoche attempted to justify non-consensual killings by arguing that notions such as the 'sanctity of life' did not apply to 'entirely unproductive persons'.

The notion of 'entirely unproductive persons' formed the basis of a new form of therapy that emerged in the 1920s known as 'occupational therapy'. The new therapy attempted to enhance the self-satisfaction of psychiatric patients. In addition, the ability to work also became an indicator of recovery. However, the individuals who did not respond to such therapy became a 'psychiatrically defined subclass'. The psychiatrists who monitored the progress of people who were discharged to work outside the asylums were encouraged – for example by Robert Gaupp in his address to the German Psychiatric Association in September 1925 – to construct genealogies of patients which could be used to identify where psychiatric problems were hereditary in nature. If individuals proved unwilling to agree of their volition not to have children, then compulsory sterilisation was advised. For Burleigh the rise of the Nazis in 1933 did not mark a decisive break in the attitude of psychiatrists towards 'entirely unproductive persons' with mental health problems; the apparatus was already in place. What the Nazi administration did was to introduce a Law for the Prevention of Heredity Diseased Progeny which led to the establishment of a series of local Heredity Health Courts. These local courts made decisions on compulsory sterilisations. However, as Burleigh points out:

> Nor did the courts confine themselves to the people who actually passed before them. For example, after he had ordered the sterilization of a young woman, the Kaufbeuen psychiatrist Hermann Pfannmuller, who was also a judge in the court at Kempton, spent a week isolating twenty-one additional 'degenerates' in her family, recommending the sterilization of ten of them as being 'highly urgent since the danger of reproduction appeared immanent'. (Ibid.: 219)

Burleigh argues that school children were encouraged to draw their family trees and identify 'defective' members, and local mayors would identify lone mothers as suitable cases for compulsory sterilisation. Burleigh quotes Hermann Pfannmuller in November 1939 saying 'The problem of whether to maintain this patient material under the most primitive conditions or to eradicate it has now become a subject for serious discussion once more' (ibid.: 220).

Hitler established Tiergartenstrass 4 (T-4) initially under Werner Heyde and later under Paul Nitsche to select, register and organise the murder of a target group of 70,000 people with a range of disabilities. The Community Patients transport service transferred people with disabilities either to gas chambers or to one of the six established killing centres. It is important to note that the people who supported this programme of genocide were not psychopaths or SS members, but ordinary people. Burleigh argues that:

> More damagingly, the Roman Catholic hierarchy entered into negotiations with T-4 to secure an 'opt-out clause' for Catholic asylum staff and the last sacraments for Catholic victims, negotiations which were only broken off when the Church's chief negotiator Bishop Wienken, went so 'native' in his dealings with T-4 as seriously to embarrass his superiors. (Ibid.: 226)

According to Robert N. Proctor (1995), the policy against people with disabilities was to lay the foundation for the Final Solution. The mechanism for the efficient mass human extermination of large populations was already in place when the destruction of the Jews became a priority for Hitler. It was the medicalisation of anti-Semitism that defined which were the 'lives not worth living'. Similarly, the Nazis also drew upon medical expertise for the extension of the euthanasia programme to gypsies, homosexuals, the tubercular, vagabonds, beggars, alcoholics, prostitutes, drug addicts, the homeless and communists.

The Nazis banned all sexual relations, both inside and outside of marriage, between Jews and non-Jews, on the grounds that the Jewish body was essentially diseased and the mixing of Jewish and non-Jewish blood would spread diseased genes. The creation of ghettos in occupied territories was justified on medical grounds. Jewish people were under quarantine for reasons of public health. As Proctor explains:

By the late 1930s, German medical science had constructed an elaborate worldview equating mental infirmity, moral depravity, criminality, and racial impurity. This complex of identifications was then used to justify the destruction of the Jews on medical, moral, criminological, and anthropological grounds. To be Jewish was to be both sick and criminal; Nazi medical science and policy united to help 'solve' this problem. (Proctor 1995: 181)

This view is supported by Paul Weindling, who argued that the gas chambers should be seen as one element of a broader *Seuchenplan Ost* 'to segregate and then eradicate the human epidemic infections' (Weindling 2000: xv).

A very important footnote to this is that at the doctors' trial at Nuremberg (1946–7) the 23 defendants were accused of murdering inmates by subjecting them to horrific involuntary experiments. However, no one stood trial for the mass human extermination of people with disabilities.

Modernity is very good at generating the otherness of strangers and it has the bureaucratic means to deal effectively and efficiently with human dirt. The bureaucracy, as outlined by Max Weber (1922), is soulless, like a machine, it has no morals and it can break down the most difficult of tasks into small discrete jobs which are easy to carry out by individuals who can still maintain their moral conscience. You may think that you could not possibly have sent train loads of people to death camps. However, could you have helped to mine the coal that was used to power the trains? Could you have maintained the track? Could you have made the Zyklon B pellets in a chemical factory, that were used amongst other things as a delousing agent? Could you have driven a train? No one task is in itself immoral, but all these tasks needed to be efficiently conducted for the death camps to be effective in their task.

ACTIVITY

Susan Wendell argues:

In most postmodern cultural theorising about the body, there is no recognition of – and as far as I can see, no room for recognising – the hard physical realities that are faced by people with disabilities (Wendell 1996: 45)

Question:

➢ Would you accept or reject the view that: 'the problem with discursive postmodern perspectives on impairment and disability is that *embodiment* is more than *conceptual*'? State the reasons for your answer.

Sexuality: Epistemes of Impairment

It is in the area of disabled people's sexuality that the epistemes of impairment are most clearly visible. Brown argues that people with disabilities are perceived as either 'asexual, or oversexed, innocents or perverts' (Brown 1994: 125). Disabled people are often in a position where other people are attempting to control:

- The level of their sexual experience
- The level of their sexual knowledge
- Their choices in relation to issues of consent
- Their access to sexual education – which in contrast to that of the able-bodied person is often solely about informing the disabled person on how to control or eliminate their sexual interest.

These conclusions are backed up by the findings of other researchers:

- **Anderson and Kitchin (2000)** in their study of family planning clinics in Northern Ireland found widely shared myths about the sexuality of people with disabilities, notably that: disabled people were unable to participate in sexual activity; unable to behave in a sexually responsible manner; unable to sustain long-term relationships with a sexual partner; unable to engage in mutually satisfying sexual practices; and had no sex drive. Anderson and Kitchin found that these assumptions also informed the clinical practice of the people who worked in Northern Ireland's family planning clinics
- **Tilly (1996)** reports that disabled women were much less likely to have received sex education; were much less likely to have breast cancer examinations; and were less likely to have cervical smear tests
- **Wolfe (1997)** found that disabled people who live in an institutionalised setting are often disciplined for any expression of overt sexuality, on the grounds that the staff view such expressions as inappropriate
- **Puri and Singh (1996)** report on how they successfully made use of pharmocotherapy with pimozide on a man with a learning disability who was a cross-dresser
- **El-Badri and Robertshaw (1998)** investigated the possible cause of sexual fetishism amongst people with learning difficulties by identifying temporal lobe dysrhythmia. The researchers conducted brain scans to identify possible biological factors as causes of what they considered to be the medical problem of sexual fetishism amongst people with learning difficulties. They assumed that there were no possible learned aspects to the sexuality of people with learning difficulties.

Gender, Sexuality and Disability

Chapter 4 on gender divisions discusses the work of Naomi Wolf (1990) who argues that women are made to feel concerns about their body shape and other aspects of their physical appearance. Wolf argues that there is a link between female liberation and female beauty and that the discourses that construct the *beauty myth* operate at a psychological and ideological level. Appearance is the central index by which men judge the value of women and ideas about what constitutes female beauty are used as political weapons to covertly control women. In this way they reinforce the glass ceiling, exclude women from power, prevent women from exercising their hard-won rights, and generate low self-esteem.

One of the most interesting studies to illustrate this interface between the beauty myth and medical discourse was conducted by Oberle and Allen (1994), who investigated the reasons why women chose to have surgery to increase their breast size. Oberle and Allen's argument is that women do this to enhance their self-esteem and self-confidence. Small-breasted women have feelings of inadequacy about their breasts. There is a history of research that supports this view (Baker et al. 1974; Clifford 1983; Goin 1983). In addition, small-breasted women exhibit a degree of sexual inhibition (McGrath and Burkardt 1984). Oberle and Allen claim that women who have breast enlargement surgery report improved self-confidence, enhanced femininity and enhanced sexuality.

This social construction of femininity is particularly harmful to women with disabilities. The discourses that construct the female beauty myth define the body of a woman with disability as unfeminine, unappealing and asexual. Disabled women are not subjected to the male gaze that Naomi Wolf describes, but to what Rosemarie Garland Thomson (1997a) defines as the *male stare*: 'If the male gaze informs the normative female self as a sexual spectacle, then the stare sculpts the disabled subject as a grotesque spectacle' (Garland Thomson 1997a: 285). In other words, the beauty myth separates the normal from the pathological body. Disabilities are signs of pathology, inferiority as well as an abnormal body. As Garland Thomson goes on to explain, the stare is the 'material gesture that creates disability as an oppressive social relationship ... the coercive valuing of certain body types over others is what lies at the heart of both disability and beauty oppression' (Garland Thomson 1997a: 285).

Morris (2001) reinforces this argument by saying that heterosexist ideas are used to inform women of what their appearance should be like and how they should behave. The bodies of women with impairments are very different from the standard imposed by the heterosexist norm. Disabled women are made to feel that they are either attractive in spite of their impairment or unattractive because of their impairment. There is little scope for women with impairments to celebrate having a body that is different; disabled women are constantly encouraged to view their impairment in negative terms – as something which detracts value from their lives. Moreover, because disabled people are less likely to be employed in the media industries, it is abled-bodied people who have control over the representation of the impaired body in television, film and literature.

Nosek (1995) in a survey of battered women's shelters in Houston, found that 64 percent of shelters were inaccessible to wheelchair users, reflecting the assumption that women with disabilities were unlikely to be in a relationship, again reflecting the assumption that sexuality is inappropriate for the disabled body.

The *stare* also has an impact on the perception of the male disabled body; the social construction of masculinity is also incompatible with disability. The disabled male body is also a pathological body, characterised by its inferiority and lacking in strength and independence.

Many young people with disabilities, who are living at home with their parents, lack the opportunities to explore their sexuality. Going to university is for many people a time to explore their sexuality. However, some people with disabilities may require assistance, what Sarah Earle (1999, 2001) calls *facilitated sex*. This term can mean a number of different things: help in attending clubs, pubs and parties where potential sexual partners can meet; assistance in having sexual intercourse with other individuals; negotiating with prostitutes; assistance with masturbation. Personal assistants were reluctant to participate in facilitating sex for people with disabilities, especially when the disabled person was attracted to same-sex relationships. The assistants did accept that sexuality was a central element in people's lives, but were unwilling to acknowledge that people with disabilities should have a need to explore their sexuality:

> Some people have the power to define and regulate the sexual practices and behaviours of others … Social groups that lack power, also lack the ability to define and regulate their own sexuality. In modern Western societies, sexuality is not seen as an integral part of the lives of disabled people. Disabled people are expected neither to reproduce nor be reproduced and the prevention of disability underpins the philosophy of eugenics. (Earle 2001: 435)

Much of the literature on the sexual experiences of people with disabilities, and particularly people with learning disabilities, is placed firmly within the medical model. Sexuality is perceived as a problem in need of a cure. In the United Kingdom, according the Sexual Offences Acts 1956 and 1967, a person with a severe learning disability is considered to be incapable of giving their consent to a sexual encounter. In addition, Cambridge and Mellan (2000) argue that men with learning disabilities are judged by different standards from other men who use pornography, which they argue, reinforces the pathological view of the sexuality of men with learning disabilities.

Cambridge and Mellan (2000) go on to argue that in the United Kingdom men with learning disabilities who engage in same-sex relationships are unlikely to be given a safe-sex education which allows them to take into account HIV risk assessment, the need to wear condoms, strategies and techniques for negotiating safer sex. Positive images of homosexuality and safe sex are not made available to men with learning disabilities because sex educators fear that providing such information would break Section 28 of the Local Government Act 1988 which prevents local authorities from *promoting* homosexuality. Cambridge and Mellan also argue that most men with learning disabilities who desire same-sex relationships become isolated, have feelings of guilt, denial and a negative self-image because they are separated from the network of self-help groups and other forms of support and information to gay men who do not have learning disabilities.

To be a person with a disability and to be homosexual is to be doubly Other, and doubly oppressed. Models of normalisation, such as *passing* for example, encourage only 'heterosexual socialisation activities' (Brown 1994: 128). The sex education for people with disabilities has a tendency to assume heterosexuality and at the same time to pathologise homosexuality. If people with learning disabilities do obtain a sex education, the emphasis is on avoiding sexual relationships and attempting to repress individual sexual feelings. Brown suggests that:

> Sex education for people with learning disabilities tends to have focused on biological rather than social issues and to have assumed a heterosexist preference and a familial context for all relationships even where neither seems applicable to the person's current life or foreseeable future. (Ibid.: 131)

Young argues that 'The culturally dominated undergo a paradoxical oppression, in that they are both marked out by stereotypes and at the same time rendered invisible' (Young 1990: 59). Yet both homosexuality and disability are socially constructed, and may be subject to reconsideration and restructuring. According to Young, 'Those living under cultural imperialism find themselves defined from the outside, positioned, placed, by a network of dominant meanings they experience as arising from elsewhere, from those with whom they do not identify and who do not identify with them' (ibid.: 59).

Feminist Perspectives on Disability

Feminists have long objected to the ways in which women are defined and judged solely on the basis of biological characteristics. In addition, feminists have long demanded that women should have control over the decisions that affect their bodies and their lives. Feminist perspectives on disability are no different. However, Jenny Morris (1993) has argued that disability was generally invisible in the mainstream feminist agenda from the 1970s onwards. Moreover, when disability became the subject of feminist research, it was the carers who were the focus of attention, rather than the people with impairments. This is a factor which Morris claims further added to the alienation of disabled women because such feminist research excluded disabled women from the category 'women'; the principle of 'the personal is political' did not seem to apply to the subjective experiences of disabled women.

In 1995 Jenny Morris launched a pointed critique against a comment by Janet Finch that disabled people should be taken out of their homes and placed in a range of residential facilities so as to de-emphasise family care, which was almost always provided by women. Morris responded to this comment by saying that 'patronizing, cavalier, *discriminatory* attitudes towards disabled people are only possible because feminists such as Finch and Dalley do not identify with our subjective reality' (Morris 1995: 72).

In her research into young women with disabilities, Barron (1997) addressed two questions:

- What societal norms and values are transmitted to physically disabled girls and young women?
- How do these norms and values affect their view of themselves and the independence they experience?

For Barron 'Disability is an aspect of identity with which gender is entwined' (ibid.: 236).

In common with the assumptions of the medical model, much of the literature on gender and impairment is based upon the assumption that disability for a young women is a personal tragedy. It is not simply the case that young women in wheelchairs are not seen as sexy. Disability becomes the primary identity of the impaired young woman. Young women thereby accept the impact that their disability will have on their life as a woman. Taking her starting point from Naomi Wolf, Barron argues that young women with disabilities are made to feel that their bodies are flawed; disabled women are made to feel that they do not live up to what is perceived as physical beauty; they are considered to lack the identity of a *woman*; most notably such women are asexual. As Barron explains:

> Gender is an important part of our identity. Not being 'seen' as a woman is not a sign of equality between the sexes, but rather a reflection of the societal view on disability. It demonstrates that disability, as well as gender, is a powerful prism through which we see and understand each other. Seeing the impairment as the primary identity of the ... young woman does not mean that they are given the same opportunities as men. Instead, it means having to strive for establishing an identity as women in a patriarchal society. (Ibid.: 229)

Kallianes and Rubenfeld (1997) argue that women with disabilities do not have the same reproductive rights as other women. The strong discourse of who is deemed suitable to be a parent does not include women with disabilities. Kallianes and Rubenfeld (1997: 203) argue that disabled women's reproductive rights are constrained by various assumptions and prejudices on the part of society:

- The assumption that women with disabilities are asexual
- A lack of equal access to reproductive health care and to contraception
- Resistance to reproduction and mothering
- Greater risk of coercive sterilisation, abortion or loss of child to custody.

Marian Corker (2001) is highly critical of the bifurcation of impairment and disability. The division between impairment and disability is similar to the division in feminist analysis between *sex* (which is commonly assumed to be a biological concept used to differentiate between people on the basis of primary and secondary sexual characteristics) and *gender* (which is a sociological concept used to denote ideas of what constitutes masculinity, femininity and the normal and acceptable ways of behaving for men and women). However, underpinning the sex/gender division is the assumption that women have a biology that has to be understood only by reference to physical science. A woman's biology is believed to have a determining influence upon her life – a view that reinforces dominant, masculinist worldviews.

In a similar fashion, the impairment/disability division also make a distinction between a given biological condition (impairment) and a sociological conception of how the disabled and able-bodied people should behave (disability). Corker argues that underpinning the impairment/disability division is the assumption that the disabled have a biology that has to be understood only by reference to physical science. Their biology is believed to have a determining influence upon the lives of disabled people – again a view that also reinforces dominant, masculinist worldviews.

To move beyond this bifurcation, we need to understand the nature of impaired ontologies. In other words, we have to recognise that impairment, as defined in Disability Studies: 'is not *of* disabled people's lives but a series of labels and their signifiers derived from scientific positivism' (Corker 2001: 35). To do this, Corker develops the notion of *sensibility* – a set of individual or collective dispositions to emotions, attitudes, and feelings which are relevant to value theory and which include ethics, aesthetics and politics. Corker claims that there is more to sensibility than perception or sensation, and that sensibility makes us question what constitutes the fixed mental or physical reality: 'Sensibility engenders ways of being in and knowing our world that are materialized in contradictory bodies in process, and performed in shifting aesthetic, ethical, and political values' (ibid.: 41).

For Corker, biological difference and socio-cultural difference are 'mutually constitutive' and what we traditionally understood as *embodied* is now no longer ontologically secure. The material world can no longer be assumed to have such a high degree of 'fixity'. Disability is not a value-neutral term – it is a label of disvalue: 'The idea that disability can be valuable is commonly greeted with philosophical cynicism … [disability is] a category of "other" designated as a dumping ground for anything that cannot be valued' (ibid.: 46–7).

The history of feeble-mindedness and the concept's transition to mental retardation provides one of the clearest examples of the convergence between masculinist and medical discourse. Carlson (2001) outlines a feminist analysis of mental retardation. She argues that mental retardation functioned as a gendered classification; there was a strong connection between stereotypes of femininity and conceptions of feeble-mindedness. Giving birth to a child outside of marriage was seen as proof of feeble-mindedness and such mothers were dangerous symbols of promiscuity and bad mothers, which justified their incarceration. At the turn of the twentieth century the feeble-minded woman became the dominant representation for feeble-mindedness in general. If a woman departed from the Victorian conception of a woman, notably in terms of her willingness to partici- pate in forms of sexual behaviour outside of marriage, then she was likely to be classified as having a moral deficiency.

The idea of the *moral imbecile* as a distinct category of feeble-mindedness emerged within medical discourse and was identified as a cause of crime, pauperism, degen- eracy and of giving birth to illegitimate children. The moral deficiency of the moral imbecile was seen as a threat to society, particularly women who were not only bad women, but also bad mothers who gave birth to children as defective as them- selves, but also were likely to be carriers of venereal disease and could pass as normal women in society. There was a need to severely control the behaviour of these women, especially to control their ability to have children. However, this form of social control was cast in terms of protection; such women could not help their immoral behaviour and were in need of society's protection. Such women needed to be taught how to be *women*. Consequently, in the asylums where they were incarcerated, they were placed within an environment that isolated them from the vice and temptation of men, where they could be provided with women's work such as caring for severely retarded women and imbecile children.

Although over 100 years have passed since women who gave birth outside of mar- riage were incarcerated in asylums in the UK, the idea that women with learning difficulties should not have children, because they are likely to be bad mothers, is still widely shared.

Resistance to the Strong Discourse of Medicalisation

Successful resistance to the strong discourse of medicalisation is rare, but one excep- tion is in the area of menstruation as a form of recurrent illness and disability. Strange (2001) draws upon the archives of the Medical Women's Federation who have collected information on women's health issues since 1916. Strange argues that in the nineteenth century, menstruation – and the menopause – were regarded as pathological and disabling for women because all women were believed to have a strong impulse to reproduce. Supported by medical opinion at the time, this was used as a reason to deny opportunities to women in education and employment. However, when the First World War was declared, increasing numbers of women were in paid employment outside of the home. It became increasingly clear to many female doctors that defining menstruation in terms of disability was with- out a sound medical foundation. As Strange explains:

> In 1922 Doctors Winifred Cullis, Enid Oppenhiem and Margaret Ross-Johnson identified a significant gap in physiological data relating to menstruation. Their study, which measured

periodic changes in basal metabolic rates in relation to the menstrual cycle, concluded that fluctuations during menstruation were sufficiently negligible to render the concept of menstrual disability obsolete. Six years later, Mrs Sourton measured levels of efficiency during the menstrual cycle among factory operatives. Whilst Sourton conceded that her results highlighted lower levels of productivity during the menstrual period, this never exceeded 5 percent. (Strange 2001: 253–54)

All medical procedures take place within such a social and cultural context. For example, many women suffer from painful periods, many women suffer from premenstrual tension. In our culture, menstruation has a very negative image and it is an experience that people are said to find shameful, hence the fact that until the late 1980s, British television companies were not allowed to show advertisements for tampons, and until the mid-1990s, the product had to be in a box or a wrapper and no discussion of the advantages of one product over another was allowed. What we have to remember is that menstruation is a natural healthy process.

In addition, the meaning of the menopause also has to be understood within a social and cultural context. Women may see the menopause as signifying a loss of femininity (Houston et al. 1979). In contrast, when women reach the menopause in Indian society, they enjoy an improvement in social standing, freedom and self-esteem (Flint 1975). Arab women in Israel also demonstrate positive attitudes to the menopause (Maoz et al. 1970). In Western society people place value on having a child (Sutherland 1990) and also a high value on youth (Ballinger 1990).

Mental Illness

Hannibal Lector from *The Silence of the Lambs*; Freddy Krueger from the series *Nightmare on Elm Street*; Michael Myers from the *Halloween* series; 'Jonny' the central character played by Jack Nicolson in *The Shining*; Robert De Niro as Max Cady in *Cape Fear*; the character Leatherface from *The Texas Chainsaw Massacre*; Jason Voorhees from the *Friday the 13th* series; Harry Warden from *My Bloody Valentine* and above all Norman Bates, the central character from Alfred Hitchcock's classic, *Psycho*, all reinforce the stigma surrounding mental illness and present a powerful picture of people who suffer from mental illness as potential psycho-killers.

What is mental illness? Unlike many countries, the United Kingdom has a legal definition of mental illness:

In this Act 'mental disorder' means illness, arrested or incomplete development of mind, psychopathic disorder, and any other disorder or disability of mind; and 'mentally disordered' shall be construed accordingly. (1959 British Mental Health Act para 4(1))

The official DSM IV list of characteristics for mental illness contains such factors as hearing voices, feeling the presence of another if a person's mother has died more than two weeks previously (for a period of two weeks the person may feel her presence and still be classed as sane), ESP, etc. In other words, mental illness is a behavioural disorder and the root of mental illness is people behaving in ways that the rest of us find unacceptable. In the United States, the American Psychiatric Association in their *Diagnostic and Statistical Manual of Mental Disorders* (DSM-IV), fourth edition (1994) is the main diagnostic reference for US Mental Health professionals.

Within the study of mental illness there are two distinct approaches:

- **The medical model**: which views mental illness as a physical impairment or real disease with physical causes and
- **The anti-psychiatric model**: which, in common with the social model of disability, views mental illness in terms of oppression and discrimination.

The Medical Model

Insanity in its various forms is now universally admitted to be a disease differing, indeed, from ordinary disease as to its nature and phenomena but a disease notwithstanding, and therefore to be viewed in the same light and treated on the same principles as those which regulate medical practice in other branches. The haze of mystery with which ignorance and superstition had invested it in former ages, and which by repelling investigation prevented proper efforts being made for its removal, has been set aside, and the more rational idea prevails that it is merely an accident of our fallen humanity, involving nothing supernatural in its occurrence so as to remove it from the range of scientific investigation and of ordinary treatment. (James F. Duncan 1875)

(*Source*: www.psychlaws.org/GeneralResources/report-nevertreated.htm)

According to medical researchers, there is ample evidence of a physical cause of schizophrenia. Dr Nancy Andreason carried out a series of positron emission tomography (PET) scans and found that there was evidence that the rate of blood flow to the prefrontal cortex of the brain was a possible cause of the loss of self-control, hallucinations and delusions that characterise schizophrenia. In addition, schizophrenia has a long history of response to drug therapy; for over 20 years antipsychotic drugs such as Clozaril, Risperdal, Zyprexa and Seroquel have all been used to control the symptoms of schizophrenia. In more recent years, drugs that restrict the level of dopamine and serotonin transmissions within the brain have also been used effectively to control symptoms.

FIVE BASIC FACTS ABOUT SCHIZOPHRENIA

Many people do not have a clear understanding of schizophrenia. Schizophrenia is a physical illness, just like diabetes or asthma. Schizophrenia has typical signs and symptoms that are recognisable in patients with this illness. Like all illnesses, the symptoms, and severity of symptoms, vary from person to person.

Five basic facts on this illness:

- Schizophrenia has diagnosable symptoms and signs
- It is a physical illness
- It can be inherited
- It gets better with medication
- It gets worse without treatment.

Further details can be accessed at: http://www2.health-center.com/mentalhealth/schizophrenia/what_is_schizo/fact.htm

Critics of psychiatry, such as Robert Whitaker (2002), have argued that the physiological differences in brain structure and function that are often found in schizophrenic patients may be caused by the antipsychotic drugs administered by psychiatrists in an effort to cure the symptoms of schizophrenia:

> The image we have today of schizophrenia is not that of madness, whatever that might be in its natural state. All of the traits that we have come to associate with schizophrenia – the awkward gait, the jerking arm movements, the vacant facial expression, the sleepiness, the lack of initiative – are symptoms due, at least in large part, to a drug-induced deficiency in dopamine transmission. (Whitaker 2002: 164–65)

In October 2002 Dr E. Torrey Fuller, the Executive Director of The Stanley Medical Research Institute in Bethesda and President of the Treatment Advocacy Center in Arlington, attempted to refute arguments such as those advanced by Whitaker by investigating the structural, neurological, neuropsychological, electrophysiological and cerebral metabolic abnormalities of the brains of people who were suffering with the symptoms of schizophrenia, but – most importantly – who had not been previously treated with antipsychotic drugs. The research is a very thorough review of 65 papers. However, although Torrey Fuller argues that his review demonstrates that schizophrenia is a disease of the brain structure and function, the papers he reviewed were unable to 'identify the predisposing genes and biological insults that interact to cause the damage'. Moreover, one of the conclusions that Torrey Fuller comes to is that:

there is no single abnormality in brain structure or function that is pathognomonic for schizophrenia. All deficits cited above can be found in some other brain diseases and, occasionally, in normal individuals, although statistically they occur more frequently in individuals with schizophrenia. Thus, we do not yet have a specific diagnostic test that points conclusively and exclusively to schizophrenia as the diagnosis. (Torrey Fuller 2002: 10)

For the anti-psychiatric perspectives, mental illness is a behavioural disorder and it is because of this that Torrey Fuller is unable to identify the predisposing genes and biological insults that interact to cause the damage.

ACTIVITY

What are the Basic Criteria for Schizophrenia?

According to the American Psychiatric Association in their *Diagnostic and Statistical Manual of Mental Disorders* (DSM-IV), fourth edition (1994), which is the main diagnostic reference for mental health professionals in the United States, schizophrenia is present if a person has two or more of the following symptoms 'for a material part of at least one month':

- Delusions: however, if the delusion is 'bizarre, such as being abducted in a space ship' then only one delusion is sufficient
- Hallucinations: however, again only one symptom is needed if the hallucination involves two or more voices talking or if the person can hear a voice 'that keeps up a running commentary on the patient's thoughts or actions'
- Incoherent speech
- Mood exclusions
- Behaviour that is severely disorganised or catatonic in nature
- Any other 'negative symptom such as flat affect, reduced speech or lack of volition'.

Question:

➢ Do the criteria outlined in DSM IV lead you to believe that schizophrenia is a behavioural disorder, rather than a disease caused by a physical impairment?

Foucault

The critique of the medical model of mental illness is most clearly argued in the work of Michel Foucault. Foucault's work on madness has to be seen as an account of how power became directly connected to the most intimate areas of the human body. For Foucault a 'regimen' refers to rules of how one ought to behave. The regimen is a sort of fiction in so far as it is used as a theory to condition which factual statements can be produced, and not the reverse. These rules covered diverse areas such as exercise, food, drink, sleep as well as sexual relations.

Foucault discusses the nature of madness in relation to passion and delirium that are said to be both of the imagination and at the same time beyond it. Madness moves outwards through the body and into the soul, causing either a continuous frenzy of irrational movement of the muscles and nerves or the pacification of melancholia. In either case madness is seen as the most damaging form of unreason. However, madness has its own discourse, in its own way logical and rigorous in its organisation – what Foucault refers to as 'the internal structure of delirium' (Foucault 1967: 97).

Delirium is for Foucault, threatening to the wider society because it is a perfectly organised discourse free of any external constraint, which has total control over the soul and the body. The mad person's perception of reality is freed from the framework of narratives, social context and belief systems that usually dominate our consciousness. The mad person becomes liberated from estrangement and apprehension. Foucault analysed the treatment of madness in terms of the development or emergence of 'discursive practices' over a long historical period from the sixteenth century until the twentieth century:

- **Renaissance** (sixteenth century): insane people were believed to be unlike the rest of the population, but not abnormal or pathological, because they had a recognised role within the community, such as village idiots
- **The Classical Age** (sixteenth to the end of the eighteenth century): the dominant 'episteme' or set of organising principles for categorising insanity at this time was built upon the dichotomy between reason–unreason together with poverty, sin, crime and disease; madness was classified as a form of unreason. Such unreasonable people were excluded from the community and forced into institutions such as the 'Hospital General'
- **The Modern Age** (eighteenth to late twentieth century): over the course of the eighteenth century, madness became a special form of unreason separated from poverty, sin, crime and disease. These four other categories had different forms of strong discourse imposed upon them, and rather than the 'Hospital General', a new and more specialised establishment was created to deal with them.

'Discourse' for Foucault, is a body of statements that is both organised and systematic, in the form of a set of rules. These 'rules of discourse' establish the parameters in areas as diverse as madness, crime and sexuality. Discursive practices are used to present knowledge as 'true' and/or 'valid'. Foucault's analysis of discourse in relation to madness is historical and is part of his wider 'archaeology' of knowledge.

For Foucault, phases of history are organised around their own distinct 'episteme' or set of organising principles for categorising what we come into contact with. Epistemes generate 'orders of discourse' or 'discursive formations' which inform us on how we should construct our view of the world. Discourse is a system of representation that regulates meaning, so that certain ways of thinking, speaking and behaving become 'natural'. Discourse is made up of statements, and one of the central purposes of the discourse is to establish relationships between statements so that we can make sense of what is being said to us. From the initial analysis of classification, in his later books Foucault developed his genealogical analysis to examine the history of how groups of ideas come to be associated with normal sexuality.

There are a number of common themes running through Foucault's work. His central concern was with how human beings become 'subjected' – are made into subjects within the modern world – by the dominating mechanisms of disciplinary technology. In addition, Foucault is concerned with how people become subjects of investigation for 'new' sciences such as medicine, psychiatry and psychology. All of this was motivated by a search for the causes of 'abnormality', searching for answers to the question: What makes some individuals perverted, sick or mischievous?

A central element for Foucault was 'the State', a political structure that emerged in the sixteenth century to look after the interests of 'the totality' – everybody within the community. The State gathered information about all forms of human activity: birth rates, death rates, unemployment, public health, epidemic diseases, crime and sexuality. All of these phenomena could be indicators of a serious threat to the community. The friend and colleague of Foucault, Paul Rabinow, in his introduction to *The Foucault Reader* (1986) explains that within Foucault's work it is possible to identify what he calls three 'modes of objectification', in other words, three organising principles used by Foucault to explain how individual human beings become subjects:

1 **Dividing practices**: this involves the exclusion of people who are viewed as a threat to the community. The insane were excluded by putting them into mental hospitals, or 'ships of fools', which were said to be ships loaded with insane individuals who were pushed out to sea to find their sanity.
2 **Scientific classification**: the Enlightenment brought with it a number of new sciences which were concerned with understanding the 'nature' of individuals. In addition, these new sciences defined what is 'normal', so that the 'abnormal' could be treated.
3 **Subjectification**: this is concerned with the process of self-formation, self-understanding and the way in which conformity is achieved by problematising activities and opening them up to observation and punishment. Foucault is concerned with what it means to be a self and how we as individuals are pressurised into creating our selves in a given fashion. From the eighteenth century onwards 'madness' became a 'police' matter, incorporated within the concept of the mode of subjection: 'the way in which the individual establishes his relation to the rule and recognizes himself as obliged to put it into practice' (Foucault 1992: 27).

The Anti-psychiatric Model

The critique of the medical model of mental illness is most clearly argued in the work of Thomas Szasz.

Thomas Szasz

In 1962 Thomas Szasz published the first edition of *The Myth of Mental Illness*. For a practising psychiatrist, Szasz came to the interesting conclusion that there is no such thing as 'mental illness'. Mental illness is a metaphor, a label phrased to resemble a medical diagnosis:

> [B]odily illness stands in the same relation to mental illness as a defective television stands to an objectional television programme. To be sure, the word 'sick' is often used metaphorically. We call jokes 'sick', economies 'sick', sometimes even the whole world 'sick' – but only when we call minds 'sick' do we systematically mistake metaphor for fact and send for the doctor to 'cure' the 'illness'. It's as if a television viewer were to send for a TV repairman because he disapproves of the programme he is watching. (Szasz 1972: 11)

It would appear that, for Szasz, people have a need for explanation. It is impossible for people to say to others: 'Your behaviour is unacceptable, you are a danger either to yourself or to others. We do not understand why you behave in the way that you do, but we are going to lock you away because of it.' As humans we need to form a rational basis to explain why people behave in the way that they do.

For Szasz, people who are evil or undeserving should not be treated as ill but should be punished. Mental illness is not merely a medical label attached to people with strange behaviour. Psychiatry is an 'immoral ideology of intolerance'. He compares the belief in witchcraft, and the persecution of witches with the belief in mental illness and the persecution of mental patients. Moreover, because mental patients have a supposed incapacity to know what is in their own best interests, they must be cared for by their families or by the state, even if that care requires intervention imposed upon the patient against their expressed wishes. There has been a gradual replacement of a theological model with a medical model. This has resulted in the transformation of a religious ideology into a scientific one. Both are equally unacceptable for Szasz as both are crimes against humanity.

According to Szasz, the practice of psychiatry can be divided into two:

1 **Institutional psychiatry**: involuntary incarceration in mental hospitals with the employed physicians as agents of social control rather than of the patients' welfare.
2 **Contractual psychiatry**: this is the preferred form of psychiatry for Szasz and it is the opposite of institutional psychiatry. Contractual psychiatry is based upon an informed consensus between two freely choosing individuals, one a therapist and the other the client. The therapist provides a service, which the client requests, in return for a monetary fee.

In contrast to the medical model of mental illness, Thomas Szasz argues that if a person behaves in such a way that they break the law, then that person should be charged with a crime. At the moment a person who behaves in a way that the rest of us find unacceptable may be taken to a place of safety, such as an asylum, and be given treatment which they neither want not desire. People who suffer from a mental illness are assumed to be unable to make decisions about their own welfare. Thomas Szasz first proposed the 'psychiatric will' in 1982, to offer some legal protection to sane people who may in the future become mental patients facing involuntary treatment.

The contractual form of psychiatry is said to be safe and presents no serious ethical problems for either the therapist or the client because, in the last analysis, it is a free exchange between equal partners. At any time the arrangement can be broken by either partner. Unlike institutional psychiatry which is dangerous, based upon coercion and is the tool of an oppressor, contractual psychiatry poses no threat to freedom or liberty.

There are a number of theoretical assumptions in the work of Szasz. As we have seen, Szasz believes that the *market* can be used to resolve social problems, unlike the intervention of the State which is likely to be coercive. In terms of perspective, Szasz has a great deal in common with the symbolic interactionists.

Szasz also views mental illness as a semiological exercise:

> Psychiatry, using the methods of communication analysis, has much in common with the sciences concerned with the study of languages and communicative behaviour. In spite of this connection between psychiatry and such disciplines as symbolic logic, semotics, and sociology, problems of mental health continue to be cast in the traditional framework of medicine. (Szasz 1972: 20)

Szasz takes his starting point from Reichenbach's *Elements of Symbolic Logic* (1947). All semiologists differ a little in the concepts they use. However, semiology is the study of signs, and is principally concerned with how meaning is generated in 'texts'. For Szasz, mental illness is a 'text'. The essential breakthrough of semiology was to take linguistics as a model and to apply linguistic concepts to other phenomena – in this case that of madness – and to treat psychiatry and madness like languages.

Szasz's application of semiology to mental illness is based upon two assumptions:

- Mental illness is a cultural phenomena, an object or set of events with meaning. In other words, mental illness is made up of 'signs'
- Mental illness does not have an basic nature in itself, but is defined by a network of social relations. Mental illness has no meaning in itself.

Reichenbach identified three types of sign:

1 **Indexical signs**: 'signs which acquire a function through their causal connection between object and sign' (Szasz 1972: 111). In this case, some types of behaviour indicate madness. Showalter (1985) gives the example of the nineteenth-century psychiatrist Henry Maudsley, who wrote: 'It would scarcely be an exaggeration to say that few persons go mad ... who do not show more or less plainly by their gait, manner, gestures, habits of thought, feeling, or action, that they have a sort of predestination to madness' (Henry Maudsley cited in Showalter 1985: 106).

2 **Iconic signs**: 'signs that stand in a relation of similarity to the objects they designate: for example, the photograph' (Szasz 1972: 112). Certain behaviours are symbolic of madness.
3 **Conventional signs**: 'signs whose relation to the object is purely conventional or arbitrary' (ibid.: 113). Szasz gives the example of mathematical symbols; there is no natural link between the sign and what it is meant to represent.

The following quote from Szasz should show how he made use of these concepts:

> When ... one's love object fails to listen and respond to verbal complaints or requests, one will be compelled, or at least tempted, to take recourse in communication by means of iconic body signs. We have come to speak of this general phenomenon, which may take a great variety of forms as 'mental illness'. As a result, instead of realising that people are engaged in various types of communications in diverse communicational (or social) situations, we construct – and then ourselves come to believe in – various types of mental illnesses, such as 'hysteria', 'hypochondriasis', 'schizophrenia', and so forth. (Ibid.: 114)

An example of what Szasz is saying would be if your girlfriend or boyfriend no longer wanted to see you, but would not give you any reason for their decision. You might ask for a reason in a fairly polite fashion, but if they continually refused to give you a reason you may start to shout, cry or adopt more and more bizzare forms of communicative behaviour, whilst continuing to request information. This behaviour could be classified as mental illness. What we believe to be mental illness may be a form of distorted communication.

In an informed critique of Szasz, R.D. Laing (1979) argues that Szasz's point that mental illness is really a form of 'illness-imitative behaviour' is in a number of cases wrong. Laing gave the examples of compulsion neurosis and psychoses. In addition, Szasz has no analysis of the structures of power or knowledge in which mental illness emerges. Finally, the notion of contractual psychiatry is in essence what most people are involved in, even if the bill is paid by the State.

It could be argued that only the mildest forms of mental disorder could be dealt with by the framework of contractual psychiatry, for example, people who need therapy but who are well enough to hold down jobs. In Szasz's vision the only people who would have access to psychiatric help would be those who needed it least. The people who need help the most would be the least likely to be in a position to afford such therapy. Even if the State were to introduce a form of voucher system, the most severely ill people would be the least likely to be able to shop around.

Erving Goffman

Goffman viewed mental illness as a stigma, which emerges through a process of labelling and not as a medical condition. However, before we can understand fully Goffman's account of mental illness, we need to look at his conception of the social order.

In *Behaviour in Public Places* (1963), Goffman outlines a model of the social order which he defines as: 'the consequences of any set of norms that regulates the way in which persons pursue objectives' (Goffman 1963: 8). There are several types of social order, including a legal order and an economic order. However, the social order in which he is interested is where people meet others face to face. Communicative behaviour takes two forms for Goffman:

- **Unfocused interaction:** in which individuals make a first assessment of the other
- **Focused interaction:** where individuals gather to sustain a focus of attention, such as having a conversation.

Goffman is concerned with how the social order is maintained. The social order has rules which he terms *situational proprieties*, moral codes that will be found in any social gathering. In addition, individuals present an image of themselves – a personal front – to show that they are willing to accept the rules. In Goffman's language, this shows that they are 'situationally present'. To break a rule, to not live up to the personal front, is to break the moral code, which in Goffman's language is to cause a 'situational impropriety'. The person who does this will be labelled, and one possible label is that of 'mentally ill'. As Goffman explains:

> [I]t may be permissible for a child on the street to suck his thumb, or lick a sucker, or inflate chewing-gum bubbles until they burst, or draw a stick along a fence, or fully interrupt his main line of activity to take a stone from his shoe. But the adult mental patients in Central Hospital who were observed conducting themselves in some of these ways were felt by staff to be acting 'symptomatically'. (Ibid.: 47)

Situational improprieties are the start of the *moral career* of the mental patient. The 'moral career' represents the stages that a person goes through, or the progression through a number of social roles, in order to become a mental patient. The social beginning of the patient's career as a mental patient begins with a complaint about behaviour; this is the first stage on the road to hospitalisation, the application of a label. The 'atrocity tales' – Goffman's term for the description of the behaviour of the labelled person – form what Goffman refers to as *career contingencies*. At this point we have what Goffman terms 'the circuit of agents' – doctors and other professionals who are requested to supply information and participate in the individual's passage from civilian to patient. In other words, the self becomes redefined.

In *Asylums* (1961) Goffman traces the ways that hospitalisation shapes an inmate's moral career. When a person enters the *total institution* of the mental hospital, they are subjected to 'rituals of degradation', in which staff and existing inmates humiliate the new inmate in an attempt to break the self-identity that the inmate may have had in the outside world.

Total Institutions

Total institutions are institutions in which people live and work in a closed community, under a single authority, according to a rational plan, which is attempting to achieve a number of approved goals. Goffman divides total institutions into five basic types, including such diverse institutions as ships, boarding schools and leper colonies. All of the total institutions have the same basic structure in Goffman's eyes. There is a strict staff–inmate division, with no social mobility between the two: staff normally work an eight-hour shift and, unlike the inmates, are fully integrated into the wider community outside the institution. Both the staff and the inmates view each other through a range of narrow stereotypes. The inmates view the staff as oppressive, patronising and mean. The staff view the inmates as resentful, circumspect and generally not to be trusted.

THE FIVE TYPES OF TOTAL INSTITUTION

1   Institutions established to care for persons felt to be incapable and harmless, for example, homes for the aged.
2   Institutions established to care for persons felt to be incapable and a threat to the community, for example, mental hospitals, leper colonies and TB sanitaria.
3   Institutions established to protect the community from intentional dangers, and where the welfare of the inmates is not the primary objective, for example, jails and concentration camps.
4   Institutions established for instrumental reasons, principally to perform some work task, for example, barracks, boarding schools, ships and oil rigs.
5   Institutions established as retreats from the world; most examples given by Goffman are training centres for the religious life – monasteries, convents etc.

One of the strengths of Goffman's work is that in his participation observation of Central Hospital, Goffman attempted to show that the behaviour of inmates was not as irrational as the hospital staff would have us believe. Goffman attempted to find rationality in what appeared to be irrational behaviour. Hoarding behaviour was at the time that Goffman was writing regarded by the hospital staff as an indicator of mental illness; after all, 'normal' people do not keep all their possessions on their person. However, in the irrational situation of the mental hospital where the inmates had no secure place to keep their possessions, then the rational thing to do was to keep their possessions with them at all times.

Critique of Goffman

One of the most interesting critiques of Erving Goffman's work was published by Alvin Gouldner in an essay: 'The Sociologist as Partisan: Sociology and the Welfare State'. Gouldner points out that Goffman takes the point of view of the underdog in society, such as the mental patient and others with stigma. Goffman speaks on their behalf, because underdogs tend not to have access to the media. Gouldner is highly critical of the partisan nature of Goffman's sociology and claims that Goffman's work is characterised by sentimentality. He goes so far as to describe Goffman's output as 'essays on quaintness': 'The danger is then, that such an identification with the underdog becomes the urban sociologist's equivalent of the anthropologist's (one time) romantic appreciation of the noble savage' (Gouldner 1974: 37).

Gouldner criticises Goffman's sociology on three levels. He contends that it is ahistorical (Goffman does not take into account the history of mental illness); that it fails to confront the matter of hierarchy; and lastly that it ignores power relationships.

However, according to Mary Rogers (1981) there is a *theory of power* at work within Goffman's oeuvre, although he is not particularly interested in the nature of power that we find in, for example, a Marxian analysis. For Goffman, power is about the ability of one person to change the behaviour of another person. People can exercise power by drawing upon two forms of resources:

- **Instrumental resources:** which include interpersonal skills such as character, presence of mind, perceived fateful circumstances, knowledge and information control
- **Infra resources:** which are concerned with perception, the skill that people have at changing the definition of the situation, use of negative stereotypes and labels.

It would appear that for Goffman power is a form of 'collusion' between people who have only a minimal stigma and who can 'pass' as normal, against others who for a variety of reasons are unable or unwilling to accept the definition of the situation. As Goffman comments, 'We must all carry within ourselves something of the sweet guilt of the conspirators' (Goffman 1959: 105).

A central flaw in the work of Foucault, Szasz and Goffman is that none of them made any comment upon the fact that it is women who are more likely to be diagnosed as mentally ill rather than men.

Gender, Sexuality and Mental Health

The statistics on mental health in both Europe and North America show that more women are diagnosed with mental health problems than are men. According to David Pilgrim and Anne Rogers (1999), there are three possible explanations for this:

- **Social causation:** society causes more female mental illness
- **Artefact explanations:** women are simply over-represented and men are under-represented in the statistics for mental health problems
- **Social labelling:** women are more likely to be labelled as having mental health problems.

From a feminist perspective, patriarchial assumptions underpin the medical model: 'man' is seen as the norm by the medical profession and 'woman' as the Other. Many feminist researchers have argued that much medical research outside of the area of reproduction is based on the assumption that 'the patient' is male; hence many health problems that specifically affect women are regarded as 'psychological' in nature because possible physiological causes are not investigated. Inhorn et al. describe this as: 'the biological essentialization of women as reproducers' (Inhorn and Whittle 2001: 559).

The medical model refuses to take racism or patriarchy into account as legitimate epidemiological risks, even though sexism, harassment and violence are all related to high blood pressure, strokes and hypertension. In addition, as Saltonstall (1993) argues, the insistence that women should be thin is built into the culture and this is a cause of a range of physical and psychiatric health problems:

> Gender norms often informed the interpretation of body insignia. Respondents used body insignia as indicators of the health of self's and other's state of womanhood or manhood ... One woman referenced norms of behaviour for women when she said: 'My mother always said that women who eat small meals are more feminine.' Female respondents regularly linked healthiness, eating, exercise, and being thin in their responses. Three women stated directly that their exercise and eating activities were motivated as much by a desire to 'not be fat' as by a desire to be healthy. (Saltonstall 1993: 11–12)

In other words, there is a decontextualisation of the female body within the medical model – a ruling out of patriarchy as a possible cause of mental illness and other more obviously physical disorders amongst women.

Elaine Showalter and the Female Malady

Showalter starts her analysis of women and mental illness by arguing that there is a fundamental alliance between 'woman' and 'madness' which is not only reflected in the statistical over-representation of women in figures for mental illness, but also in the ways in which the notion of feminine is represented in the culture as irrational. She argues that from the early nineteenth century onwards, in both Britain and the United States, women who rebelled against the narrow constraints of what was expected of a woman, who attempted to resist the patriarchal constraints of bourgeoisie femininity and display a defiant womanhood, were much more likely to come into contact with the psychiatric services.

Showalter (1985) identifies three historical phases of English psychiatry, each of which was shaped by social disorder:

Psychiatric Victorianism (1830–1870)

The foundations of psychiatry in the victorian period were built upon the concepts of moral insanity, moral management and moral architecture. *Moral insanity* was a condition invented in 1835 by James Cowles Prichard to describe what was considered at the time to be significant deviation from socially acceptable behaviour. This unacceptable behaviour included masturbation, a 'morbid perversion of the natural feelings'. A distinction was made between physical and moral causes of insanity; physical causes included masturbation, epilepsy and fever. Many psychiatrists argued that mental illness was caused by masturbation and that the surgical removal of the clitoris would allow women to better control their behaviour. Dr Isaac Baker Brown, a member of the Obstetrical Society, removed both the clitoris and labia to cure a number of problems: eye problems, paralysis, epilepsy and even women who wanted to take advantage of their rights under the 1857 Divorce Act, which he interpreted as evidence of mental illness.

Key biological phases in a woman's life were also identified as important points when insanity could emerge: puberty, pregnancy and menopause. Sexual desire in menopausal women was considered to be particularly problematic and one psychiatrist W. Tyler Smith administered treatments such as inserting ice into the vagina, placing leeches onto the cervix and a course of ice water injections into the rectum.

Moral causes of insanity included domestic grief, jealousy and 'over-excitement at the Great Exhibition'. However, as Showalter argues:

> But while doctors blamed menstrual problems or sexual abnormality, women writers suggested that it was the lack of meaningful work, hope, or companionship that led to depression or breakdown. (Showalter 1985: 61)

Moral management involved attempting to impose high standards through re-education to enhance a person's self-esteem. Work and religious observance were believed to be therapeutic and humanitarian. A woman's appearance was also an important element in moral management, and as Showalter argues, psychiatrists at the time believed that it was abnormal for a woman to neglect her appearance and women who did so ran the risk of being diagnosed as mentally ill for falling short of the middle-class standards of fashion.

The layout of asylum buildings also had a role to play in the moral management of inmates. Large gardens were believed to be therapeutic. Males and females were separated. People who were diagnosed with different conditions were also separated, with opportunities for staff to observe even the most intimate aspects of a person's daily routine.

Psychiatric Darwinism (1870–1920)

Psychiatric Darwinism took its starting point from Darwin's book *The Descent of Man* (1871) in which he argued that men were superior to women and that women were of a lesser order of civilisation. Herbert Spencer in *Principles of Sociology* (1876) argued that women were often depleted of energy because of their reproductive process which left them intellectually handicapped. These assumptions were embedded within the psychiatric approach developed by Henry Maudsley and T.S. Coulston, who viewed mental illness as a product of evolution. They believed that some individuals had inherited or developed a biological defect, or alternatively that mental illness could be a product of the local environment. In contrast to this view, Elaine Showalter argues that it was with the emergence of the women's suffrage movement that there was a parallel emergence of a range of nervous disorders among women, notably hysteria and anorexia nervosa.

Psychiatric Modernism (1920–1980)

The period of Psychiatric Modernism brought with it a range of new techniques and approaches. Electro convulsive therapy (ECT) was invented by Ugo Cerletti who initially did ECT experiments on pigs. The lobotomy was also developed and first used in 1935 by Egas Moniz as a cure for schizophrenia. Moniz later went on to use the technique in an effort to cure homosexuals, alcoholics and political dissidents. In the United States the technique was developed by Dr Walter Freeman, who devised the 'transorbital lobotomy' in which the surgeon used an instrument similar to an ice pick to enter the brain from behind the eyelid. Once inside, nerve fibres in the front of the brain were cut, which reduced or eliminated the patient's emotional reaction capabilities, sexual and homosexual drives. Lobotomies for homosexuality were performed until the 1950s in the US.

However, Showalter argues that it was women who were most likely to be subjected to psychosurgery. She quotes from Sergeant and Slater's psychiatric textbook published in 1972 which stated that a depressed woman: 'may owe her illness to a psychopathic husband who cannot change and will not accept treatment' (Sergeant and Slater 1972 cited in Showalter 1985: 210).

Most of Showalter's discussion of Psychiatric Modernism focuses upon the work of R.D. Laing. There are three key influences upon the work of R.D Laing, all of which helped to politicise his work: phenomenology, the Marxian theory of power and ideology, and Freud.

Laing was a practising psychiatrist and one of his first patients was an 18-year-old man who believed that he was Julius Caesar. Laing talked to the young man at great length sharing his fantasies. In his book *The Divided Self* (1960), Laing developed this technique of sharing the fantasies of patients. He argued that psychosis had a lawful shape that the patient developed to cope with a threatening personal environment. People suffered from 'ontological insecurity' in which they were uncertain about the boundaries between themselves and the world. The behaviour of the mad person should be seen as meaningful rather than odd or irrelevant. In addition, mad people had a career; madness developed through a number of distinct phases.

The final chapter of *The Divided Self* was about a single schizophrenic patient named Julie. Laing investigated her family background and found that she had gone through a three-stage progression from 'good girl' to 'bad girl' who rejected the instructions of her parents on how to behave, to 'mad girl' who was blamed for all of the problems of the family. In his latter works this became the 'double-bind theory' of schizophrenia. In the double-bind family, the entire family problems are blamed on one single person, usually the youngest female. From the mid-1960s onwards, in place of traditional psychiatric techniques, Laing started to view schizophrenia as a healing process rather than a psychiatric problem. Schizophrenic patients were said to be engaged in a lonely voyage through the inner space of their minds.

Research into Women and Mental Health

- **Chesler (1972)** and **English and Ehrenreich (1976)** argued that medical practice was partiarchial and male doctors had a tendency to regard symptoms presented to them by women as psychological in nature. In addition, many male doctors viewed women as psychologically impaired
- **Broverman et al. (1970)** found that behaviour described by doctors as 'male' was more likely to be regarded as 'healthy' than behaviour that was described as 'female'
- **Busfield (1982)** found extensive gender stereotyping in medical textbooks
- **Milliren (1977)** found that older women were more likely to be prescribed minor tranquillisers for anxiety than were the rest of the population
- **Sheppard (1991)** found that GPs were more likely to section women under the Mental Health Act for compulsory admission to a mental hospital
- **Nazroo (1998)** and **Brown and Harris (1978)** found that women are more at risk of depression than are men if they experience a severe life event
- **Sutherland (1990)** and **Atkinson et al. (1990)** found that 86 percent of menopausal women were diagnosed as suffering from psychiatric conditions and a significant number of these were diagnosed as 'clinically depressed'. In addition, **Hinchliff and Montague (1988)** found that the highest number of female suicides was amongst women in their 50s
- **Coleman (1993)** found that a number of severe life events occur during middle age, such as children leaving home
- **Gulledge (1991)** and **McGhie (1979)** found that women find the loss of their parental role depressing
- **Sutherland (1990), Martinson (1990)** and **Bevan (1978)** found that physical changes to the body may also play a causative role in the onset of depression, loss of athletic skills, a tendency to gain weight and to tire more easily
- **Houston et al. (1979)** and **Flint (1975)** found that in Europe and North America women may see the menopause as signifying a loss of femininity, leading to depression
- **Sutherland (1990)** and **Ballinger (1990)** argued that in Western society people place value on having a child and also a high value on youth. However, the meaning of the menopause has to be understood within a social and cultural context; in Indian society it brings an improvement in social standing, freedom and self-esteem
- **Maoz et al. (1970)** found that Arab women in Israel also evinced positive attitudes towards the menopause.

It is important to note too that amongst the female population, women with young children, and especially divorced women with young children, are more likely to experience mental health problems.

Most of the research on the relationship between gender and the use of the psychiatric health services shows that women make greater use of the services than men, especially for emotional problems. Such research includes Veroff (1981); Shapiro et al. (1994); Leaf et al. (1986, 1987); Wells et al. (1986); and Bland et al. (1990). However, according to Albizu-Garcia et al. (2001), none of these studies was designed to explain how women differ from men in their help-seeking behaviour. The studies generally assume that:

- Women are more likely to recognise a mental health problem
- Women are more likely to report a mental health problem
- Women are more receptive to psychiatric services
- Women have more opportunity to seek professional help.

Verbrugge (1985) suggests a number of possible explanations for women's greater help-seeking behaviour:

- Women have a greater burden of illness – a greater need for health care
- Women are socialised to recognise symptoms whereas men are not
- Men's greater involvement in the labour market reduces their opportunities to seek help
- Women are more likely to report symptoms
- Previous experience of health services influences future use.

All of these issues have been addressed by feminist researchers. Belenky et al. (1986) for example, in support of the point that women are socialised to recognise symptoms in a way that men are not, argue that women have a distinct ontology and epistemology. Women are receptive to knowledge and experience 'reality' differently than men. There are distinct 'women's ways of knowing' which Belenky traces from ways that women understand the meaning of silence, the acceptance of authority, the grounds for trusting subjective knowledge, and the ability to synthesise external and subjective knowledge. Women have knowledge that men do not possess and women experience a reality to which men do not have access.

Albizu-Garcia et al. (2001) also found that women were more likely to report physical complaints to the health service. However, when all possible sources of care for psychiatric and emotional problems were taken into account – such as in the Veterans Associations in the United States – Albizu-Garcia found that men and women had similar rates of seeking help for emotional problems, suggesting that women are simply over-represented in the statistics for emotional or psychiatric problems (the artefact explanation).

However, there is very little research on the use of mental health services by lesbians, gay men or bisexuals. Before the publication of DSM III (1980), homosexuality was regarded as a psychiatric disorder and medical professionals would attempt to 'cure' homosexuality by aversion therapy or electric shock treatment. Even within DSM III there was a category of mental disorder named 'ego-dystonic homosexuality'. In other words, unhappy lesbians and gay men were deemed to be suffering from a psychiatric disorder. According to Golding:

> Many lesbians, gay men and bisexual men and women who use mental health services do not feel safe enough to come out or disclose their sexuality to both staff and users within them ... 73 percent reported actual experiences of prejudice, discrimination, harassment and even physical and sexual violence or rape. (Golding 1997: 17)

Because many lesbians and gay men view counselling or psychotherapy, or similar psychotherapeutic methodologies as approaches that pathologise gay sexuality, there is a natural reluctance on the part of lesbians and gay men to access these services. The MIND report *Lesbians, Gay Men, Bisexuals and Mental Health* by Jackie Golding (1997), updated by George Stewart in 2002, found that many people believe that their doctors or therapists see a person's sexual orientation as a problem or cause of their mental health problems. In addition, many gay men face stigma and discrimination because of their sexuality, leading to feelings of isolation and depression. Golding argues that this societal oppression may be a cause of the high level of substance abuse within the gay community.

ACTIVITY

'Cures' for Homosexuality

Don Romesburg in the Journal *Out in All Directions: An Almanac of Gay and Lesbian America*, outlines the following 'cures' for homosexuality which were popular from the nineteenth century onwards: Prostitution Therapy, Marriage Therapy, Cauterization, Castration/Ovary Removal, Chastity Hypnosis, Aversion Therapy, Psychoanalysis, Radiation Treatment, Hormone Therapy, Lobotomy, Psycho-Religious Therapy, Beauty Therapy. With respect to Beauty Therapy, Romesburg discusses Dr Arthur Guy Matthew's book *Is Homosexuality a Menace?* (1957), which explains how he cured a lesbian by getting her hair 'professionally coiffured,' showing her how to apply cosmetics and employing a fashion expert who selected the most elegant feminine styles to bring out her charm and beauty.

(Source: www.law.harvard.edu/studorgs/lambda/l_13theo.html)

Question:

➢ Why do you believe that the medical profession has invested so much time, effort and resource into attempts to find a 'cure' for homosexuality?

Mental Illness and Ethnicity

Cross-cultural diagnosis of mental health problems is always going to be difficult, not least because if mental illness is about inappropriate ways of behaving, diagnosis is likely to involve the imposition of Western forms of behaviour on people who may choose to reject key aspects of the lifestyle and culture. In a nutshell, certain behaviour is regarded as evidence of mental illness, even though that behaviour might be considered normal within a person's own culture. In addition, there may be important cultural differences in the way that people experience and communicate ideas about mental illness. Finally, the social control aspects of these issues should not be under-estimated. It is well documented that in Britain, people of Afro-Caribbean heritage are much more likely to come into contact with the psychiatric services via the police or the courts, or via the prison psychiatric service.

People of Afro-Caribbean heritage are much more likely to be diagnosed with a range of mental illnesses than the white population and a number of factors have been suggested to account for this: biological factors that might make the people more susceptible to mental illness; for first-time migrants the psychological stress of migration, low income, poor housing and other material disadvantage; cultural factors such as stress induced by the exposure to racism; and racially motivated misdiagnoses. However, it would be reasonable to expect that such factors would affect all ethnic minorities equally, but this is not the case. People of Asian heritage have lower rates of mental illness than people of Afro-Caribbean heritage, and there are higher rates for people of Pakistani heritage than for people of Indian heritage. In addition, second- and third-generation Afro-Caribbean and Asian people have higher rates than the initial migrants.

David Pilgrim and Anne Rogers (1999) suggest that in the case of schizophrenia, the apparent under-representation of Asian groups could be caused by the reluctance of people from this group to make use of psychiatric services as schizophrenia has a stigma attached.

Frederick (1991) has identified a number of factors that may cause mental health problems for ethnic minority members:

- Recurrent racism
- Few positive images of black people in the media, which in turn has a detrimental effect upon self-image and expectations
- Problems in the education system leading to educational under-achievement.

Hutchinson et al. (1997) found that the risk of developing schizophrenia is no greater in the first-generation relatives of Afro-Caribbean patients than it is in the population as a whole. However, there is an increased risk of second-generation Afro-Caribbean relatives of patients with schizophrenia themselves becoming schizophrenic patients. According to Gavin et al. (2001), this finding supports the view that environmental factors may act synergistically with genetic predisposition to produce schizophrenia in people of Afro-Carribean heritage.

In a survey of the available evidence, Gavin et al. (2001) found that there are several possible reasons for the increased risk of schizophrenia in migrants. Research by Bhugra and Jones (2001) found that schizophrenia occurred more commonly in the country of origin of immigrants. However, Gavin et al. (2001) argue that epidemiological data from Hickling and Rodgers-Johnson (1995) and Mahy et al. (1999) do not support this view. There is no convincing evidence of increased rates of biological risk factors in immigrants' countries of origin.

Obstetric complications were once believed to be a risk factor for schizophrenia. Early research had assumed that women of Afro-Carribean heritage had more obstetric complications than the general population, thus accounting for the increased rate of schizophrenia. However, Hutchinson et al. (1997) found that women of Afro-Carribean heritage actually have a lower rate of obstetric complications compared to other women in the population. The increased susceptibility of women of Afro-Carribean heritage to rubella infection could be a causal factor, but Glover (1989) could find no substantial evidence to support this view.

Sharpley et al. (2001) found that undesirable social circumstances, such as social isolation, overcrowding or unemployment, often found in urban areas, are strongly related to the development of schizophrenia following migration. In addition, people of Afro-Carribean heritage are more likely to live in single-parent families; this suggests that a lack of social cohesion is a possible factor.

Institutional racism was also thought to be a factor as people of Afro-Carribean heritage are more likely to have low educational attainment and to have been imprisoned. Davies et al. (1996) found that people of Afro-Carribean heritage had a high rate of involuntary admission via the police. In addition, there are few black self-help groups to support people with mental health problems and to campaign on their behalf.

Saffron Karlsen and James Nazroo (2000) argue that in the United States and Britain, health care professionals fail to take into account the central aspects of ethnic minority experience that may influence health, such as the multi-dimensional and contextual nature of cultural identity, socio-economic disadvantage and the impact of racial harassment and discrimination. Racial harassment and discrimination can affect health in two ways: first, the physical and psychological consequences of facing harassment and, second, in the way racism devalues individuals, leading to exclusion and social disadvantage.

Measures of 'ethnic group' used, particularly in health research, still tend to employ crude assessments of country of origin and skin colour, which, not surprisingly, lead to discussions that focus on, or at least imply, genetic and cultural explanations for the relationship between ethnicity and health. (Karlsen and Nazroo 2000: 8)

Are assessment levels of schizophrenia among black British people exaggerated? During his time at Queens Medical Centre (Nottingham), Professor Glynn Harrison carried out extensive research on the high incidence of schizophrenia amongst Nottingham's 'black' population. Although his work can be challenged on methodological grounds, notably that he had problems estimating the size of the 'black' population, Harrison explored some of the possible reasons for the differences: genetic factors. biological differences, viruses, failure of the immune system, neurochemistry, pre- and perinatal problems, high unemployment and low income. One possibility is misdiagnosis. There is always a danger that physical symptoms may be believed to be psychological in nature when there is a physical cause. Haemoglobin E disease can generate symptoms which may be classed as mental illness.

In sharp contrast to Glynn Harrison's research, *Ethnic Minority Psychiatric Illness Rates in the Community* is a detailed analysis of the mental health problems of ethnic minority groups compared to the general population. The report contains data on a range of widespread mental disorders. James Nazroo and his team, (2002) argue that people of Afro-Caribbean heritage do not have significantly higher rates of schizophrenia than other groups in the population.

Whereas Harrison argued that people of Afro-Caribbean heritage are between three and five times more likely to suffer from schizophrenia than other groups, Nazroo's research suggests that the differences in the rate are not statistically significant:

> We think the figures are different because we assessed rates of mental illness in the community. Previous research has looked at the numbers of people actually in contact with treatment services. These findings are crucial to our understanding of the relationship between mental illness and ethnicity.

The research also found that practitioners have problems in identifying and treating mental illness amongst some ethnic groups, because ways of recounting mental illness differ. In particular, people born in the Indian subcontinent were found to describe experiences in terms that were unfamiliar to mental health professionals. The report also draws attention to the problems faced by people of Irish heritage.

Despite being white, people of Irish heritage experience racism within the psychiatric service. According to Bracken (1998), people of Irish heritage have the highest rates of admission to psychiatric hospitals, particularly for schizophrenia, of any ethnic minority in Britain. They are almost twice as likely to be hospitalised as the rest of the population. Psychiatric services, and other public services such as education, the police and criminal justice, simply do not recognise the distinct culture of people of Irish heritage. In addition to their over-representation in statistics for use of psychiatric services, people of Irish heritage are statistically more likely to be socially disadvantaged; to leave school at the earliest opportunity, with few qualifications; to be unemployed or in low-paid, low-skilled occupations;

and to experience high levels of long-term disability. Police harassment is a problem both for people of Afro-Caribbean heritage and people of Irish heritage. Legal protection has, to some extent, been eroded as police powers to stop, search and detain are often carried out under the Prevention of Terrorism Act where the police do not have to provide evidence to support their suspicion.

People of Irish heritage are far more likely to reside in the private rented sector, while homelessness amongst single people of Irish heritage is more common than it is for other ethnic minorities. However, because they are classified with the indigenous population as 'British' or 'white', the problems that people of Irish heritage experience are often invisible. Research by Cochrane et al. (1996) demonstrates that Irish men are the only migrant group whose life expectancy worsens on emigration to England.

Nazroo's (2002) report also concluded that there were no discernible differences in mental illness between groups, though rates were low for Bangladeshi women and high for Irish men and Pakistani women. With the notable exceptions of Bangladeshi and Irish people, in most ethnic groups women experienced higher rates of mental illness than men. Experience of racism and discrimination were identified as causal factors in mental illness as were marital relationships, work and money problems, and family problems.

Labelling may be the most important factor. Ways of behaving which are both common and acceptable in the Caribbean, for example, may be treated with hostility in Britain. For example, within most cultures of the Caribbean there is a tendency to always stress the positive when speaking and not to mention any negative words; such neologisms could be defined as symptoms of mental illness in a different culture. It is also possible to extend R.D. Laing's theory of the double-bind family to cover the whole of the host society in an effort to explain mental illness among ethnic minorities. People were invited to live and work in Britain after the Second World War, but once people settled here they experienced racism. Such contradictory messages and the culture shock that it brought for some may be a possible cause of mental illness.

Conclusion

In this chapter we have argued that the social division of disability is based upon strong discourses that the able-bodied or sane impose upon the mentally ill or disabled to segregate them and place them in particular social niches. The voices of people experiencing disability have brought about a definite shift away from the 'medical model' – which assumed that disability is a personal tragedy and has nothing but a negative impact on people's lives – towards a social model. The medical model assumes that both mental health problems and impairment are disagreeable, a source of legitimate stigma, a barrier to full participation in the consumer society and a problem for the wider social system. In contrast, the social model of disability assumes that the problem is to be found in the *social constructions* of prejudices that surround disability and not in the bodies of disabled people. These arguments are embedded within much disability legislation, notably the Americans with Disabilities Act (1990). However, some people with disabilities suffer physical or psychological burdens that no amount of social justice can abolish.

'Strong discourse' for Foucault, is a body of statements that is both organised and systematic, and is in the form of a set of rules. However, according to Hughes and Patterson (1997), *pain* is a concept drawn from medical discourse, and is viewed as a product of anatomy and physiology. However, pain is both an experience and a discursive construction in that it has phenomenological parameters where our bodies meet with our minds and culture. It has to be defined and packaged as an unpleasant experience, and the people who get pleasure from experiencing pain are defined as having a mental health problem. In a range of areas, as diverse as physical impairment, learning difficulties and schizophrenia, there is limited evidence of biological impairment as a legitimate and objective category; rather such categories are behavioural in nature – in other words *epistemes of assumed* impairment. Unacceptable behaviour is discursively reframed as a biologically based functional impairment. In the case of mental illness we find that the medical model plays a central role in the mode of subjectivation; a chemically induced and medically approved attempt to impose the power of the norm.

References

Abberley, P. (1998) *The spectre at the feast: disabled people and social theory*, in T. Shakespeare (ed.) *The Disability Reader: Social Science Perspectives* Cassell, London.

Albizu-Garcia, C.E., Alegria, M., Freeman, D. and Vera, M. (2001) 'Gender and Health Services Use for a Mental Health Problem', *Social Science and Medicine* 53(7): 865–78.

Albrecht, G.L. (1992) *The Disability Business*, Sage, London.

Albrecht, G. and Bury, M. (2001) 'The Political Economy of the Disability Marketplace' in Albreht, G. Seelman, K., and Bury, M., (eds) *Handbook of Disability Studies*, Sage, London.

Anderson, P. and R.M. Kitchin. (2000) *Disability, space and sexuality: Access to family planning services*, Social Science and Medicine 51: 1163–73.

Andreason, N. (1997) 'More Evidence of Physical Cause of Schizophrenia', *The Lancet* 353 (9162): 1425.

Antle, B.J. (2000) 'Seeking Strengths in Young People with Physical Disabilities'. Dissertation abstracts International A (Humanities and social sciences) 60(10-A): 3795.

Apperley, P. (1998) 'The Spectre at the Feast: Disabled People and Social Theory' in Shakespeare, T. (ed.) *The Disability Reader: Social Science Perspectives*, Cassell, London.

Atkinson, R.L., Atknison, R.C., Smith E.E., Benn, D.J. and Hilgard, E.R. (1990) *Introduction to Psychology*, (10th edn) Harcourt Brace Jovanovich, San Diego, Cal.

Ballinger, C.B. (1990) 'Psychological Aspects of the Menopause', *British Journal of Psychiatry* 156: 652–59.

Barnes, C (2003) *Independent Living, Politics and Implications,* Internet publication URL: www. independentliving.org/docs6/barnes2003.html

Barker, J.L., Jr Kolin I.S. and Bartlett E.S. (1974) 'Psychosexual Dynamics of Patients Undergoing Mammary Augmentation', *Plastic and Reconstructive Surgery* (53): 652–59.

Barron, K. (1997) 'The Bumpy Road to Womanhood', *Disability and Society* 12(2): 223–39.

Bauman, Z. (1989) *Modernity and the Holocaust.* Cambridge: Cambridge University Press.

Bauman, Z. (1997) *Postmodernity and its Discontents,* Cambridge, Polity Press.

Bauman, Zygmunt (1998) *Globalization: the Human Consequences,* Columbia Press, New York.

Bauman, Zygmunt (2001) *Community: Seeking Safety in an Insecure World,* Polity, Cambridge.

Beauboeuf-LaFontant, T. (2003) 'Strong and Large Black Women? Exploring Relationships between Deviant Womanhood and Weight', *Gender and Society* 17(1): 111–21.

Belenky, M.F., Clenchy, B.M., Goldberger, N.R., and Torule, J.M. (1986) *Women's Ways of Knowing: The Development of Self, Voice and Mind,* New York, Basic Books.

Bell, D. (1973) *The Coming of Post-Industrial Society,* New York, Basic Books.

Berman, B. and Gritz, E. (1991) 'Women and Smoking: Current Trends and Issues of the 1990s', *Journal of Substance Abuse* 3: 221–338.

Bevan, J. (1978) *A Pictoral Handbook of Anatomy and Physiology,* Mitchell Beazley, London.

Berger, P.L. and Luckman, T. (1973) *The Social Construction of Reality,* Harmondsworth: Penguin.

Best, S. (2000) *Active Sociology,* Longman, London.

Bhugra, D. and Jones, P. (2001) 'Migration and Mental Illness', *Advances in Psychiatric Treatment* 7: 216–23.

Bhugra, D., Leff, J. and Mallet, R. (1997) 'Incidence and Outcome of Schizophrenia in Whites, African-Caribbeans and Asians in London', *Psychological Medicine* 27: 791–98.

Bland, R.C., Newman, S.C. and Orn, H. (1990) 'Health Care Utilization for Emotional Problems', *Canadian Journal of Psychiatry* 35: 397–400.

Bordo, S. (1993) *Unbearable Weight: Feminism, Western Culture and the Body,* University of California Press, Berkeley, Cal.

Bracken, P. (1998) 'Mental Health and Ethnicity: The Irish Dimension', *British Journal of Psychiatry* 172: 103–5.

Braddock, D.L. and Parish, S.L. (2001) 'An Institutional History of Disability', in Albrecht, G., Seelman, K. and Bury, M. (eds) *Handbook of Disability Studies,* Sage, London.

Broverman, D., Clarkson, F. and Rosenkratz, P. (1970) 'Sex Role Stereotypes and Clinical Judgements of Mental Health', *Journal of Consulting and Clinical Psychology* 34: 1–7.

Brown, D. (1994) 'An Ordinary Sexual Life? A Review of the Normalisation Principle as It Applies to the Sexual Options of People with Learning Disabilities', *Disability and Society* 9(2): 123–144.

Brown, G.W. and Harris, T.O. (1978) 'The Social Origins of Depression', Tavistock Press, London.

Burleigh, M. (1994) 'Psychiatry, German Society and the Nazi 'Euthanisa' Programme', *Social History of medicine* 7: 213–28.

Busfield, J. (1982) 'Gender and Mental Illness', *International Journal of Mental Health* 11(12): 46–66.

Cabot, M. (1990) 'The Incidence and Prevalence of Schizophrenia in the Republic of Ireland', *Social Psychiatry and Psychiatric Epidemiology* 25: 210–15.

Cahill, S. and Eggleston, R. (1995) 'Reconsidering the Stigma of Physical Disability: Wheelchair Use and Public Kindness', *The Sociological Quarterly* 36: 681–98.

Cambridge, P. and Mellan, B. (2000) 'Reconstructing the Sexuality of Men with Learning Disabilities: Empirical and Theoretical Interpretations', *Disability and Society* 15(2): 293–311.

Carlson, L. (2001) 'Cognitive Ableism and Disability Studies: Feminist Reflection on the History of Mental Retardation', *Hypatia* 16(4): 124–46.

Casper, R. and Offer, D. (1990) 'Weight and Dieting Concerns in Adolescents. Fashion or Symptom?', *Pediatrics* 86: 384–90.

Chesler, P. (1972) *Women and Madness,* Doubleday, New York.

Cochrane, R., Pearson, M. and Balarajan, R. (1996) *The Irish in Britain: Socio Economic and Demographic Conditions.* Occasional Papers in Irish Studies No. 3, Institute of Irish Studies, Liverpool.

Coleman, P.M. (1993) 'Depression during the Female Climateric Period', *Journal of Advanced Nursing* 18: 1540–46.

Cooper, Charlotte (1997) 'Can a Fat Woman Call Herself Disabled?', *Disability and Society* 12(1): 31–41.

Corker, M. (2001) 'Sensing Disability', *Hypatia* 16(4): 34–52.

Clayton, E.W. (2002) 'The complex relationship of genetics, groups, and health: what it means for public health', *J Law Med Ethics* 30: 290–97.

Clifford, E. (1983) *'Augmentation, Reduction, and Reconstruction: Psychological Contributions to Understanding Breast Surgery'*, in Geogiade N.G. (ed.) *Aesthetic Breast Surgery*, Williams and Wilkins, Baltimore, Maryland.

Davies, S., Thornicroft, G., Leese, M., Higgingbotham, A., and Phelan, M. (1996) 'Ethnic Differences in Risk of Compulsory Psychiatric Admission among Representative Cases of Psychosis in London', *British Medical Journal* 312: 533–37.

Deleuze, G. and Guattari, F. (1987) *A Thousand Plateaus: Capitalism and Schizophrenia*, UMP, Minneapolis.

Deshan, Shlomo (1992) *Blind People: The Private and Public Life of Sightless Israelis*, State University of New York Press, New York.

Doyal, L. and Pennel, I. (1982) *The Political Economy of Health*, Pluto, London.

Duncan, James (1875), President's Address, *Journal of Mental Science* 21: 316. Cited at: http://www.psychlaws.org/GeneralResources/report-nevertreated.htm

Earle, S. (1999) 'Facilitated Sex and the Concept of Sexual Need', *Disability and Society* 14(3): 309–23.

Earle, S. (2001) 'Disability, Facilitated Sex and the Role of the Nurse', *Journal of Advanced Nursing* 36(3): 433–40.

El-Badri, D. and Robertshaw, D. (1998) 'Sexual Fetishism associated with Temporal Lobe Dysrhythmia and Learning Disability: Two Case Studies', *British Journal of Learning Disabilities* 26(3): 110–14.

English, B. and Ehrenreich, D. (1976) *Complaints and Disorders: The Sexual Politics of Sickness*, Writers and Readers Publishing Co-operative, London.

Finkelstein, J. (1996) *After a Fashion*, Melbourne University Press, Melbourne.

Finkelstein, V. (1980) *Attitudes and Disabled People*, World Rehabilitation Fund, New York.

Flint, M.P. (1975) 'The Menopause: Reward or Punishment?', *Psychosomatics* 16: 161–63.

Foucault, M. (1967) *Madness and Civilization: A History of Insanity in the Age of Reason*, trans. R. Howard, Tavistock, London. First published, in French in 1972 as *Histoire de la Folie*.

Foucault, M. (1972). *The Archaeology of Knowledge*, trans. A.M. Sheridan-Smith, Tavistock, London. First published in French in 1969.

Foucault, M. (1977) *Discipline and Punish: The Birth of the Prison*, trans. A. Sheridan, Allen Lare, London. First published in French as *Surveilleret Punir*, 1975.

Foucault, M. (1979) *The History of Sexuality*, Vol. 1, trans. R. Hurley, Allen Lare, London. First published in French as *La Volonté de Savoir* in 1976.

Foucault, Michel (1986) *The Foucault Reader* (ed. Paul Rabinow) Penguin, Harmondsworth.

Foucault, Michel (1992) *The Use of Pleasure: The History of Sexuality*, Vol. 2, trans. Robert Hurley, Penguin, London.

Frank, G. (1988) 'Beyond Stigma: Visibility and Self-empowerment of Persons with Congenital Limb Deficiencies', *Journal of Social Issues* 44: 95–115.

Frederick, J. (1991) *Positive Thinking for Mental Health*, The Black Mental Health Group, London.

Fuller Torrey, E. (2002) 'Studies of Individuals with Schizophrenia Never Treated with Antipsychotic Medications: A Review', *Schizophrenia Research*, October. Accessed at: http://www.psychlaws.org/GeneralResources/report-nevertreated.htm

Garland Thomson, R. (1997) *Extraordinary Bodies*, New York, Columbia University Press.

Gavin, B.E., Kelly, B.D., O'Callaghan, E. and Lane, A. (2001) 'The Mental Health of Migrants', *Irish Medical Journal* 94(8): 8–11.

Geyer, Robert (2000) *Exploring European Social Policy*, Polity Press, Oxford.

Gill, C. (1996). 'Becoming visible: Personal health experiences of women with disabilities', in D. Krotoski, M. Nosek and M. Turk (eds) *Women with Physical Disabilities*, Paul H. Brookes, Baltimore.

Gleeson, B.J. (1997) 'Disability Studies: a Historical Materialist View', *Disability and Society* 12(2): 179–202.

Glenn, S. and Cunningham, C. (2001) 'Evaluation of Self by Young People with Downs Syndrome', *International Journal of Disability, Development and Education* 48: 207–32.

Glover, G.R. (1989) 'The Pattern of Psychiatric Admissions of Caribbean-born Emigrants in London', *Social Psychiatry and Psychiatric Epidemiology* 24: 49–56.

Goffman, Erving (1963) *Stigma: Notes on the Management of a Spoiled Identity*, Penguin, Harmondsworth.

Goffman, E. (1959) *Presentation of Self in Everyday Life*, Penguin, Harmondsworth.

Goffman, E. (1961) *Asylums: Essays on the Social Situation of Mental Patients*, Penguin, Harmondsworth.

Goin, M.K. (1983) 'Psychological Aspects of Aesthetic Surgery', in Geogiade N.G. (ed.) *Aesthetic Breast Surgery*, Williams and Wilkins, Baltimore Maryland.

Golding, Jackie (1997) *Lesbians, Gay Men, Bisexuals and Mental Health*, MIND, London.

Goodley, D (2001) 'Learning Difficulties: the Social Model of Disability and Impairment: Challanging Epistemologies', *Disability and Society* 16(2): 207–32.

Gouldner, A.W. (1968) 'The sociologist as partisan: sociology and the welfare state', American Sociologist 3: 103–16.

Gouldner, A. (1974) *For Sociology*, Penguin, Harmondsworth.

Gudex, C. and Lafortune, G. (2000) *An Inventory of Health and Disability-related Surveys in OECD Countries*, Labour Market and Social Policy Occasional Papers No. 44, OECD, Paris.

Gulledge, A.D. (1991) 'Depression and Chronic Fatigue', *Primary Care* 18(2): 263.

Haraway, D. (1991) 'Situated knowledges: the science question in feminism and the privilege of partial perspective', in Haraway, D. (ed.) *Simians, Cyborgs and Women: The Reinvention of Nature*, Routledge, New York.

Hart, N. (1982) 'The Political Economy of Health', *British Journal of Sociology* 33(3): 435–443.

Harrison, G. (1990) 'Searching for the Causes of Schizophrenia: the Role of Migrant Studies', *Schizophrenia Bulletin* 16: 663–71.

Harrison, G., Owens, D., Holton, A., Neilson, D. and Boot, D. (1988) 'A Prospective Study of Severe Mental Disorder in Afro-Caribbean Patients', *Psychological Medicine* 18: 643–57.

Harrison, G., Amin, S., Singh, S.P., Croudace, T. and Jones, P. (1999) 'Outcome of Psychosis in People of African-Caribbean Origin', *British Journal of Psychiatry* 175: 43–49.

Hart, N. (1985) *The Sociology of Health and Medicine*, Causeway Press, Ormskirk.

Hartmann, H. (1979) 'Capitalism, Patriarchy and Job Segregation by Sex', in Z.R. Eisenstein (ed.) *Capitalist Patriarchy and the Case for Socialist Feminism*, New York, Monthly Review Press. pp. 206–47.

Hickling, F.W. and Rodgers-Johnson, P. (1995) 'The Incidence of First-contact Schizophrenia in Jamaica', *British Journal of Psychiatry* 167: 193–96.

Hinchliff, S. and Montague, S. (1988) *Physiology for Nursing Practice*, Bailliere-Tindall, Oxford.

Houston, J.P., Bee, H., Hatfield, E. and Rimm, D.C. (1979) *Invitation to Psychology*, Academic Press, London.

Hughes, B. (1999) 'The Constitution of Impairment: Modernity and the Aesthetic of Oppression', *Disability and Society* 14(2): 155–72.

Hughes, B. (2002) 'Bauman's Strangers: Impairment and the Invalidation of Disabled People in Modern and Post-modern Cultures', *Disability and Society* 17(3): 571–84.

Hughes, Bill and Paterson, Kevin (1997) 'The Social Model of Disability and the Disappearing Body', *Disability and Society* 12(3): 325–40.

Hutchinson, G., Takei, N., Bhugra, D., Fahy, T.A., Gilvarry, C., Mallett, R., Moran, P., Leff, J. and Murray, R.M. (1997) 'Increased Rate of Psychosis among African-Caribbeans in Britain Is Not Due to an Excess of Pregnancy and Birth Complications', *British Journal of Psychiatry* 171: 145–47.

Inhorn, M.C. and Whittle, K.L. (2001) 'Feminism Meets the 'New' Epidemiologies: toward an Appraisal of Antifeminism Biases in Epidemiological Research on Women's Health', *Social Science and Medicine* 53(5): 553–67.

Jameson, F. (1991) *Postmodernism, or the Cultural Logic of Late Capitalism*, Duke University Press, Durham.

Johnston, M. (1996) 'Models of Disability', *The Psychologist* 9: 205–10.

Kallianes, V. and Rubenfeld, P. (1997) 'Disabled Women and Reproductive Rights', *Disability and Society* 12(2): 203–21.

Karlsen, Saffron and Nazroo, James (2000) 'The Relationship between Racism, Social Class and Health among Ethnic Minority Groups', *Health Variations: The Official Newsletter of the ESRC Health Variations Programme* 5: 8–9.

Kearney, P.M. and Griffin, T (2001) 'Between Joy and Sorrow: Being a Parent of a Child with Developmental Disability', *Journal of Advanced Nursing* 34(5): 582–92.

Laing, R.D. (1960) *The Divided Self*, Penguin, Harmondsworth.

Laing, R.D. (1979) Review of Szasz book 'Schizophrenia', *New Statesman*, February.

Leaf, P.J., Bruce, M.L. and Tischler, G.L. (1986) 'The Differential Effects of Attitudes on the Use of Mental Health Services', *Social Psychiatry* 21: 187–92.

Leaf, P.J. and Livingston-Bruce, M. (1987) 'Gender Differences in the Use of Mental Health-Related Services: A re-examination', *Journal of Health and Social Behaviour* 28: 171–83.

Lenane, J.K. and Leanne, R.J. [1973](1982) 'Alleged Psychogenic Disorders in Women – a Possible Manifestation of Sexual Prejudice', in Whitelegg et al. (1982) *The Changing Experience of Women*, Martin Robertson, London.

Levine, S. (1987, November) 'Peer support for women in middle management', *Educational Leadership* 74–75.

Lomas, J. (1998) 'Social Capital and Health: Implications for Public Health and Epidemiology', *Social Science and Medicine* 47: 1181–88.

McGhie, A. (1979) *Psychology as Applied to Nursing* (7th edn), Churchill Livingstone, Edinburgh.

Mahy, G., Mallett, R., Leff, J. and Bhugra, D. (1999) 'First Contact Incidence Rate of Schizophrenia in Barbados', *British Journal of Psychiatry* 175: 28–33.

Maoz, B., Dowty, N., Antonosky, A. and Wijsenbeek, H. (1970) 'Female Attitudes to Menopause', *Social Psychiatry* 5(1): 35–40.

Martinson, E.W. (1990) 'Physical Fitness, Anxiety and Depression', *British Journal of Hospital Medicine* 45(5): 301–2.

McGrath, M.H. and Burkhardt, B.R. (1984) 'Safety and Efficacy of Breast Implants for Augmentation Mammaplasty', *Plastic and Reconstructive Surgery* 74: 550–60.

Milliren, J.W. (1977) 'Some Contingencies Affecting the Utilisation of Tranquillisers in the Long-Term Care of the Elderly', *Journal of Health and Social Behaviour* 18: 206–11.

Morris, J. (1993) 'Feminism and Disability', *Feminist Review* 43 (Spring): 57–70.

Morris, J. (1995) 'Creating a Space for Absent Voices: Disabled Women's Experience of Receiving Assistance with Daily Living Activities', *Feminist Review* 50 (Autumn): 68–93.

Morris, J. (2001) 'Impairment and Disability: Constructing an Ethic of Care that Promotes Human Rights', *Hypatia* 16(4): 1–16.

Nazroo, J. (1998) 'Genetic, Cultural or Socio-economic Vulnerability? Explaining Ethnic Inequalities in Health', *Sociology of Health and Illness* 20(5): 710–30.

Nazroo, James (2002) *Assessments of Levels of Schizophrenia Among Black British People Are Exaggerated* (EMPIRIC Report). Accessed at: http://www.doh.gov.uk/public/empiric/empiric.htm

Nazroo, James and Sproston, Kerry (2002) *Ethnic Minority Psychiatric Illness Rates in the Community*, EMPIRIC Report; April.

Nichter, M. (2000) *Fat Talk: What Girls and Their Parents Say about Dieting*, Harvard University Press, Cambridge, Mass.

Nosek, M. (1995) 'Sexual Abuse of Women with Physical Disabilities', *Physical Medicine and Rehabilitation* 9(2): 487–502.

Oberle, K. and Allen, M. (1994) 'Breast Augmentation Surgery: A Woman's Health Issue', *Journal of Advanced Nursing* 20: 844–52.

Oliver, M. (1983) *Social Work with Disabled People,* Macmillan, London.

Olney, M.F. and Kim, A. (2001) 'Beyond Adjustment: Integration of Cognitive Disability into Identity', *Disability and Society* 16: 563–83.

Olney, M.F. and Brockelman, K. (2003) 'Out of the Disability Closet: Strategic Use of Perception Management by Select University Students with Disabilities', *Disability and Society* 18: 35–50.

Orbach, S. (1989) *Fed Up and Hungry*, Women's Press, London.

Oswin, M. (1991) *Am I Allowed to Cry? A Study of Bereavement amongst People who have Learning Difficulties,* Human Horizons, London.

Paroski, P.A. (1987) 'Health Care Delivery and the Concerns of Gay and Lesbian Adolescents', *Journal of Adolescent Health Care* 8: 188–92.

Parsons, Talcott (1951) *The Social System*, Free Press, New York.

Parsons, Talcott (1978a) *Action Theory and the Human Condition*, Free Press, New York.

Parsons, Talcott (1978b) 'The Gift of Life and its Reciprocation', in *Action Theory and the Human Condition*, Free Press, New York.

Parsons, Talcott (1978c) 'Health and Disease: a Sociological and Action Perspective', in *Action Theory and the Human Condition*, Free Press, New York.

Patrick, D.L. Wickizer, T.M. (1995) 'Community and Health', in Amick, B.C., Levine, S., Tarlove, A.R. and Walsh, C.D. (eds) *Society and Health,* Oxford University Press, New York.

Pilgrim, D. and Rogers, A. (1999) *A Sociology of Mental Health and Illness* (2nd edn), Open University Press, Buckingham.

Pinder, R.M. (1997) 'The pharmacologic rationale for the clinical use of antidepressants', *Journal of Clinical Psychiatry* (58): 501–8.

Proctor, R.N. (1995) *Cancer Wars. How Politics Shapes What We Know and Don't Know About Cancer.* Basic Books, New York.

Puri, B. and Singh, I. (1996) 'The Successful Treatment of a Gender Dysphoric with Pimozide', *Australian and New Zealand Journal of Psychiatry* 30(3): 422–25.

Rapley, M., Kierman, P., and Antaki, C. (1998) 'Invisible to Themselves or Negotiating Identity? The Interactional Management of Being Intellectually Disabled', *Disability and Society* 13: 807–27.

Reichenbach, H. [1947](1961) 'The Elements of Semiology', cited in Szasz (1961) *The Myth of Mental Illness*, Paladin, New York.

Rogers, M. (1981) 'Goffman on Power', in Ditton, J. (ed.) *The View from Goffman*, Macmillan, London.

Romesburg, D. (2000) 'Thirteen Cures for Homosexuality', in *Out in All Directions: An Almanac of Gay and Lesbian America*. Accessed at: www.law.harvard.edu/studorgs/lambda/l_13theo.html

Saltonstall, R. (1993) 'Healthy Bodies: Men's and Women's Concepts and Practices of Health in Everyday Life', *Social Science and Medicine* 36(1): 7–14.

Selten, J.P., Slaets, J.P. and Kahn, R.S. (1997) 'Schizophrenia in Surinamese and Dutch Antillean Immigrants to The Netherlands: Evidence of an Increased Incidence', *Psychological Medicine* 27: 807–11.

Shakespeare, T. and Watson, N. (1997) 'Defending the Social Model', *Disability and Society* 12(2): 293–300.

Shapiro, S., Skinner, E.A., Kramer, M., Steinwachs, D. and Regier, D. (1984) 'Measuring Need for Mental Health Services in a General Population', *Medical Care* 23: 1033–43.

Sharpley, M., Hutchinson, G., McKenzie and Murray, R.M. (2001) 'Understanding the Excess of Psychosis among the African-Caribbean Population in England', *British Journal of Psychiatry* 178 (suppl. 40): 60–68.

Sheppard, M. (1991) 'General Practice, Social Work and Mental Health Sections: the Social Control of Women', *British Journal of Social Work* 21: 663–83.

Shilling, Chris (2002) 'Culture, the "Sick Role" and the Consumption of Health', *British Journal of Sociology* 53(4): 621–38.

Showalter, Elaine (1985) *The Female Malady: Women, Madness and English Culture, 1830–1980*, Virago, London.

Stocker, S. (2001) 'Problems of Embodiment and Problematic Embodiment', *Hypatia* 16(3): 30–55.

Strange, Julie-Marie (2001) 'The Assault on Ignorance: Teaching Menstrual Etiquette in England c.1920s to c.1960s', *Social History of Medicine* 14(2): 247–65.

Stone, E. and Priestley, M. (1996) 'Parasites, Pawns and Partners: Disability Research and the Role of Non-disabled Researchers', *British Journal of Sociology* 47(4): 699–716.

Sutherland, F.N. (1990) 'Psychological Aspects of the Menopause', *Maternal and Child Health* 15(1): 13–14.

Szasz, T. (1972) *The Myth of Mental Illness* (2nd edn), Paladin, New York.

Szasz, T. (1982) 'The Psychiatric Will: a New Mechanism for Protecting Persons against "psychosis" and Psychiatry', *American Journal of Psychology* 37: 762–70.

Taylor, S.M. (1989) 'Community Exclusion Of The Mentally Ill', in J. Wolch and M. Dear (eds.) *The Power Of Geography: How Territory Shapes Social Life*, Unwin Hyman, London.

Taylor, I. and Robertson, A. (1994) 'The Health Care Needs of Gay Men: A Discussion of the Literature and Implications for Nursing', *Journal of Advanced Nursing* 20(3): 560–66.

Tilly, C. (1996) *Workfare's Impact on the New York City Labour Market: Lower Wages and Worker Displacement*, found at http://www.endpage.com/Archives/Mirrors/Aufheben/auf_8_work.html

Verbrugge, L. (1985) 'Gender and Health: An Update on Hypotheses and Evidence', *Journal of Health and Social Behaviour* 26: 156–82.

Veroff, J.B. (1981) 'The Dynamics of Help-seeking in Men and Women: A National Survey Study', *Psychiatry* 44: 189–200.

Walls, P. (1996) 'Researching Irish Mental Health Issues and Evidence – A Study of the Mental Health of the Irish Community in Haringey', London, Muintearas.

Watson, N. (1998) 'Enabling Identity: Disability, Self and Citizenship', in Shakespeare, T. (ed.) *The Disability Reader: Social Science Perspectives*, Cassell, London.

Webb, C. (1986) 'Women as Gynaecology Patients and Nurses', in Webb, C. (ed.) *Feminist Practice in Women's Health Care*, Wiley, London.

Weindling, P. (2000) *Epidemics and Genocide in Eastern Europe 1890–1945*, Oxford University Press, Oxford.

Wells, K., Manning, W., Duan, N., Newhouse, J.P. and Ware, J. (1986) 'Sociodemographic Factors and the Use of Mental Health Services', *Medical Care* 24(10): 2475–85.

Wendell, S. (2001) 'Unhealthy Disabled: Treating Chronic Illness as Disabilities', *Hypatia* 16(4): 17–33.

Whitaker, R. (2002) *Mad in America: Bad Science, Bad Medicine, and the Enduring Mistreatment of the Mentally Ill*, Perseus Publishing, New York.

Wolfe, P. (1997) 'The influence of personal values on issues of sexuality and disability', *Sexuality and Disability* 15(2): 69–89.

Young, I.M. (1990) *Justice and the Politics of Difference*, Princeton University Press, Princeton NJ.

UPIAS (1976) *Fundamental principles of disability*. Union of the Physically Impaired Against Segregation.

World Health Organisation (2001) *International Classification of Functioning, Disability and Health (Icf)*. World Health Organisation, Geneva.

Three

Chapter Outline

By the end of this chapter you should have a critical understanding of:

- The notion of 'race' as an essential category

- The major contributions to the study of race, racism and ethnic diversity: Talcott Parsons; Oliver Cromwell Cox; Charles Husband; Richard Miles; Stuart Hall; Michael Omi and Howard Winant; Frantz Fanon; Homi Bhabha; Floya Anthias

- The notion of 'racialisation'

- The social construction of whiteness

- The concept of Islamophobia: the creation of new *others* post the events of 11 September 2001.

Race, Racism and Ethnic Diversity

Introduction: Creating Racial Categories

Modernity is driven by a striving for stable classifactory systems and for order. Modernity has an uneasiness with ambiguities and ambivalence which disturbs and destabilises neat boundaries and borders. Modern people do not respond to each other as individuals but have a tendency to view others in terms of a category. These modern classifications are essential in character: we assume that a surface difference reflects a deeper understanding of the nature of a person. The idea that some groups of people are biologically different and can be defined as 'races' is well established as a classificatory device but has little or no scientific basis. However, the founder of eugenics, Sir Francis Galton, believed that the notion of 'race' reflected a natural intellectual and evolutionary hierarchy. This view, now almost universally discredited, lends credence to the argument that people have a tendency to change any form of classification into a basis for prejudice. A number of questions arise from this: Does the process of classification generate racism? Are people racist because they choose to categorise people as the Other? To what extent are our identities constructed rather than given? The last question is one of the central issues of this chapter. Much of the research since the early 1990s has been concerned with decentring, de-essentialising the social, including the racist subject and the Other.

Cruz-Janzen et al. (2003) argue that it is commonly assumed that *race* is a biologically determined factor, based upon the physically determined differences between people that are outside of their control, such as genetics and heredity. However, before the colonial expansion by European powers, informed opinion within Europe was that all humans were of one race and species. The ranking of people by skin colour, mental ability and moral qualities was simply a justification for their harsh and differential treatment.

As St Louis (2002) makes clear, we have been aware for a long time that race has no real biological foundation and is socially constructed through discourse, which acts to racialise different groups. However, although race may no longer be regarded as a biological fact, it is still a social fact. People are still very keen to identify differences between themselves and the Other. According to Alexander and Alleyne (2002), race is still a primary signifier for exclusionary practices:

> [R]ace (and its non-identical twin, ethnicity) has lost none of its power to draw its borders, legislate its citizens and police its Others, through violence: symbolic or, too often, embodied. Racial and ethnic difference remains definitive of our times. (Alexander and Alleyne 2002: 541)

However, racial social divisions are notoriously difficult to draw. Claire Alexander (2002) discussed how surprised many people in the United States were that she included people of Afro-Caribbean and Asian heritage together in the category 'black'. By the 1990s, it was no longer possible to have such a diverse category of 'black', because as Alexander explains; 'black' is no longer about structural positioning and disadvantage, as people of Afro-Caribbean and Asian heritage often have very different socio-economic experiences, with people of Asian heritage having far more financial security. There is also a much greater degree of 'cultural segmentation' between people of Afro-Caribbean and people of Asian heritage; Alexander argues that the notion of *difference* is now much more significant than before the 1990s. Finally, the boundaries between people of Afro-Caribbean and of Asian heritage are more likely to be categorised by opposition, antagonism and fragmentation. Alexander argues that since the 1990s the notion of *Asian* has emerged as a politicised category with an emphasis upon *cultural difference*, whereas the notion of 'black' or 'a black identity' is associated with a 'politics of difference'.

Up to the 1990s, studies of 'black' communities focused mainly upon discrimination and inequality, with the underpinning assumption that the 'black' community had a weak culture and pathologised family structure which generated young 'black' people who were likely to be far less successful in the education system and much more likely to be involved in crime. How and why young 'black' males developed a pathologised identity was the main focus of research in the area. At the end of the twentieth century, Alexander argues the 'black' identity had something of a 'postmodern makeover'; under the influence of African-American culture such as hip-hop, the 'black' identity became streetwise and the 'epitome of dangerous and desirable marginality' (Alexander 2002: 557).

Charles Husband

Charles Husband traces the history of the concept of 'race', racism and racist ideology in an attempt to identify the point at which Europeans first came to consider people with darker skin as socially inferior rather than physically different and why these definitions of social inferiority persisted over time.

In the medieval world, unflattering images of non-Europeans were common; Husband cites the way in which Shakespeare plays with racial stereotypes, and his audience's expectations in *Othello*. From this time *blackness* was associated with evil, whereas *whiteness* was associated with purity and goodness. Scriptural explanations for the emergence of race, such as the theory of blackness advanced by George Best in 1578, argued that blackness was God's curse upon Noah's son Ham for having sexual intercourse whilst the Ark was afloat, against God's expressed wishes. However, for Husband as for many theorists in the area, the decisive twist came with the emergence of slavery. The economic significance of slavery for a country such as Britain is highlighted in the example given by Husband that in the eighteenth century the British Government considered handing back Canada to the French in exchange for the island of Guadeloupe, a Caribbean island measuring only 532 square miles.

The European colonial powers gained enormous revenues from the exploitation of the colonies. It was from this material base of the slave-plantation production that racist ideas and assumptions of the genetic inferiority of black people derived. Such assumptions were supported by a range of other sources of evidence, widely accepted at the time, such as the strong Protestant belief that God had created different races with different levels of intelligence, and social Darwinism, which parallels animal evolution with national development. Darwin introduced the notion of natural selection, which allowed people to view race in terms of a scientific basis for inferiority and superiority.

Colonisation was justified on the grounds that it spread civilisation to peoples who would otherwise suffer as a consequence. Husband gives the example of the nineteenth-century Tory politician Thomas Carlyle, who published *Discourse on the Nigger Question*, in which he argued that idleness is a central element of the black person's psychological make-up and that an explicit work ethic needed to be imposed. Other 'scientific' accounts at the time included: Hamilton Smith (1848) *The Natural History of the Human Species*; Knox (1850) *The Races of Man*; Gobineau (1853) *Essai sur l'inégalité des races humaines*; and Nott and Gliddon (1854) *Types of Manhood*. The legacy continued up to and including Arthur Jensen's influential paper in the *Harvard Educational Review* (1969) 'How Much Can We Boost IQ and Scholastic Achievement?', and Hans Eysenck's (1971) *Race, Intelligence and Education*, which presents the argument that 'race' is a real category which can be used to identify different 'types' of people and differences in intelligence. Such 'scientific' accounts, Husband argues, reinforced the pre-nineteenth century *race-thinking*, with its notions of purity, sexuality and Christian virtue:

> The essential part of race-thinking is the common sense assumption that 'race' is a real and self-evidently neutral fact, not to be confused with racism which is a special condition of a few disturbed bigots who abuse reality with their prejudice. (Husband 1981: 21)

Alternative arguments in the nineteenth century were positive but equally as racist in the assumptions made. For example, the idea of the *noble savage* was a paternalistic idea, shared by many people in the nineteenth century, that black people were closer to nature than white Europeans and in need of the latter's guardianship. Husband argues that such ideas are not interesting relics of how people used to think, rather such ideas live on in our perspective of non-white people today. This can be seen in popular culture and entertainment, which reject multiculturalism and maintain the colonial symbolism of white superiority. In contrast to the assumption that racial prejudice is caused by the abnormal psychology of a minority of racists who incite racial conflict – which is the assumption that underpinned the television and newspaper coverage of riots in Blackburn, Burnley and Oldham in the early years of the twenty-first century, Husband and Hartman argue that the prejudice resides within the culture:

> we find a willingness to accept interpretations of racial prejudice that suggest that such prejudices are the product of the abnormal psychology of a minority of individuals. In this way responsibility for such prejudice as is recognized can be detached from society as a whole and be attributed to a minority of social and psychological defectives who inevitably are found in every society. ...
>
> [...]
>   The essence of prejudice was the belief or assumption, conscious or unconscious, that coloured people have less entitlement to resources than whites, and that they are somehow less important, worthwhile or desirable than whites. (Hartman and Husband 1974: 20, 54)

For Husband, racism is built into the culture of Western societies. Communication between people is only possible if they share common frameworks of interpretation, if they share the same meanings for the same symbols. For Husband, this framework of interpretation is a structure of shared mental categories that allow us to make sense of the world. The common framework is built upon the colonial past that makes all white people have a predisposition to accept unfavourable images and beliefs of black people. In simple terms, all white people are racist because they are born and brought up within a racist culture. White people have to make a conscious effort to break away from the common culture in order not to be racist.

ACTIVITY

Racism is a psychological condition deeply embedded within *white* culture at an unconscious level. Moreover, racism refers to both the action and inaction of deluded white people. All white people are racist.

Questions:

➤ Do you accept or reject the summary above of Husband's analysis? Give reasons for your answer.

➤ Do you believe racism to be the prerogative of white people?

Talcott Parsons: The Functionalist Perspective on Race

For Parsons, 'race' is a biologically determined fact, which has a central defining role for the personality and self of an individual. Writing in 1965, Parsons argued that the 'American Negro' is a second-class citizen. Parsons's position was that a 'race' is a group of people who are biologically distinct, but who should be treated as belonging to the same humanity. However, in the American context of the 1950s and 1960s, skin colour symbolised inferiority, and this was used as the justification for placing black Americans at the bottom of the class and status ladder. Parsons argues that because the United States has a pluralistic social structure, in which power is widely shared, a person's status as a member of an ethnic minority does not significantly affect their other statuses in life, such as employment status, education or rights before the law. Taking his starting point from Marshall and Rawls, Parsons argues that citizenship is understood as full membership of the *societal community* – a term he developed to describe the underpinning solidarity and mutual loyalty of the total society – membership of which is central to being an American. The societal community is linked to the political organisation of the State; revolution occurs when the links are severed or there is conflict between the societal level and the political organisation of the State; however, the societal community is not identical with the political organisation of the State. In the last analysis, for Parsons, full citizenship should include a fundamental equality of rights.

In Parsons's analysis there is a synthesis of citizenship and territoriality, as societal communities are differentiated as nations. In societal communities people are linked to each other by *associational* – or non-ascriptive – criteria in which three elements are integrated: government, community and ascriptive bases, such as family ties. The process by which previously excluded groups achieve full membership of the societal community as a citizen is what Parsons calls *inclusion*. Parsons assumes that the United States is pluralistic in nature and membership of an ethnic group 'is necessarily by hereditary ascription' (Parsons 1965: 715). However,

> [i]n a pluralistic social structure, membership in an ethnic group or religious group does not determine *all* of the individual's social participations. His occupation, education, employing organisation, and political affiliation may in varying degrees be independent of his ethnicity or religion. On the whole, the trend of American development has been toward increasing pluralism in this sense and, hence, increasing looseness in the connections among the components of total social status. (Ibid.: 715)

Parsons makes a distinction between necessary and sufficient conditions to bring about full citizenship inclusion. For the society to have a set of pluralistic rules is one of the necessary conditions for full inclusion, but it is not in itself sufficient to guarantee full inclusion. Formal opportunity needs to be accompanied with the capacity to take advantage of that opportunity. In addition, Parsons also recognised that the United States had deeply ingrained notions of individualism and free market competition, which for people at the bottom of the social scale could combine to produce 'a vicious circle of cumulative *disadvantage*, which becomes accentuated the more marked the "competitiveness" of the society becomes ... It almost goes without saying that the Negro in this country is very deeply caught up in this vicious circle' (1965: 719).

The discrimination faced by black Americans, claims Parsons, forced them to be subservient but also prevented them from developing sufficient capacities to take advantages of new anti-discrimination legislation. Full citizenship inclusion comes about by a change in the *common value system*, together with a commitment to association, mobilisation of political power and the mobilisation of influence. As Parsons explains: 'The ultimate social grounding of the demand for inclusion lies in commitment to the values which legitimise it' (ibid.: 722).

Resistance to inclusion is also found within the common value system. Parsons argues that there is a symbolisation of black Americans as inferior, which forms the basis of the resistance of some sections of American society to their full inclusion. The fear is, claims Parsons, that the inclusion of inferior black Americans into the societal community will devalue the societal community. For Parsons, 'The most important single condition of avoiding inflationary "debasement" is the general upgrading not only of the Negro but of all elements in the population falling below the minimum acceptable standards of full citizenship' (ibid.: 744).

In Parsons's view, the definition of any group of people as inherently inferior is incompatible with the basic principles of a democratic society – it is immoral and illegitimate. The Civil Rights Movement has done a great deal to highlight the immoral and illegitimate nature of racial exclusion, as Parsons explains:

> [The Civil Rights Movement] has dramatized the moral issue in terms which make concrete continuance of the old practices morally intolerable ... Not least important among the consequences of the movement has been its contribution to the current moral 'reenergizing' of American society. (Ibid.: xxvi)

What Parsons is outlining here is a concrete example of what he would later refer to as 'cultural and motivational sources of change' (Parsons and Smelser 1967), in which people identify an aspect of the common value system as unacceptable and bring about change by campaigning. They do this by drawing upon like-minded people from the widest possible range of American society for alternative goals for the polity to aim for in their campaigning. The Federal Government is a powerful agency for change, but only when the elected officials feel that there is a general movement for change from amongst wide and diverse groups in the population. Parsons argues that Federal Government-sponsored programmes – such as anti-discrimination legislation and social programmes similar in nature to New Deal – can raise the human capital of the population sufficiently to ensure that no category of people is excluded from full participation in the societal community.

What Parsons believes the Civil Rights Movement and all minority people, are aiming to achieve, is full assimilation into the racial order of the United States – what people in the 1960s referred to as 'the melting pot'. This is in stark contrast to the conceptions of disapora that became popular at the end of the twentieth century. Patterson (1965) shares Parsons's liberal/pluralistic assumptions and also identifies the common value system as the place where an explanation for racism can be found.

IMMIGRANTS: THE CHOICE BETWEEN ASSIMILATION AND INTEGRATION

All migrants to a society are initially faced with a degree of hostility because they have been socialised into a different set of cultural values that may not be compatible with the values of the host society. In the case of the United Kingdom, Irish, Jewish and Flemish migrants all faced discrimination.

However, the relationship between migrants and hosts changes over time, either through a process of *assimilation* or *integration*. With processes of assimilation, the migrants change the particularistic nature of their cultural values and adopt the universalistic value system of the host society; in other words a process of resocialisation occurs in which old values are replaced by the values of the new society. Alternatively, the value system of the host society can change in an effort to incorporate elements of the migrant culture within the culture of the wider society. Foreign food, for example, is no longer viewed as *foreign* and instead becomes accepted as a normal part of the diet.

A less optimistic functionalist view was presented by Robert Merton (1949), who also identified the common value system as the starting point for his analysis; Merton argued that prejudice and discrimination were independent of each other and that it was possible to identify four relationships between prejudice and discrimination:

Table 2   Merton's typology of personalities

Personality Type	Prejudice	Discrimination
Bigot	+	+
Timid bigot	+	−
Fair-weather liberal	−	+
All-weather liberal	−	−

Source: Adapted from Merton (1949)

- The bigot is a racist person who is prejudiced and does discriminate
- The timid bigot is also a racist in that this person is prejudiced, but does not discriminate. Possibly on the grounds that it is wrong to discriminate even against people whom one does not like, or perhaps because this type fears the consequences of being seen to discriminate
- The fair-weather liberal is a person who is not prejudiced, but who does discriminate; for example, people who allow themselves to take advantage of indirect forms of discrimination
- Finally, the all-weather liberal is not a racist, a person who is not prejudiced and does not discriminate.

The important point about Merton's typology is that prejudice does not necessarily lead to discrimination, and that people discriminate for a range of reasons which may not be based upon prejudice, but upon such things as material advantage.

The standard critique of the functionalist perspective of race relations rejects the notion that the problems that ethnic minorities face will eventually disappear because of the processes of long-term evolution that underpin the social system, and in particular the common value system. The persistence of racism and racial disadvantage in areas such as employment, health and education were not explained. Similarly, functionalists assumed consensus as the basis for the social system, which ignores the various subcultural groups who reject 'core' American or European values. However, Talcott Parsons in particular recognised that State intervention was needed to change the position of black Americans; he both admired and supported the Civil Rights Movement and the Johnson Administration's programmes for creating the 'Good Society', such as bussing and Operation Headstart. It is important to note that Lyndon Johnson wrote the preface to Parsons and Clark's book *The Negro American* (1966), in which he specifically stated that simply providing equality of opportunity for black Americans was not enough, people needed to be given the skills and abilities to make full and effective use of the opportunities that the Government provided for them.

The state may be in a position to provide goals and attempt to encourage some forms of goal attainment rather than others, however, it is other institutions, notably the family, that has the central role to play in the process of socialisation, which is the ongoing process in which the individual learns the pattern variables (common culture, dominant ideas and ways of thinking) that underpin the social system. bell hooks (1992) argues that the home is the place where white women are socialised into white supremacist values. This bourgeois notion of *womanhood*, what it means to be a woman, has a central role to play in the reproduction of what it means to be a white person. Irrespective of class background, all white girls are encouraged to accept a racialised notion of bourgeois respectability. Frye (1992) explains this in the following terms:

> The white girl learns that whiteliness is dignity and respectability ... Adopting and cultivating whiteliness as an individual character seems to put it in the woman's power to lever herself up out of a kind of nonbeing (the status of woman in a male supremacist social order) over into a kind of being (the status of white supremacist social order). (Frye 1992: 160)

In addition, Drema Moon (1999) argues that white people are socialised into *whitespeak*: a form of subjectification (ways of behaving, understanding and relating to others that the person incorporates in order to make sense of who they are as a person) in which white people are encouraged to think and talk about racial issues in a way that separates them as individuals from the processes of racialisation.

There are some question marks against Parsons's ultimate goal for the Johnson Administration. Parsons's ultimate aim was progressive universal inclusion; however by the 1980s, this aim was seen as an approach that involved the repression of local and national heritages. With the rise of multiculturalism, Parsons's aim was treated with some distain. Many multiculturalists would agree with Frantz Fanon's comment:

I am not a potentiality of something. I am wholly what I am. I do not have to look for universal. No probability has any place inside me. My Negro consciousness does not hold out as a lack. It *is*. It is its own follower. (Fanon 1952: 135)

Finally, under the New Right Regan–Bush Senior and Bush Junior Administrations, attempts at assimilation and greater integration gave way to the view of black Americans as the cause of many urban problems: black drug abuse, young black male gangs, welfare cheats. As Gray (1995) made clear, in contrast to the Johnson Administration, the Regan and Bush Administrations 'had to take away from blacks (and other persons of color) the moral authority and claims to political entitlements won by the civil rights movements of the 1960s' (Gray 1995: 17–18).

Traditional Marxian Approaches

The traditional Marxian view of race was based upon the assumption that racism was a function of capitalist development and that there was racial harmony before the development of capitalism, and that there would be again under socialism. Oliver Cromwell Cox is widely regarded as one of the first and most influential Marxian researchers in the area of race. In a paper published in 1945, Cox attempted to undermine the established position that racial issues should be seen in terms of caste:

'race relations' developed in modern times as our own exploitative system developed. Moreover, race relations or problems are variants of modern political class problems – that is to say, the problems of exploitation of labour together with the exploitation of other factors of production ... the fact that the race problem in the United States arose, from its inception in slavery, out of the need to keep Negroes proletarianized. (Cox 1945: 427)

This argument was later reinforced when he wrote:

Our hypothesis is that racial exploitation and race prejudice developed among Europeans with the rise of capitalism and nationalism, and that because of the world-wide ramifications of capitalism, all racial antagonisms can be traced to the policies and attitudes of the leading capitalist people, the white people of Europe and North America. (Cox 1948: 322)

Race relations are brought about by the economic interests of the bourgeoisie that led to exploitation; racial prejudice was a means to that end. Cox made it clear that racial prejudice was generated by the bourgeoisie 'for the purpose of stigmatising some group as inferior' (Cox 1945: 393), to justify exploitation. The same underlying assumption can be identified in Castles and Kosack's work:

Prejudice hinders communication and prevents the development of class solidarity. The basic cause of this phenomenon is to be sought in the prevailing socio-economic conditions. (Castles and Kosack 1985: 7)

Wallerstein went one stage further, claiming that ethnicity was a product of capitalist development, when he argued that:

> Both the process of state-formation and the process of labour formation have involved the creation and shaping of peoples as 'nations' seeking territories that conform with state boundaries and as 'ethnic groups' seeking privileges and/or reserved rights within states. (Wallerstein 1983: 18)

Cashmore and Troyna (1990) show how the arguments of Gunder-Frank (1967) and Wallerstein (1979) can be used to explain how 'race' is a central factor in the processes of class formation. The first world keeps the third world poor by exercising monopoly power over world markets. Capitalist countries continue to exploit the labour and resources of the third world and this relationship of dependency has a determining effect upon the shape and structure of social class and other economic structures in the first world.

The underdevelopment of the third world was caused by the continual exploitation of third world resources. Therefore, the development of the first world and the underdevelopment of the third world are outcomes of one and the same process. The third world supplied raw materials to the developed world at very low prices and in return imported expensive manufactured goods. This unequal exchange was possible because the first world was said to control world markets. In Marxian terms, surplus value created in the world passed along the chain to the first world. Moreover, the political leaders in the third world supported this 'chain of dependency', because they were co-opted into the service of the first world.

'RACE' AS A CENTRAL FACTOR IN THE PROCESSES OF CLASS FORMATION

1   'Push' of the periphery or 'pull' of the centre brings migrants to the metropolis.
2   The migrant has only a limited range of employment opportunities available.
3   The migrant takes low-level 'cellar jobs' unwanted by white workers and becomes suspicious of white-dominated trade unions.
4   The migrant earns less than white workers, has less spending capacity, leading to: (i) poor accommodation; (ii) inadequate education; (iii) poor diet and poor health; and (iv) likelihood of becoming involved in crime and insurgence.
5   Two effects follow from the above: (i) the migrant is judged by the white population as unsuccessful, only capable of cellar jobs, suited to poor living conditions, limited intellectually, in sum inferior; and (ii) the migrant has self-doubt and self-hatred and views her/himself as inferior.
6   The two judgments of inferiority based on stereotypes become rationales for prejudice and racial discrimination and working-class division.

(Source: adapted from Cashmore and Troyna 1990: 94)

Key exponents of dependency theory, such as Andre Gunder-Frank (1967) have made little or no use of key Marxian concepts. In their view, the relationship between the first world and the third world is one of unequal exchange in the world market, rather than exploitation as explained by Marxists with the Labour Theory of Value. In a similar fashion, Wallerstein (1979) argues that capitalism was never confined by national boundaries; it created a new world order with global interconnections that spread across the earth. He made a distinction between two types of world system:

1 **World empires:** historical political units that colonised areas of the world by military means and imposed a rigid bureaucracy to extract taxes from local people.
2 **World economies:** capitalistic in nature and based upon capital accumulation, the world economy is neo-colonial in nature, and is largely free from any influence of nation states.

Moreover, all power and wealth are transferred to the core of the world system while the periphery and semi-periphery are left relatively poor and powerless. However, not only are Gunder-Frank and Wallerstein's accounts both *functional* and *economically reductionist* in nature, but in addition racial divisions – with economic consequences – are found outside of global capitalism, notably in the Hindu doctrine of Creation and its link to the caste system. Brockington (1997) points out:

> Brahma created just Brahimins but those who were short-tempered and violent left their Varna, turned red and became Kshatriyas, those who took to cattle-rearing and agriculture turned yellow and became Vaisyas, and those who in their delusion took to injury and untruth turned black and became Sudras; those who diverged still further from the proper norms and did not recognize them became Pisacas, Raksasas, Prefas and various sorts of Mlecchas (foreigners, barbarians). (Brockington 1997: 99)

For the traditional Marxist approaches, racism is seen as a key element in the creation of a false consciousness – a class ideology that is used by the bourgeoisie to divide and rule over the working class. However, historical evidence presented by Husband (1981) and Miles (1989) clearly demonstrates that racism pre-dates the emergence of capitalism. Finally, the Marxian argument is teleological in nature: racism structures production and at the same time production structures racism.

Robert Miles: A Neo-Marxian Approach

For Robert Miles (1980), the relationship between the capitalist class structure and racial categories is unclear in Cox's work, it is insufficiently theorised. Given his assumptions, Cox has difficulty explaining racism amongst working-class people. How and why do working-class people internalise racist ideas? In addition, Miles challenges Cox's assumption that racism is reducible to class conflict. Racism might have its origins in slavery, but slavery did not proletarianise the black population, it turned them into slaves – the possessions of slave owners not a free proletariat in the Marxian sense of the term. Cox does not draw upon Marx's Labour Theory of Value, but rather has a sociological notion of exploitation. In contrast to Cox, Miles argues that

[f]or a Marxist, the 'Negro' in the contemporary social formation of the USA must be conceived as being within the class structure, even if excluded from access to certain social and economic positions: the correct concept is therefore that of a black working class. (Miles 1980: 485)

Weberian approaches to the study of race and ethnicity attempt to locate race and ethnicity within the context of Weber's theory of stratification. In Weberian accounts the emphasis is on individual social actors looking at any factor they consider to be significant and making a judgement about the qualities of a person on the basis of that fact. Individual people create and recreate racial disadvantage and racial ideas and there is little or no emphasis upon structural factors that might determine how people perceive race.

As we discussed in the Chapter 2 on Class Division, in contrast to Marx, Max Weber outlined a theory of stratification that included three elements.

- **Social classes:** formed in the marketplace on the basis of supply and demand for skills and which included *market situation* (the amount of money one can earn) and *work situation* (the conditions of service a person can enjoy at work)
- **Status:** the social estimation of honour
- **Party:** the amount of political power that a person has.

For Weber, a social class is a group of people who share the same class position. By this Weber meant that a social class is made up of a group of people who have similar market and work situations. In addition to the Marxian bourgeoisie, Weber also said that the people who own large amounts of land – whom he named the *rentier class* – also had significant power. The class groupings that did not own property could be divided into different classes on the basis of the level of skill that they had and the demand for that skill in the marketplace. If a skill is in short supply, in other words if only a few people have a particular ability and there is a big demand for that skill or ability, then such people will be in a position to demand high financial rewards. In a similar fashion, if people have few skills or skills that are easily acquired, then such people are not in a position to demand high financial rewards. However, for Weber, social class was only one aspect of a person's *stratification position*: 'status' in the Weberian analysis is what people think of a person in terms of the amount of prestige that a person enjoys. Weber argued that status was independent of both social class and party, in other words, a person could have a high social class position but this does not guarantee that they will have a high status position. Similarly, a person may have low social class position but high status. Moreover, in contrast to Marx, the people who hold political power can come from any social class and may or may not have a high status.

Race and ethnicity are important in a Weberian analysis because their perception as significant does impact directly upon the life chances of an individual. Meaning is given to race and ethnicity and the perception that people hold of Others from a different race or ethnicity directly impacts upon market situation, work situation, status and party.

John Rex in his influential book *Race Relations in Sociological Theory* (1983) draws upon these Weberian insights to generate a sociology of 'race relations'. Rex describes 'race' as 'a distinct group of social phenomena, with demonstrably different attributes from other phenomena' (ibid.: 7) and 'race relations' as 'situations in which one or more groups with distinct identities and recognisable characteristics are forced by economic and political circumstances to live together in a society' (ibid.: 160). The end result is that the labour market, as defined in terms of market and work situation becomes *racialised* – a dual labour market is formed in which people are given differential rewards on the basis of their race and ethnicity. People of Asian and West Indian heritage are recruited into occupations that are lower paid and have below average conditions of service. In addition, similar processes are at work in terms of consumption, residential areas of towns and cities become areas where people of Asian and West Indian heritage are more likely to live because of similar discriminatory processes.

Miles takes his starting point from a critique of traditional Marxist approaches (which under-emphasised the role of the human agent in racial ideas and practices) and from a critique of Weberian approaches (which under-emphasised the history of racial ideas and practices and the factors outside the immediate control of the individual human agent in *racialised* practices. Miles looks at racism as a process of *signification* – the categorisation of people into a hierarchy on the basis of the attribution of meanings to phenotypical or genetic characteristics. It is this categorisation of people that forms the basis for a range of exclusionary practices. Moreover, it was this categorisation that underpinned such diverse historical events as: the slave trade, the holocaust, segregation in the southern United States, and South African apartheid. For Miles, this process of signification is in the last analysis: 'always a component part of a wider structure of class disadvantage and related exclusion' (Miles 1989: 9). Miles's analysis of *racialisation* (process of signification) 'linked racism and capitalism in some sort of causal dependency' (ibid.: 67) whereby 'racism is expressed within a structure of class differentiation and exploitation' (ibid.: 55).

The process of the subordination of black people and their definition as the Other, is inextricably linked to the spread of imperialism and later globalisation. Colonialism in the eighteenth and nineteenth centuries created at the peripheries, on plantations and other places or work in the colonies, unfree relations of production in which black people were forced to work under the threat of violence. The justification for this harsh treatment came from a range of scientific accounts, widely accepted at the time, that black people were biologically inferior and in need of harsh supervision. Black people were placed in 'a subordinate position to the emergent proletariat at the centre' (ibid.: 67). The process of racialisation was central to the process of primary accumulation in the colonies, in other words it was central to the continued development of the capitalist mode of production.

WHAT IS RACIALISATION?

Racialisation is a concept that attempts to decentre the idea of an essential notion of race, the idea that people have a given and identifiable biological component that defines the nature of that person. Miles separates the concept of 'race' from the 'ideas of race' which form a cultural resource that people can draw upon to maintain social divisions. Bolaffi et al. (2003) explain that racialisation assumes that race is socially constructed and is used to refer to any situation to which racial meanings are attached. If individuals are looking at events from the perspective of race, assuming that race is a significant factor in a situation, then they are involved in a process of racialisation.

Miles describes the arbitrary nature of the processes of signification very clearly when he states:

> 'races' are either 'black' or 'white' but never 'big-eared' and 'small-eared'. The fact that only certain physical characteristics are signified to define 'races' in specific circumstances indicates that we are investigating not a given natural division of the world's population, but the application of historically and culturally specific meanings to the totality of human physiological variation. … Thus, the use of the word 'race' to label the groups so distinguished by such features is an aspect of the social construction of reality: 'races' are socially imagined rather than biological realities. (Miles 1989: 71)

In the last analysis, racialisation is the process by which the unique individual is placed within a category of Others who are assumed to have one essential defining feature. However, when a person defines the Other in terms of ascribed racial characteristics and makes assumptions about how those given characteristics will determine some aspect of that person's life, one is also making assumptions oneself. Making use of the term 'race' generates a barrier or division between self and Other.

Despite its arbitrary nature, the term 'race' is widely used in everyday life: newspapers run features about institutionalised racism; organisations have policies to combat racism and promote equality of opportunity; and the term is well established within legislation. Moreover, as Carter et al. (2000) explain, people who criticise the use of 'race' as a concept run the risk of being labelled as denying racism and racial discrimination. The effect of this rationalist bullying, argues Carter, is to ensure that the concept of *race* evades any serious sociological scrutiny. An example of this reasoning is Miles and Torres (1999), who object to attempts such as that by Omi and Winant (1993) to develop a critical theory of 'race', on the grounds that such an attempt serves merely to racialise the world.

<hr/>

ACTIVITY

The Aftermath of the Stephen Lawrence Case: The Macpherson Report

Read the passage below, and then attempt the questions that follow:

On the 22 April 1993, black teenager Stephen Lawrence was murdered in South East London. The way in which the investigation was handled by the police raised the issue of whether there was institutional racism within the police force. In July 1997 the Government asked Sir William Macpherson to investigate what lessons needed to be learned about the police investigation and prosecution of racially motivated crimes in general. When the Macpherson Report was published in February 1999, it made 70 recommendations on how to break down institutionalised racism. The report also raised the important issue of the links between citizenship rights and race.

In 2000 the Government revised the 1976 Race Relations Act in response to the recommendations made by the Stephen Lawrence Inquiry Report, and the Commission for Racial Equality (CRE) reviewed of the workings of the 1976 Act and the European Union Directive 2000/43/EC. This European Union Directive established, for the first time in Europe, the principle of racial equality between persons within the European Union; a minimum standard of legal protection against racism. The Act makes both direct racial discrimination and indirect racial discrimination illegal:

- **Direct racial discrimination:** when a person is treated less favourably on racial grounds, i.e. on grounds of colour, race, ethnic origin or nationality
- **Indirect racial discrimination:** where treatment is formally equal, but has discriminatory consequences.

The 2000 Race Relations Act gives the police, local councils, tax inspectors and other public bodies the duty to eliminate racial discrimination and promote equality of opportunity. In addition, the CRE has the power to issue a *compliance notice* to any public body that it believes is not providing good relations between racial groups. Chief police officers are *vicariously liable* for acts of racial discrimination by police officers.

The 2000 Act redefines the role of the CRE. The duties of the CRE are now:

(Continued)

(Continued)

- To move towards the elimination of racial discrimination
- To promote equality of opportunity
- To promote good relations between racial groups
- To review the effectiveness of the race relations legislation and suggest amendments to the Government
- To conduct formal investigations into cases of alleged racial discrimination.

Questions:

➢ Is race a useful concept for social scientists to employ in their research?

➢ Is the concept of racism a valuable tool to explain certain types of behaviour and the motivations of some people?

➢ Re-read the section on racialisation above in the light of your answers and come to some conclusions.

Racial classification detaches the body from the self, as irrespective of who the person is or what characteristics, skills or abilities they may have, we view them through the racial category. In addition, we must keep in mind the comments from Carter:

> Race may refer to a symbolic categorization rather than to a biological classification, but a belief in it carries real social effects […] [C]ritiques of the concept race seriously underestimate its power as a discursive category. (Carter 2000: 12, 22)

For Carter, the relationship between 'agency' and 'structure' is unclear within Miles's notion of racialisation. If racialisation is a process of categorisation, then individual people (the human agents) must be the categorisers, and the nature of the 'structure' is unclear. However, if the notion of racialisation refers to a historical shift, people have their perceptions shaped by determining factors within the structure. In other words, people have racialised ideas placed within their heads.

Anthias (1990) argues that racism can never be located as the product of class division or the capitalist mode of production. Moreover, a central problem with Marxian approaches, including that of Miles, is the failure to examine the impact of racial categorisation upon the labour process and class formation. If it is 'race' or racial discourse and practice that underpins exclusion from areas of the labour market, then economic processes within capitalism, such as the Labour Theory of Value, will always be secondary.

Read the following comment from Floya Anthias:

> So race is neither a class nor not a class and becomes merely some form of representation of the economy. (Anthias 1990: 33)

Question:

➢ To what extent do you accept that Anthias's comment applies to the following analyses:

— Cox's analysis?
— Castles and Kosack's analysis?
— Wallerstein's analysis?
— Cashmore and Troyna's analysis?
— Miles's analysis?

State the reasons for your answers.

Stuart Hall

In the 1990s, Stuart Hall developed an anti-essentialist critique of national, ethnic and racial conceptions of identity. Taking his point of departure from Foucault, Hall looked at identity in terms of discursive practice, what he referred to as a *narrativisation of the self*, rather than from the point of the knowing subject. Race is practical social formation, a category used to describe people and as the basis for discrimination. Postmodern perspectives have been used to raise ontological issues about the nature of race and to challenge the essentialist reductionism. As Adler explains, *essentialism* is the idea that 'our complex, multiple and sometimes fragmented identities could be reduced to one attribute only which somehow constitutes the central core of our very being' (Adler 1999: 439). However, as Carter et al. (2000) ask, if Hall argues that the 'black identity' should not be viewed in terms of a essential black nature, or any other essentialising guarantee, then what is the 'black identity' built upon?

Postmodernism and its theoretical aversion to essentialism brings with it a change in how we view the Other. Stuart Hall (1992a) developed the concept of *new ethnicities* to challenge the essentialist reductionism of race. He argues that we should move away from the conceptual autonomy of race, end the essential black subject, dismantle the simple distinction of white oppressor/black oppressed. Race becomes a linguistic categorisation, constituted outside of a pre-social biologically determined 'nature'. This was a significant shift away from the position that Hall had adopted in the late 1970s and 1980s, when the emphasis was very much provided by the distinct Marxism of Antonio Gramsci, who rejected the economic determinism contained in traditional Marxian approaches. Writing from his prison cell in the 1930s, Gramsci made a distinction between two parts of the state:

1 **Political society:** which contained all the repressive state institutions, such as the police and the army
2 **Civil society:** which contained all the institutions, such as the mass media, which attempted to manipulate our ideas.

For Gramsci, the state rules by consent, although it has the ability to use force if necessary. However, the state would always prefer to use negotiating skills to produce a compromise. The state attempts to form a historic bloc, which involves making compromises with different groups in an effort to maintain solidarity. Consent is maintained by hegemony, a body of ideas which becomes part of our consciousness and which we accept as right. Gramsci maintained that capitalism could only be overthrown by challenging and reformulating hegemony and establishing a new historic bloc.

Drawing upon Antonio Gramsci's notion of hegemony, Stuart Hall in the 1970s and 1980s consistently argued that culture was used to reproduce capitalist society and induce consent. In addition, with the transformation of traditional society into modern society, Hall argued that new communities were constructed that developed their own discourses, ideas, religion, symbols, views of the art and traditions, that is the resources from which *identity* developed. Hall and the others at the CCCS (Birmingham Centre for Contemporary Cultural Studies) distanced themselves from the traditional Marxian approach to ideology on the grounds that it was too deterministic.

In place of ideology, Hall and his colleagues developed the Gramscian notion of hegemony and of the 'relative autonomy' of the superstructure that allowed young people in particular to develop their own forms of cultural resistance to authority. One of the many interesting books that came out of the CCCS was Dick Hebdige's *Subculture: The Meaning of Style* (1979), which made use of a range of semiological concepts to read the youth subcultures from teddy boys in the 1950s to punks in the late 1970s as a form of resistance. These groups, although radically different in the styles that they adopted, were concerned with the same thing: showing their contempt for authority and capitalist ideology by developing forms of resistance through loud music with radical lyrics, forms of dress and aggressive behaviour. Youth culture was then a deliberate resistance to capitalist ideology. There were always problems with this position: conflict between groups of working-class people, for example mods and rockers. Problems of theorising about middle-class youth cultures, together with a failure to take into account the views of people who make use of the culture, were flaws in the early work of Hall and the CCCS. Many young people did not see youth culture as a form of resistance to capitalism, it was simply about having a good time.

In the 1980s, Stuart Hall developed the 'New Times' thesis that was a sign of a loss of confidence in Marxism and the growing significance of post-Fordism. Hall looked at Thatcherism as 'Authoritarian Populism', where Thatcher recreated commonsense in the minds of the working class by the use of 'hegemonic messages'. The Thatcher Administrations also ruled by consent, although they too demonstrated their ability to use force where it was thought necessary. However, the Thatcher Administrations, in the same fashion as the state in the Gramscian analysis, always preferred to use negotiating skills to produce a compromise.

In the 1990s, Hall moved away from what he saw as the increasingly redundant Marxian concepts towards concerns with identity that have a more postmodern feel to them. In *New Ethnicities* (1992a) Stuart Hall argues that the notion of 'black' is now uncertain. Black politics in the 1970s and 1980s was based upon the notion of an essential black subject, or fixed black identity. However, there are significant differences within the black community in terms of ethnic backgrounds, religions and culture. Moreover, there are significant political differences between 'black' people based upon these differences. This deconstruction of the category 'black' has generated a significant literature that suggests that racism is based upon skin colour. 'Racial formations' or the 'process of racialisation' should include factors such as religion and nationality.

A number of people have attempted to save the Marxian analysis from which Hall moved away. Raymond Williams, for example, has attempted to argue that within the Marxian analysis, individual people were responsible for producing culture. However, to remain within a Marxian framework, Williams still had to make comments such as:

> At one level, 'popular culture' ... is a very complex combination of residual, self-made and externally produced elements, with important internal conflicts between these. At another level, and increasingly, this 'popular' culture is a major area of bourgeois and ruling class cultural production, moving towards an offered 'universality' in the modern communications institutions. (Williams 1981: 228)

In other words, according to Williams (1981, 1990) people have an active role to play in culture, even popular culture. However, in the last analysis, people have their ideas manipulated by the capitalist media.

Hall's Anti-Essentialist Critique

What is the nature of Stuart Hall's anti-essentialist critique of national, ethnic and racial conceptions of identity? Hall takes his point of departure from Foucault's argument that we should look at identity in terms of a theory of discursive practice, what Hall refers to as a *narrativisation of the self*, rather than from the point of the knowing subject. In other words, 'identities are constructed within, not outside, discourse' (Hall 1996a: 4). Hall draws upon the problematic conception of identity in terms of strategic and positional *identifications*. Such identities are never wholly coherent or unified and are constructed by the coming together of a range of discourses, practices and positions. The identity of a self is always at least partly imaginary in nature and is sutured into its historical and institutional locations. Identities are both points of identification and at the same time are drawn upon as a device to exclude others.

The 'new ethnicities' project continued to make use of Gramsci's conception of hegemony, but with a very definite shift away from its original Marxian assumptions and towards a non-essentialist reading that had much in common with the position of Ernesto Laclau and Chantal Mouffe. In their book *Hegemony and Socialist Strategy* (1985), Laclau and Mouffe cast doubt upon the basic assumptions of the Marxian tradition, arguing that it is based upon a 'totalising' logic, an attempt to theorise about the whole of society that is both flawed and anti-democratic. In contrast, they argue that society is highly pluralistic in nature and that people have an identity that is independent of economic forces. New social movements provide the basis for bringing about social change and a source from which individuals can build an identity.

In addition to the Gramscian notion of hegemony, Laclau and Mouffe's explicitly post-Marxist analysis also draws upon poststructuralism and Lacanian subject theory in order to explore fully the question of how our social and political identity is constructed. Laclau and Mouffe reject what they call the rationalist 'dictatorship' of the Enlightenment and attempt to devise a form of postmodern theorising. They argue that they have overcome the two central problems of traditional Marxism:

1 **Epiphenomenalism:** the theory that the legal, political and ideological factors are determined by the economic base
2 **Class reductionism:** the idea that all aspects of a person's life can be reduced to their class location.

The problems of epiphenomenalism and class reductionism are brought together in the phrase *the problem of essentialism*. These essential elements can be identified clearly in the work of Poulantzas (1979) on ideology, when he argues that by nature:

• All people are class subjects
• All ideology is class based
• All classes have pure and coherent ideologies.

Class, ideology and identity, for Poulantzas, have a fixed and predetermined quality. In contrast, for Laclau and Mouffe neither our identity nor our values are fixed.

Identity is viewed in terms of discursive practices, what Hall was later to refer to as the *narrativisation of the self*. Identity and the values we hold are constituted within ideological discursive formations, with reference to politics and ideology, but without the economistic determinism of the traditional Marxian approach. In the last analysis, for Poulantzas and others such as Althusser (1981), ideology is never independent of the economic base and is always a distorted reflection of social reality.

The failure of Marxism to account for a politics that is independent of the determining force of class leads to the disappearance of politics in the Marxian analysis. Laclau and Mouffe draw upon Gramsci's notion of the *integral state* in order to give their theorising an ethical and political dimension. The integral state is built upon civil society; the State educates people by forming attractive moral and political ideas, which the people are made to feel are necessary for the continued existence of civilisation. Hegemony, for Gramsci, takes the form of an intellectual and moral reform, which is only achieved when the ruling class have created the *historic bloc* – a set of institutional arrangements and ideas that win the consent of the people because they are believed to give both moral and intellectual leadership and successfully eliminate the opposition. For Laclau and Mouffe, the discursive construction of hegemony ceases to be a superstructure and is independent of the economic base. Identity is also constructed independently of the economic base, and is formed through a process of struggle and articulation within hegemony. This struggle for the successful articulation of an identity and the antagonism that it generates, replaces the class struggle for Laclau and Mouffe.

Hall argues that Laclau and Mouffe do not use the notion of hegemony in a truly Gramscian way. He maintains that if we view identity in terms of hegemony, then identity should not be fixed, but at the same time should not be viewed as nothing. Identity is a point of *suture*: 'between the social and the psychic. Identity is the sum of the (temporary) positions offered by a social discourse in which you are willing for the moment to invest' (Hall 1997: 401).

In contrast to this view, Wood explores Hall's use of the Gramscian notion of hegemony. He argues that hegemony 'is a complex discursive field that takes shape across various social locations' (Wood 1998: 404). The exercise of hegemony was about people thinking of themselves in Thatcherite terms. In other words, hegemony repositions people with identities into relations that are already secured. Hall attempts to distance his analysis from that of Laclau and Mouffe's 'fully discursive position' on the grounds, claims Wood, that Laclau and Mouffe's discursive analysis ignores the 'social' – the organisational features that cannot be reduced to discourse, what Hall refers to as 'structuring lines'. Wood goes on to argue that Hall has a poorly developed theory of social solidarity, in that 'the State' is linked to 'discourse' by use of the concept of 'articulation' – a concept that can be dissolved and replaced by an effective agency making new *connections* drawn from a reservoir of 'elements'. The concept of 'articulation' leads Hall to exaggerate the role of ideology. Agency itself turns out to be a discursively constituted subjectivity. In addition, *ideology* is at the base of all groups and attempts at group formation – Hall presents no account of group formation independent of ideology. Wood concludes that Hall has taken the political malleability of social relations too far.

Wood's analysis is fine, as far as it goes, but the analysis is only fine if the reader shares his view of the social as totalising, objectivist and realist in nature and rejects all notions of social construction. If we refuse to make these assumptions about the 'social', then Hall has no case to answer. It is also important to take into account that Hall has a very selective reading and application of Gramsci. In an interview with Peter Osbourne and Lynne Segal in June 1997, Hall explained:

> I am perfectly well aware of making Gramsci up, of producing my own Gramsci. When I read Perry Anderson's classic piece on Gramsci, 'The Antinomies of Antonio Gramsci,' – Gramsci, the true Leninist – I recognize that there are many aspects of Gramsci's life and work that my Gramsci doesn't take on. (Hall 1997: 393)

Hall took up many of these selective Gramscian ideas in his *New Ethnicities* project which emphasised that ideological discursive formations have no fixed or otherwise predetermined quality. In any given situation there will be a complex combination of ideological elements, discourses and institutional practices that we experience as the social context. That context can be read and re-read in any number of different ways, with some readings gaining dominance through the successful manipulation of economic policy, education and the mass media. However, the consciousness of North America and Europe is still deeply embedded with what Stuart Hall (1992b) called the division between 'the West' and 'the Rest'.

The *West* argues Hall, is a historical, not a geographical construct; it describes a modern, industrial, urban and secular society. The term West is also:

- A tool to classify types of society
- A set of images that form a system of representation
- A set of criteria for ranking societies, judging the advancement of the West.

Hall argues that the 'ideal' of the West was a central factor in the formation of *the West*. Moreover, it is the difference between the *West* and the *Rest* that gives the West its meaning – how Europeans represent non-Europeans as 'Others'; they 'became related elements in the same discourse' (ibid.: 279). This is a discourse that divides the world as a simple binary opposition or dichotomy. The *Rest*, had an important role to play in the formation of a 'Western' sense of identity: 'Europe brought its own cultural categories, languages, images and ideas to the New World in order to describe and represent it … [as] a "regime of truth"' (ibid.: 293, 295).

By 1997, Hall was moving away from looking at ethnicity and identity in terms of binarism, which he started to see as a quality that was intrinsic to essentialism. In a rather confusing passage that draws upon the Derridian notion of *différance*, Hall argues:

> Having refused the binarism which is intrinsic to essentialism, you have to remind yourself that binaries persist. You've questioned them theoretically, but you haven't removed their historical efficacy. Just because you say there is no absolute distinction between black and white doesn't mean that there aren't situations in which everything is being mobilized to make an intractable difference between black and white. (Hall 1997: 403)

This statement is unclear, but it also raises for Hall the question: Where do identities come from? Is our identity simply a product of a 'regime of truth' – structurally shaped by the bio-power of the state imposing subjectivation upon individuals and turning them into categories of Other? Or is identity to be seen in terms of a Deleuzian notion of *becoming*, where individuals step off the line of organisation that consititutes the state's preferred socialisation outcomes within a given identity, and literally become the identity they prefer?

More general critiques of the Stuart Hall and the CCCS have included the following:

- **Blummaert and Verschueren (1998)** who argued that the CCCS was solely concerned with ways in which white people attempted to make Caribbean style objective; a process *Othering* black people which was little more than an 'abnormalization of the immigrant' (Blummaert and Verschueren 1998: 20)
- **Harris (1996)** argued that Stuart Hall and the CCCS largely ignored the members of the black community who were not highly visible, reactive and rebellious, for example, older people, conformist youth
- **Wright (2000)** argued that academics, including Stuart Hall and the CCCS, only looked at black people in terms of racism and social disadvantage, and largely ignored the varied aspects of Afro-Caribbean culture.

Racial Formation Theory: Michael Omi and Howard Winant

In the 1980s Michael Omi and Howard Winant developed Racial Formation Theory, an approach to the study of 'race' that attempted to 'specifically address the shifting meanings and power relationships inherent in race today' (Winant 1994: 23). Omi and Winant rejected approaches that looked at race in terms of:

- Racial reductionism, i.e. that race is a 'natural' attribute
- Race as a epiphenomenon of class relationships
- Race as a product of 'national oppression'.

Racial Formation Theory is primarily concerned with the role and purpose of racial ideas and practices in the relationship between agency and structure. Racial Formation Theory looks at race as a 'phenomenon whose meaning is contested throughout social life' (ibid.: 23). Race is constituent both of an individual's psyche and of relationships between individuals at the same time – it is an 'irreducible component of collective identities and social structures' (1994: 23). Racial signification they argue, is 'inherently discursive' – we are all involved in *racial projects*, which are discursive formations that we use to make sense of race. As Winant explains, 'A racial project is simultaneously an interpretation, representation, or explanation of racial dynamics and an effort to organize and distribute resources along particular racial lines' (ibid.: 24). Racial projects change over time and Winant outlines some of the key historical phases.

The Pre-Civil Rights Era

This was an era in which racial projects had domination as their focus and this domination was achieved by the use of coercion, racial violence and segregation.

THE DRED SCOTT CASE

In the *Dred Scott v. Sanford* case (1857), the US Supreme Court declared that all black people, whether slaves or not, were not citizens of the United States. According to Justice Taney, the negro: 'had no rights which the white man was bound to respect; and that the negro might justly and lawfully be reduced to slavery for his benefit. He was bought and sold and treated as an ordinary article of merchandise and traffic, whenever profit could be made by it.'

'All men are created equal'. However, Taney explained that 'it is too clear for dispute, that the enslaved African race were not intended to be included, and formed no part of the people who framed and adopted this declaration. ...'

(Source: Africans in America http://www.pbs.org/wgbh/aia/part4/4h2933.html)

Even as late as 1950, the Fugitive Slave Act meant people who escaped to the North were not legally safe. In addition, Michael Omi and Howard Winant argue that the Dred Scott Case denied full citizenship rights to black Americans irrespective of where they were born in the United States or if they were born as slaves or free persons – a legally supported racial project of inferiority.

The Black Civil Rights Movement

The Civil Rights Movement challenged the legitimate use of violence for political ends and successfully raised awareness and brought many black Americans into the political process. The domination of the pre-Civil Rights era was successfully challenged. For black Americans at this time, racial projects could be viewed as having two distinct components: war of manoeuvres and the war of position.

- **War of manoeuvre:** with the absence of any real legal or civil rights and limited access to employment and less than adequate wages, black Americans looked inward upon their everyday lives, drawing upon their resources to endure hardship and maintain family and community life
- **War of position:** black Americans campaigned for the enforcement of the legal and civil rights that they had already won such as: the Thirteenth Amendment (1865), which legally at least abolished slavery across the entire United States; the Fourteenth Amendment (1868), which gave all persons born in the US equal status under the law and full citizenship; and the Fifteenth Amendment (1870), which extended the franchise to all male citizens. The campaign to enforce these legal rights was used as a vehicle to gain greater access to areas such as education and employment.

Black Americans were allowed to vote and there were new opportunities for economic and social mobility. People's identity was also politicised and this changed American culture. Michael Omi and Howard Winant argue that the Civil Rights Movement enhanced people's awareness of racial identities.

Many on the political Right rejected what they saw as the intrusion of egalitarian racial awareness into everyday and personal lives, and attempted to redefine the source of the Civil Rights Movement in terms of opposition to the traditional American values of individualism and personal freedom.

The 'Decentring' of Racial Conflict

The rejection of the *essential* or *totalising* conception of 'race' as a biological entity has given rise to what Winant (1994) refers to as 'pragmatic liberals', people who have no coherent 'racial' politics because they have no durable or concrete vision of 'race'. There is a high degree of uncertainty about what should constitute 'race' in the United States. There is no longer any one 'single axis' of racial domination. However, there is a form of 'racial hegemony' that, although not explicitly racist in nature, draws upon moral discourse to provide a racial backdrop to discussion of a range of issues such as tax, crime and poverty. Race is used as a:

> Key cultural marker, a central signifier in the reproduction and expression of identity, collectivity and agency itself. Race generates an 'inside' and an 'outside' of society, and mediates the unclear border between these zones. (Ibid.: 31)

The economic recession in the United States during the Regan–Bush Senior era hit the black American population the hardest. Winant argues that the notion of 'race' still has a central role to play within the processes of class formation. Winant's argument is that we should view discrimination:

as a racial process with class consequences. The reactionary redefinition of the nature of racial discrimination (in the 'reverse discrimination' arguments of the 1970s and 1980s) as something that only happened to individuals and thus is disconnected from history and from preponderant collective logic in the present, conveniently suppresses the fact that discrimination drives all wages down. (1994: 34)

Postcolonial Accounts of Blackness

As long as you think you are white, there's no hope for you. (James Baldwin quoted in Bonnet 1999)

Frantz Fanon's (1952) contextualist argument for the social construction of blackness and whiteness has influenced a generation of postcolonial theorists and others such as Toni Morrison (1992) in her analysis of American literature. Morrison argues that it was the colonial representation of the black person that allowed Americans to construct a white identity. Fanon foresaw and supported movements towards struggles over cultural hegemony, hybridity, intercultural and diasporic relations as forms of 'imagined community'. Colonialism was not only an objective set of institutions, economic arrangements and historical conditions; colonialism is also about the shaping of people's attitudes and perceptions of these things. Colonialism imposed an existentially false and humiliating way of life upon black people and demanded their conformity to a set of distorted values that were in the last analysis degrading to black people. In addition, Fanon argues that *blackness* and *whiteness* are mutually reinforcing cultural categories; when we construct the Other we also construct ourselves. 'The Negro' is a socially constructed identity which white colonisers – the dominant strangers – have successfully essentialised as a dominant form of '"corporeal malediction" ... battered down by tom-toms, cannibalism, intellectual deficiency, fetishism, racial defects, slave ships and above all else, "Sho'good eatin"' (Fanon 1952: 111, 112). Fanon's contribution to the development of postcolonial studies has been described by Steven Connor as 'an analysis which, instead of obediently adopting a marginal place itself, brings the margins into the centre by applying deconstructive critique to the dominant self-histories of the West' (Connor 1997: 265).

ACTIVITY

Question:

➢ What do think Frantz Fanon means when he states:
  'The Negro is not. Any more than the white man' (Fanon 1952: 231)?

Black Skin White Masks (1952), originally entitled 'An Essay for the Disalienation of Blacks', is a highly personal and disturbing account of what it means to be a black person. Based upon his own experience and that of his patients, Frantz Fanon attempts to identify how racism emerged historically and culturally within a colonial context and how white European cultural domination persists in a post colonial world: 'to enable the man of color to understand, through specific examples, the psychological elements that can alienate his fellow Negroes' (Fanon 1967: 79). For Fanon, 'race' is not based upon any natural factor or human nature. In a number of statements that appear to anticipate both Edward Said's notion of Orientalism – the idea that the West created the notion of the Orient via a set of ideologies and brutal colonial power – and Stuart Hall's *New Ethnicities* project of the latter years of the twentieth century, Fanon argued that white people created the 'Negro'. Fanon, rejected what we would now call the essentialist definition of 'race': 'the man who adores the Negro is as "sick" as the man who abominates him' (Fanon 1967: 10). In his 1967 work entitled *The Wretched of the Earth*, Fanon explains:

> Ontology – once it is finally admitted as leaving existence by the wayside – does not permit us to understand the being of the black man. For not only must the black man be black; he must be black in relation to the white man. Some critics will take it on themselves to remind us that this proposition has a converse. I say this is false. The black man has no ontological resistance in the eyes of the white man. (Ibid.: 110)

From a personal perspective, Fanon outlined his dilemma:

> I made a complete audit of my ailment. I wanted to be typically Negro – it was no longer possible. I wanted to be white – that was a joke. And, when I tried, on the level of ideas and intellectual activity, to reclaim my negritude, it was snatched away from me. (Ibid.: 132)

For Fanon, cultural imposition constructs an undifferentiated whiteness and a conception of the Negro as Other, defined only in terms of being non-white. Being classified as a Negro by white people was a central factor in how people experienced the world, including their social relationships and their consciousness of inferiority and often feelings of non-existence.

A key concept for Fanon is the collective unconscious, which is found in the unreflected imposition of a white colonial culture that defines the Negro as black, ugly, sinful, dark, immoral. The Negro becomes the victim of white civilisation and culture as Fanon explains: 'If I order my life like that of a moral man, I simply am not a Negro' (Fanon 1952: 192). Fanon delineates his position by arguing that it is white people, through their socialisation in white families, who define the limits of the black person's psychic structure, stop the black person from becoming an *actional* person, and make the black person define their own self-worth, self-esteem and morality on the white person's terms. The black person is faced with a feeling of non-existence unless over a period of time he or she learns to think and see in ways that are fundamentally white. In Fanon's terms: 'A normal

Negro child, having grown up within a normal family, will become abnormal on the slightest contact with the white world' (ibid.: 143).

Black people suffer because they are not white, argues Fanon. White people impose discrimination, rob black people of their worth, or their individuality, forcing them to obey an imposed dependency/inferiority complex, shattering both black people's horizons and psychological mechanisms. Nowhere is this more clearly expressed by Fanon than in his discussion of sex and sexuality:

> I wish to be acknowledged not as *black* but as *white*.
> Now – and this is a form of recognition that Hegel had not envisaged – who but a white woman can do this for me? By loving me she proves that I am worthy of white love. I am loved like a white man.
> I am a white man.
> Her love takes me onto the noble road that leads to total realization … .
> I marry white culture, white beauty, white whiteness.
> When my restless hands caress those white breasts, they grasp white civilization and dignity and make them mine. (Ibid.: 63)

This area has also been explored by Jo Eadie (2001), who in the course of discussing the film *Shivers* discusses the issue of: What do white people think about when they fuck? Drawing upon the work of Robert Reid-Pharr (1996), Eadie argues that white people are haunted by the fear that the expression of strong sexual desire is stigmatised as animalistic black passion, a perception that is always waiting in the shadows of the white consciousness, threatening to take away a person's whiteness the further they descend into strong passion.

This argument draws upon Fanon's argument that white people have developed the idea that they have socially limited desire, whereas black people have biologically determined lust. The black person is perceived in the popular consciousness as having no *bodily becoming* outside of their animalistic passions. Fanon's work can be described as an 'anti-foundationalist theory of hope'. Some commentators have suggested that his work has a number of essentialising tendencies contained within it, notably his tendency to locate 'cultural imposition' as the central element in the formation of the Negro's identity.

Homi Bhabha

One of the many thinkers whom Fanon has influenced is Homi Bhabha. For Bhabha it is possible to identify a space between 'coloniser' and 'colonised' where there is both overlap and tension. Bhabha attempts to unravel such thinking by challenging the binary oppositions that underpin it: coloniser and colonised; black and white; rural and urban; gay and straight; men and women. He does this by focusing upon the fault lines of the binary oppositions, the border situations where identities are constructed and contested. He describes this space as a *liminal space* that does not separate but rather mediates mutual exchange and relative meanings, where hybridity can be found:

> The pact of interpretation is never simply an act of communication between the I and the You designated in the statement. The production of meaning requires that these two places be mobilized in the passage through a Third Space, which represents both the general conditions of language and the specific implication of the utterance in a performative and institutional strategy of which it cannot 'in itself' be conscious. (Bhabha 1994: 36)

Drawing upon the ideas of Jacques Derrida in *Writing and Difference*, Bhabha posits that Western thinking contains a 'linear narrative of the nation', which claims to explain the whole of culture. However, writing does not passively record social 'realities' but in fact precedes them and gives them meaning through a recognition of the differences between signs within textual systems.

Bhabha views English writing, and in particular 'the English book' – a term used to include a range of cultural products such as novels, cinema, music, but above all the Bible – as having the discursive capacity to 'narrate' colonial power. The English book is a mode of colonial domination, a symbol of English 'cultural rule' because it is a vehicle for the imposition of central elements of Western culture upon colonial people: empiricism, idealism, mimeticism, monoculturalism. For Bhabha, writing is also the site of resistance to such colonial rule. In his essay 'Signs Taken for Wonders' (in Bhabha 1994) Bhabha argues that the colonised subject still has linguistic agency, the ability to make use of the language of the powerful to undermine the psychological structures and linguistic devices that help to maintain the colonial mindset that persists in postcolonial societies. The English book contains the fragility of colonial discourse because of its vulnerability to 'mimetic' (linguistic) subversion through hybrid mimicry:

> If the effect of colonial power is seen to be the production of hybridization rather than the noisy command of colonialist authority or the silent repression of native traditions, then an important change of perspective occurs. The ambivalence at the source of traditional discourses on authority enables a form of subversion, founded on the undecidability that turns the discursive conditions of dominance into the grounds of intervention. (Bhabha 1994: 112)

Bhabha views this as a 'narrative struggle' to liberate the 'repression of a "cultural" unconscious; a liminal, uncertain state of cultural belief when the archaic emerges in the midst of margins of modernity' (ibid.: 143).

In a similar fashion to Fanon, Gayatri Chakravorty Spivak's essay 'Can the Subaltern Speak?' draws upon Gramsci's concept of the 'subaltern' and Derrida's concept of 'deconstruction' in order to locate and re-establish a 'voice' for the economically dispossesed of postcolonial India:

> So right from the beginning, the deconstructive move. Deconstruction does not say there is no subject, there is no truth, there is no history. It simply questions the privileging of identity so that someone is believed to have the truth. It is not the exposure of error. It is constantly and persistently looking into how truths are produced. That's why deconstruction doesn't say logocentrism is a pathology, or metaphysical enclosures are something you can escape. Deconstruction, if one wants a formula, is among other things, a persistent critique of what one cannot not want. And in that sense, yes, it's right there at the beginning. (Spivak 1988: 28)

Homi Bhabha, Gayatri Chakravorty Spivak and others have drawn upon Fanon's pioneering work to reject notions of cultural purity and instead celebrate hybrid notions of *diasporic* culture, with its resultant identities, lifestyles and cultural forms, which reject the assimilationist ambitions of Talcott Parsons and others.

The Social Construction of *Whiteness*

It was stated earlier that racial classification detaches the body from the self. Irrespective of who the person is or what characteristics, skills or abilities they may have, we view them through the category. However, 'whiteness' is not seen as a category; if anything it is the absence of a category, it is constructed as a person without ethnicity – normal, a non-label. As Martin et al. (1999: 31) explain: 'Whites just "are"'. Similarly, Gallagher argues that:

> Racial dominance means that whites do not have to think about being white because white privilege and white standards are so culturally embedded that whiteness has been 'naturalized'. As the racial norm, being white or acknowledging one's whiteness need never be recognized or analysed by whites because whites generally view themselves as the racial yardstick with which other racial groups are compared. (Gallagher 1994: 167–68)

However, this is not to say that 'whiteness' has no influence upon identity; it does. Moreover, many groups who are now considered white were classified as 'non-white' in the nineteenth century. Irish, Jewish and East European immigrants to both the United States and Britain had to fight for recognition as 'white'.

Whitespeak

Dreama Moon (1999) argues that not only is the white identity invisible, but in addition, white people make use of the passive voice to indicate that 'things' happen to non-white people. *Whitespeak* allows white people to discuss the problems of non-white people without identifying the factors and historical agents that came together to cause the problems in the first instance. Moon gives the following example: 'Africans were brought to the United States to work as slaves' (Moon 1999: 189). The passive voice of *whitespeak* allows the white person to identify historical events without having to identify their ancestors' racist behaviour as causing the events to happen.

Consider the following example: Blance makes the following observation about Native American children in school:

> 'I had a group of Native American kids come to campus for a tour. They were relatively intelligent kids, but had been cloistered on the reservation to the point that they were afraid to come to campus.'

The sentence fragment, '[they] had been cloistered', obscures the responsible agent as well as the history surrounding such segregationist actions. We understand cloistering as a problem, but fail to glimpse the historical conditions that have made this cloistering a present-day reality. In this reversal, Blance fails to consider a long history of fear and distrust of white people and reservationization of Indian nations by the (white) US government, and at the same time, the comment seems to suggest that Native Americans have somehow failed to prepare their children adequately for entry into the white world of the university. By failing to engage with other possible ways of understanding the behavior of these children, she is free to demonstrate her racial tolerance (which translates into 'personal empathy'), while avoiding social responsibility for, and awareness of, the historical conditions and power relations that have contributed to the present state of many Native nations. (Moon 1999: 190)

Questions:

➤ Do you accept or reject Moon's argument? Give the reasons for your answer.

➤ Have you ever come across an instance of *whitespeak* in your everyday life?

Frantz Fanon's (1967) contextualist argument has also played a central role in the social construction of whiteness because, as we have seen, Fanon argues that blackness and whiteness are mutually reinforcing cultural categories; when we construct the Other we also construct ourselves.

What does it mean to be a white person? If you are a white person, do you feel that you belong to a race? In 1997, Richard Dyer published his book *White,* in which he argued that 'race' is something that is only applied to non-white people. Race may be about the biological classification of people on the basis of the differences that can be observed, notably skin colour. However, for Dyer, being a white person and viewing oneself as 'human' rather than 'raced' helps to secure a position of power for white people. 'Other' people are 'raced' but white people are 'just people', as he explains:

> There is no more powerful position than being 'just' human. The claim to power is the claim to speak for the commonality of humanity. Raced people can't do that – they can only speak for their race. But non-raced people can, for they do not represent the interests of a race. (Dyer 1997: 2)

It is the objectified and until recently largely invisible category of whiteness as simply 'people' that is the vehicle for masking a range of assumptions that maintain racism within the culture.

White people have more control over the definition of themselves and are highly unlikely to be classed as Other on racial grounds, even when in a tiny minority. In the United States a number of groups whom we would now consider to be 'white' such as the Irish, Italians and Jews had to struggle and campaign to be recognised as 'white', which reinforces the argument that 'whiteness' may appear to be a 'natural' and neutral category, but in the last analysis the concept is historically constructed through discourse. Taking our starting point from Foucault, as we have done in previous chapters, discourses of *whiteness* are again viewed in terms of *exteriority*, in which we do not search for the true meaning – or essential nature – of what it means to be white, but rather in terms of the rhetorical character of what people say it means to be white. Dyson (1999) develops the following arguments:

- Whiteness is regarded as the positive universal whereas blackness is the negative particular
- Whiteness represents ethnic cohesion and is the instrument of nation-building
- Whiteness limits and distorts our conceptions of blackness.

As Dyson (1999: 220) explains 'Through this meaning of whiteness, whites were able to criticize blacks for their failure to be human, not explicitly for their failure to be white, although in principle the two were indistinguishable.'

Alistair Bonnett (1999) argues that the term 'white' is one that we strongly associate with 'European' and that anti-racism often ignores the underpinning colonial assumptions of the category 'whiteness', which reinforces the objective view that most people have of whiteness:

[w]hiteness has developed, over the past two hundred years, into a taken-for-granted experience structured upon a varying set of supremacist assumptions (sometimes cultural, sometimes biological, sometimes moral, sometimes all three). Non-white identities, by contrast, have been denied the privileges of normativity, and are marked within the West as marginal and inferior. (Bonnett 1999: 213)

Bonnett looks at the emergence of 'whiteness' as the creation of racialised capitalism in relation to two interrelated historical processes:

- The marginalisation of non-European whiteness and the marginalisation of any 'racial' connotation to the whiteness of Europeans
- The identification of the white European as a privileged identity.

Whiteness can never be a 'free-floating signifier', it is always a form of oppression linked with the capitalist social and economic structures from which it emerged. For the white population, the hegemony of whiteness is internalised and experienced as freedom and pleasure and possibility. However, as Fanon (1967) pointed out, to experience the world as non-white is to be acted upon by whites to feel the oppressive agency of white folks and to experience a sense of inferiority and powerlessness.

ACTIVITY

Read the exchange below, which is part of a dialogue between Samuel L. Jackson and his two young cousins in the film *Die Hard with a Vengeance*.

Uncle Zeus: So who are the bad guys?
Cousins: People with guns. People with drugs.
Uncle Zeus: So who's gonna help you?
Cousins: We are.
Uncle Zeus: So who's not gonna help us?
Cousins: White people.
Uncle Zeus: That's right.
(Quoted in Denzin 2002: 86)

Question:

➢ What do you consider to be the significance of this exchange?

Thomas Nakayama and Robert Krizek (1999) argue that whiteness should be seen as a form of strategic rhetoric. In other words, whiteness is a rhetorical construction, not an essential category. By drawing upon Deleuze and Guattari's (1987) notion of *assemblage*, Nakayama and Krizek attempt to uncover the ways in which whiteness is used to exercise power within the social fabric. Whiteness is a territorialising machine which identifies the places where white and non-white people can and cannot place themselves within the society. The work of Deleuze and Guattari is fully explained in the concluding chapter.

Raka Shome looks at whiteness through: 'the interlocking axes of power, spatial location, and history' (Shome 1999: 109). What Shome means by this is that whiteness has to be understood against a background of colonialism and neo-colonialism, which has historically placed white people in a position of global dominance and racial superiority. This historical global dominance is facilitated by the global distribution of Eurocentric worldviews, which is manifest in 'the white gaze'. The white gaze functions in the same way for postcolonial theorists as the male gaze functions for third-wave feminists; its use both demonstrates and maintains the body of the Other as objectively different – both a look and a judgement.

Islamophobia: The Creation of New *Others*

'Racism is like a Cadillac; they make a new model every year.' (Malcolm X)

Following the collapse of communism, Francis Fukuyama in *The End of History and the Last Man* (1992) argues that history, in terms of new great historical epochs (such as socialism, communism, fascism, etc.), has come to an end and from this moment on we shall have 'events' that take place within a form of liberal capitalism which we all share. Fukuyama suggests that cultural globalisation is bringing about a homogenisation of all civilisations upon one liberal democratic model and that liberal democracy is the terminus of history; from now on there will be no more great historical epochs.

However, a contrasting and very pessimistic view that many people believe gives a clear indication of the root causes of September 11, has been suggested by Samuel Huntington. In *The Clash of Civilizations* (1996) Huntington argues that the confrontation of the Cold War between the USA and the Soviet Union has been replaced by multiple confrontations, primarily between Western democracy and Islam. Since the end of the Cold War, conflict along what Samuel Huntington describes as the fault line between Western and Islamic civilisations, or the *clash of civilisations,* has come to dominate international politics. The differences between Western (Modern European and North American democratic societies) and non-Western civilisations (Islamic societies) have moved into sharper focus with an increased awareness of cultural differences between civilisations that exacerbate economic conflict.

As George Bush Jr.'s declared War on Terrorism, including the War in Afghanistan and the Gulf War, have clearly demonstrated, modern Western societies, notably the United States, expect to make use of international institutions, notably the United Nations, the military power of its allies and economic resources to maintain Western dominance, to protect its interests and promote modern Western values. In other words, these clashes are not based on politics, economics or the demands of the nation state, but rather on culture. The next world war, if there is one, Huntington argues will be between these contrasting civilisations.

For Huntington, civilisation has a number of objective elements: language, history, religion, custom, institutions and 'subjective self-identification of people' (Huntington 1996: 41). However, for Huntington it is religion that is the central defining element of any civilisation. Western civilisation is characterised by:

- The separation of religious from secular authority
- Pluralism and representative government
- Rule of law
- Individual rights and civil liberties.

For Huntington, all of the above are missing from Islamic civilisation.

These divisions have great depth, they are old and embody basic differences between people. Moreover, claims Huntington, these conflicts will become more passionate as people struggle to keep hold of their cultural identity against the globalising tendencies of the modern world which are seen to be Western in origin.

Huntington assumes that there is a single anti-American, fundamentalist Islamic culture that stretches across the globe. In contrast to Huntington's view, Al-Azmeh (1993: 1) has argued that 'there are as many Islams as there are situations that sustain it'. Fuller (2002) has argued that it is not possible to generalise about Islam in the way that Huntington does. The Islamic world contains a variety of different cultures and traditions because of issues such as ethnic divisions, economic development, colonial history and the power of Islamic fundamentalism.

Norris and Inglehart also take issue with the Huntington thesis. Drawing information from the *World Values Survey* and the *European Values Survey 1995–2001*, which conducted research into the values of people in 72 nation states across the world, Norris and Inglehart (2003) argue that there is general agreement between peoples in the Western world and the Islamic world on questions that relate to democratic performance, democratic ideals and strong leadership. However, there is disagreement on questions that relate to gender equality, homosexuality, abortion and divorce. The prime division between the West and Islam is over gender equality and in particular sexual liberation. As Norris and Inglehart explain:

> Just as it would be a mistake to understand the 1995 bombing in Oklahoma City as a collective attack on the federal government by all Christian fundamentalists, rather than the work of a few individuals, it may [be] inappropriate to view the attack by Al Qaeda

terrorists on symbols of American capitalism and financial power as a new 'clash of civilizations' between Islamic and western cultures. (Norris and Inglehart 2002: 239)

Jihad vs. McWorld: A Clash of Cultures?

In a similar vein to Huntington, Benjamin Barber (1996) argues that in the future we are likely to see major conflicts between Western commerce and consumerism (McWorld) and more localised nationalistic and religious conflicts (*jihad*). The notion of McWorld is derived from George Ritzer's conception of the process of McDonaldisation. The production line approach which has been common in a number of industries for many years and has been applied to the hospitality industries. Ritzer views this process as a bad thing because it is seen as reducing both diversity and choice. McDonaldisation has four key components:

1 **Efficiency:** 'choosing the optimum means to a given end' (Ritzer 1996: 36). This efficiency is defined by the organisation rather than the individual and is in effect imposed upon the individual.
2 **Calculability:** 'an emphasis on the quantitative aspect of products sold (portion size, cost) and service offered (the time it takes to get the product)' (ibid.: 9).
3 **Predictability:** 'discipline, order, systemization, formalization, routine, consistency and methodical operation. In such a society, people prefer to know what to expect in most settings and at most times' (ibid.: 79). The experience is the same in every shop for the consumer and work becomes very routine for the workers.
4 **Control:** management have a need to control both the workers and the customers in an effort to reduce the level of uncertainty within the organisation.

However, Ritzer is critical of these processes, which he argues have their own irrational outcomes: 'Rational systems inevitably spawn a series of irrationalities that limit, eventually compromise, and perhaps even undermine their rationality' (ibid.: 121). The inefficiencies generated by these rational processes include:

• Longer waiting times and more work for the customer – having to make your own salad in the salad bar, or fill up your own drink in the fast food restaurant
• Dehumanisation of the worker and of the customer
• The emergence of unforeseen anomalies.

In contrast to Huntington, Barber does not see *jihad* as a throwback to premodern times, rather as a reaction to the Western processes of McDonaldisation:

Jihad stands not so much in stark opposition as in subtle counterpoint to McWorld and is itself a dialectical response to modernity whose features both reflect and reinforce the modern world's virtues and vices – *jihad* via McWorld rather than *jihad* versus McWorld. The forces of *jihad* are not only remembered and retrieved by the enemies of McWorld but imagined and contrived by its friends and proponents. *Jihad* is not only McWorld's adversary, it is its child. (Barber 1996: 157)

Before we can evaluate this, we need to have a closer look at the nature of Islam.

What Is Islam?

In the West, there is a clear distinction between the political sphere and the religious sphere, with politics regarded in the eyes of most people as a totally secular activity. Not so with Islam: religion and politics are one and the same activity. The word *Islam* is derived from two roots: *Salm* (peace) and *Silm* (submission). Therefore, Islam stands for a commitment to surrender one's will to the will of God. For the Muslim it is through this submission to God that peace is brought about.

Islam is more than a simple faith, on the Western model of religion. Nor is it a simple political doctrine or ideology. It is all of these, as well as a social movement complete with an ethical code that is found in the holy book the *Qur'an*, which is believed by Muslims to be the word of God, and contains the philosophical basis of a political system and the *Hadiths* or traditions that were passed down from the Prophet Muhammad and his companions.

Three main principles are of significance:

- **Tawhid:** the idea that there is one God who is the Creator, whom we should worship alone as master of the universe. In other words, Muslims have no conception of political sovereignty outside the law of the Qur'an (*shari'a*). The purpose of government in the Islamic state is to fulfil the word of God
- **Risala:** the medium through which Muslims receive the law of God. These are to be found in the *Qur'an* which provides an established model of how to lead a good Muslim way of life
- **Khilafa:** this third element, means 'representation'. If people have any power in society they should exercise their power as the representatives of God on earth. Responsibility for the maintance of Khilafa falls upon the whole Muslim community, and not upon any single individual or section of society. The leader, *emir*, ideally, should be guided by an advisory council (*shura*), elected by universal suffrage, of all the people who accept the fundamentals of the constitution. In the Islamic State, all citizens have the right to be critical of the Government, and the Government maintains its legitimacy by seeking the active cooperation of the masses.

ISLAM'S FIVE ARTICLES OF FAITH

Underpinning the Islamic state is the principle of *La ilaha illallah* – there is no deity but God. It is from *La ilaha illallah* that the five articles of faith are derived:

1 Belief in one God – the *shahada*.
2 The *salat* – the need to pray formally five times each day.
3 The *zakat* – having concern for the poor and giving them help.
4 Fasting during the month of Ramadan.
5 The pilgrimage to Mecca – the *hajj*.

Individuals have free will and can choose not to be Muslim. However, to choose not to be Muslim is to become an unbeliever (a Kafir), and the state of being Kufir is seen to be one of ignorance, ingratitude and infidelity. However, Islam has laid down rights for non-Muslims, referred to as *dhimmis* (the covenanted), living within the Islamic state. Moreover, these rights are an important part of the constitution; the *dhimmis* are to be respected in the same way as Muslims, with no difference in either civil or criminal law. Human rights in an Islamic society are rights conferred by God, and for a Muslim not to accept the validity of the rights of non-Muslims, or not to give non-Muslims respect is to become one of the Kafirun. However, traditionally Muslims have accepted three clear forms of political inequality: between Muslims and non-Muslims; between men and women; and between masters and slaves. In more recent years Muslim social movements have expressed hostility towards equal rights for lesbian and gay people.

Many people in the West view Islamic states with mistrust and even fear, believing that the spread of Islamic fundamentalism – principally from Iran – is one of the major threats to the West. This view is reinforced by the idea of *jihad*, and the suggestion of world domination by the use of terrorism, which this concept seems to have underpinning it. The stereotyping of Islam in recent years has been related to:

- The Iranian Revolution in 1979, in which the Ayatollah Khomeini and his supporters overthrew the violent and corrupt regime of the Shah and introduced a new constitution, legal code (*shari'a*), judicial system, education system etc., all of which were based upon Islamic principles
- The *Satanic Verses* controversy (1989), in which Ayatollah Khomeini ordered that author Salman Rushdie should be executed for comments he had made about the Prophet Muhammad in his novel
- The Gulf War (1991) in which Iraq occupied Kuwait and annexed the country as Iraq's nineteenth province
- Attacks on the twin towers of the World Trade Center, New York on the 11 September 2001, in which two hijacked planes were flown into two large office blocks in New York, a third into the Pentagon in Washington and a fourth crashed in Pennsylvania.

Since the terrorist attacks in the United States on September 11, the international War on Terrorism has been the main focus of international cooperation. Was there a religious motive behind the September 11 attacks? Let us look briefly at the events running up to this momentous day.

In 1998 Osama bin Laden the leader of the terrorist group al-Qaeda, declared a *jihad* against the United States. 'To kill Americans and their allies, both civil and military, is an individual duty of every Muslim who is able, in any country … until their armies, shattered and broken-winged, depart from all the lands of Islam.' Bin Laden believes that violence, including killing civilians, is justified as a means to restore *sharia* (Islamic law) and maintain Islamic cultural identity. However, while bin Laden often quotes the Koran and promotes a fundamentalist interpretation of Islam, bin Laden is not a certified Islamic cleric and most Muslims do not accept his fundamentalist radical and politicised interpretation of Islam. In addition, few Muslims support these extreme views. The September 11 attacks were widely condemned across the Muslim world.

WHAT IS JIHAD?

Jihad is not one of the central pillars of Islam. However, if the citizens of an Islamic state are attacked by a non-Muslim power, then there is an obligation on all Muslims to come forward for *jihad*. In addition, it is the religious duty of the neighbouring Muslim countries to help and if they fail, then the Muslims of the whole world must fight the common enemy.

The use of *jihad* is part of the defence of Islam, and is used in particular to describe a war that is waged in the name of God against people who practise oppression against Islam.

It is important to recognise that there is a great diversity within Islam. There are two main groups within the Muslim world: the majority Sunni, who make up an estimated 90 percent of the Muslim population, and the Shi'i. The two groups split after the death of the Prophet Muhammad, concerning a disagreement over the status of his brother in law, Ali, as the only legitimate leader after the Prophet Muhammad. In addition, within these two broad groups there is much diversity. Many Shi'ites such as the late Ayatollah Khomeini believe that sovereignty does not lie with the people but with God. This gives many in the West the view that all Muslims are hostile to democracy.

ACTIVITY

The War Against Terror

Re-read the final sections above on Islam and Islamophobia.

Question:

➢ In your opinion, what were the reasons for the wars in Afghanistan and Iraq? A number of reasons have been proposed by different commentators:

(Continued)

(Continued)

— Was it an act of revenge for September 11, inflicted by evil and corrupt Western powers, and particularly the US, in a drive for world domination?

— Was it to remove the threat of Weapons of Mass Destruction (WMD) and secure global peace?

— Was it to gain control of oil assets and maintain stability in the price of oil to safeguard national economies?

— Was it an attempt by the West to (perhaps misguidedly) impose their view of democracy and liberty on societies that are culturally and politically not ready or not aligned to their system?

➢ Now try to imagine how you would respond to this question if you were a Muslim living in Baghdad during the bombings. Give reasons for your answers.

Floya Anthias: Rethinking Social Divisions

According to Floya Anthias, the key element in any valid understanding of 'race' is the notion of *ethnos*: 'race can only be considered as an analytically valid category if it is incorporated within the more inclusive, albeit highly heterogeneous, category of ethnos' (Anthias 1990: 21). Anthias argues that *ethnos* provides 'race' with its 'analytical axis' and ontological validity. The characteristics of *ethnos* include:

• Inclusion and exclusion
• Difference and identity
• The construction of entities
• A historical point of origin or essence
• The construction of a collective difference from an 'other'.

Anthias (1990) makes a distinction between *discursive* and *systemic* forms of racism:

• **Discursive racism**: racism embedded in the worldview of Western cultures, as seen in the use of language about people of colour, representations, and the practices that take place within institutions, such as the law and education
• **Systemic racism**: the racism that is the product and consequence of structures.

Racist discourse draws upon social categorisation of people around a range of linguistic and cultural boundaries that we experience as a set of naturalising assumptions believed to have a biological origin. As Anthias explains:

> Racism is a form of discourse and practice that can be harnessed to different political projects but whose ontological and analytical status of 'race' derives from modes by which communal difference and identity are attributed and proclaimed. (Ibid.: 37)

The problem with Anthias's analysis at this point is that the notion of *ethnos* is ill defined and in the last analysis means nothing more than 'people'.

The social categorisation of people into separate social divisions has always had a central role to play in the social sciences. According to Floya Anthias's later argument (1998), such categorisation is a fundamental part of any system of classifying principles found in society (Durkheim and Mauss 1962; Lévi-Strauss [1949] 1969). She argues that although there are no consistent ways in which societies categorise people, these categories bestow individuals with characteristics of 'otherness' and/or 'sameness'; in other words, a constructed *difference* which is then seen to have recognised social effects in terms of determined outcomes.

Sociological theory has traditionally focused on class relations and has examined all other forms of stratification as, in the last analysis, dependent upon class divisions. Anthias and Yuval-Davis (1998) argue that these non-class based forms of stratification are equally significant in determining our life chances in a Weberian sense. Non-class based forms of stratification are central to our understanding of power relations, the structure of inequality and the organisation of social formations. Moreover, although we tend to think of such categories in a binary way and as mutually exclusive, social categorisation and social identification are not mutually exclusive and any one individual may cross several different dimensions of otherness and sameness at the same time. Social divisions have a central role to play in the development of social relationships, stretching *closure* where one group has resources it wishes to protect, to forms of subordinated inclusion in which exploitation is central. People are placed in a system of 'hierarchical production and organisation differently according to different grids' (Anthias 2003: 523) that underpin social divisions.

Anthias and Yuval-Davis (1998) strive to create a framework for theorising the social divisions of gender, ethnicity and class 'in terms of parameters of differentiation and inequality that lie at the heart of "the social"'. They argue that there are common parameters to the social divisions of gender, ethnicity, 'race' and class in terms of categories of *difference* and *positionality*. They use the concept of *ontological spaces* or domains of gender and ethnos to claim that their study must be undertaken in local and specific contexts with attention given to their construction. Within the complex interweaving of social relations, they identify social divisions as the parameters of social inequality and exclusion and these can be identified through local analyses of differentiated social outcomes. Drawing upon the postmodernist proliferation of identities, their argument is that the creation of specific social outcomes of different social processes is a product of what happens locally to people at several levels: the experiential, intersubjective, organisational and representational levels.

SOCIAL OUTCOMES OF DIFFERENT SOCIAL PROCESSES

Experiential: this focuses on the experiences of persons (within specific locatable contexts, say in the school, the workplace, or the neighbourhood) being defined as different, identified as belonging to a particular category.

Intersubjective: this arises from the level of intersubjective relations: the actions and practices that take place in relation to others (including non-person actors such as the police, the social security system and so on).

Organisational: this focuses on the institutional and other organisational ways in which the ontological spaces are played out: for example, family structures and networks, educational systems, political and legal systems, the state apparatus and the system of policing and surveillance. For example, how are sexuality, biological reproduction or population categories organised within institutional frameworks and in terms of the allocation of resources?

Representational: what are the symbolic and representational means, the images and texts, the documents and information flows around the ontological spaces? (Anthias and Yuval-Davis 1998: 6).

Anthias argues that experiential, intersubjective, organisational and representational factors should be seen as a series of connecting threads that make it possible for us to concentrate our analysis at different levels: the personal (experience), the action (interaction/practice, intersubjectivity), the institution/structure (the organisational), and the symbolic, discursive (representational).

The two problematics of *differentiation* and *positionality* are then brought together within an analysis of a context or habitus and field (Bourdieu 1990). Social divisions can then be seen as mutually reinforcing systems of domination and subordination, particularly in terms of processes and relations of unequal resource allocation, hierarchisation and inferiorisation. Such an analysis, Anthias argues, can indicate the connections between differentiation and positionality in producing specific social outcomes:

> In my understanding of social divisions, the specification of essential unities of identity and difference is abandoned in favour of the identification of ontological spaces or domains, which are contingent and variable in their specificities. A relational ontological space, or social domain, constitutes the framework for investigating the social relations of difference and inequality. The ontological spaces are not essentialist but themselves social in as much as they have experiential, intersubjective, organisational and representational forms. The concepts relating to the ontological spaces are merely signposts. Ethnos, for example, is a concept that can be a heuristic device enabling the delineation and specification of those experiential, intersubjective, organisational and representational processes related to the ontological space of collectivity. It is an abstraction. Nor need it

> emerge in any specific form. It enables the investigation of patterned social relations and
> their outcomes at a number of different levels. (Anthias and Yuval-Davis 1998)

The concepts of gender and ethnicity/race (ethnos) are related to ontological spaces by the use of *heuristic devices* (hypothesis-generating concepts) or a set of concepts about social divisions that Anthias claims have the following characteristics:

- The concepts do not purport to be a model with the aim of comparison
- The concepts do not overstate any extreme feature of observable phenomena
- By designating the *ontological territory* of a series of social relations, we are able to use the concepts to reflect on the experiential, intersubjective, organisational and representational aspects that relate what is observed to its local context and recognise variability
- Unlike categories, concepts are tools of analysis and, as such, do not claim to either exist or to be known or understood. These concepts allow us to view the social world in terms of a number of grids that can be organised or a set of problematic of assumptions about the nature of social division.

As Anthias explains:

> Gender, ethnos (ethnicity and 'race') and class may be seen as crosscutting and mutually
> interacting ontological spaces which entail social relations and social processes (having
> experiential, intersubjective, organisational and representational dimensions) that coalesce
> and articulate at particular conjunctures to produce differentiated and stratified social out-
> comes. Any analysis at the level of social outcomes cannot look at each social division in
> isolation from the other, therefore. The analogy of a grid may be useful which can be over-
> laid onto individuals. The different grids are experienced contextually and situationally as
> sets of simultaneous and mutually effective discursive instances and social practices. (Ibid.)

In the case of minority working-class women who are positioned differentially within a number of contradictory locations (family, labour market, sexuality and politics for example), social divisions come together to produce a coherent set of practices of subordination. In this way, such women occupy the worst social spaces – economic to political and cultural – in a range of social contexts. In contrast, white working-class men may be seen to be in a relation of dominance over minority women but are themselves in a relation of subordination in class terms. This leads to highly contradictory processes in terms of positionality and identity. Anthias argues that: 'This is one reason why Western feminism, organising around the category "woman", was unable to address issues of racism and economic subordination.'

Conclusion

This chapter has highlighted a number of questions that lie at the heart of the issue of racial division: What is 'race'? Should the concept/category be related to traditional approaches to stratification? Should 'race' be related to the emergence of capitalism? Is the central issue that of the struggle around resource allocation, or does this struggle comprise a diverse range of exclusions and inclusions that are independent of capitalism? Is the central issue one of identity? Is it in the nature of people to want to classify others as *Others* and does racism emerge from the very classification of people into races?

The scientific evidence suggests that there is no such thing as 'race', there are only people. However, there are racial discourses – processes of racialisation – and there are victims of racism. What the notion of institutional or systemic racism shows very clearly is the ability of human agency to create structures. Even though we may feel successful in our attempt to decentre the notion of race, this does not mean that we have banished racist discourse from the world or that we have successfully invalidated racism in the mind of the racist.

References

Adler, F.H. (1999) 'Antiracism, Difference and Xenologica', *Cultural Values* 3(4): 492–502.

Al-Azmeh, A. (1993) *Islams and Modernities,* Verso, London.

Alexander, C. (2002) 'Beyond Black: Re-thinking the Colour/Culture Divide', *Ethnic and Racial Studies* 25(4): 552–71.

Alexander, C. and Alleyne, B. (2002) 'Framing the Difference: Racial and Ethnic Studies in Twenty-first Century Britain', *Ethnic and Racial Studies* 25(4): 541–51.

Althusser, L. (1981) 'Marx's New Science', in Bottomore, T. (ed.) *Modern Interpretations of Marx,* Basil Blackwell, Oxford.

Anthias, F. (1990) 'Aspects of Ethnicity, Class and Generation amongst Greek Cypriots in Britain', in *Proceedings of the First International Conference on Cypriot Immigration: historical and sociological approaches,* Nicosia.

Anthias, F. and Yuval-Davis, N. (1998) *Women – Nation – State,* Macmillan, Basingstoke.

Barber, B. (1996) *Jihad vs. McWorld,* Ballantine Books, New York.

Barot, R. and Bird, J. (2001) 'Racialization: the Genealogy and Critique of a Concept', *Ethnic and Racial Studies* 24(4): 601–18.

Bhabha, H. (ed.) (1990) *Nation and Narration,* Routledge, London.

Bhabha, H. (1994) *The Location of Culture,* Routledge, London.

Blummaert, J. and Verschueren, J. (1998) 'The Role of Languages in European Nationalist Ideologies', in Schieffelin, B.B., Woolard, K.A. and P.V. Kroskrity (eds) *Language Ideologies: Practice and Theory,* Oxford University Press, New York & Oxford.

Bolaffi, G., Bracalenti, R., Braham, P. and Gindro, S. (eds) (2003) *Dictionary of Race, Ethnicity and Culture,* Sage, London.

Bonnett, A. (1999) *White Identities: Historical and International Perspectives,* Routledge, London.

Bourdieu, P. (1990) *Homo Academicus,* Polity Press, Cambridge.

Brockington, J.L. (1997) *The Sacred Thread,* Oxford University Press, New Delhi.

Carter, K., Edwards, K. and Herring, C. (2000) 'Not by the Color of Their Skins: Skin Tone Variations and Discrimination Against People of Color'. Paper presented at the Annual Meeting of the Association of Black Sociologists, Washington, DC.

Cashmore, E. and Troyna, B. (1990) *Introduction to Race Relations* (2nd edn), The Falmer Press, London.

Castles, S. and Kosack, G. (1985) *Immigrant Workers and Class Structure in Western Europe*, Oxford University Press, Oxford.

Connor, M. (1997) 'An African American Perspective on Generative Fathering', in Hawkins, A.J. and Dollahite, D.C. (eds) *Generative Fathering: Beyond Deficit Perspectives*, Sage, Thousand Oaks, Cal.

Cox, O.C. (1945) 'Race and Caste: A Distinction', *American Journal of Sociology* 50: 360–68.

Cox, O.C. (1948) *Caste, Class and Race: A Study in Social Dynamics*, Modern Reader Paperbacks, New York.

Cruz-Janzen, M.I., King, E.W. and Wardle, F. (2003) 'The Challenge of Declaring an Interethnic and/or Interracial Identity in Postmodern Societies', *SAGE Race Relations Abstracts* 28(1): 5–21.

Deleuze, G. and Guattari, F. (1987) *A Thousand Plateaus: Capitalism and Schizophrenia*, Minneapolis, UMP.

Denzin, Norman K. (2002) *Reading Race*, Sage, London.

Durkheim, E. and Mauss, M. [1903] (1962) *Primitive Classifications*, trans. Rodney Needham, University of Chicago Press, Chicago, Ill.

Dyer, R. (1997) *White*, Routledge, London.

Dyson, A.H. (1999) 'Transforming Transfer Unruly Children, Contrary Texts, and the Persistence of the Pedagogical Order', in Nejad, A. and Pearson, P.D. (eds) *Review of Research in Education* 24: 141–72.

Eadie, J. (2001) 'Shivers; Race and Class in the Emperilled Body', in Holliday, I. and Hassard, J. (eds) *Contested Bodies*, Routledge, London.

Fanon, F. (1952) *Black Skin White Masks*, Grove Press, New York.

Fanon, F. (1967) *The Wretched of the Earth*, Grove Press, New York.

Frye, M. (1992) 'White Woman Feminist', in *Willful Virgin: Essays in Feminism*, Crossing Press, Freedom, Cal.

Fukuyama, F. (1992) *The End of History and the Last Man*, Free Press, New York.

Fuller, G. (2002) 'The Future of Political Islam', *Foreign Affairs* 81(2): 48–60.

Gallagher, C.A. (1994) 'White Reconstruction in the University', *Socialist Review* 24: 165–87.

Gray, H. (1989) 'Television, Black Americans and the American Dream', *Critical Studies in Mass Communication* 6: 376–87.

Gray, H. (1995) *Watching Race: Television and the Struggle for 'Blackness'*, University of Minnesota Press, Minneapolis.

Green, K. (2002) 'The Other and Another Other', *Hypatia* 17(4): 1–15.

Gunder-Frank, A. (1967) *Capitalism and Underdevelopment in Latin America. Historical Studies of Chile and Brazil*, Monthly Review Press, New York.

Hall, S. (1992a) 'New Ethnicities', in Donald, J. and Rattansi, A. (eds) *Race, Culture and Difference*, Sage, London.

Hall, S. (1992b) 'The West and the Rest: Discourse and Power', in S. Hall and B. Gieben (eds) *Formations of Modernity*, Polity in association with Open University, Oxford.

Hall, S. (ed.) (1996a) *Representation: Cultural Representations and Signifying Practices*, Sage & Open University Press, London.

Hall, S. (1996b) 'Gramsci's Relevance for the Study of Race and Ethnicity', in Morley, D. and Kuan-Hsing, Chean (eds) *Critical Dialogues in Cultural Studies*, Routledge, London.

Hall, S. (1997) 'Interview with Peter Osbourne and Lynne Segal', *Radical Philosophy* 67: 32–39.

Harris, A. (1996) 'Life after Welfare, Women Work and Repeat Dependency', *American Sociological Review* 61 (June): 407–26.

Hartman, P. and Husband, C. (1974) *Racism and the Mass Media*, Davis-Poynter, London.

Hebdige, D. (1979) *Subculture: The Meaning of Style*, Routledge, London.

hooks, bell (1992) *Yearning: Race, Gender and Cultural Politics*, Turnaround, London.

Huntington, S. (1996) *The Clash of Civilizations*, Simon & Schwsters, New York.
Husband, C. (ed.) (1981) 'Race', in *Britain, Continuity and Change*, Hutchinson, London.
Laclau, E. and Mouffe, C. (1985) *Hegemony and Socialist Strategy*, Verso, London.
Lévi-Strauss, C. [1949] (1969) *The Elementary Structures of Kinship*, trans. J.H. Bell, Beacon Press, Boston, Mass.
Martin, A. (1999) 'A Meeting of Minds', *Adults Learning* 10(9): 16–27.
Merton, R. (1949) *Social Theory and Social Structure*, Free Press, New York.
Miles, R. (1980) 'Class, Race and Ethnicity: A Critique of Cox's Theory', *Ethnic and Racial Studies* 3(3): 169–87.
Miles, R. (1989) *Racism*, Routledge, London.
Miles, R. and Torres, R. (1999) 'Does "Race" Matter? Transatlantic Perspectives on Racism after "Race Relations"', in Torres, R., Miron, L. and Inda, J.X. (eds) *Race, Identity and Citizenship*, Blackwell, Malden, Mass.
Moon, D. (1999) 'White Enculturation and Bourgeois Ideology: the Discursive Production of "Good (White) Girls"', in Nakayama, T. and Martin, J.N. (eds) *Whiteness: The Communication of Social Identity*, Sage, London.
Nakayama, T. and Krizek, R. (1999) 'Whiteness as a Strategic Rhetoric', in Nakayama, T. and Martin, J.N. (eds) *Whiteness: The Communication of Social Identity*, Sage, London.
Norris, P. and Inglehart, R. (2002) 'Islamic Culture and Democracy: Testing the "Clash of Civilizations" Thesis', *Comparative Sociology* 1(3–4): 235–63.
Norris, P. and Inglehart, R. (2003) *Rising Tide: Gender Equality and Cultural Change Around the World*, Cambridge University Press, New York.
Omi, M. and Winant, H. (1993) 'On the Theoretical Status of the Concept of Race', in McCarthy C. and Crichlow, W. (eds) *Race Identity and Representation in Education*, Routledge, New York.
Parsons, T. (1965) 'The Normal American Family', in Farber, S.M., Mustacchi, P. and Wilson, R. (eds) *Man and Civilization: the Family's Search for Survival*, McGraw-Hill, New York.
Parsons, T. and Clark, K.B. (eds) (1966) *The Negro American*, Routledge, London.
Parsons, T. and Smelser, N. (1967) *Economy and Society*, Routledge, London.
Patterson, S. (1965) *Dark Strangers*, Pelican, London.
Poulantzas, N. (1979) *State, Power, Socialism*, Verso, London.
Rattansi, A. (1994) 'Western Racisms, Ethnicities and Identities in a "Postmodern" Frame', in Rattansi, A. and Westwood, S. (eds) *Racism, Modernity and Identity on the Western Front*, Polity, Cambridge.
Reid-Pharr, R. [1996] (2001) 'Bodily Becoming', in Holliday, I. and Hassard, J. (eds) *Contested Bodies*, Routledge, London.
Rex, J. (1983) *Race Relations in Sociological Theory* (2nd edn), Routledge and Kegan Paul, London.
Rex, J. and Moore, R. (1967) *Race, Community and Conflict*, Oxford University Press, Oxford.
Ritzer, G. (1996) *The McDonaldization of Society*, Pine Forge Press, Cal.
Shome, R. (1999) 'Postcolonial Interventions in the Rhetorical Canon: An "Other" View', in Lucaites, J.L., Condit, C.M. and Caudill, S. (eds) *Contemporary Rhetorical Theory: A Reader*, Guilford, New York.
Spivak, G.C. [1998] (1995) 'Can the Subaltern Speak?', in Ashcroft, B., Griffiths, G. and Tiffin, H. (eds) *The Post-Colonial Studies Reader*, Routledge, London.
St Louis (2002) 'Post Race/Post Politics? Activist – Intellectualism and the Reification of Race', *Ethnic and Racial Studies* 25(4): 652–75.
Wallerstein, I. (1979) *The Capitalist World-Economy*, Cambridge University Press, Cambridge.
Wallerstein, I. (1983) *Labor in the World Social Structure*, Sage, Beverly Hills, Cal.
Williams, R. (1981) *Culture*, Fontana, London.
Williams, R. [1975] (1990) *Television: Technology and Cultural Form*, Routledge, London.

Winant, H. (1994) *Racial Conditions: Politics, Theory, Comparisons*, University of Minnesota Press, Minneapolis.

Wood, B. (1998) 'Stuart Hall's Cultural Studies and the Problem of Hegemony', *British Journal of Sociology* 49(3) 399–414.

Wright, L. (2000) 'The Academic Pendulum and Self-Esteem of African American Males', *Perspectives* (Fall): 74–78.

Four

Chapter Outline

By the end of this chapter you should have a critical understanding of:

- The work of Michel Foucault on the history of sexuality

- The analysis of sex, gender, patriarchy, heterosexuality, sadomasochism and bisexuality

- The emergence of women's rights and the legal framework in a global context

- The functionalist and Marxist accounts of gender and sexuality

- The contribution of Queer Theory

- The impact of the emergence of the postmodern family on sexuality and gender relations

- The beauty system: Naomi Wolf

- The relationship between class, gender and images of beauty in the work of Beverley Skeggs

- Intellectual sexism and women's social mobility: the work of John Goldthorpe

- Gender classification in the risk society and 'The Normal Chaos of Love'

- The feminist critique of heterosexuality: Monique Wittig, Luce Irigaray and Judith Butler

- Maxine Sheets-Johnstone and the 'corporeal turn'

- Camille Paglia on sex and nature.

Gender and Sexuality

This chapter is an introduction to the sociology of sexuality; the major discourses surrounding sex, sexuality, sexual acts, identities and relationships. The connection of sexuality to gender will also be explored.

Sex is the site of one of our most strongly policed social divisions. It is the social division most likely to generate moral outrage and state intervention, for our culture, in common with most other cultures, attempts to exclude specific people from engaging in sexual relations. In addition, people who do choose to engage in sexual relationships will find that society prescribes a rigid, but arbitrary, set of rules on where and how to use either a vagina or a penis, and what one is not supposed to do with it or whom to share it with.

Before and throughout most of the twentieth century it was commonly assumed that social inequalities between men and women were biologically determined. Women were assumed to have a natural inferiority compared to men. Differences in 'sex' were assumed to be the cause of a range of social inequalities. Men were assumed to be stronger, more aggressive, yet more rational and superior in intelligence, whereas women were assumed to be more caring in nature, primarily because of their 'natural' child-bearing and child-rearing roles, more irrational and emotional. As a consequence, women had far fewer legal rights, political rights and career opportunities than did men.

Feminists were always highly sceptical of this argument. Oakley (1971) highlighted the significance of gender – our shared ideas of masculinity and femininity – and pointed to the ways in which gender roles (the roles men and women play) varied both over time and from place to place. In other words, there is nothing inevitable about male or female behaviour. Gender roles were culturally defined and socially produced rather than biological in origin.

The temptation to have romantic and or sexual relationships with members of the same sex is frowned upon, as are transsexuals, transvestites, people who regard themselves as transgendered, S&M participants or even people who at the same time exhibit masculine and feminine characteristics such as forms of dress. No discussion of these issues would be complete with looking first at the work of Michel Foucault.

Foucault on Sexuality

The most influential theorist on matters concerning the sexual body is Michel Foucault. In *The History of Sexuality*, Foucault politicises sexuality and its role within the processes of self-formation. Foucault shows how heterosexuality encodes and structures everyday life. In Foucault's work the 'social' and the 'sexual' become linked, through the notion of 'normal' behaviour.

Foucault's work on sexuality has to be seen as an account of how power became directly connected to the most intimate areas of the human body. Foucault analysed sexuality in terms of the development or emergence of 'discursive practices'. A 'discourse' for Foucault, is a body of statements that is both organised and systematic, and is in the form of a set of rules. Foucault referred to this historical analysis of discourse as an 'archaeology' of knowledge, which he used to show the history of truth claims.

From the initial analysis of classification, in his later books Foucault develops his *genealogical analysis* to examine the history of how groups of ideas come to be associated with normal sexuality. One of the central themes of Foucault's work was how discursive power works on bodies, and is seen most clearly in *The History of Sexuality*. In terms of his discussion of discipline, Foucault described the spreading notion of what constituted 'normal' through society as the 'carceral continuum'. The Enlightenment saw the development of bio-power, new forms of control over the bodies of people (by the use of new disciplinary technology). In the area of sexuality bio-power manifest itself as: new scientific disciplines which were concerned with 'an anatomo-politics of the human body' (Foucault 1990: 139) and regulatory controls or a 'bio-politics of the population' (ibid.).

Foucault developed what he called a *capillary* model of power in which he attempted to understand the 'relations of power' by looking at struggle and resistance:

- Struggles are concerned with resisting the effects of power on bodies
- Struggles are concerned with resisting the role of government in individual self-formation
- Struggles are concerned with the politics of self-definition and self-formation.

There are a number of common themes running through Foucault's work on sexuality. In the first volume of *The History of Sexuality*, Foucault explains that he wants to trace the origins of our 'restrained, mute, and hypocritical sexuality' (ibid.: 3) in which silence about sexuality became the norm (ibid.: 38). For Foucault a 'regimen' refers to these rules of how one ought to behave. The misuse of sexual pleasure could lead to death. Foucault draws upon the classical Greek text *The Interpretation of Dreams* by Artemidorus, who argues that nature had established the principle that there was a definite form of sexual act for each species, which was the one natural position. Other activities that Artemidorus disapproved of include: relations with gods, relations with animals, relations with corpses, relations with oneself and relations between women.

A number of sexual practices were 'problematised' and subjected to a rigid set of 'epistemic' rules, discursive and punitive practices that together formed a 'disciplinary' model. Critique of Foucault's work has revolved around the issue of whether Foucault had overstated the extent to which people could be 'subjected', leaving them little scope for resistance. Such resistance has become the point of departure for 'Queer Theory' (see below).

Women's Rights

In the nineteenth century British women had very few rights, and feminism – the movement for social, economic and political equality between men and women – has a long history. Towards the end of the seventeenth century, perhaps because of the chaos brought about by the English Civil War, there was a distinct increase in the production of social and political texts by women, particularly women from a working-class background. This phase of the feminist movement provided the foundation for what later became known as *first-wave feminism*. Many women were expressing their opinions about social and political issues in public for the first time. One such text was Mary Astell's (1694) *A Serious Proposal to the Ladies*, which criticised the institution of marriage and is unexpectedly 'modern' in both its tone and argument.

Women could not vote and as Sir William Blackstone explained: 'By marriage, the husband and wife are one person in law: that is, the very being or legal existence of the woman is suspended during that marriage'. Practically, this meant that, on marrying, normally 'both possession and control of a woman's property – including any monies she might earn from paid labour – passed to her husband' (cited in Levine 1987: 134). In the United Kingdom, it was only with the 1857 Matrimonial Causes Act that women obtained limited access to divorce, usually on a specific cause other than adultery. Women were also granted limited rights of access to children after divorce. In addition, women were granted rights to their property after a legal separation or a protection order given as a result of a husband's desertion. However, it was not until the 1937 Divorce Act that desertion and insanity became grounds for divorce.

After the First World War, British women began to acquire rights, including the right to vote, but they only won these rights very slowly. It has only been since 1990 that married women have been taxed independently on their own income with their own personal allowance. The right to be paid the same as a man for the same work, for example, was only given to women by the Equal Pay Acts, 1970 and 1983. However, employers could still legally discriminate against female workers and the right to be treated equally was granted by the Sex Discrimination Act (1975).

Equal Pay Acts 1970 and 1983

The purpose of the Equal Pay Act (1970) was to end discrimination in pay between men and women in the United Kingdom. The Act (1970) was based upon the concept of 'like work'; this meant that if a man and a woman were doing the same job, then they should be on the same pay scale. The problem with the 'like work' concept was that within a company men and women often do different tasks. Many work tasks were divided into male jobs and female jobs; often jobs done primarily by men were graded as more highly skilled and as a consequence overall pay discrimination continued. In 1983 the Act was amended to include the concept of 'equal pay for work of equal value', in other words if a man and a woman have different work tasks but the tasks add equal value to the end product or service, then the people doing the different tasks should be on the same pay scale.

Sex Discrimination Act 1975

The Sex Discrimination Act 1975 established, in the United Kingdom, the Equal Opportunities Commission which would investigate cases of sex discrimination and also campaign for greater gender equality. The 1975 Act made it illegal to discriminate on grounds of sex, and identified a number of different forms of discrimination:

- **Direct discrimination:** which occurs when a person is treated less favourably on grounds of sex
- **Indirect discrimination:** takes place when a condition must be satisfied in order to get a job or promotion, but one sex can satisfy the condition far more easily. The employer has to justify that condition as essential, otherwise indirect discrimination will be said to have taken place
- **Victimisation:** which is also covered by the Act.

Kingsmill Report on Women's Employment and Pay

In April 2001, the British government commissioned Denise Kingsmill to investigate the state of women's employment and pay. Kingsmill consulted the top management of 100 of the UK's leading private and public sector organisations. In December 2001 she published her Report which found an 18 percent earnings gap between men and women in the UK.

Why Narrow the Pay Gap?

Commenting on the Report, Kingsmill said:

> The Report highlights the demand for better human capital management in the UK. The overwhelming business case for the effective use of the talents and abilities of women offers the greatest potential for reducing the pay gap. My recommendations are aimed at helping organisations to achieve their strategic objectives and develop best practice processes which best serve their needs.

Question:

➢ According to the above quotation, what is the motivation for reducing the pay gap between men and women?

Kingsmill's recommendations included:

- Providing more information to staff within organisations, through voluntary pay reviews, which cover all aspects of women's employment
- The establishment of a Standards Board to look at the ways in which people are managed at work
- The commissioning of research on loss to the economy of not making the best use of women's skills in the labour market
- The use of training tax credits for employers who recruit and train women
- The introduction of rights of disclosure for individual employees to establish whether they are receiving pay equal to named colleagues.

EQUAL PAY: SOME GLOBAL COMPARISONS

Discrimination against women in the labour market is a controversial issue not only in the United Kingdom. According to The American Federation of Labor-Congress of Industrial Organizations, around the world, women are more likely than men to hold low-paid jobs.

(Continued)

(Continued)

- **Japan:** 37 percent of working women hold low-wage jobs compared with only 6 percent of men
- **United States:** 33 percent of working women hold low-wage jobs compared with 20 percent of men
- **United Kingdom:** 31 percent of working women hold low-wage jobs compared with 13 percent of men
- **France:** 25 percent of working women hold low-wage jobs compared with 8 percent of men
- **Sweden:** 8 percent of working women hold low-wage jobs compared to 3 percent of men.

Worldwide, women hold only 14 percent of administrative and managerial jobs and less than 6 percent of senior management jobs.

(Source: http://www.aflcio.org/front/faqs.htm)

What is Feminism?

Inspired and radicalised by the events leading up to the French Revolution, Mary Wollstonecraft argued against the forces that kept women ignorant and against the superficiality of activities that ladies were encouraged to engage in. Mary Wollstonecraft was an early proponent of educational equality between men and women, and her *Vindication of the Rights of Woman* (1792) was the first great feminist tract. In Paris, where she lived with the American Gilbert Imlay during much of the French Revolution, she was close to many of the Revolution's leading political figures.

ACTIVITY

Vindication of the Rights of Woman (1792)

Read the passage below and attempt the questions that follow:

To account for, and excuse the tyranny of man, many ingenious arguments have been brought forward to prove, that the two sexes, in the acquirement of virtue, ought to aim at attaining a very different character; or, to speak explicitly, women are not allowed to have sufficient strength of mind to acquire what really deserves the name of virtue. Yet it should seem, allowing them to have souls, that there is but one way appointed by Providence to lead mankind to either virtue or happiness.

If then women are not a swarm of ephemeron triflers, why should they be kept in ignorance under the specious name of innocence? Men complain, and with reason, of the follies and caprices of our sex, when they do not keenly satirise our headstrong passions and grovelling vices. Behold, I should answer, the natural effect of ignorance! The mind will ever be unstable that has only prejudices to rest on, and the current will run with destructive fury when there are no barriers to break its force. Women are told from their infancy, and taught by the example of their mothers, that a little knowledge of human weakness, justly termed cunning, softness of temper, outward obedience, and a scrupulous attention to a puerile kind of propriety, will obtain for them the protection of man; and should they be beautiful, everything else is needless, for at least twenty years of their lives.

(Source: Wollstonecraft [1792] accessed at
http://www.pinn.net/~sunshine/march99/wollstn3.html)

Questions:

➤ What is Mary Wollstonecraft suggesting is the cause of women's inequality?

➤ List the reasons Mary Wollstonecraft gives for women's inequality and state if you agree or disagree with each reason.

➤ Is Mary Wollstonecraft's argument still relevant today?

From this initial work of Mary Astell and Mary Wollstonecraft, we saw the emergence of what has become known as first-wave feminism, a social movement that focused on obtaining legal and political equality for women. In other words, first-wave feminism had the objective of campaigning for a society in which women should be able to do whatever men do. This movement informed later second-wave feminist work, such as Simone de Beauvoir's *The Second Sex* (1949) and Betty Friedan's *The Feminine Mystique* (1963).

With the introduction of equal pay legislation (1970 and 1983) and equal opportunities legislation (1975), feminist campaigning moved beyond looking at political and legal inequality. A key book in this change to second-wave feminism was Kate Millett's *Sexual Politics* (1971). Millett demonstrated that what appeared as natural was in fact socially constructed. This argument gave rise to *gynocentric feminism* – recognition that there is a sexual difference that feminists should celebrate.

However, what unites first-wave and second-wave feminism is the use that these feminists made of the concept of patriarchy.

Sylvia Walby: Theorising Patriarchy in a Global Context

In her early work, Sylvia Walby (1989) argues that much second-wave feminist theorising was seriously flawed because it was large-scale and assumed one sole basis upon which patriarchal practice had its foundation or causal base. She gives examples of such theorising:

- **Firestone (1974)**: who views reproduction as the basis of patriarchal relations
- **Delphy (1984)**: who views expropriation of women's labour by men in the home as the basis of patriarchal relations
- **Hartmann (1979)**: who argues that patriarchal relations operate at the level of the expropriation of women's labour by men
- **Rich (1980)**: who views the institution of compulsory heterosexuality as the basis of patriarchal relations
- **Brownmiller (1976)**: who views male violence and especially rape as the basis of patriarchal relations.

In contrast, Walby argues that patriarchy needs to be conceptualised at different levels of abstraction. She contends that it can take different forms and that it need not be a universalistic notion which is true in one form at all times and in all places. Drawing upon the processes that make up Giddens's theory of structuration, she attempts to construct a more flexible model of patriarchy which can either be in a 'public' or a 'private' form, and constructed out of six partially interdependent structures which have different levels of importance for different women at different times and places, rather than a simple universal base-superstructure model.

At its most abstract level, patriarchy exists as a system of social relations, built upon the assumption that whenever a man comes into contact with a woman, he will attempt to oppress her. The second level of patriarchy is organised around six patriarchal structures:

1 The patriarchal mode of production.
2 Patriarchal relations in paid work.
3 Patriarchal relations in the state.
4 Male violence.
5 Patriarchal relations in sexuality.
6 Patriarchal relations in cultural institutions, such as religion, the media and education.

Patriarchy is not universal; it can take different forms and is dependent upon a range of structures. If one structure of patriarchal relations is challenged and becomes ineffective, another can easily replace it. Men draw upon the structures of patriarchy in order to empower themselves and make their social actions more likely to be effective. By doing so, men reinforce these very patriarchal structures;

hence Walby's argument that patriarchal relations are not simply given, but are created by individual people as a medium and an outcome of the practices that make up their everyday lives. The structures of patriarchy are in constant flux as they are drawn upon by men, reinvented, reinforced and recreated.

ACTIVITY

Rosemary Crompton was highly critical of Sylvia Walby's position on patriarchy. Consider the following quotes by Crompton:

- 'However, it may be argued that Walby has not established the theoretical basis of a *system* of patriarchy.' (Crompton 1989: 114)
- 'the theoretical coherence of the patriarchal "mode of production" cannot be sustained ... neither can Walby's claims to have established a "theory" of patriarchy as such.' (Ibid.: 115)
- '... the assumption that men as a category are driven to oppress women as a category – a position which is profoundly unsociological.' (Ibid.: 115)

Question:

➤ Do you accept or reject the above comments that Rosemary Crompton makes about Sylvia Walby's arguments? State the reasons for your answer.

In recent years a number of personal accounts of second-wave feminism and feminist movements have appeared. One good example is Susan Brownmiller's book *In Our Time: Memoir of a Revolution* (1999) in which she outlines her motivation behind becoming a feminist activist in New York in the late 1960s and her attitude to such issues as abortion. Rosen (2000) argues that the origins of second-wave feminism in the United States are to be found in the politicising of people's identity in the 1950s, when there was a major concern, in governmental circles, about how to contain communism. It was during this time that many American women came to realise that 'their identity as females had become the basis for their exclusion' (Rosen 2000: 36). However, she is critical of the consequences of the second wave:

Paradoxically, the exposure of so many crimes and secrets did little to cast feminists as agents of change. Although activists challenged all kinds of received wisdom, including the language permitted by men on the street, in the bedroom, in the office, and in political office, the cumulative impact of all these revelations also helped implant an image of women as passive victims of villainous men. (Ibid.: 195)

In her more recent work, Sylvia Walby (2002, 2003) argues that many of the ambitions and struggles that second-wave feminism was concerned with have been accomplished. As a consequence feminism has changed because of the changing global context in which it now operates: 'Feminism is being re-shaped by its articulation through a global discourse of human rights and an increased focus on state intervention' (Walby 2002: 533).

For Walby there has been a 'transition' in the gender regime that has provided women with greater opportunities for participation in the political process and also to have what were previously seen as 'feminist demands' incorporated within the political mainstream. Since the Treaty of Amsterdam (1999) equality of opportunity has become a central organising principle of the European Union. There is legal protection for women against male violence, employment protection and a range of other issues initiated by governmental bodies such as the United Kingdom's Women's Unit. These initiatives reflect the success of the various women's social movements over the previous decades.

EQUAL TREATMENT FOR MEN AND WOMEN: THE TREATY OF AMSTERDAM

Article 141 (former Article 119) of the Treaty of Rome (1957) established the principle that men and women should get equal pay for equal work. From 1975 onwards there was a series of EU directives aimed at ending all forms of discrimination at work.

Article 2 of the Treaty of Amsterdam seeks to expand gender equality. As the EU make clear in their briefing notes:

The Charter of Fundamental Rights of the European Union, adopted in December 2000, includes a chapter entitled 'Equality' which sets out the principles of equality between men and women. It states that 'Equality between men and women must be ensured in all areas, including employment, work and pay.'

In June 2000, the Commission also adopted a Communication entitled *Towards a Community Framework Strategy on Gender Equality* (2001–05). Its purpose is to establish a framework for action within which all Community activities can contribute to attaining the goal of eliminating inequalities and promoting equality between women and men.

Walby argues that globalisation has 'facilitated new spaces, institutions and rhetoric' based upon the development of human rights discourses derived from the United Nations which have a 'hybridized rather than purely Western form'

(Walby 2002: 534). Gender issues have also become mainstream in economics, again notably in terms of equal opportunities policies and employment regulation. She argues that there are four elements that have brought about the new feminist politics:

1 The 'movement from separatist autonomous groups to engagement with the state'.
2 The 'fading of radical feminist and socialist discourse' and the movement towards 'equal rights discourse'.
3 Increased global communication between feminist networks.
4 Utilisation of new political spaces developed by global institutions such as the European Union and the United Nations.

In contrast to Walby's optimistic view of globalisation, many other feminist writers have pointed to the link between processes of globalisation and neo-liberal reform of welfare provision, IMF structural adjustment programmes, the expanding global sex trade, the expansion of the prison industrial complex, and the migration of women into low-paid domestic service – all factors that are hostile to women's interests and concerns.

Ursula Biemann (2002) argues that globalisation is a highly gendered process and that there has been a 'feminization of migration', in that compared with migrants in previous decades, a significant number of economic migrants in the world today are women. Biemann argues that the processes of globalisation directly address women as sexual beings, in that women's labour is being sexualised. The migration politics of European states, including European Union member states, and North America, directly encourage migrant women into the sex industry. The Swiss Government, argues Biemann, will only issue 'cabaret' visas to non-European female migrants that are dependent upon employment contracts with the cabaret sector. Each year there are 500,000 migrant women recruited into the European entertainment industry, mainly from the former communist countries of Eastern Europe. Biemann argues that 'The official policy of the EU and the European states is to fight human trafficking, but migration politics allow the sex trade to enjoy an increasing supply of marginalized and economically disadvantaged women.'

The civil rights and sexual governance of the EU that Walby describes as a major defender of women's interests ignores those of marginalised and economically disadvantaged women, particularly if they have chosen to go into sex work. The people who draw up the policies and protocols of the European Union cannot understand why a woman would want to be a sex worker and therefore cannot understand the need for employment regulation. For those non-EU female migrants who do not go into the sex industry, the other main avenue of employment is domestic service.

The employment protection and other legal/political advantages that Walby describes have not benefited all women. If some women are freed from the drudgery of housework and the demands of child care, it is often because another woman has been employed to do it instead. Although no reliable figures exist for the number of global migrants working as domestic servants, Simone Odierna (2001) calculated that in Germany alone there were 2.4 million people working as domestic servants in private houses; earning less than the minimum wage and with no social security; 90 percent of these people were women. Helma Lutz explains:

> Due to globalization, house and care work is a cheap product that can be 'bought in': the impoverished and completely de-regularized labour markets of the world offer a large reservoir for these services. The global care chain has become an aspect of the international division of labour. (Lutz 2002: 100–1)

Anderson and Phizacklea (1997) found the following common problems for women in this situation:

* Working unpaid hours
* Low income
* Less than minimum wage
* Denial of wages in cases of dismissal following a trial period
* Refusal by employers to arrange legal resident status – usually for tax purposes
* Control and sexual harassment
* Pressure to do additional work outside of the family for friends or colleagues
* Excessive workloads, especially in relation to child care and care of the elderly.

Anderson and Phizacklea argue that all countries have employment hierarchies built upon racial assumptions and stereotypes that determine people's rate of pay. In this schema, marginalised and economically disadvantaged women from outside the EU are at the very bottom of the ladder.

The US-led global-war-on-drugs is another area where the interests of marginalised and economically disadvantaged women come face-to-face with the processes of globalisation. The number of women in prisons across the world has significantly increased because of the global-war-on-drugs. As we saw in our previous discussion of the underclass, across Europe and North America being in paid employment is seen as the norm, irrespective of how many people are without work. Moreover, paid work is deemed both a duty and a responsibility and it is a central element of the work ethic that gainful employment is morally superior to all the alternative lifestyle options – it has become an abnormal moral failing not to work. Julia Sudbury (2002) argues that in both Europe and North America social problems have become redefined as criminal problems, in other words there has been a general criminalisation of the lifestyles of poorer people. The cost of 'tough-on-crime' policies is borne by reducing the cost of providing welfare and the increase in the prison population is mainly female. Again, it is marginalised and economically disadvantaged women, particularly black women, who bear the cost of neo-liberal processes of globalisation. As Sudbury (2002: 61) explains: 'Criminalization therefore became the weapon of choice in dealing with the social problems caused by the globalization of capital and the problems it engendered'.

Sudbury goes on to argue that this process of criminalisation gave rise to the *prison industrial complex*:

> ... a symbiotic and profitable relationship between politicians, corporations, the media and state correctional institutions that generates the racialized use of incarceration as a response to social problems rooted in the globalization of capital.' (Ibid.: 61)

The process of economic globalisation has resulted in the 'unhindered super-exploitation of predominantly young women of colour' (ibid.: 60).

In the United Kingdom in 1980, 4.4 percent of women serving prison sentences were convicted of drug-related offences, however, by 2001 the figure had increased to 39 percent. Many women, Sudbury argues, are coerced into importing drugs into Europe and North America, however, many choose to do so in an effort to support their families. As Sudbury's research concludes: 'The failure of the legal economy to provide adequate means for women's survival is the incentive for those who choose to enter the drug trade as couriers' (ibid.: 70).

GROWTH IN FEMALE PRISON POPULATIONS – GLOBAL PRESS COVERAGE

Iowa, US

Iowa's female prison population jumped 228 percent between 1990 and June 2002, while the men's population grew 105 percent, state records show.

The number of female inmates in Iowa's prisons is projected to continue rising over the next decade, according to a new report by the Iowa Division of Criminal and Juvenile Justice Planning.

In June 2002, 670 women were being held in state prisons. By 2012, that number is expected to grow to 994, an increase of 48 percent, according to the division.

Lettie Prell, a state analyst and the report's chief author, said the increase is driven by the same factors that also have caused the male population to grow.

'It's an increase in prison admissions, particularly for drug offenses; the long-term effect of abolishing parole for certain crimes; and an increase in average lengths of stay in prison,' Prell said.

(Source: http://www.dadi.org/femprisn.htm)

(Continued)

(Continued)

United Kingdom

The female population is the fastest-growing section of the prison estate. It has more than doubled in six years, rising to 3,392 in 1999. It is an extraordinary increase, particularly when the facts about women and prison are considered … the number of women sentenced for drug offences has risen dramatically.

(Source: http://society.guardian.co.uk/crimeandpunishment/
story/0,8150,431172,00.html)

California

Since mandatory sentencing laws went into effect in the mid 1980s, the California female prison population has skyrocketed. At the end of 1980, women in California's prisons totaled 3,564. In 1998 the population rose to 10,876 an increase of 305 percent in 12 years.

Every prison for women in California is 160 percent or more above its designed capacity. Although African-American women make up roughly 13 percent of California's female population, they constitute 33.6 percent of the California female prison population. Although white females are around 48 percent of the females of California, they make up only 37 percent of the state's female prison population. Latinas constitute 22.3 percent of the female prison population.

(Source: http://www.women-as-allies.org/Conference2002.htm)

UK: The Centre for Crime and Justice Studies Report

Since 1995, 12,000 additional prison places have been made available at a cost to the tax payer of £1.28 billion, an average of £100,000 per place.

The prison population as of 26 July 2002 was 71,723, up by 4,464 for the same month last year. Of these 3,785 were adult women, 623 were female young offenders (under 21), 56,363 were adult men and 10,952 were male young offenders. The prison population is continuing to rise. The number of female prisoners is now at an all-time high.

Young offenders in prison are aged between 15 and 21 years. Those aged 15–17 are separated from those aged 18–21 and resources have been poured into improving facilities for the 15–17 year olds. There is still considerable room for improvement in facilities for 18–21s.

(Source: The Centre for Crime and Justice Studies;
http://www.kcl.ac.uk/depsta/rel/ccjs/crimescene/sept2002.html)

Australia

Another indicator pointing to an underlying social malaise is that between 1994 and 1998 the number of NSW [New South Wales] women convicted of stealing without violence dropped by 13 percent, but the number convicted of credit card and social security fraud increased by 37 percent. These are offences directly related to economic need. Far fewer women are jailed than men, but the number of female inmates is rising sharply – in NSW it trebled over the same four-year period. The three major crimes were fraud, stealing without violence and drug offences.

(Source: http://www.wsws.org/articles/2000/nov2000/pris-n01.shtml)

The EU may offer employment and other legal protection for many women, but not for all, as Walby made clear in her early work; if one structure of patriarchal relations is challenged and becomes ineffective, another can easily replace it.

What Is Heterosexuality?

The terms 'heterosexual' and 'homosexual' did not exist until the late nineteenth century; neither term appeared in the first edition of the *Oxford English Dictionary*. However, because heterosexual intercourse can result in pregnancy and reproduction, there is an assumption that heterosexuality is both the norm and superior to any alternative sexuality. However, for most heterosexuals having sex is largely divorced from the act of procreation, and most of the time heterosexuals have sex for reasons other than having children. So what is sex and why do people want to have sex?

Identifying the functions and purposes of sex is problematic as the question assumes that there is an impersonal purpose beyond individual human agency. Antonio Gramsci does look at such impersonal deterministic factors that underpin the functions and purposes of sex. However, most commentators such as Don E. Marietta Jr (1997) argue that there is a rich variety of reasons why people engage in sexual activities, but it is *people* who have purposes, not sex itself; sex has no agency. Sex is used by people as a means to an end of their own choosing. The functions and purposes of sex then become diverse, argues Marietta, including:

• Procreation
• To satisfy a range of individual physical, mental and emotional aspects of a person's life
• To express affection

- To express a feeling of unity between two people
- To give pleasure
- To exercise power or humiliate another
- To make money.

ACTIVITY

What Is Sex? The Clinton/Lewinsky Débâcle

In 1998, the then American President Bill Clinton was said to have lied under oath about a sexual relationship with former White House intern Monica Lewinsky. Throughout his testimony to the Grand Jury, President Clinton steadfastly insisted that in his view he did not have a sexual relationship with Monica Lewinsky. However, in her evidence to the Starr Report, Monica Lewinsky's story was very different:

> According to Ms Lewinsky, she performed oral sex on the President on nine occasions. On all nine of those occasions, the President fondled and kissed her bare breasts. He touched her genitals, both through her underwear and directly, bringing her to orgasm on two occasions. On one occasion, the President inserted a cigar into her vagina. On another occasion, she and the President had brief genital-to-genital contact.

> (Source: The Starr Report quoted from
> http://news.bbc.co.uk/1/hi/events/clinton_under_fire/starr_report/169555.stm)

In his testimony to the Grand Jury, President Clinton argued that most Americans would define a sexual relationship as 'sleeping together ... having intercourse':

> If you said 'Jane and Harry had a sexual relationship' – and we are not talking about people being drawn into a lawsuit and being given definitions and great efforts being made to trip them in some way, but you are just talking about people in ordinary conversation – I bet that the Grand Jurors, if they were talking about two people they knew and said they had a sexual relationship, they meant they were sleeping together, they meant they were having intercourse together. ... I believe that that is the definition that most ordinary Americans would give. ... I believe that the common understanding of the term, if you say, two people are having a sexual relationship, most people believe that includes intercourse. ... I would have thought that that's what nearly everybody thought it meant.

> (Source: President Clinton quoted from
> http://news.bbc.co.uk/1/hi/events/clinton_under_fire/starr_report/169555.stm)

According to *Black's Law Dictionary*, a married person committing 'adultery' is involved in an act of sexual intercourse with someone other than his or her spouse.

Questions:

➤ Did President Clinton have a 'sexual relationship' with Monica Lewinsky or was it simply 'inappropriate intimate contact'? Or sexual gerrymandering? Outline the reasons for your answer.

➤ Is sex always sexual intercourse? Or would kissing count as sex?

The Social Construction of Heterosexuality

What does it mean to be a *heterosexual* person? Being a heterosexual person is being a 'normal' person. 'Other' people have 'sexuality' but heterosexual people are 'just people'. However, we need to look at heterosexuality through the interlocking axes of power, spatial location and history.

The notion of heterosexual is objectified and although publicly displayed in film, other media and on the streets, it remains a largely invisible category. What constitutes heterosexual sex is problematical. Heterosexual people are simply 'people', that is, the category is almost devoid of any objective meaning except for masking a range of assumptions about what people should not do in terms of their sexuality that maintain sexual divisions within the culture. Historically, heterosexuals have more control over the definition of themselves and are highly unlikely to be classed as Other.

In the 1990s there was a significant increase in the level of political activism amongst gays and lesbians who had 'come-out' since the beginning of AIDS. In Britain, the activist group Outrage captured the news headlines because of their tactic of 'outing' closet homosexuals (using a number of methods to force unwilling individuals to admit publicly that they were homosexual). Outrage has also been active in other areas fighting anti-gay discrimination, prejudice and violence. In particular, building on the work of Michel Foucault (1977), Outrage has attempted to remake and remodel the identity of the homosexual man and lesbian woman, moving away from the notion of 'gay' and labelling themselves as 'queer'. Individuals who describe themselves as 'homosexual', in the eyes of Outrage, are accepting a heterosexual and false-scientific view of sexuality, in which the homosexual is marginalised and can only be accepted as a person if they reject their 'queerness' or deny the legitimacy of their chosen sexuality. People who describe themselves as homosexuals are merely attempting to assimilate themselves into heterosexual life by accepting a role as a member of a distinct minority who ask for tolerance but will always be regarded as sexually wrong.

WHAT IS HETEROSEXISM?

The assumption that all people live and behave as heterosexuals and that people who do otherwise are abnormal. Heterosexism generates social division by judging non-heterosexuals as inadequate, incapable and inferior.

In contrast, heterosexuality appears to be a 'natural' and neutral category, but in the last analysis the concept is historically constructed through discourse. Taking our starting point from Foucault, as we have done in previous chapters, discourses of heterosexuality are again viewed in terms of *exteriority*, in which we do not search for the true meaning – or essential nature – of what it means to be hetero-sexual, but rather in terms of the rhetorical character of what people *say* it means to be heterosexual:

- Heterosexuality is identified as a privileged essential identity
- Heterosexuality is regarded as the positive universal whereas any other way of conducting oneself sexually is the negative particular
- Heterosexuality represents sexual cohesion and through procreation is the instrument of nation-building
- Heterosexuality limits and distorts our conception of sexuality.

These assumptions reinforce the view that most people would be heterosexuals unless something unfortunate had happened to them: hormone imbalance, mental illness, sexually abused as children, etc.

Heterosexuality is a taken-for-granted experience structured upon a varying set of supposed supremacist assumptions: biological, cultural, moral. Sexualities that differ from heterosexuality, by contrast, have become margin-alised and have been denied the privileges of normativity; they are marked as inferior – sexually wrong. In terms of homosexuality in the United Kingdom, up until 1861 sodomy was still punishable by execution. In that year the death penalty for this crime was replaced by a prison term of between ten years and life. However, the 1885 Criminal Law Amendment Act widened the range of sexual activities defined as offences, by introducing the catch-all phrase 'gross indecency', which criminalised such activities as men masturbating each other, any form of contact between male genitalia or two men kissing in public. Perhaps surprisingly, even given the changes to the law in 1967 which decrim-inalised such activities between consenting adults in private, in 1990 almost 5,000 gay men were convicted for consenting homosexual relations. Sexual relationships between females are not as criminalised an activity as between men; this may well be based upon the legal prejudice that women have little interest or desire for sex. In a similar fashion, men who are penetrated are free from prosecution, because they are assumed to be passive, playing a female role.

In addition, the law does not recognise transsexuality, and only a man and a woman can marry. Any transition from female to male or male to female has no legal standing, and post-operative transsexuals are unable to marry or take up the rights of their new gender with the social security system.

Heterosexuality can never be a 'free-floating signifier', it is always a form of oppression linked with the patriarchal social and economic structures from which it emerged. For the heterosexual population, the hegemony of heterosexuality is internalised and experienced as freedom and pleasure and possibility.

In contrast, 'queer' activism has a number of characteristics that both highlight the arbitrary and historically constructed nature of the heterosexual identity:

- 'Queer' activism is highly political, but above party politics
- 'Queer' activists reject the rational sexual categories imposed upon us all, both homosexual and straight, male and female, in which we are asked to define our selves as sexually 'normal'/ heterosexual or otherwise
- 'Queer' activism aims to destabilise the power relations that maintain these categories' that force homosexuals into a private world
- 'Queer' activism refuses to accept homosexuals as a minority group in the population.

Drawing upon Deleuze and Guattari's (1987) notion of *assemblage*, from the point of view of the 'queer' activists, heterosexuality should be seen as a form of strategic rhetoric. In other words, heterosexuality is a rhetorical construction, not an essential category. Heterosexuality is used to exercise power within the social fabric, it is a territorialising machine which identifies the places where people can and cannot place themselves within the society. The work of Deleuze and Guattari is explained in the concluding chapter.

ACTIVITY

Queer Identity

Many lesbians and gays have questioned the notion of 'queer' and the identity that goes with it. Consider the following examples:

> Assimilationism, as a term used to apply to minority groups in society, is the desire to merge – or the practice of merging – with the dominant majority. (Toby Manning, *Gay Times*, April 1995: 19, 20)

> Assimilationism is generally used in a slightly pejorative way to describe efforts amongst lesbian and gay men to become part of society. My own feeling is that [at Stonewall]

(Continued)

(Continued)

we're not aiming towards a situation where everyone becomes the same – it's all about recognition and respect for difference. That's what makes life and society interesting. We're campaigning for social justice and equality. I don't see that as collaborating. (Angela Mason, Executive Director of the Stonewall Group. Source: *Gay Times*, April 1995: 19, 20)

Assimilationism has been the dominant lesbian and gay rights strategy for the last 30 years, emphasising law reform, and the idea that the best way to advance our interests is by quietly blending in with mainstream heterosexual society. However, since the legal system has been devised by and is dominated by heterosexuals, that inevitably means that we win equality on terms which are dictated by straights. The end result is the phenomenon of 'hetero homos' – queer versions of heterosexual lifestyle and morality. The opposite of assimilation is not separatism. It is the proud assertion of a distinctive queer identity and culture. Assimilation implies that there is nothing worthwhile or valuable in the lesbian and gay experience. Queer emancipation does not depend on us adapting to the heterosexual status quo, but on us radically transforming it. In questioning and rejecting the predominant social view that homosexuality is wrong and inferior, many of us also end up challenging other social assumptions. While equal rights are an important first step, they do not amount to full queer emancipation. There's a need for a complete overhaul for all the laws and values around sex – a post-equality agenda. This would benefit both heterosexuals and homosexuals and it creates the possibility of a new radical consensus for social change which transcends sexual orientation. (Peter Tatchell, Outrage activist. Source: *Gay Times*, April 1995: 19, 20)

Question:

➤ Do you accept or reject Peter Tatchell's arguments? Give the reasons for your answer.

Functionalism and Marxism on Sexuality

The traditional heteronormative sociological approaches such as functionalism and Marxism have said little about sexuality outside of the context of the family. For functionalism and Marxism, the family, and in particular the social practices of mothers, has important functions for the reproduction of the wider society. In addition, these theories assume that motherhood represents the central biological difference between men and women.

For Parsons, the nuclear family had two key functions to perform in the modern world:

1   The socialisation of young children – providing guidance and opportunities for children to internalise the culture of the wider society.
2   The stabilisation of adult personalities – which included the sexual relationship between a heterosexual married couple.

For the Marxist, the structure of society is capitalist, and the role of the patriarchal family is to maintain that structure by reproducing labour power; in numerous ways mothers prepare the future workforce. From the point of view of the capitalist, this is the cheapest and most efficient way in which capitalism can produce a new generation of workers. In addition, because the man is forced by economic necessity into the role of the breadwinner, the patriarchal family facilitates economic dependence.

Engels's *The Origin of the Family, Private Property and the State* as the primary Marxist text on gender is regarded by Jennifer Pen as:

> theoretically inadequate not only to the immediacy and totality of the Women's Liberation Movement, but in Engels's heterosexism as well. The determinism of … much Marxism, combined with the prudery and heterosexism of most Leftist organizations, provoked many gay and lesbian activists to eschew Marxism entirely. (Pen 2003)

Drawing upon the work of Raya Dunayevskaya, who has explored Marx's *Ethnological Notebooks*, Pen argues that there is a significant rift between Marx's reading of anthropological authors such as Henry Lewis Morgan, and Engels's use of these same authors. Dunayevskaya argues that Marx's notebooks contain a powerful Hegelian-Marxist dialectic that is capable of producing:

> multiple revolutionary subjectivities and pathways to revolution across human history. … contrasted … with Engels's reduction of the anthropological evidence to a unilinear determinism. Engels's rigidity about historical movement was a philosophic error which muted Marx's dialectics and led to biologism: the belief that our biology determines our fate. Engels's theories about gender in *Origin of the Family* were too inflexible, hence not open to the subjectivity of the actual Women's Liberation Movement when women loudly declared that biology is NOT destiny. (Pen 2003)

Engels argued that the respect given to women in ancient societies flowed from the material base of their reproductive powers. 'This already reduces women's subjectivity and universality, since it implies that women are seen only through their child-bearing capacities.' (Pen 2003). In his discussion of modern individual sex love, Engels makes it clear that the only legitimate sexuality is heterosexuality. In addition, the notion of *woman* is conflated with *mother*, which in itself is bad for the women's movement, but also such an approach can be used to silence gay men and lesbians as sexual beings, Pen maintains:

> Biological determinism is vulgar materialism, not historical dialectics. False naturalizing is a by-product of biologism. Categories of 'natural' and 'unnatural' are consistently formulated and used against les-bi-gay people, and against all women who defy the pretensions

of bourgeois morality. So, it is hardly surprising that when Engels does refer to homosexuality, he categorizes it as a 'perversion,' 'degradation,' and an 'unnatural vice.' (Ibid.)

Pen concludes by saying the complexity of human social relations cannot be contained in Engels's rigid categories or strictly functional conceptions of gender.

Antonio Gramsci (1957) rejected the traditional Marxian economic deterministic argument. As we saw in the chapter on stratification and class, writing from the prison cell in the 1930s, Gramsci made a distinction between two parts of the state:

1 **Political society**: which contained all the repressive State institutions, such as the police and the army.
2 **Civil society**: which contained all the institutions, such as the mass media, which attempted to manipulate our ideas; the nuclear family had a central role to play here because of its emphasis on socialisation.

The state rules by consent although it has the ability to use force if necessary. However, the state would always prefer to use negotiating skills to produce a compromise. The state attempts to form a *historic bloc*, which involves making compromises with different groups, in an effort to maintain solidarity. Later Marxists such as Ernesto Laclau and Chantal Mouffe argue that the notion of *hegemony* involves the 'privileging of the political moment in the structuration of society' (Laclau and Mouffe 2001: xii). Social division is the product of democratic politics: 'Politics, we argue, does not consist in simply registering already existing interests, but plays a crucial role in shaping political subjects' (ibid.: xvii).

Laclau and Mouffe are highly critical of Erik Olin Wright and Nicos Poulantzas's attempts to redefine the working class within new boundaries. Mouffe (2000) develops this argument about the nature of social division. This provides the essential condition for the emergence of an antagonism that becomes *political* in nature, as people are given collective identities which establish them as on either side of a political divide. Gramsci's arguments formed the basis of the Regulation School's conception of Fordism.

For Gramsci, sexuality had an important role to play within Fordism.

The Emergence of the Postmodern Family

In the last few decades there has been a series of demographic shifts that have significantly impacted upon family patterns.

- A rising divorce rate
- A growth in the illegitimacy rate especially amongst young mothers who are still children themselves

- A significant increase in lone parenting, surrogate mothers, and gay and lesbian families
- An increasing number of woman in the workforce and a consequent economic decline in the need for women to marry
- And with the greater liberation of women, the knocking down of what Shorter (1975) refers to as the 'nest' conception of nuclear family life.

These changes highlighted the arbitrary nature of family roles and undermined the assumed biological nature of motherhood. In contrast to the Marxian and functionalist view of motherhood as the product of biologically determined differences, postmodern perspectives view motherhood as a patriarchal and heterosexual construct; motherhood is a contested social category that can only be understood within the given gender regimes of modernity. Family relationships and other living arrangements within a range of households not traditionally classed as *families*, have become more ambivalent, diverse, contested, fluid and undecided in nature. Within modernity, individuals were always carriers of a gendered culture; now they were seen to be this.

Households now reflect multiplicity of relationships in which people find themselves and household structures reflect the values, attitudes, opinions, lifestyles and personalities of the household members/participants. In the late twentieth century there was a lesbian baby boom in the industrialised countries. Lesbian households with children, either via donor insemination, adoption or fostering can be variously named: the reinvented family, dual-orientation households, lesbian-led families, planned lesbian mother families, etc. However, there remain both legal obstacles and prejudice against lesbians and gay men adopting children. Charlotte J. Patterson found that lesbian and gay parents and their children are a diverse group. However, courts in the United States have expressed a number of concerns about the possible effects on children of having gay or lesbian parents:

- The development of sexual identity may be impaired among children of lesbian or gay parents so that children themselves are more likely to become gay or lesbian
- Children's personal development may be impaired; children may be less psychologically healthy
- Children may experience difficulties in social relationships, be stigmatised or teased
- Children with gay or lesbian parents may be more likely to be sexually abused by the parent or by the parent's friends or acquaintances.

The research in the area suggests that there is no foundation to any of these concerns.

> In summary, there is no evidence to suggest that lesbians and gay men are unfit to be parents or that psychosocial development among children of gay men or lesbians is compromised in any respect relative to that among offspring of heterosexual parents. Not a single study has found children of gay or lesbian parents to be disadvantaged in any significant respect relative to children of heterosexual parents. Indeed, the evidence to date

suggests that home environments provided by gay and lesbian parents are as likely as those provided by heterosexual parents to support and enable children's psychosocial growth. (Patterson 2003. http://www.apa.org/pi/parent.html)

This is an interesting area. However, what is significant for us is how lesbian-parented families together with the more general changing nature of families/households, challenge the traditional theoretical understandings of family intimacy and undermine the belief in a biologically determined gender division that traditionally was used as the foundation for the privileged position of heterosexuality. The appeal to a biologically determined motherhood can no longer be seen as valid and, as such, the heterosexuality/homosexuality division becomes questionable.

Although lesbian and gay activists have had a great deal of success in removing the derogatory labels, some activities are still regarded as perverted.

Marriage: An Inequitable Institution?

In 1976, Jessie Bernard published her influential study *The Future of Marriage*, in which she argued that men benefited much more than women from being married. Married men were much more likely to have better health – both physically and mentally – than single men; higher incomes, higher status and generally more successful careers. In contrast, single women were much less likely to suffer ill-health and depression than married women. Moreover, single women had more successful careers, higher incomes and more status. Bernard attributed this to the 'Pygmalion effect' – women change their lifestyle and personalities to fit in with their husbands' needs. This was a theme taken up by a number of feminists in the 1980s and 1990s, such as: Hartmann (1981), Chafetz (1990), Lengermann and Niebrugge-Brantley (1990) and Delphy and Leonard (1992) who argued that:

> Within the context of the family system specifically, we see men exploiting women's practical, emotional, sexual and reproductive labour. Loving women does not prevent men from exploiting them. (Delphy and Leonard 1992: 258)

The argument here is that:

- Women still have the *responsibility* for housework – men may help but this help is discretionary
- Home is a place of leisure for men
- Women provide most of the emotional care within families
- Women are expected to please men and organise their own lives around other members of the family.

However, one of the criticisms of this approach is that feminists have a tendency to express rather than establish the exploitation within marriage. Feminists assume that women cannot redefine the housewife role and exercise power over men.

Who Benefits the Most from Marriage?

Ken Dempsey (2002) published a survey of 85 people, both male and female, which examined their perceptions of fairness regarding the division of labour within the home, child care, feeling loved, leisure opportunities, and if they were happy with their marriages at the moment. Dempsey found that 75 percent of tasks performed outside of the home, such as cutting the grass, were performed by men, but 90 percent of indoor tasks – notably cooking and cleaning – were performed by women. Indoor tasks often took twice as much time to perform and had to be carried out much more often. In addition, women were responsible for child care in 90 percent of cases.

When asked 'Who gets the best deal from marriage?', 78 percent of women said men got the best deal, whilst 40 percent of men said they got the best deal. Only 25 percent of men and 16 percent of women said that women got the best deal from marriage. When asked to explain the reasons for their answers, one male respondent said: 'Well, I say women get the best deal because in a lot of cases they are provided for in a marriage' (32-year-old man).

In contrast, many women argued that men benefited the most:

> They don't have the full responsibility of running a house like we do. They have their job [paid] and their outside jobs at home, but they don't have all the mental stress and worry of the problems to do with the kids and sorting out different things in the household. (47-year-old woman)

> Husbands [have the best deal because they] are exempted from responsibility for household chores and jobs to do with the children. (23-year-old woman)

However, some respondents argued that both men and women benefited from marriage but in different ways:

> It is not possible to say because the man gets what he gets from a marriage and a woman gets what she gets. If you're both happy and in love then it's neither gets the better deal. (49-year-old female)

When asked about their own marriages, women expressed more dissatisfaction with marriage; the reasons given included:

(Continued)

(Continued)

- Division of labour
- Child care responsibilities
- Opportunities for leisure
- Inadequate communication
- Spending insufficient time with their partner.

Questions:

➤ Does the information presented above confirm what you have observed in families that you are familiar with?

➤ What explanation do you have for the ways women are treated within marriage?

➤ What is your answer to the question: Who gets the best deal from marriage: women or men? Give reasons for your answer.

Sadomasochism: A Form of Perversion?

Masochistic or sadomasochistic activities are generally regarded as perverted, dangerous and illegal. However, the notion of perversion is difficult to define and historically was discussed in relation to sexual activities that cannot result in the birth of a child: oral sex, anal sex and masturbation. Such activities used to be regarded as neither honest nor well intentioned although in the recent past they have been largely mainstreamed into the area of 'normal' sexual practice for both heterosexual and homosexual couples. The concept of perversion is rooted in Christian ideas that sex without the possibility of conception is morally wrong. As St Augustine argued, sex is a shameful activity and has to be justified by the possibility of creating a new life. Even what appear to be less judgmental definitions of perversion, such as statistical definitions, often single out sadomasochistic activities. Alan H. Goldman (1977), who argues in favour of a statistical definition, identifies perversion in terms of the desire for physical contact that is motivated by the desire to harm or be harmed as a means of sexual gratification; it is the absence of reciprocal arousal that makes masochistic or sadomasochistic activities incomplete and morally wrong.

Bill Thompson begins his analysis of sadomasochism by investigating the 'Spanner' trial in the United Kingdom during 1990–91. The case involved a group of 15 gay men mainly from the northern town of Bolton who got together to have sex. The group videoed their activities, but when a copy fell into the hands of the police, an investigation started which resulted in prosecution on grounds of assault, even though all the participants gave their consent. The police believed that the group were a 'perverted sadomasochistic sex-ring' who was interested in producing snuff movies.

For Thompson the case highlights the prejudice, discrimination and misconception faced by devotees of S&M. The Spanner judgment, argues Thompson:

> amounted to legalizing prejudice and moral beliefs about various forms of sexual pleasure, rather than the application of the law as it stood: and that these show trials will enable 'society' to pretend it is doing something about violent sex crime by criminalizing people who enjoy 'kinky sex' rather than catching real criminals. (Thompson 1994: 7)

Discrimination against people who are involved in sadomasochism is based upon the perception that sadomasochists enjoy giving and receiving pain. This contravenes the core Christian belief that pain should be the punishment for sin rather than a stimulant to pleasure. In contrast, Thompson argues, sadomasochism has little to do with pain; it is about role-play, fantasy and above all emotional pleasure. If any pain is inflicted on a person, it is only as a stimulant and only with the informed consent of all the participants.

Weinberg and Kanel (1983) drew upon the work of Erving Goffman to make sense of sadomasochism. In Goffman's approach, social actors always attempt to control what they consider to be the central aspects of a setting in order to present a coherent front. Goffman's approach was later described as dramaturgical in character. In developing his dramaturgy, in his early work Goffman argued that there were social rules and rituals which people drew upon to 'define the situation'. In his latter works he developed the notion of the *Frame*, which moved away from the type of analysis that Mead had pioneered and rested on a structuralist approach.

GOFFMAN: BASIC CONCEPTS

Goffman's work involves the examination of particular instances of social life as they occur in their usual settings:

The Self: In *The Presentation of the Self in Everyday Life* (1959) Goffman explains that selves reside in social roles, and that the self can be divided into the Official and Unofficial self. All social behaviour, Goffman believed, is based upon intentionality; every social action has meaning for the social actors.

Moral Career: All social roles constitute a 'moral career'. Internally, the moral career involves an image of self and felt identity. Externally, the moral career involves social location, lifestyle and 'is part of a publicly accessible institutional complex' (Goffman 1961: 127). The term *moral career* refers to the progression through a number of social roles.

Defining the Situation, Social Occasion, Frame: If social actors define the situations in which they find themselves as real, then for Goffman, the situation *is* real. Social situations are a 'negotiated order'; a process of negotiation between the social actors involved creates the definition of the situation.

In his later work Goffman develops these themes into the notion of a *frame*. In his *Frame Analysis* (1974), Goffman divides up what he refers to as primary frameworks into two types:

- Natural primary frameworks
- Social primary frameworks.

For Goffman, these primary social frameworks constitute the central element in a social group's culture. From his notion of the primary framework, Goffman develops the notions of *Key* and *Keyings*. Goffman explains that a rough musical analogy is intended. However, the notion of 'Keying' means that social activity is vulnerable to fabrication. Goffman refers to Keying and fabrications as 'basic transformations' upon the untransformed activity of the primary social framework, which set the terms for experience.

The frame provides the group with the organising principles of its culture, the primary framework provides a negotiated foundation upon which submissive and dominant roles are performed: governess/child; teacher/pupil; and an example from Tom Sharpe's novel *Blott on the Landscape* ... sister cathetar the wicked nurse/patient. S&M is 'social' rather than 'private' in nature, and the primary framework allows the participants to participate within a set of negotiated social arrangements, to share fantasy and separate the activities from other aspects of their everyday lives. The primary framework provides a shared fantasy pathway from everyday life to role-playing fantasy. The theatrical or dramaturgical nature of the activities is all-important. As Thompson argues:

> Given that all sexual fantasies involve some form of role-play, the only real difference between SM devotees and the rest of the population is that the former's fantasies involve overt elements of power relationships. In many cases, knowing that the imagination is often more stimulating and satisfying than reality, SM devotees would not attempt to realize them; but when they do enact fantasy role-play, the imagination is still the most important feature. It is this feature which helps to distinguish SM devotees from those who commit violent sexual crimes against unwilling victims, and ensures that devotees are perfectly harmless. (Thompson 1994: 178)

Whatever our sexual preferences, and whatever we think about Goffman's work on presentation of self, physical appearance is widely recognised as significant in gender relations.

The Beauty System

The argument that women are constrained by ideas of beauty was first suggested by Jane Fonda in her book *Jane Fonda's Workout*. Fonda argued that Vietnamese women were having plastic surgery to various parts of their bodies in an effort to make themselves look more American. Dean MacCannell and Juliet Flower MacCannell developed Jane Fonda's observation into a systematic critique of what they termed *the beauty system:*

> There is no other cultural complex in modern society which touches upon individual behaviour that is as rigorously conceived and executed, total, and minutely policed by collective observation and moral authority, than are feminine beauty standards. (MacCannell and Flower MacCannell 1987: 208)

The beauty system polices all aspects of a women's appearance:

- Face paint colour
- Body size and weight
- Breast size and shape
- Upper arm measurement
- Head and body hair texture, colour and visibility
- Facial expression
- Garment and accessory selection and coordination.

MacCannell and Flower MacCannell view the beauty system as both an ideology and a social fact, what they describe as an: 'amazing feat of cultural engineering' (ibid.: 218). The ideologies that constitute the beauty system operate at a psychological and highly personal level; women are made to feel that their purpose in life is getting and keeping a man. Any woman can accept herself as she is, but to do so is to stand in opposition to almost every image in popular Western culture:

> She is drawn into the beauty system by the force of her entire culture, by the design of the overall relation between the sexes. When she looks in the mirror and sees ugliness reflected back upon herself, what she is actually experiencing is the value that her society has placed upon her gender. (Ibid.: 214)

Interestingly, MacCannell and Flower MacCannell argue that no similar system is applied to men, men present themselves as they are, in a wonderful phrase: 'Men are real. Women are "made up"' (ibid.: 212). When a woman looks in the mirror and sees what she perceives to be a flaw, she is in no position to challenge Western ideas of beauty, rather she will view the flaw as a personal problem. One of the central themes of the beauty system is that 'every beauty flaw can be corrected by rigorous adherence to beauty discipline' (ibid.: 216).

This is an interesting but problematical contribution to the issue of beauty and its social impact. However, their argument is a little thin that the beauty system is partiarchial in nature, it is ideological in nature and it is a social fact. MacCannell and Flower MacCannell simply assume that the beauty system emerges from patriarchal relations, for the benefit of men and to the detriment of women. How and why could an ideology, so effective at a personal level, arise objectively in a society and benefit one group? This important question is not addressed. In addition, the important question about the nature of masculinity and its impact upon the lives of men is not addressed.

Naomi Wolf and the Beauty Myth

The year 1990 saw the publication of Naomi Wolf's influential book *The Beauty Myth* (1990). Wolf argues that even though the Women's Movement has won significant victories in a range of areas of social life over the 1970 and 1980s, women do not feel as free as they perhaps should. The beauty system is used effectively to prevent full female liberation, constraining women from exercising their hard-won rights and generating low self-esteem. Women are made to feel concerns about such things as body shape, hair and other aspects of their physical appearance:

> The more legal and material hindrances women have broken through, the more strictly and heavily and cruelly images of female beauty have come to weigh upon us ... During the past decade, women breached the power structure; meanwhile, eating disorders rose exponentially and cosmetic surgery became the fastest-growing medical speciality. ... It is no accident that so many women, potentially powerful women, feel this way. We are in the midst of a violent backlash against feminism. (Wolf 1990: 10)

Wolf argues that the beauty myth is a key element in a powerful backlash against feminism. Ideas about what constitutes female beauty are used as political weapons to covertly control women, reinforcing the glass ceiling, excluding women from power. However, it is commonly assumed that notions of female beauty are ahistorical and, claims Wolf, operate 'objectively' and 'universally'. This common assumption is not true. Wolf claims that the ideologies of beauty are 'determined by politics' and are 'culturally imposed' by men. Such ideologies have no legitimate or biological justification. The myth is a 'social fiction that masqueraded as natural components of the feminine sphere' (ibid.: 15).

The myth operates in a similar fashion to the Iron Maiden, an instrument of torture found in Germany during medieval times. This instrument was a casket, shaped and painted with the limbs and smiling face of an attractive young woman. The victim was placed inside the casket where she would die of starvation or by being stabbed by the metal spikes that held the victim in place. The present-day Iron Maiden is much more subtle and is composed of 'emotional distance', politics, finance and sexual repression. It is used to impose ways of behaving upon women and is not simply about appearance. However, a key element of both the Iron Maiden then as now is the desire that women have to be thin, to lose one stone.

In terms of critique, Wolf's argument about who controls the beauty myth is unclear. At various points in the text she talks about 'the traditional elite' (1990: 55);

'the elite of power structure' (1990: 138), the elite who maintain a 'caste system' (ibid.: 87, 286). The workings of these institutions are not explained or fully described. Moreover, the motive behind these institutions is also unclear. Wolf appeals to women to reject the artificial nature of the myth by their 'natural solidarity' (ibid.: 282). She seems to suggest that it is women themselves who are to blame for the upholding of the beauty myth. In other words, her argument that our conceptions of 'beauty' are built upon a false set of patriarchal representations imposed upon women by male-dominated institutions lacks theoretical complexity.

In contrast to the lack of theoretical rigor in Wolf's analysis, Paula Black (2002) draws upon the Beck/Giddens conception of individualisation to make sense of the beauty system. Beauty therapy is linked to the wider social transformations that Beck and Giddens have described as *reflexive modernisation*. In terms of beauty therapy, these processes impact upon women in terms of transformations in the workplace that demand a much higher degree of self-monitoring and much more reflexive individualisation. The grooming process that many women have to be involved in as part of their working lives is highly gendered in nature and is highly policed. In her ethnographic account of 'the salon', Black quotes several women's accounts of how they have encountered 'appropriate femininity' at work, for example:

> I hadn't realized I had got so scruffy. It was embarrassing. They [employer] literally compared me with this other woman who is immaculate and groomed and they just said, 'well look at her'. And I just stood there in reception and I felt really humiliated. I just wanted the ground to swallow me up. Did I look that scruffy? I couldn't have looked that bad but it really hurt. (Cited in Black 2002: 11)

For Black (2002) the salon is a space in which women gather the resources to present an 'appropriate' gendered performance as a woman. Pampering, grooming and corrective treatments are used by women who visit the salon to underpin their coping strategies in the workplace. What many men in the workplace see as a naturalised way of being is a highly skilled performance. Women in the workplace have to be feminine but not over-feminine, sexual but not over-sexual, they have to cultivate an appropriate level of feminisation and normality. A central part of this gendered performance is the use of corrective treatments, notably the removal of facial hair, which as Black points out, 'is always and everywhere experienced as inappropriate' (ibid.: 14). Other corrective treatments include treatment for acne and the removal of thread veins. The purpose of corrective treatment, claims Black, is 'to achieve normality within the bounds of an ascriptive heterosexual femininity' (ibid.: 14).

Beauty therapy – pampering, grooming and corrective treatments – are cultural products that are directly linked to processes of individualisation and self-regulation. The notion of 'appropriate femininity' at work has been explored by Melissa Tyler and Philip Hancock. Tyler and Hancock (2001) use the concept of the 'organisational body' to refer to the 'mode of embodiment, the manipulation of the presentation of the body, which must be maintained in order to become and remain an employee of a particular organisation and to "embody" that organization' (Tyler and Hancock 2001: 25).

In their analysis of female flight attendants, Tyler and Hancock (2001) argue that the female body is 'incorporated' into the organisation; the female fight attendant is expected to learn a number of corporeal management techniques that are expected of her in the gendered organisation of work. Her body becomes the material signifier for the organisation and its ethos, but the women are not paid extra for this body work because it is what is expected of any normal woman. Drawing upon Erving Goffman's dramaturgical model, Tyler and Hancock argue that 'the airline industry demands of its employees a presentation of self through which the lived body is scripted, staged and performed in accordance with a standardized role, namely the "organizational body"' (ibid.: 30).

Tyler and Hancock found the following reasons why some women were unsuccessful in their application to become a flight attendant:

- The applicant was too old
- Her skin was blemished
- Her hair was too short, messy or severe
- Her nails were too short or bitten
- Her posture was poor
- Her legs were too chubby
- Her weight was not in proportion to her height
- She lacked 'poise and style'.

The female flight attendant had to conform to a strict dress code that included not only clothing, but shoes, hair, make-up and weight restrictions. However, similar corporeal management techniques that are expected of female employees in the gendered organisation of work were found by:

- **James (1989) (1992):** in relation to nursing
- **Davies (1979):** in relation to waitressing and bar work
- **Hall (1993)** and **Adkins (1995):** in relation to betting and gaming industries
- **Filby (1992)** and **Pringle (1989) (1993):** in relation to secretarial work.

Such expectations about how to look and how to dress are an attempt by the organisation to impose corporate standards and corporate control over a woman's subjectivity.

Efrat Tseelon (1995) has also made use of Erving Goffman's dramaturgical model, in particular the notion of stigma – notably *abominations of the body* – to evaluate some of the key research findings on the beauty myth. She argues that a woman is more likely to be judged on the basis of her attractiveness, and to be more harshly rejected when thought to be deficient in it. 'The beauty system is naturalised by the ideology of sexual differences, and is made to feel essential to femininity' (Tseelon 1995: 90). She suggests that according to the empirical evidence:

- Women have a lower body image than men
- Women perceive themselves to be heavier than they are
- Women are more concerned about their body attractiveness than men
- Women have a lower body satisfaction than men
- Women are more dissatisfied with some aspect of their appearance – and this includes not only mature women but children as young as 6 years of age
- For women body image has a significant effect upon psychological health, romantic relationships and femininity.

In addition, feeling unattractive and/or obese can make a woman become *socially* unattractive. The 'socially unattractive' withdraw from a range of social situations because encounters with others are painful. Women are made to feel both dependent upon their attractiveness and insecure about it. For this reason women are much more likely to do dangerous things to improve their appearance, such as constant dieting and surgery. Goffman's analysis suggests that women are made to feel 'on-stage' and self-conscious about the impression of themselves they are giving. Secondly, women are made to feel a permanent insecurity about becoming ugly. Tseelon's conclusion is that women are stigmatised by the very expectation to be beautiful; this becomes a woman's 'master status', which is independent of the real characteristics of the person herself.

Underpinning the beauty myth hypothesis is an assumption of a dominant masculinist discourse that bolsters the male gaze. One might want to argue that there is not one essential gendered male identity, and moreover many men are made to feel – by both women and other men – that they have a marginal set of male characteristics and as such a defective masculine identity.

ACTIVITY

Victims of Beauty?

Feminine bodily discipline has this dual character: on the one hand, no one is marched off for electrolysis at the end of a rifle, nor can we fail to appreciate the initiative and ingenuity displayed by countless women in an attempt to market the rituals of beauty. Nevertheless, insofar as the disciplinary practices of femininity produce a 'subjected and practiced', an inferiorized body, they must be understood as aspects of a far larger discipline, an oppressive and inegalitarian system of sexual subordination. (Bartky 1997: 103)

Question:

➤ What is Bartky's argument in the passage above?

Class, Gender and Images of Beauty

A number of feminist writers have argued that images of beauty directly link gender and sexuality with class. These links can be seen most clearly in the discourses surrounding female underwear. You might ask, what does underwear have to do with class analysis? The simple answer is, more than you might think. Dana Wilson-Kovacs's (2001) analysis of the suspender belt argues that the development of women's underclothes is a product of a range of complex factors, not least of which is the middle-class invention and domination of *'the shame frontier'*. This is a moral definition of what constitutes appropriate female underwear and appropriate forms of desire aroused when reflecting about what women are wearing under their dresses.

In her ethnographic account of Ann Summers parties, Merl Storr (2002) explains that there is a complex link between gender and class for many women. The women in her study were unable or unwilling to identify themselves within a given class position or class category. Class was something imposed upon women, something *'they* work out', rather than something *she* as a woman lives through. One possible reason for this is suggested by Beverley Skeggs (1997), who argues that the term 'working class' has stigmatised connotations for many women. The term can mean: ignorant, dirty, slag or bad mother. Skeggs describes this as the *emotional politics of class*:

> [T]he label working class when applied to women has been used to signify all that is dirty, dangerous and without value. In the women's claims for a caring/respectable/responsible personality class was rarely directly figured but was constantly present. It was the structuring absence. Yet whilst they made enormous efforts to distance themselves from the label of working class, their class position (alongside their other social positions of gender, race and sexuality) was the omnipresent underpinning which informed and circumscribed their ability *to be*. (Skeggs 1997: 74)

She quotes Bourdieu: 'Taste classifies and it classifies the classifier' (Bourdieu 1984: 6). Our taste helps to inform others about our class position and status, but this class position is not simply reflected in our tastes. Our tastes *make* class distinctions and for Bourdieu such distinctions are often the basis for conflict. Wearing one style or type of item or hairstyle does not reveal that one is 'common'; it makes one 'common'.

Hair is particularly in the beauty system. In the nineteenth century if a woman's long hair was pinned up into a neat bun and covered, this suggested virtue. Dishevelled hair, in contrast, was suggestive of sexual impropriety, strong sexual urges and sexual availability. The covering of the hair by women in the Catholic, Jewish and Muslim faiths during religious events is seen as respectable.

Before we look at Skeggs's conclusions, let us look at what Bourdieu has to say about class, taste and cultural capital.

Pierre Bourdieu

Bourdieu has three key concepts that he uses to explain the nature of social life: *practice, habitus* and *field*. Bourdieu takes his starting point from Marx's eight theses on Feuerbach:

> Social life is essentially *practical*. All mysteries which mislead theory to mysticism find their rational solution in human practice and in the comprehension of this practice. (Marx 1845)

Bourdieu attempts to construct a model of social practices, which are made up of processes that are partly conscious and partly not. Practices often act as signifiers of taste that people draw upon in an effort to make a distinction between themselves and others. People invest in certain practices in an effort to gain a reward. Bourdieu rejects dualisms such as agency and structure and views practice as both a medium and an outcome of an agent's living in a structure. As individuals we acquire habits, either knowingly or unknowingly, from a structural context. We use these practices to live out our everyday lives. In a similar fashion to Giddens, Bourdieu argues that practices are not random, and also like Giddens he views practices as a *practical accomplishments*, yet we experience practice as a having a rule-like quality. Once we have learned a practice, most often we do not reflect upon that practice that we are engaged in, rather we have a habitual response to most practice. Practice both enables and constrains us in our everyday life, including what we think and feel about things as well as our actions. Habitus is a set of dispositions that bring about a unity between the personal histories of people within a community. Bourdieu defines it as 'an acquired system of generative schemes objectively adjusted to the particular conditions in which it is constituted.' (Bourdieu 1977: 95).

People who live in the same area are more likely to share the same *social field*, to share the same habitus and engage in similar practices. In other words:

Habitus + Field = Practice

However, socialisation into a particular habitus does not mean that there will be no conflict within the field. People will have their own interpretation of the habitus and their own idea on the appropriate practice to follow. Habitus is a constructed system of structuring qualities that are found in the 'active aspect' of practice. Or as Bourdieu defines it, 'an acquired system of generative schemes' (Bourdieu 1990: 55). Although habitus has no specific design or rule that it has to follow in advance, by its nature 'practice' has a structuring quality and generates regular and durable social relations, including ideas of what is 'reasonable' and what is 'common-sense'; we internalise the habitus as a second nature. These social relations are cognitive and motivational in nature, but 'arbitrary' in that there is no natural or inevitable form that social relations should take. However, at the same time, habitus makes our actions mutually intelligible. Our perception of the world, including its economic relations, family relations and the division of labour are shaped by the habitus. In other words, the habitus is constituted by practice and at the same time our future practice is shaped by the habitus. Bourdieu explains the significance of this by saying:

> The *habitus* contains the solution to the paradoxes of objective meaning without subjective intention. It is the source of these strings of 'moves' that are objectively organised as strategies without being the product of a genuine strategic intention. (Bourdieu 1990: 62)

There is a link between taste and class habitus. Lifestyle choices, such as leisure patterns and taste – from the type of holiday we go on, to the sports we play, the music we enjoy, the food we eat and the books we read – reflect the class we belong to. The activity of people in the higher-class positions restricts the access of lower-class people to certain forms of less desirable lifestyle and taste choices. Bourdieu identifies three broad class/taste groupings:

- **The legitimate:** classical music, broadsheet newspapers, non-fiction books, Tuscany
- **Middle-brow:** Inspector Morse, Daily Mail, Skiing
- **Popular:** TV soaps, tabloid (red top) newspapers, commercial music, Lloret De Mar.

For people to successfully engage in practice, they have to work within an identifiable habitus. People feel an obligation to share in the lifestyle, tastes and dispositions of a particular social group. However, at the same time people have to improvise beyond its specific rules and conventions. The habitus structures but does not determine choice of practice.

The women in Skeggs's study spent a great deal of time generating, accumulating or displaying their cultural capital. The motivation behind this 'improvement discourse' was the need to display their cultural capital in order to demonstrate that they could improve, that they were not like the working-class women who lacked respect and either could not or would not do anything to improve their situation in life. Not only were the women's bodies markers of social class and respectability but also their homes, relationships and the clothes they wore. The imaginary judgements of others were important for the women and signifiers of respectability told others that it would be wrong to classify them as tasteless, vulgar or tarty. As Skeggs explains:

> The surface of their bodies is the site upon which distinctions can be drawn. Skills and labour such as dressing-up and making-up are used to display the desire to pass as not working class.
>
> [...]
>
> Clothing and objects are experienced intimately: they signify the worth of the person. This is not just about difference but also about deflecting associations of negative value.

They are ways of protecting and distancing oneself from the pathological and worthless. (Skeggs 1997: 84, 86)

Heterosexuality was a central organising principle in this process, as to be seen without a man was undesirable and carried a social stigma that increased as the woman grew older. However, as Skeggs points out, 'playing the field' or 'being part of the meat market' were also to be avoided, as was the strong temptation for the women to settle for inadequate partners.

Women and Stratification

With the emergence of second-wave feminism, 'the personal' was seen as 'political' and many feminists assumed that abstract or *gender-blind* class analysis was infused with intellectual sexism.

Writing in 1973, Joan Acker argued that gender was rarely considered to be a factor in the processes of class formation, even though it was widely seen as the basis of one of the observable forms of division and discrimination. Acker argued that sociologists, including both functionalists and Marxists, make six assumptions about the link between gender and class-based forms of stratification:

1 The family, rather than the individual, is the unit of analysis in class-based forms of stratification.
2 The social position of the family is determined by the status of the male head of household.
3 Females live in families and, as such, the male head of household determines a woman's status.
4 The status of the female is the same as the male head of household.
5 Only single women determine their own social status.
6 Women are unequal to men on the basis of their gender and biological sex, but this is irrelevant to class-based forms of stratification analysis.

Acker draws together evidence to challenge these assumptions. On the basis of American census data from as far back as 1960, women headed approximately two-fifths of American households. In addition, many women do not live in families and instead determine their status on the basis of their own status resources. Therefore, it is wrong to suggest that women have no status resources of their own, or that such resources become inoperative if a woman chooses to live with a man.

By using the individual rather than the family as the unit of analysis in class analysis, Acker claims that it is possible to integrate 'sex' into stratification models. Women 'have certain common interests and life-patterns' and 'share certain disabilities and inequities'. Therefore, argues Acker, they should be viewed as a 'caste-like grouping' within social class. Her argument is based upon a number of assumptions:

1   Sex is an enduring ascribed characteristic which (a) has an effect upon the evaluation of persons and positions, and (b) is the basis of the persisting sexual division of labour and of sex-based inequalities.
2   The sex dichotomy cuts across all classes and strata. (Acker 1973: 6)

Christine Delphy argues that such assumptions should not be regarded as 'methodological errors' by male sociologists, but rather as 'unintentional indices of a hidden social structure' (Delphy 1981: 15). She goes on to explain:

> The purported theoretical aim [of stratification studies that use the family rather than the individual as the unit of analysis] is to study women as members of social groups and as subjects of their relationships. But these groups are *operationally* defined as being made up exclusively of men, and women are *operationally* defined as being mediators and not subjects in social relationships with men. (Ibid.: 19)

No man, Delphy argues, has his position in the class system defined by the occupation of his wife or any other woman. However, Delphy rejects the essentialist argument that women's differences should be the starting point for a feminist analysis.

It was Christine Delphy who coined the term 'materialist feminist' in the 1970s to describe a form of analysis that looks to Marx's analysis of capitalism to explain the origins of women's oppression. Women provide unpaid labour within the home and although such labour may have no 'exchange value', it allows capitalism to run smoothly and efficiently.

Nicky Hart argues that masculinity – which she defines as a set of rights and duties of breadwinners – is a central element in the processes of class formation, but it is often overlooked and in contrast to Delphy's use of Marxian terminology, she argues that:

> The social force of class is not a pure and single-stranded material phenomenon but a blended compound which, in its heyday, depended for theoretical propulsion on normative as much as material constituents.
>
> [...]
>
> ... The substance of gender oppression cannot be confined to what women add to the domestic quantity of surplus-value through domestic production. Women's oppression has lain historically in the 'natural' rights of men to own the 'second sex', their labour, their children, their property. (Hart 1989: 71, 96)

Men used the rights and duties associated with masculinity to form a near occupational monopoly during the nineteenth century; this diminished the financial power of women and increased their dependency upon men.

John Goldthorpe: Intellectual Sexism, Social Mobility and Class Structure in Modern Britain

In this study Goldthorpe and his team measured the absolute and relative mobility rates of 10,309 men aged between 16 and 64 resident in England and Wales. In contrast to absolute mobility rates, which simply inform us on how many men were upwardly or downwardly mobile within the class structure; relative mobility rates measure relative mobility chances – in this case the chances of a man from a working-class background being upwardly mobile, compared with a man from a higher-class position remaining there. Goldthorpe used a Weberian conception of social class that he defined in terms of *market* and *work* situation. The team devised a new scale that is made up of seven classes which they often collapsed into three: the service class, the intermediate class and the working class. The exclusion of women from the study caused a long-running debate about intellectual sexism within class analysis. Before we explore this, let us look briefly at the key elements of the study.

The team were interested in testing three hypotheses about the class structure in modern Britain:

- **The Closure Thesis:** which suggests that the top of the class system is closed to people from the bottom end of the occupational ladder: 'Elite groupings will contain no more than quite negligible proportions of men whose recruitment has entailed long-range upward movement as, say, from a working-class social background.' (Goldthorpe et al. 1987: 44)
- **The Buffer-Zone Thesis:** which suggests that the chances for sons of skilled manual workers to be upwardly mobile into non-manual occupations are less than for sons of semi-skilled or unskilled manual workers becoming skilled
- **The Counterbalance Thesis:** which suggests that 'any increase in upward mobility achieved in recent decades via educational channels will have been offset by a decrease in chances of advancement in the course of working life.' (Ibid.: 55).

A man may experience *inter*generational mobility, in that he has a better job than his father had, but is less likely to experience *intra*generational mobility; in other words he is unlikely to experience upward social mobility over the course of his working life. A manual worker, for example, may have a son who goes on to become a schoolteacher but during the course of the son's career, he is unlikely to become a head teacher.

For Goldthorpe, social mobility is about measuring the mobility of the head of the household and this is a man. For Goldthorpe, women have a *derived* class position, their class position is determined by the occupation of their husband or father. Women have no independent class position.

Goldthorpe attempted to defend his position by making the following points. First, he argued that functionalist accounts of stratification, such as that of Talcott Parsons, view the family as the unit of analysis in stratification studies because the division of labour within the home – where men go out to work and women stay at home doing child care and domestic work – is functional for the smooth running of the social system. Goldthorpe argues that he makes no such assumption in his analysis; rather his reason for using the family as the unit of analysis reflects the fact that 'within Western capitalist societies women still have to await their liberation from the family' (Goldthorpe 1983: 29). He goes on to explain that:

> what is essential to class analysis is the argument that family members share in the same class position, and that this position is determined by that of the family 'head' in the sense of the family member who has the greatest commitment to, and continuity in labour market participation. (Ibid.: 31)

There are very few cross-class marriages according to Goldthorpe, who acknowledges that if significant numbers of married couples were both involved in the labour market with different class positions, this would be a serious challenge to the conventional view. However, Goldthorpe points out that 'It should not be overlooked that the increase in the proportion of women in paid employment since 1951 is attributable *entirely* to the growth of part-time working' (ibid.: 35). In addition, Goldthorpe argues that only a small minority of married women are continuously part of the workforce throughout their working lives. Most women enter and withdraw from the labour force with the birth of their children. Women with children are not committed to the labour market: 'labour market participation of married women is typically of an intermittent and limited kind, and is moreover conditioned by the class context in which it occurs' (ibid.: 36).

Finally Goldthorpe suggests that whether a woman chooses to work or not is largely dependent upon her husband's performance as a breadwinner: 'The timing and extent of wives' work may often form part of a family plan, whether aimed at social advancement or social survival, which is developed in response to the husband's career possibilities or problems' (ibid.: 40).

David Lockwood (1986) has also defended the conventional view of class. For Lockwood, occupation is important for understanding the class system, and the sex of the person who holds a given occupation is irrelevant for class analysis. The status a woman derives from her man, or that she acquires herself, is more significant than the status she shares with other women. In addition, women do not form a status group because the notion of patriarchy is so vague, and the divisions between women are so great. In this way, women cannot be said to form a group with an identity that could engender a social movement to bring about social change or form the basis of a politics in the same way as for classes and class-based politics. Lockwood explains that:

Beyond Male Mobility Models

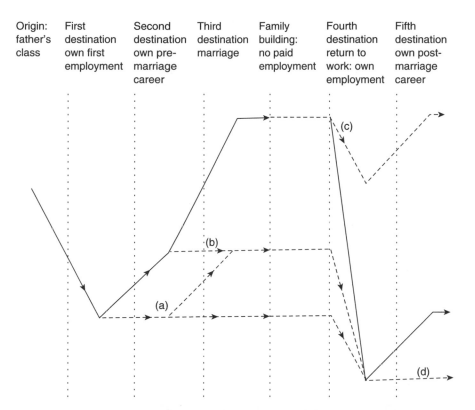

| Origin: father's class | First destination own first employment | Second destination own pre-marriage career | Third destination marriage | Family building: no paid employment | Fourth destination return to work: own employment | Fifth destination own post-marriage career |

Source: Geoff Payne and Pamela Abbott 'Beyond Male Mobility Models' (1991: 165). In the figure the unbroken line shows the typical mobility experiences of a women. The variations are (a) no early career mobility (b) limited mobility because of marriage to a lower class male (c) advantageous return to the labour market after childbirth (d) no career progression on later life.

> the most important question regarding claims about the significance of sexual inequality is whether societies can be differentiated according to the predominance of systems of gender relations, that is, structures of social action comparable to those within the range of class polarization and status-group consolidation. (Lockwood 1986: 12)

The conflict and divisions between men and women are not large classes of men and women but, argues Lockwood, are rather at an individual level, between individual men and individual women.

My view is that we do have a women's movement, but it is divided, although in the past women have come together around common issues, such as the

Suffrage Movement. In addition, Lockwood has exaggerated the coherence of classes and class-based politics.

Although women were excluded from the Goldthorpe study, they are not totally excluded from the data. Later studies, notably the Essex Mobility Study, found that women who enter the labour market are much more likely to experience downward social mobility compared to their fathers. Although single women and married women without children were generally likely to experience worklife upward mobility, when a woman had a break in her career to have children she usually experienced extreme downward social mobility to a market and work situation that was worse than the first occupation she had when she joined the labour market. This means that because women entering the labour market for the first time and women with children hold significant proportions of the jobs at the bottom end of the occupational class structure, for a man to get a job at all he must experience social mobility. However, the relative upward mobility chances for men are enhanced by the significant proportion of the jobs at the bottom end of the occupational class structure occupied by women. If women and men had been included as individuals in Goldthorpe's study, there would have been significantly less upward mobility and significantly more closure.

The class analysis of John Goldthorpe and the people who contributed to the critique of his work is firmly rooted in a modernist conception of the 'industrial society'. Towards the latter decades of the twentieth century a number of researchers started to look beyond the traditional industrial forms of modernity.

Risk, Female Individualisation and Zombie Categories

Ulrich Beck (1992) argues that modernity is breaking free from the contours of classical industrial society and that we are in the midst of a transition from an industrial society to a risk society. This means that we are moving from a social situation in which political conflicts and divisions were defined by a logic of the distribution of 'goods' to a social situation in which conflicts are becoming defined by the distribution of 'bads' – in other words the distribution of hazards and risks.

Beck's analyses are based upon a three-stage historical periodisation of pre-industrial, industrial and risk societies. Each of these three types of society contains risk and hazards, but there are qualitative differences between them in terms of the types of risk encountered. In pre-industrial societies, risks were not man-made; they were 'natural', for example, crop-destroying weather. In modern industrial societies, there are industrially produced hazards. However, the insurance principle provides some support in the form of accountability and compensation. The risk society, however, is a society in which:

- 'Risks' become the axial principle of social organisation. In other words, coping with risk is becoming an essential element in the way we organise our society
- 'Risks' take on a form that is incalculable, uncompensatable, unlimited and unaccountable.

A central feature of the risk society is the process of *individualisation*; individual people are cut loose from previously supportive social forms, for example family, social class, neighbourhood or fixed gender roles. According to Beck, individualisation involves a 'new mode of societalisation' involving a redefinition of the relationship between the individual and society. As individuals we now compose our own life narrative, we create a biography that we want. Our biography is not determined or forced upon us. As individuals we may not be free to form a society, but society becomes one more variable that we attempt to manipulate in an effort to create the biographies that we desire. Although we may view this as human liberation, at the same time the support and security previously offered by tight-knit communities and secure family groupings also diminish. The very context of our lives is within the processes of Individualisation.

Beck outlines an abstract or 'a historical model of individualisation' which involves three components:

1   **The Liberating Dimension** or disembedding: which involves the breaking down of socially and historically prescribed commitments.
2   **The Disenchantment Dimension** or loss of traditional security: which involves the breaking down of 'practical knowledge, faith and guiding norms' (Beck 1992: 128).
3   **The Control/Reintegration Dimension** or re-embedding: which involves the creation of new forms of social commitment.

In Beck's view, individualisation is about placing the logic of individual design at the centre of our life narrative:

> Individualization is understood as a historical process that increasingly questions and tends to break up people's traditional rhythm of life – what sociologists call the normal biography. As a result, more people than ever before are being forced to piece together their own biographies and fit in the components they need as best they can. They find themselves bereft of unquestionable assumptions, beliefs or values and are nevertheless faced with the tangle of institutional controls and constraints which make up the fibre of modern life. (Beck and Beck-Gernsheim 2002: 88)

Our individual biography becomes an 'elective biography' or 'risk biography' (ibid.: 3); our biographies become self-reflexive as the given determinations over our future paths or life narratives that dominated industrial society are dissolved and our destinies are placed in our own hands. The 'inherited recipes for living' – the historical role advice and models passed on from our parents and neighbourhoods on how to conduct oneself in any given situation – are no longer accepted without question. We may still have tradition to guide us, but we no longer accept such tradition without question. How to live a life is in a constant process of re-negotiation and dialogue based upon, often contradictory, information: 'the nationally fixed social categories of industrial society are culturally dissolved or transformed. They become "zombie categories", which have died yet live on' (ibid.: 27).

This is perhaps nowhere more clearly seen than in the area of sexuality. With the advent of the risk society, the female biography has undergone an 'individualisation boost'. The foundational assumptions that underpinned the heterosexual married couple as the only legitimate arena for the expression of sexuality have dissolved, allowing a *post-familial family* to emerge which allows individuals greater opportunity to make lifestyle choices to a degree unheard of in previous generations. Women are no longer expected to get a husband, have a family, provide a caring relationship for family members and to do a host of other types of emotional work. As Beck and Beck-Gernsheim explain, in the past: 'if they were disappointed, women used to abandon their hopes; nowadays they cling to their hopes and abandon the marriage' (ibid.: 62).

There are new opportunities, as well as new risks, as women are liberated from their traditional ascribed roles of homemaker and mother. The power of husbands has been restricted, women no longer need marriage to secure their economic future or their social status. The impetus for this individualisation of the female biography, argue Beck and Beck-Gernsheim, has come from the changing nature of work, education, legal changes and the changing nature of the family bond. Women do not need men to provide for them. However, the *feminisation* of poverty is one of the central risks faced by women who are free of the patriarchal family – single women with children and few marketable skills are the fastest growing group in poverty.

'The Normal Chaos of Love'

In their 1995 book *The Normal Chaos of Love*, Ulrich Beck and Elisabeth Beck-Gernsheim argue that in the conditions of reflexive modernity – impersonal, free from tradition, uncertain and risky – love has become more important for us, but at the same time more difficult to achieve:

> 'love' is the new centre round which our detraditionalized life revolves. It may manifest itself as hope, betrayal, longing, jealousy – all addictions which affect even such serious people as the Germans. This, then, is what we mean by the normal chaos of love. (Beck and Beck-Gernsheim 1995: 3)

Individualisation releases both women and men from their traditional gender roles found in industrial society. Even in the 1960s, marriage, family and a steady job were seen as the cornerstones and aspirations of the nuclear family. Now lifestyle choice presents itself in all aspects of our everyday life. Individuals are expected to create a life of their own choosing, on the basis of their own skills and abilities that they – as individuals – present to the labour market. However, this is not to say that people have abandoned or lost the need for emotional commitment; rather, individual women and men:

> are *driven* into seeking happiness in a close relationship because other bonds seem too tenuous or unreliable ... As a consequence the direct route away from marriage and family usually leads, sooner or later, back to them again.
>
> [...]
>
> Individualisation may drive women apart, but paradoxically it also pushes them back into another's arms. As *traditions become diluted, the attractions of a close relationship grow.* Everything that one has lost is sought in the other. (Ibid.: 24, 32)

Motherhood is also redefined within reflexive modernisation. Having children is no longer seen as the expected natural path or inclination for a woman, instead it is a lifestyle choice. Women's social movements have politicised issues in relation to contraception and abortion to the degree that motherhood can no longer be seen as a woman's natural destiny. In the same way that the motivation for sex has no inevitable link with childbirth.

Feminism and Postmodernism

In common with many second-wave feminists writing in the 1970s and 1980s, Acker, Delphy and Hart assume that the category of 'woman' is an 'essential category'. In other words, that 'sex' is a naturally given category and that by its 'nature' the category determines the important aspects of our personality, identity and central aspects of our life chances.

WHAT IS ESSENTIALISM?

According to Diana Fuss, the traditional Aristotelian definition of essentialism was 'a belief in true essence – that which is most irreducible, unchanging, and therefore constitutive of a given person or thing' (Fuss 1989: 2). In addition:

> [an] essentialist assumes that innate or given essences sort objects naturally into species or kinds, whereas a constructionist assumes that it is language, the names arbitrarily affixed to objects, which establishes their existence in the mind. (Ibid.: 5)

However, it is important to note Diana Fuss's observation that: 'They still share a common classification *as essence*' (ibid.).

(Continued)

(Continued)

The philosopher John Locke made a distinction between a 'real' essence and a 'nominal' essence. The real essence is unchanging and given by nature, whereas the nominal essence is a linguistic classification or name given. Moreover, it is important to note that even a real essence has to be *read* or made sense of by the use of linguistic categories.

Critics of the second wave from within the feminist movement were, by the mid-1980s, claiming that an essential conception of 'woman' was an attempt by white radical feminists to impose a category of identity upon 'Others', such as lesbians and women of colour. In her discussion of *difference*, Denise Thompson (2001) argues that women may experience male domination differently. However, she also makes clear that comparing the different experiences of women of colour or class is not in women's interests. The reason for this is that such comparison 'deflects attention away from the *real problem* by disguising or ignoring the workings of male supremacy, or by reducing feminism to nothing but the trivial preoccupation of the privileged' (Thompson 2001: 131, emphasis added). Second-wave radical feminism ascribed all forms of oppression to men and Thompson clearly states that she wants to resurrect that argument. All forms of domination are rooted in masculinity; if we end male supremacy we will have freedom for all:

> Imperialism, whether it takes the form of outright slavery, of the colonial dispossession of indigenous peoples, of the multinational control and exploitation of distant lands and their national economies, or of the forcible imposing of foreign cultures, requires the defining of subjugated populations as less than human ... Hence imperialism requires dehumanisation. But so does masculinity in the sense that it is a 'human' status bought at someone else's expense. Domination already has a model of human beings who are not fully human – women. (Ibid.: 139).

The objection to this view is that racism and economic exploitation are *real problems* and should be treated as such. One can understand why there is an argument within the social sciences about feminist complicity with Western imperialism.

Many radical feminists assume that white middle-class women are the norm for understanding women's oppression, which is often inappropriate for understanding the experiences of women of colour. Chris Beasley gives the following example to highlight the point:

> [T]he rape of Australian Aboriginal women by Aboriginal men is not necessarily a subject appropriate for white feminists to discuss publicly and at a distance from the relevant Aboriginal communities in terms of men's brutal oppression of women ... this kind of discussion reinstates whites as the interpreters of Aboriginal experience while evading the significance of the context of racism in generating violence. (Beasley 1999: 109)

In 1996, Patricia Hill Collins, in a similar fashion to bell hooks, drew upon the thoughts, experiences, music and literature of black women to developed what she called a *black women's standpoint epistemology* which attempts to break the images of black women that white feminists use to inform their racism. Collins is interested in the relationship between white feminism and the structures of power. This standpoint epistemology attempts to describe the subjugated knowledge of black women that has for so long been regarded as not *real or valid* intellectual knowledge.

White radical second-wave feminists were recast from within the increasingly diverse women's movement into the role of oppressors. Second-wave feminists had to explore the notion of 'difference' as it became increasingly clear that feminist accounts of women's experience did not apply to all women. As Rudy (2001) in her personal account of being a lesbian in the radical women's movement in the 1980s explains:

> By the mid-1980s, it had become clear that most generalizations about women did not hold true especially across racial, class, or ethnicity lines. African American lesbians and other lesbians of color told white radical feminists in no uncertain terms that the female nature they had theorised did not represent difference.
>
> [...]
>
> It was a politically retrograde fantasy to think that all women could exist under the sign of 'woman' with no references to other realities, other experiences, other identities. (Rudy 2001: 201, 204)

Under the influence of texts such as Judith Butler's (1990) *Gender Trouble: Feminism and the Subversion of Identity*; Diana Fuss's (1989) *Essentially Speaking: Feminism, Nature and Difference* and Eve Sedgwick's (1990) *Epistemology of the Closet*, the anti-essentialist and explicitly postmodern Queer Theory emerged. The emerging Queer Theory of the 1990s put forward the argument that not only 'gender' but also 'biological sex' was socially constructed. Queer theorists challenged the assumption that individuals had a simple and straightforward relationship with their sexual organs, and that in turn, possession of one type of sexual organs rather than another type determines our relationship to a binary reality as a woman or a man. By deconstructing biological sex, gender and sexual preference, individuals were liberated from the confines of a given identity. It was individuals who were in a process of sexually *becoming* that groups such as Outrage were making increasingly politicised. As Rudy explains:

> [M]any aspects of queer culture show intense interest in alternative sex practices such as sadomasochism, pornography, man-boy love, group sex, cross-dressing, leather bars, and other erotic subcultures that exist in America today, affirming in every case the perverse, the chaotic, and the nonmonogamous. Queer theory challenges not only the construction of female and male as 'normal', but it also disputes the idea that sexuality has any 'normal' parameters at all. (Rudy 2001: 215)

In her contribution to *Feminist Contentions*, philosopher Seyla Benhabib (1995) presents herself as a critic of the synthesis of feminism and postmodernism. Benhabib takes her outline of what constitutes postmodernism from Jane Flax's book *Thinking Fragments: Psychoanalysis, Feminism and Postmodernism in the Contemporary West*. For Flax, postmodernism embraces three positions, all of which have impacted on feminist analysis:

- **The Death of Man:** in contrast to the notion of 'man' as natural phenomena, Flax argues that the concept of 'man' is socially constructed, historically located and a discursive artefact. The task of the postmodernist is to identify the 'chains of signification' and 'webs of fictive meaning', in other words the grand narratives, that are drawn together to construct 'man'. The idea behind this form of deconstruction is to undermine the essentialist conception of 'man'
- **The Death of History:** the notion of 'history' and 'progress' are rational Enlightenment concepts that have been used to create and maintain the essentialist conception of 'man'
- **The Death of Metaphysics:** in the history of the Enlightenment, philosophy has a privileged place in the rational search for the 'truth'; it is assumed that it is possible to find, identify and describe an absolute and ultimate foundation of being upon which the world rests. Such a foundation would incorporate all knowledge within a rational and scientifically valid system of thought.

Taking her point of departure from Nietzsche, Judith Butler uses the notion of the 'death of man' to think beyond gender categories; to do away with what Nietzsche referred to as the 'doer beyond the deed'. As Butler posits: 'There is no gender identity behind the expressions of gender; that identity is performatively constituted by the very "expressions" that are said to be its results' (Butler 1990: 25).

For Benhabib, Butler's use of Nietzsche's arguments in this way 'can only lead to self-incoherence' (Benhabib 1995: 21). For Benhabib, we might want to accept and recognise the self as constituted in performance, but not to go beyond that in the way that Nietzsche urges us to. Rather, we need to be in a position to change the 'expressions' out of which we are constituted and have a greater say in the production of our own gender performance. In other words, we need to adopt a weak version of the 'death of man'.

Similarly, Benhabib argues that we should be critical of grand narratives, but not dispense with them altogether. Grand narratives provide people with a link between politics and historical memory, and to dispense with them is to lose the possibility of emancipation and would bring to an end the chance of a successful campaign against oppression. Again Benhabib argues there is a need to reject the strong version of postmodernism.

In summary, Benhabib's (1995) argument is based on the assumption that Butler's *strong* postmodern account leads to the dissolution of the subject, the end of intentionality, self-reflexivity and independence. This gives rise to an 'identity crisis' for feminism, the implications of which signal the end of feminism as a coherent social movement. For Benhabib, female emancipation is not possible without a female human agency defined in terms of selfhood and situated within a grand narrative.

In response, Butler argues that it is commonly assumed that politics is unthinkable without a foundation of being:

> To claim that politics requires a stable subject is to claim that there can be no *political* opposition to that claim. Indeed, that claim implies that a critique of the subject cannot be a politically informed critique but, rather, an act which puts into jeopardy politics as such ... [This argument] enforces the boundaries of the domain of the political in such a way that enforcement is protected from political scrutiny. ... an authoritarian ruse by which political contest over the status of the subject is summarily silenced. (Butler 1995: 36)

Contrary to the argument of Benhabib and others, the 'death of the man' does not mean the end of politics or the end of agency. The modern concept of 'woman' is situated within maternal and racialist concepts of reality. Butler argues that subjects are formed through such processes of exclusion, and politically it is important to trace how such exclusionary processes work. *Women* have to be redefined, in a self-critical fashion, using resources other than the exclusionary processes of the identity categories of modernity: 'To deconstruct is not to negate or dismiss, but to call into question and, perhaps most importantly, to open up a term, like the subject, to a reusage or redeployment that previously has not been authorized' (ibid.: 49).

Deconstruction allows feminists to expand the meaning of what it means to be a woman, to liberate the notion of *woman* from maternal and racialist ontologies. In modernity, argues Butler:

> sex does not *describe* a prior materiality, but produces and regulates the *intelligibility* of the *materiality* of bodies ... this kind of categorization can be called a violent one, a forceful one, and this discursive ordering and production of bodies in accord with the category of sex is itself a material violence. (Ibid.: 52)

Butler argues that the power of the performative is a structural condition of language, but as Amy Hollywood (2002) argues, if the performative has the power to act, where does that power come from? Does it come from outside the speech act? Or is it, rather, internal to that performance? Judith Butler's analysis is primarily concerned with the ways in which the binary notions of sex/gender have traditionally been mistakenly viewed as 'pre-linguistic' and a form of 'ontological essentialism', which allows gender to be formed with partiarchial power relations that cannot be challenged. As White explains:

> There is no entity – whether the subject, the gendered subject, the body, or whatever – which hovers, as it were, behind its acts; rather such entities are always 'produced or generated' in the very performance of linguistic actions. The continual reiteration of social scripts – and thus regimes of power – is what gives life and specific shape to what are then mistakenly identified as pre-existing entities with ontological status. (White 1999: 158)

There are however, a number of problems with Butler's analysis, which White identifies:

- How human beings have bodies seems to have become an epiphenomenon of performativity
- It is not clear how discursive power 'produces' subjects

- Despite Butler's claims that subjects can resist power, it is not clear how, in Butler's own theory, critical agency emerges.

Butler's answer to these critical points is similar to Althusser's theory of interpellation, in which a subjective notion of guilt can emerge from being hailed by a police officer. Butler argues that discipline, particularly religious authority, is central to the understanding of subjection; various forms of prohibition within religious authority are influential in shaping a person's own subjection. The subject for Butler is formed in terms of condemnation.

Judith Butler: Subjectification

As individuals we are used to the idea of an external power attempting to exert influence upon us as subjects, attempting to make us do things that we may not want to do. However, since Foucault, we have also come to understand power as something that has a central role to play in the formation of the subject. Power is also something that we depend upon to help make us who we are. As Judith Butler explains: 'Subjection consists precisely in this fundamental dependency on a discourse we never chose but that, paradoxically, initiates and sustains our agency' (Butler 1997: 2).

A central concept for Butler is *alterity*. The social construction of alterity is directly related to both order and social division. The word *alterity* is derived from the German word 'alter' and means *Otherness*, in the sense of a systematised narrative for the construction of categories or social divisions rather than a distinction between the individual self and others based upon individual differences. In this process we institutionalise the cultural assumptions or prejudices that make us who we are into our laws and customs.

FOUCAULT ON SUBJECTIFICATION

Friend and colleague of Foucault, Paul Rabinow in his introduction to *The Foucault Reader* (1986) explains that within Foucault's work it is possible to identify several 'modes of objectification', organising principles used by Foucault to explain how individual human beings become subjects. A central 'mode of objectification' for Foucault is *subjectification*. Foucault is concerned with what it means to be a self and how we as individuals are pressurised into creating our selves in a given fashion.

Foucault uses the word '*regimen*' to refer to these rules of how one ought to behave. Individuals define themselves as 'normal' in relation to a number of factors: sex, health,

(Continued)

(Continued)

race and many more. This is primarily concerned with what Foucault was to call the *power of the norm*. All individual actions are now within 'a field of comparison' which both pressurises people and *normalises* them. Normal people can legitimately regard themselves as members of a homogeneous social body – the society. Normalisation may impose homogeneity upon people, but it also allows us – as members of society – to categorise and measure people, and place people in hierarchies on the basis of widely accepted rules.

Butler argues that Hegel attempted to make the case that in the relationship between master and slave, the master becomes the slave's 'psychic reality'. The slave requires recognition from the master, becomes dependent upon subordination to develop any sense of 'self'. In the first instance the master is seen as an 'external' force but soon re-emerges as the slave's own conscience. The 'individual' becomes a linguistic category of the 'subject', a place or category within a structure of power relationships established through language. Firstly, power makes 'the subject' possible by generating a structure with sites that can be occupied by 'subjects', and secondly power makes possible the emergence of subjects to occupy the sites within the structure. Power creates the linguistic category of the 'subject' and provides the resources that the subjects draw upon to view themselves as a 'subject'. However, Butler argues that 'Agency exceeds the power by which it is enabled' (Butler 1997: 15).

The subject cannot be reduced to the power that was used to create it and, similarly, the power cannot be reduced to the subject. The subject gets its power from opposing the power that brought the category of subject into being. Power then is not simply about oppression of subjects, but is also about the process of subject formation. When Foucault talks about the *power of the norm*, we assume that he is arguing that subjects internalise norms. However, the notion of an interior and exterior social life are merely the way in which we attempt to make sense of the world through categorisation. Norms are a medium and an outcome of power, as Butler explains: 'one makes oneself an object for reflection; in the course of producing one's own alterity, one becomes established as a reflexive being, one who can take oneself as an object' (ibid.: 22).

In summary, in Butler's analysis subjection involves:

- Regulatory power that sustains subjects in a position of subordination
- The subject is located with a structure that sets limits to its subjectification
- The agency of the subject is formed in opposition to the power that maintains the site – or place in the structure – for the subject.

Richard Sennett has developed a similar Hegelian argument concerning 'authority' in the relationship between master and slave. As in Butler's analysis, the master is essential in the definition of the slave's 'psychic reality'. For Sennett, authority need not be legitimate in the eyes of the population. However, the desire to be under some authority is regarded as indispensable, and although people fear the damage that authority can do to our liberties, the emotional bonds of authority are seldom stable in nature. Authority relationships require recognition from the master, and as such the slave becomes dependent upon subordination to develop any sense of 'self'.

Sennett outlines a number of 'bonds of rejection' which people use to counter authority, but which simultaneously allow us to depend upon the authority and be used by that authority.

- **Disobedient dependence:** this is a situation in which people rebel 'within' authority, rather than 'against' authority. The practice of 'transgression' involves more than simply saying 'no' to the authority, but proposing an alternative that the authority cannot accept. Individuals have a need to be given some recognition by the authority
- **Idealised substitution:** the authority serves as a negative model; whatever the authority does, the opposite is what we want. Individuals feel secure with the anchor that authority can provide.

What is significant about Sennett's work on authority in this area is that he demonstrates that the state authority can have a important role to play in the processes of alterity and subjectification. In addition, Sennett makes clear that the authority of the state need not be regarded as legitimate for its authority still to have a considerable role to play in the process of alterity and subjectification.

ACTIVITY

According to Judith Butler:

[S]ubjection is the paradoxical effect of a regime of power in which the very 'conditions of existence', the possibility of continuing as a recognizable social being, requires the formation and maintenance of the subject in subordination. ... Only by persisting in alterity does one persist in one's 'own' being. (Butler 1997: 28)

Question:

➢ Summarise in your own words what Judith Butler is saying about *subjectification*. Make a list of things you find convincing about Butler's analysis and a list of things you find unconvincing.

The processes of alterity/subjectification are the essence of social division and the purpose of these processes is to restrict the individual agency from fully *becoming*. Social division is about the creation and maintenance of sites within a structure, inhabited by individuals who *become* agents who exercise their agency in appropriate ways. Social division is about shaping who we are as individuals, what is appropriate for us, from the clothes we wear, the music we enjoy, the food we eat, to the thoughts we have. Social division lends the process of subjectification a degree of objectivity it might otherwise lack and links subjectification to alterity.

When Butler argues that 'agency exceeds the power by which it is enabled' (Butler 1997: 15), she is highlighting the crucial point where the process of *becoming* meets the processes of subjectification. Individuals have the restriction of social division placed upon them, which they experience directly through the processes of subjectification. Subjectification is fundamental to any conception of social division because without it there can be no alterity, and alterity is fundamental to any conception of social division because without it there can be no subjectification. The purpose of the dual processes of alterity/subjectification is to restrict the process of *becoming* within the parameters of becoming.

In the United Kingdom, citizenship education is a good example of the ways in which the state directly involves itself in the processes of restricting becoming by directly involving the state in the processes of alterity/subjectification.

The Corporeal Turn: Maxine Sheets-Johnstone

In sharp contrast to the linguistic turn of Michel Foucault, Judith Butler and other postmodern and poststructuralist writers, Maxine Sheets-Johnstone's underlying argument is that *thinking* is modelled on the functioning of the body. She maintains that corporeal experience is derived from an anatomical source, and that the central concepts that we use today to guide our practice as people are in the last analysis corporeal concepts: 'Indeed, it is clear from history that our hominid ancestors bequeathed to us *a corporeal legacy that is not more ancient than thought but coincident with it.*' (Sheets-Johnstone 1990: 288; italics in original).

In contrast to the linguistic turn, for Sheets-Johnstone the concepts we use in our everyday lives are not language-dependent; rather, human thought is structured in and by the pre-linguistic bodily experiences of our early ancestors. Our early ancestors had a basic system of corporeal meanings upon which our advanced forms of thinking are based. Traditionally, philosophers have dealt with issues of being (mind and thought), whilst scientists have dealt with the body. Sheets-Johnstone wants to break down that traditional division of labour. In particular, Sheets-Johnstone argues that we need to develop a corporeal analysis of the tactile-kinesthetic nature of the body; the living body is a *semantic template* of bodily logos:

> [T]here is an indissoluble bond between hominid thinking and hominid evolution, a bond cemented by the living body ... The *tactile-kinesthetic body* is the sentiently felt body, the body that knows the world through touch and movement. (Ibid.: 4–5; italics in original)

It was the basic system of corporeal meanings derived from the tactile-kinesthetic body that gave rise to the invention and use of verbal language, upright walking, mathematical reasoning, tool-making and the construction of buildings that symbolise belief. In contrast, the linguistic turn has no theory of the nature and origin of language:

> Although not recognized as such, the ontologies of many existential and analytic philosophers are ontologies in which, precisely, humans arrive on the scene as Special Creations. In many of these instances language is something of a pied piper. It comes from nowhere and so charms those who hear it that they follow it anywhere, mesmerized. (Ibid.: 15)

In terms of tool-making, Sheets-Johnstone argues that the hardness of the teeth, compared with the softness of the tongue, is a binary tactile opposite. In addition, teeth have an edge that can be used to transform objects, bite, chew and grind. The idea that stones with an edge and teeth share the common properties of hardness and sharpness triggers the possibility in the minds of the early hominids of a functional similarity, that tools could extend the power of the body to transform objects. By the use of analogical thinking, where meaning is transferred from one framework to another, the early hominids started flaking stones to make tools that were hard with edges in a similar fashion to teeth: 'Whether a tool was fashioned by trial and error or by (in Piagetian terms) "an operational intelligence," it would in either case have involved the concept of causal order' (ibid.: 54). Sheets-Johnstone claims that such analogical thinking in the first instance is tactile-kinesthetic in nature and the roots of such thinking are basically corporeal.

Similarly, Sheets-Johnstone argues that the answers to the questions 'Where did numbers come from?' and 'How did hominids come to count?' are also to be found in analogical thinking; counting also has a tactile-kinesthetic nature and the roots of mathematical thinking are also basically corporeal. She argues that counting, in the first instance, is matching and noticing similarities, notable simple one-to-one correspondences. When hominids started to walk with an upright body, rather than with a quadrupedal posture, they walked with 'locomotor binary periodicities' – striding legs and swinging arms. The upright posture gave the body a binary structure: two hands, two arms, two legs, two feet, two eyes, two nostrils, two breasts, two testicles, two ears, two buttocks. In addition, bodies inhale and exhale, eat and excrete and because hominids did not have litters, but tended to produce one child at a time, there was the binary relationship between mother and child. The upright posture also automatically exposes the penis and makes it starkly visible, reinforcing the binary male/female division. These binary pairs gave the body a 'proto-numerical meaning': 'enumeration takes place only on and with the tactile-kinesthetic body ... One-to-one corporeal ratios were the conceptual ground of numerical thinking' (ibid.: 85–6).

Drawing upon Piaget's example of a young child opening its mouth in harmony with its opening of a matchbox, Sheets-Johnstone similarly argues that the ability of paleolithic people to create cave drawings and other pictorial art forms also developed from corporeal meanings derived from the tactile-kinesthetic body.

Death is a concept that is particularly difficult for the linguistic turn to explain, claims Sheets-Johnstone because:

> public criteria validate the use of any word, and there is no behavior coincident with the concept of *death*. The concept entails something far more complex than any particular behavior ... it entails certain compounded experiential understandings of the tactile-kinesthetic body. (Ibid.: 15–16; italics in original)

If individuals were isolated from each other at birth, they would have no conception of death. In addition, developing an understanding that we inhabit a physical body does not in itself allow us to invent a concept of death. In order to understand death, an individual has to think beyond the death of an Other, has to develop an awareness that seeing the lifelessness of the Other leads to an awareness of one's own lifespan as time limited. In other words, Sheets-Johnstone argues, the hominid had to develop a complex, non-linguistic understanding of bodily life. However, there is a contradiction here, on the one hand Sheets-Johnstone argues that 'the mere perception of a physical body as such does not lead a creature to conceive of death' (ibid.: 217). On the other hand, in relation to 'natural' death as opposed to 'accidental' death, she argues that the early hominids realised that:

> [L]ike the Other, I too will change radically and become a merely visual body ... In other words, only with the experiences of natural deaths might the concept of death have taken root. Only through such experiences might it have been realized that a certain nullifying fate was inevitable and mine. (Ibid.: 221)

The difficult conceptual issue of how an individual develops the ability to think beyond the death of an Other, to develop an awareness that in seeing the lifelessness of the Other, one becomes aware that one's own lifespan is time limited, is left unexplained by Sheets-Johnston's analysis. She offers no explanation of how corporeal meanings derived from the tactile-kinesthetic body can generate an understanding of death.

ACTIVITY

Sheets-Johnstone on Death

How does anyone develop a conception of death? Read the passage below.

> If death is bad for the one who died, then it must be a very peculiar kind of misfortune indeed. It is certainly not the kind the 'victim' could conceivably know, nor appreciate, nor in any possible way experience any effects of death. What could be bad which could have no bad effects – in fact, no effects at all? Would it not be more reasonable to say with Epicurus that, rightly understood, 'death is nothing to us'? (Suits 2001: 69)

Question:

> ➤ What significance do you think the passage has for Sheets-Johnstone's comments regarding death?

ACTIVITY

Sheets-Johnstone on Concepts

On the important question of how people get from corporeal experiences to concepts, Maxine Sheets-Johnstone provides the following explanation:

> In primordial language, corporeal representation is yet again produced in order to mean, but the analogical transfer of sense is *meta*corporeal: iconicity is between the articulatory (tactile-kinesthetic) gestures of speech and the spatio-kinetic character of the worldly processes or events referred to. Iconic spatio-kinetic corporeal representation is thus evident all the way from mimicry through display and gestural language to hominid primordial language. At the level of *symbolic* corporeal representation it defines an evolutionary semantics and places animal communicative systems within a conceptually analysable and appropriately broad spectrum; biological modes of meaning. It suggests *contra* Noam Chomsky that human and non-human forms of communication can be understood within a common *non-abstract* frame of reference. ... The two basic features of this evolutionary semantics are semanticity and iconicity, both of them clearly the work of symbolic corporeal representation. (Sheets-Johnstone 1990: 116; italics in original)

(Continued)

(Continued)

Questions:

➤ Outline what you believe Sheets-Johnstone is saying.

➤ State if you agree or disagree with the account given. In your answer consider how Sheets-Johnstone would deal with ideas of race and racism, disability, gender and sexuality. Do racism, disability, sexism or homophobia for example, have corporeal origins?

In summary, in *The Roots of Thinking* (1990) Maxine Sheets-Johnstone argues that the human concepts and symbols that we use in our everyday lives to shape our practices, beliefs and interactions with others can be traced back to an anatomical source that is older than human speech and which is central to understanding the nature and source of human thinking.

Pilloud and Louis-Courvoisier argue that the body is a historical object and should not be viewed as a universal thing that is essentially the same at all times and in all places. They argue that the body is a constructed phenomenon, developed within a given historical and cultural context. This is unlike Butler's work, which in the opinion of many commentators still holds that 'the body' is a biologically given thing, but surrounded and understood by discourses of the body. Pilloud and Louis-Courvoisier (2003) argue that bodily experience can either be external, as Maxine Sheets-Johnstone suggests, or internal, including such sensation as itching. Such sensations and experiences are subjective and individual, but are understood because they are shared within a common frame of reference. However, bodily experiences remain unique, conditioned by an individual's biography and personality.

In the eighteenth century it was common for doctors to consult with patients by letter. This allows the researcher to read, in the individual's own words, an account of these highly subjective and intimate sensations. Subjective reality has an impact upon an individual's perception of their own body. In their analysis of eighteenth-century patients' letters, Pilloud and Louis-Courvoisier (2003) found that many patients viewed their body like a machine that needed the right balance of air, food, sleep – free from disturbing and often erotic dreams that could lead to tiredness, tension or involuntary ejaculations. In contrast, many patients believed they had a humoral body, in which an overabundance of bodily liquids was the cause of poor health – such retention needed to be addressed. There were believed to be many humours within the body, and illnesses were caused by humours mixing with one another, taking a wrong turn and/or leaving the body by the wrong or an inappropriate orifice. Alternatively again, some patients believed themselves to have a nervous body – these patients were in poor health because of limp or flabby nerves or similar nervous ailments.

The significance of Pilloud and Louis-Courvoisier's research for Sheets-Johnstone's argument is that she assumes that she can view the body in the same manner as the first hominids and that there was one valid and commonly accepted hominid vision of the body. The hominid perspective on corporeality could be as many and varied as patients in the eighteenth century; it is also unknown to us if hominids thought in the ways that we think. We certainly cannot make any valid assertions on the hominid perspective of their own body in the way that Sheets-Johnstone suggests.

Monique Wittig: A Lesbian Is Not a Woman

Monique Wittig describes herself as a 'materialist feminist' and cites the central influences upon her work as Marx and Rousseau. Labour power is to be found within bodies, and capitalists, inside the context of patriarchal domination, appropriate that labour power from women. Patriarchal domination is a political set of arrangements organised around the web of compulsory heterosexual relations for the non-economic oppression of women. Women form a social class in the economically defined exploitative sense that Marx describes, but women have social interests in relation to issues of non-economic oppression that are in conflict with the interests of men. Patriarchal domination can only be overcome by taking up the lesbian standpoint, the only position from which women can identify the non-essential and constructed nature of the category 'woman' without which patriarchal domination cannot be challenged. By political action we need to challenge the arbitrary and oppressive categories of 'man' and 'woman'.

The categories 'man' and 'woman' are not products of nature and neither is heterosexuality, rather they are the products of 'the straight mind'. Only lesbians can escape this web of heterosexual relations. The purpose of Wittig's social analysis is to *lesbianise* patriarchal heterosexual relations and, by doing so, destroy the socio-political system that produces and institutionalises such forms of oppression. Wittig's argument is summed up in the following passage from 'One Is Not a Woman Born':

> Lesbian is the only concept I know which is beyond the categories of sex (woman and man), because the designated subject (lesbian) is *not* a woman, either economically, or politically, or ideologically. For what makes a woman is a specific social relation to a man, a relation that we have previously called servitude, a relation which implies personal and physical obligation as well as economic obligation ('forced residence', domestic corvee, conjugal duties, unlimited production of children, etc.), a relation which lesbians escape by refusing to become or to stay heterosexual. We are escapees from our class in the same way as the American runaway slaves were when escaping slavery and becoming free. For us this is an absolute necessity; our survival demands that we contribute all our

strength to the destruction of the class of women within which men appropriate women. This can be accomplished only by the destruction of heterosexuality as a social system which is based on the oppression of women by men and which is the doctrine of the difference between the sexes to justify this oppression. (Wittig 1981: 36)

Colette Guillaumin

Guillaumin (1988, 1995) also describes herself as a 'materialist feminist' and her work developed against the background of the debate within feminist circles about essentialism and social constructivism. Guillaumin argues that categories such as 'race' are not 'natural', but rather emerge through the exchange of discourse about race. In other words, 'race' and ideas about the characteristics that 'given' races are said to possess are a product of racist ideologies and racist discourse. In a similar fashion, Guillaumin attempts to define a non-essential category of 'woman'. She argues that the Marxian conception of labour power is far too narrow and proposes her own conception of *sexage* to describe the appropriation of women's labour power. For Guillaumin, labour power is found within bodies, and bodies are categorised in different terms, along grounds of gender or race, for example, to allow greater or lesser levels of exploitation. If a body is categorised as 'woman', then that body is expected to be engaged in a range of domestic and caring roles, because such roles are a reflection of the 'natural' or 'innate' facts of nature, the natural abilities of a woman. The 'imaginary' categories are given legal sanction within the social system, so that the State polices and maintains the idea of such 'natural' groups.

Luce Irigaray

Luce Irigaray examines the phallogocentric system, the relationship between nature and patriarchy. The phallus is not the penis or a natural fact of difference, rather the phallus is a *signifier*, a representative symbol of patriarchal domination. However, much if not all of the symbolic logic of the phallus is derived from the thing it symbolises, the penis. Irigaray questions the assumptions upon which the phallogocentric system is based. She asks, why is female sexuality as it is? And why is female sexuality located as it is? The phallogocentric system establishes masculine parameters around sexuality and is based upon the binary opposition:

penis/vagina

or

penis/nothing

Within this binary opposition the penis is culturally privileged over the vagina, female sexuality always refers back to the penis. Women are sexual objects of male desire, women do not define their own sexuality, the vagina is viewed simply as a small hole that the penis goes into in order to facilitate ejaculation. Men gain pleasure from vaginal intercourse, women get pleasure by giving a man pleasure. The penis then becomes a metaphor not only for gender but also for sexuality.

Karen Green (2002) argues that Irigaray assumes that *man* is the subject and woman *the Other*; she quotes Irigaray as saying: 'I was the other of/for man, I attempted to define the objective alterity of myself for myself as belonging to the female gender' (Irigaray 1995: 63). Irigaray argues that she speaks from the point of view of the Other – a place that does not exist from the male point of view. Her first book was *Speculum of the Other Woman*. A speculum is an instrument used by gynaecologists to examine the inside of the vagina, but it can also mean 'mirror'. Green (2002) suggests that Irigaray uses the term to refer to the female identity as the identity of the Other; that an authentic feminine subjectivity cannot be constructed within the patriarchial discourse of which they are typically constructed. Irigaray's use of the concept of alterity is central to her analysis. Individuals need to be able to identify the identity aspects of their life narrative by reference to something significant. However, as Butler and Cornell (1998) argue, Irigaray has placed too much emphasis upon the role of patriarchal discourse in the construction of a 'woman'. The notion of *woman* for Irigaray is a construct formed solely by the activities of distinct discourse communities.

In *Sexes and Genealogies*, Irigaray argues that fathers and other men in positions of authority restrict female desire. This restriction of female desire is said to be a matter of good health and of good virtue. The maternal function of women underlies the social order, and this is believed to be a woman's only 'order of desire'. Patriarchy is underpinned by a mythology of matricide, which according to Irigaray is necessary for the foundation of the social order. She argues that we live in sacrificial societies. The use of sacrifice was traditionally one of the ways in which men attempted to control nature. Men have always had a need to kill, break and eat. Matricide is said by Irigaray to pre-date the murder of the father outlined by Freud in *Totem and Taboo* (1913) and signifies the sacrificial nature of patriarchy. The religion's rites of sacrifice, she argues, including the social ceremonies, are almost universally performed by men, even though such activities 'serve as the basis and structure for the society' (Irigaray 1995: 78). This exclusion of women from the culture of sacrifice demonstrates that the hidden sacrifice of our society is the *extradition* of women – a ban on women's participation in the processes of social decision-making. Women are 'paralysed in and by cultural bonds that are not their own' (ibid.). Moreover, women who attempt to fight this patriarchy will be eliminated because they cause trouble. Often it is claimed that such women attempting to disrupt the libidinal economy are mad, because they will not obey the phallic order. Creativity has, claims Irigaray, been forbidden to women for centuries – women are seen as mothers only. In addition, women are 'subjected to a normative heterosexuality' (ibid.: 20) which they must reject if they are to rediscover their genealogy. Women need to discover the history of their desires, and hence rediscover their identity and their desires free from the phallic order.

Luce Irigaray: *Je, Tu, Nous* – Towards a Culture of Difference

Irigaray argues that the area of sex is important for reproduction, culture and the preservation of life: 'The issue ... is one of whether our civilizations are still prepared to consider sex as pathological, a flaw, a residue of animality, or if they are finally mature enough to give it its human cultural status' (Irigaray 1993: 36).

Women should come to accept that they have an identity that is different from that of men. Women can only enjoy any rights won by the Women's Movement if they find value in being a woman and not just in motherhood. Women must learn both to respect and to enjoy female sexuality, outside of the male sexual parameters that are imposed upon women. A woman must recognise that 'the geography of her pleasure is far more diversified, more multiple in its differences, more complex, more subtle, than is commonly imagined – in an imaginary rather too narrowly focused on sameness' (Irigaray 1985: 28). To achieve this, centuries of socio-cultural values about what it means to be a woman need to be changed. However, traditionally a women's sexuality was defined as a use-value for a man, so there are layers of sexual oppression to overcome before a woman can fully enjoy her needs and desires.

The biggest factor preventing this liberation of women's consciousness is the hold that patriarchy has on our civilisation. Patriarchal values appear to be both neutral and universal, yet these values involve the destruction of female genealogies. Patriarchy involves '*one part of humanity having a hold over the other*, here the world of men over that of women' (Irigaray 1993: 16; italics in original). Both men and women are 'conditioned' (ibid.: 21) to feel that the father–son genealogy is superior to the mother–daughter relationship, so much so that feminine becomes treated as simply non-masculine. We live in a between-men culture, which is seen most clearly in the use of grammar, where the appropriation of language by men has made 'feminine' syntactically secondary. Sexual justice cannot come about without changing the rules of language and the conceptions of truth and value that go with this: 'Man seems to have wanted, directly or indirectly, to give the universe his own gender as he wanted to give his own name to his children, his wife, his possessions' (ibid.: 31).

Irigaray goes on to explain that by the term 'possessions', she includes such diverse things as both women's and children's bodies, natural space, living space, the economy of signs, images, social and religious representation. Women need to involve themselves in *parler femme*; they must be involved in 'speaking as a woman', disrupting the discursive logic of male syntax.

What is the *culture of difference*? The culture of difference is for Irigaray 'a respect for the non-hierarchical difference of the sexes: *he* means *he*, *she* means *she*. *He* and *she* cannot be reduced to complementary functions but correspond to different identities' (ibid.: 48). The establishment of a culture of difference would involve a questioning of the categories upon which currently accepted discourses and truth are based. Women would contribute to the creation of culture on equal terms with men; therefore we would have the establishment of new rules and new subjective identities. Liberation from the phallogocentric system for women is by attaining *le parler femme*, a language for women that emerges spontaneously whenever women are together without the presence of men. *Le parler femme* represents the *lesbian continuum*, a form of sociality among and between women.

However, not all feminist writers are convinced that the feminist project of overturning patriarchy or the phallogocentric system is the correct approach.

Camille Paglia

'If civilization had been left in female hands, we would still be living in grass huts.' (Paglia 1990: 38)

Camille Paglia is often described as an 'antifeminist' and is certainly highly critical of feminist theories influenced by Foucault or by postmodernism and post-structuralism, which she describes as 'trendy' French social theories, but she has much in common with Maxine Sheets-Johnstone. Paglia regards academic feminism as a 'rickety house of cards' (Paglia 1992: 84). She argues that feminism has a simplistic view of patriarchy and never recognises the positive contributions that men have made to the world. However, Paglia has a tendency to call people names rather than present a coherent critique. For example, she has described feminists as puritanical about sex, fascist in their thought processes, unable to understand or relate to men, and having no knowledge of history. Consider the two quotes below:

A major failing of most feminist ideology is its dumb, ungenerous stereotyping of men as tyrants and abusers, when in fact – as I know full well, from my own mortifying lesbian experience – men are tormented by women's flirtatiousness and hemming and hawing, their manipulations and changeableness, their humiliating rejections. Cock teasing is a universal reality. It is part of women's merciless testing and cold-eyed comparison shopping for potential mates. Men will do anything to win the favor of women. Women literally *size up* men – 'What can you show me?' – in bed and out. If middle-class feminists think they conduct their love lives perfectly rationally, without any instinctual influences from biology, they are imbeciles. (Paglia 1992: 35)

[Andrea] Dworkin's blanket condemnation of fellatio as disgusting and violent should make every man furious. [Catharine] MacKinnon and Dworkin are victim-mongers, ambulance chasers, atrocity addicts. MacKinnon begins every argument from big, flawed premises such as 'male supremacy' or 'misogyny,' while Dworkin spouts glib Auschwitz metaphors at the drop of a bra. Here's one of their typical maxims: 'The pornographers rank with Nazis and Klansmen in promoting hatred and violence.' Anyone who could write such a sentence knows nothing about pornography *or* Nazism ... In arguing that a hypothetical physical safety on the streets should take precedence over the democratic principle of free speech, MacKinnon aligns herself with the authoritarian Soviet commissars. She would lobotomize the village in order to save it.

(Source: Paglia http://www.dimensional.com/~randl/camille.htm)

Paglia argues that she supports political and legal equality for women. However, she has serious reservations about the consequences of overturning or completely dismantling patriarchy, which she argues is the foundation of people's protection against the violence of nature. For Paglia, people are animals, they are part of nature and in a state of nature life is nasty, brutish and short. In her first book *Sexual Personae* (1990), she draws upon the work of Hobbes, Nietzsche and Sade, in order to identify the character and origins of patriarchal civilisation. Social organisation is an artificial creation, built as a defence against nature's power. Sexual power takes the form of Nietzsche's *the will to power* and this force is contained by Hobbesian social arrangements for strong government, as found in the Commonweal. As she later very forcefully explains: 'It is nature, not society, that is our greatest oppressor' (Paglia 1992: 45). And again: 'Society is not the enemy, as feminism ignorantly claims. Society is woman's protection against rape' (ibid.: 51).

In sharp contrast to Irigaray, Paglia argues that sex is not a matter of social convention, as feminists have mistakenly suggested; rather, sex is the interconnection between the social and nature: 'Sex is chthonian' (Paglia 1990: 295), which is described as a 'pre-Christian form of the malevolent nature mother' (ibid.: 364). Meaning that sex is from the earth, sex is from the muck; muddle and danger that are found in nature. In a delicious Shakespearean phrase that clearly demonstrates her view that sex involves surrender to nature, she observes that 'Two people making love are the beast with two backs' (ibid.: 297). This danger is seen in the many 'daemonic' models of women found within mythology, such as the siren and the *femme fatale*. These women are depicted as 'vampires', whose ability to drain and paralyse men, by wielding nature's power, is a key element in all-female physiology. Such women are deadly to men and represent the fear that we still have of nature. All cultures contain within them the fear amongst men of the toothed vagina. As Paglia argues: 'Metaphorically, every vagina has secret teeth, for the male exits as less than when he entered ... Physical and spiritual castration is the danger every man runs in intercourse with a woman' (ibid.: 13). The idea that the penis is power, she explains, is a lie that men tell themselves in order to overcome their fear of intercourse. The prostitute, in contrast to the feminist view, is not 'the victim of men but rather their conqueror, an outlaw who controls the sexual channel between nature and culture' (Paglia 1992: 18).

Contemporary feminists have a naïve and prudish view of sex. However, on the one hand she argues that women do not need legal protection from men, yet on the other hand, both sexual freedom and sexual liberation are modern feminist delusions: 'Society is our frail barrier against nature' (Paglia 1990: 3). As she goes on to explain: 'Men, bonding together, invented culture as a defense against female nature' (ibid.: 9).

This invented patriarchal culture represented a shift from 'belly magic', the magical power of nature as demonstrated in the biological functioning of the female body, to 'head magic'. This head magic was a male invention which stressed logic, and in particular the use and application of number. This logic was central in the creation of male civilisation and its attempt to control nature. It is with some irony that Paglia argues: 'The very language and logic modern woman uses to assail patriarchal culture were the invention of men' (ibid.: 9).

In addition, the notion of 'beauty' was an invention against nature. In contrast to the arguments in opposition to 'the beauty system', Paglia argues that ideas of 'beauty' allow us to categorise and conceptualise nature. Such conceptions allow us to feel that the daemonic nature of sex is under our control. This gives greater emphasis to what can be seen and undervalues the unseen dangerous 'chthonian' nature of the female: 'Female genitalia are not beautiful by any aesthetic standard … the idea of beauty is a defensive swerve from the ugliness of sex and nature' (ibid.: 286).

However, Paglia is at pains to explain that she is not a biological determinist. Her argument is that 'civilisation', as found in abstract law for example, marks our transition from barbarism to order. The issue here is that if people have the ability to liberate themselves from nature, as Paglia clearly explains that they do, then why does she claim that both sexual freedom and sexual liberation are modern feminist delusions? This delusion can be brought into reality by the same learning 'to behave as civilized beings' (Paglia 1992: 67) that brought about patriarchy.

In other words, if people have the ability to liberate themselves from nature, then such liberation can take a variety of forms. The relation between 'the social' and 'nature' implies that the social contains some form of agency, exercised by people, which acts as a constraint upon nature. Patriarchy is not the only form of liberation/protection from nature, and not the only form of hierarchy. To make anatomical sexual differences significant is an act of human decision-making, not the inevitable outcome of 'the will to power'. If people choose to liberate themselves from nature, they can do so in a variety of ways.

Finally, although Paglia explains that she is not a biological determinist, at times her argument is clearly just that. In a discussion of hormones she argues: 'If you are in any doubt about the effect of hormones on emotion, libido, and aggression, have a chat with a transsexual, who must take hormones medically. He or she will set you straight' (ibid.: 186).

Joseph Bristow (1997) argues that Camille Paglia's arguments are based upon the assumption that people's achievements are rooted in energies that are naturally occurring within human nature. Rather than providing any sociological insight on why gender inequality persists, Paglia argues that men achieve success because of their anatomy.

In terms of the nature of social division, sex is a biological fact for Paglia and patriarchy is a social construction invented by people to defend us all from the violence that nature would inflict upon us.

Theorising about Bisexuality

Writing in the pre-AIDS era, Jill Johnston's *Lesbian Nation* (1973) argued very strongly for a form of political lesbianism that was based upon the separatist assumption that women who slept with men were 'sleeping with the enemy' and helping to maintain the hegemonic institution of heterosexuality, which was one of the central drivers behind women's oppression. This separatist stance raises serious issues for bisexuality. There is a high degree of hostility towards bisexuality both in the lesbian and gay communities and amongst heterosexuals across the political spectrum. Right-wing Christian fundamentalists in Colorado in the 1990s attempted to make 'bisexual orientation' a basis for legal discrimination. Exclusion is a typical tactic; the term 'bisexuality' for example is not found in the index of Ken Plummer's influential book *Modern Homosexualities*.

Does bisexuality divide homosexuality from heterosexuality or does it unite them? Bisexuality destabilises the hetro/homo division. Post AIDS, bisexuals have become cast by many as misfits, outsiders, carriers of HIV from the gay community to the 'innocent' heterosexual community. The bisexual is always 'the Other' in terms of the boundary markers of difference. However, bisexuality is itself a highly fluid concept that disrupts the monosexual modes of identity rigidly codified in terms of sexuality rooted in gender, because as Yasmib Prabhudas explains, 'To be bisexual is to be both gay and straight' (Prabhudas 1996: 36). Similarly, 'To be mixed race is to be both black and white' (ibid.: 38).

According to Jo Eadie (1993), bisexuals are said to have 'heterosexual privilege' and are assumed to behave in heterosexist ways. The lack of a coherent bisexual identity, claims Eadie, is a product of dominant heterosexual and homosexual epistemologies that attempt to exclude bisexuality because it has no accepted – by which she means policed – characteristics. For Eadie, bisexuality has elements of 'hybridity' in the sense that Bhabha uses the term – as a product of systems of separation and organisation, but at the same time the hybrid generates a paranoid threat because it has the ability to break down central concepts for identity: self/other; inside/outside.

Elisabeth Daiumer (1992) argues that bisexuality is not an identity, but an epistemological and ethical vantage point. The painfulness of adapting to bisexuality, seen by both gay and straight people as a personal flaw, highlights the coercive nature of sexuality rooted in gender and the homo/hetero sexual framework. Bisexuals, by defending their sexual framework within affectional choices, politicise all sexual identities. Bisexuality opens up the possibility of having a heterosexual relationship without the 'heterosexualism' normally associated with it.

The relationship between bisexuality and gender for the bisexual has been spelt out by Ann Kaloski (1997), who argues that there are three broad positions:

1   Gender is irrelevant, or such an insignificant difference between people as to be discountable.
2   Bisexuals are not bi-gendered and are erotically attracted to both sexes.
3   Gender is a mutable, but nevertheless important way of recognising and expressing particular human differences.

Conclusion

Before the twentieth century it was commonly assumed that social inequalities between men and women were biologically determined. Women were assumed to have a natural inferiority compared to men. As a consequence women had far fewer legal rights, political rights and career opportunities than men. In the nineteenth century British women had very few rights, and feminism – the movement for social, economic and political equality between men and women – has a long history. Many women were expressing their opinions about social and political issues in public for the first time. Women were also granted limited rights of access to children after divorce. There is now legal protection for women against male violence, employment protection, and a range of other issues initiated by governmental bodies such as the United Kingdom's Women's Unit. These advances reflect the success of the various women's social movements over the previous decades. However, the employment protection and other legal/political advantages have not benefited all women.

In addition, some feminists argue that the processes of globalisation directly address women as sexual beings, in that women's labour is being sexualised. It is marginalised and economically disadvantaged women, particularly black women, who bear the cost of neo-liberal processes of globalisation.

We also saw that the beauty system polices all aspects of a women's appearance. Feminists assume that the beauty system simply emerges from patriarchal relations, for the benefit of men and to the detriment of women. Wolf argues that even though the Women's Movement had significant victories in a range of areas of social life during the 1970s and 1980s, women do not feel as free as they should, given the gains they have made. It is no accident that so many women, potentially powerful women, feel this way. Ideas about what constitutes female beauty are used as political weapons to covertly control women, reinforce the glass ceiling and exclude women from power; women are made to feel a permanent insecurity of becoming ugly.

Many women are unable or unwilling to identify themselves within a given class position or class category. Class is something imposed upon women; something '*they* work out' rather than something *she* as a woman lives through. Only single women determine their own social status. There is a debate around the issue of whether women are unequal to men on the basis of their gender and biological sex, and whether this is relevant or not to class-based forms of stratification analysis. The power of husbands has been restricted; women no longer need marriage to secure their economic future or their social status. Women no longer need men to provide for them. Individualisation releases both women and men from their traditional gender roles found in industrial society.

Second-wave feminists explored the notion of 'difference' as it became increasingly clear that feminist accounts of women's experience did not apply to all women. The social construction of alterity was seen as directly related to both order and social division. A number of feminists argue that labour power is to be found within bodies; and capitalists, inside the context of patriarchal domination, appropriate that labour power from women. Women form a social class in the economically defined exploitative sense that Marx describes, but women have social interests in relation to issues of non-economic oppression that conflict with the interests of men. For many this is an absolute necessity; our survival demands that we contribute all our strength to the destruction of the class of women within which men appropriate women.

Irigaray (1995, 1996) argues that women are sexual objects of male desire, women do not define their own sexuality, the vagina is viewed simply as a small hole that the penis goes into in order to facilitate ejaculation. Men gain pleasure from vaginal intercourse, women get pleasure by giving a man pleasure. This marginalisation of women in the culture of sacrifice demonstrates that the hidden sacrifice of our society is the *extradition* of women – a ban on women's participation in the processes of social decision-making; women are seen as mothers only.

Liberation from the phallogocentric system for women is achieved by attaining *le parler femme*, a language for women that emerges spontaneously whenever women are together without the presence of men. *Le parler femme* represents the *lesbian continuum*, a form of sociality among and between women. However, both the phallogocentric system and the *lesbian continuum* are monosexual in nature and are viewed by many bisexual individuals as the basis for a form of discrimination, oppression and the foundation of otherness.

Like all of the most effective social divisions, sexual division is assumed to be biological in origin; men and women have different bodies in terms of primary and secondary sexual characteristics. However, do these biological differences determine the 'nature' or essence of what it means to be a man or a woman?

In addition, is it possible to understand biological difference outside of the discourses of gender and sexuality? Sex, gender and sexuality have become increasingly difficult to define, increasingly politicised, and are tied up with the processes of alterity/subjectification that are the essence of all social division. The effect of these processes is to restrict the individual agency from fully *becoming*. Individuals as sexual being have the restriction of social division placed upon them, which they experience directly through the processes of subjectification.

References

Acker, J. (1973) 'Women and Social Stratification: A Case of Intellectual Sexism', *American Journal of Sociology* 78: 936–45. Also found in Scott, J. (ed.) (1996) *Class: Critical Concepts*, Vol. III, Routledge, London.

Adkins, L. (1995) *Gendered Work: Sexuality, Family and the Labour Market*, Open University Press, Milton Keynes.

Adkins, L. (2001) 'Cultural Feminisation: Money, Sex and Power for Women', *Signs: Journal of Women in Culture and Society* 26(3): 669–95.

Anderson, B. and Phizacklea, A. (1997) *Migrant Domestic Workers. A European Perspective*. Report for the Equal Opportunities Unit, DGV, Commission of the European Communities.

Astell, Mary [1694] (1997) 'Serious Proposal to the Ladies' parts 1 and 2, Pickering & Chatto, London.

Bartky, S.L. (1997) 'Femininity and Domination: Studies in the Phenomenology of Oppression', Routledge, London.

Bartky, Sandra Lee (1988) 'Foucault, Femininity and the Modernization of Patriarchal Power', in Diamond, I. and Quinby, L. (eds) *Feminism and Foucault: Reflections on Resistance*, Northeastern University Press, Boston, Mass.

Beasley, Chris (1999) 'What is Feminism?', Sage, London.

Beck, U. (1992) *The Risk Society*, Sage, London.

Beck, U. and Beck-Gernsheim, E. (1995) *The Normal Chaos of Love*, trans. Mark Ritter and Jane Wiebel, Polity Press, Cambridge.

Beck, U. and Beck-Gernsheim, E. (2002) *Individualization: Institutional Individualism and its Social and Political Consequences*, Sage, London.

Benhabib, S. (1995) 'Feminism and postmodernism', in S. Benhabib, J. Butler, D. Cornell and N. Fraser *Feminist Contentions: A Philosophical Exchange*, Routledge and Kegan Paul, London.

Bernard, J. (1976) *Family and Relationships*. London: Penguin.

Best, Shaun (2001) 'Just Like a Girl: Do We Still Need Feminism?', *The Social Science Teacher* 30(1): 20–5.

Biemann, U. (2002) 'Remotely sensed: a topography of the global sex trade', *Feminist Review* 70: 75–88.

Black, P. (2002) 'Ordinary People Come Through Here: Locating the Beauty Salon in Women's Lives', *Feminist Review* 71: 2–17.

Bourdieu, P. (1977) *Outline of a Theory of Practice*, Cambridge University Press, Cambridge.

Bourdieu, P. (1984) *Distinction: A Social Critique of the Judgement of Taste*, Routledge, London.

Bourdieu, P. (1990) *The Logic of Practice*, trans. R. Nice, Polity, Cambridge.

Bristow, Joseph (1997) *Sexuality*, Routledge, London.

Brownmiller, Susan (1976) *Against Our Will: Men, Women and Rape*, Random House, New York.

Brownmiller, Susan (1999) *In Our Time: Memoir of a Revolution*, Dial Press, New York.

Butler, Judith (1990) *Gender Trouble: Feminism and the Subversion of Identity*, Routledge, London.

Butler, Judith (1993) *Bodies that Matter: On the Discursive Limits of 'Sex'*, Routledge, London.

Butler, Judith (1997) *The Psychic Life of Power: Theories in Subjection*, Stanford University Press, Stanford, Cal.

Butler, J. and Cornell, D. (1998) 'The future of sexual difference: an interview with Judith Butler and Drucilla Cornell', *Diacritics* 28(1): 19–42.

Carter, Angela (1984) *Nights at the Circus*, Picador, London.

Chafetz, J.S. (1990) *Gender Equity: An Integrated Theory of Stability and Change*, Sage, Newbury Park, CA.

Chodorow, N. (1978) *The Reproduction of Mothering: Psychoanalysis and the Sociology of Gender*, University of California Press, Berkeley, Cal.

Collins, Patricia Hill (1986) 'Learning from the Outside Within: The Sociological Significance of Black Feminist Thought', *Social Problems* 33: S14–S32.

Collins, Patricia Hill (1996) *Black Feminist Thought: Knowledge, Consciousness, and the Politics of Empowerment*, Unwin Hyman, Boston, Mass.

Coward, Rosalind (1983) *Patriarchal Precedents: Sexuality and Social Relations*, Routledge & Kegan Paul, London.

Crompton, R. (1989) 'Class, Theory and Gender', *British Journal of Sociology* 40: 565–87. Also found in Scott, J. (ed.) (1996) *Class: Critical Concepts Vol. III*, London, Routledge.

Daiumer, E. [1992] (1999) 'Queer Ethics, or the Challenge of Bisexuality to Lesbian Ethics', in Storr, E. (ed.) *Bisexuality: A Critical Reader*, London, Routledge.

De Beauvoir, Simone [1949] (1974) *The Second Sex*, trans. and ed. H.M. Parshley, Vintage, New York.

Davies, M. (1979). 'Woman's place is at the typewriter: The feminization of the clerical labour force, in Z.R. Eisenstein (ed.) *Capitalist Patriarchy and the Case for Socialist Feminism*, Monthly Review Press, New York.

Delphy, C. [1981] (1996) 'Women in Stratification Studies', trans. Helen Roberts, in Scott, J. (ed.) *Class: Critical Concepts Vol. III*, London, Routledge.

Delphy, C. (1984) 'The Main Enemy', in *Close to Home: A Materialist Analysis of Women's Oppression*, trans. and ed. D. Leonard, Hutchinson, London.

Delphy, C. and Leonard, D. (1992) *Familiar Exploitation: A New Analysis of Marriage in Contemporary Western Societies*, Polity Press, Cambridge.

Dempsey, K. (2002) 'Who Gets the Best Deal from Marriage: Women or Men?', *Journal of Sociology* 38(2): 91–110.

Derrida, Jacques (1991) *A Derrida Reader*, ed. P. Kamuf, Columbia University Press, New York.

Dworkin, A. (1987) *Pornography: Men Possessing Women*, Basic Books, New York.

Eadie, J. [1993] (1999) 'Activating Bisexuality: Towards a Bi/Sexual Politics', in Storr, E. (ed.) *Bisexuality: A Critical Reader*, Routledge, London.

Felski, R. (1997) 'Judith Krantz: Author of "The Cultural Logics of Late Capitalism"', *Women's Cultural Review* 8(2): 129–42.

Filby, M.P. (1992) '"The Figures, the Personality and the Bums": Service Work and Sexuality', *Work, Employment and Society* 6: 23–42.

Firestone, S. (1974) *The Dialectic of Sex: The Case for Feminist Revolution*, Bantam Books, New York.

Flax, J. (1990) *Thinking Fragments: Psychoanalysis, Feminism, and Postmodernism in the Contemporary West*, University of California Press, Berkeley.

Foucault, M. (1969a) *The Order of Things: An Archaeology of the Human Sciences*, trans. Alan Sheridan-Smith, Tavistock Publications, London.

Foucault, M. [1969] (1986) 'What Is an Author?', in Rabinow, P. (ed.) *The Foucault Reader*, Peregrine/Penguin, Harmondsworth.

Foucault, Michel (1977) *Discipline and Punish: The Birth of the Prison*, trans. Alan Sheridan-Smith, Penguin, London.

Foucault, Michel (1990a) *The History of Sexuality Vol. 1*, trans. Robert Hurley, Penguin, London.

Foucault, Michel (1990b) *The Care of the Self: Vol. 3 of The History of Sexuality*, trans. Robert Hurley, Penguin, London.

Foucault, Michel (1992) *The Use of Pleasure: The History of Sexuality Vol. 2*, trans. Robert Hurley, Penguin, London.

Fuss, D. (1989) *Essentially Speaking: Feminism, Nature and Difference*, Routledge, New York.

Goffman, E. (1959) *The Presentation of Self in Everyday Life*, Doubleday Anchor, New York.

Goffman, E. (1961) *Asylums*, Doubleday, New York.

Goldman, Alan H. (1977) 'Plain Sex', *Philosophy and Public Affairs* 6: 267–88.

Goldthorpe, J.H. (1983) 'Women and Class Analysis: In Defence of the Conventional View', *Sociology* 17: 465–88. Also in Scott, J. (ed.) (1996) *Class: Critical Concepts Vol. III*, Routledge, London.

Goldthorpe, J.H., Llewellyn, C. and Payne, C. (1987) *Social Mobility and Class Structure in Modern Britain*, (2nd edn) Clarendon Press, Oxford.

Green, Karen (2002) 'The Other as Another Other', *Hypatia* 17(4): 1–15.

Guillaumin, C. (1988) 'Race and Nature: The System of Marks', trans. M.J. Lakeland, *Feminist Issues* 8(2): 25–43.

Guillaumin, C. (1995) *Racism, Sexism, Power and Ideology*, Routledge, New York.

Gullette, M.M. (1994) 'All Together Now: The New Sexual Politics of Midlife Bodies', in Goldstein, L. (ed.) *The Male Body: Features, Destinies, Exposures*, University of Michigan Press, Michigan.

Hall, E.J. (1993). 'Waitering/waitressing: engendering the work of table servers', *Gender and Society* 17: 329–46.

Hart, N. (1989) 'Gender and the Rise and Fall of Class Politics', *New Left Review* 175: 19–47. Also in Scott, J. (ed.) (1996) *Class: Critical Concepts, Vol. III*, Routledge, London.

Hartmann, H. (1979) 'Capitalism, patriarchy and job segregation by sex', in Z.R. Eisenstein (ed.) *Capitalist Patriarchy and the Case for Socialist Feminism*, Monthly Review Press, New York: pp. 206–47.

Hartmann, H. (1981) 'The family as the locus of gender, class and political struggle', *Signs* 6(3): 366–94.

Hollywood, A. (2002) 'Performativity, Citationality, Ritualization', *History of Religions* 42(2): 93–113.

hooks, bell (1990) *Yearning: Race, Gender and Cultural Politics*, South End Press, Boston, Mass.

Irigaray, Luce (1982) *Je, Tu, Nous: Towards a Culture of Difference*, trans. Alison Martin, Routledge, London.

Irigaray, Luce (1985) *This Sex Which Is Not One*, trans. Catherine Porter and Carolyn Burke, Cornell University Press, Ithaca, NY.

Irigaray, L. (1993) *An Ethics of Sexual Difference*, trans. Carolyn Burke and Gillian C. Gill, Cornell University Press, Ithaca, NY.

Irigaray, Luce (1995) *Sexes and Genealogies*, trans. Gillian C. Gill, Cornell University Press, Ithaca, NY.

James, N. (1989) 'Emotional labour: skill and work in the social regulation of feelings', *Sociological Review* 37: 15–42.

James, N. (1992) 'Care = Organisation + Physical labour + emotional labour', *Sociology of Health and Illness* 14(4): 488–505.

Johnston, Jill (1973) *Lesbian Nation: The Feminist Solution*, Simon & Schuster, New York.

Kaloski, A. [1997] (1999) 'Bisexuals Making Out with Cyborgs: Politics, Pleasure, Confusion', in Storr, E. (ed.) *Bisexuality: A Critical Reader*, Routledge, London.

Laclau, E. and Mouffe, C. (2001) *Hegemony and Socialist Strategy* (2nd edn), Verso, London.

Lengermann, P.M. and Niebrugge-Brantley, G. (1990) 'Feminist sociological theory: the near-future prospects', in Ritzer, G. (ed.) *Frontiers of Sociological Theory: The New Synthesis*, Columbia University Press, New York.

Levine, S. (1987). 'Peer support for women in middle management', *Educational Leadership*, November: 74–75.

Lockwood, D. (1986) 'Class, Status and Gender', in Crompton, R. and Mann, M. (eds) *Gender and Stratification*, Polity, Cambridge.

Lutz, L. (2002) 'Government and the life course', in Jeylan, T. Mortimer and J. Michael Shanahan (eds) *Handbook of the Life Course*, Kluwer, New York.

MacCannell, D. and Flower MacCannell, J. (1987) 'The Beauty System', in Armstrong, N. and Tennenhouse, L. (eds) *The Ideology of Conduct: Essays on Literature and the History of Sexuality*, Methuen, New York.

MacKinnon, Catherine, A. (2001) *Sex Equality*, Foundation Press, New York.

Marietta, Don, E. (1997) *Philosophy of Sexuality*, M.E. Sharpe, Armonk, NY.

Miller, James (1993) *The Passion of Michel Foucault*, HarperCollins, London.

Millett, Kate (1970) *Sexual Politics*, Hart-Davis, London.

Mouffe, C. (2000) *The Democratic Paradox*, Verso, London.

Oakley, Ann (1972) *Sex, Gender and Society*, Maurice Temple Smith in association with New Society, London.

Oliver, K. (2000) *French Feminist Reader*, Rowman & Littlefield, New York.

Paglia, Camille (1990) *Sexual Personae: Art and Decadence from Nefertiti to Emily*, Dickinson, Penguin, London.

Paglia, Camille (1992) *Sex, Art and American Culture*, Vintage Books, New York.

Paglia, Camille (1993) *Vamps and Tramps*, Vintage Books, New York.

Patterson, Charlotte J (2003) *Lesbian and Gay Parenting*, American Psychological Association, http://www.apa.org/pi/parent.html

Pen, Jennifer (2003) *Heterosexism and Sexism in Engels*, http://www.graphicgirlz.com/qniii/engels.htm

Pilloud, M. and Louis-Courvoisier, M. (2003) 'La petite marchande de prose, conflit delirant autour d'une mort cerebrale', *Medecine et Hygiene* 2463: 2506.

Prabhudas, Y. [1996] (1999) 'Bisexuals and people of mixed-race: arbiters of change', in Storr, E. (ed.) *Bisexuality: A Critical Reader*. Routledge: London.

Pringle, R. (1989). *Secretaries Talk: Sexuality, Power and Work*, Verso, London.

Pringle, R. (1993). 'Male secretaries', in C. Williams (ed.) *Doing 'Women's Work': Men in Nontraditional Occupations*, Sage, London.

Rich, A. (1980) 'Compulsory Heterosexuality and Lesbian Existence', *Signs* 5(4): 38–51.

Rosen, R. (2000) *The World Split Open: How the Women's Movement Changed America*, Viking, New York.

Rudy, K. (2001) 'Radical Feminism, Lesbian Separatism and Queer Theory', *Feminist Studies* 27(1): 191–222.

Sedgwick, E.K. (1990) *Epistemology of the Closet*, University of California Press, Berkeley.

Sennett, R. (1990) *Authority*, Faber & Faber, London.

Sheets-Johnstone, M. (1990) *The Roots of Thinking*, Temple University Press, Philadelphia.

Shorter, E. (1975) *The Making of the Modern Family*, Basic Books, New York.

Skeggs, B. (1997) *Formations of Class and Gender*, Sage, London.

Storr, M. (2002) 'Classy Lingerie', *Feminist Review* 71: 18–36.

Sudbury, J. (2002) 'Celling black bodies: black women in the global prison industrial complex', *Feminist Review* 70: 57–74.

Suits, D. (2001) 'Why Death Is Not Bad for the One Who Died', *American Philosophical Quarterly* 38(1): 69–84.

Thompson, Bill (1994) *Sadomasochism*, Cassell, London.

Thompson, Denis (2001) *Radical Feminism Today*, Sage, London.

Tseelon, E. (1995) *The Masque of Femininity*, Sage, London.

Tyler, M. and Hancock, P. (2001) 'Flight Attendants and the Management of Gendered "Organizational Bodies" ', in Backett-Milburn, K. and McKie, L. (eds) *Constructing Gendered Bodies*', Palgrave, Basingstoke.

Walby, Sylvia (1990) *Theorizing Patriarchy*, Blackwell, Oxford.

Walby, Sylvia (1989) 'Flexibility and the Changing Sexual Division of Labour', in Wood, S. (ed.) *The Transformation of Work*, Unwin Hyman, London.

Walby, S. (2002) 'Feminism in a global era', *Economy and Society*, 31(4): 533–58.

Walby, S. (2002), 'Myth of the nation-state: theorizing society and politics in a global era', *Sociology*, 37(3): 529–47.

Weinberg, T. and Kamel, G.W. (1983) *S&M: Studies in Sadomasochism*, Ptometheus Books, Buffalo, NY.

White, S.K. (1999) 'As the World Turns: Ontology and Politics in Judith Butler', *Polity* 32(2): 155–76.

Wilson-Kovacs, D. (2001) 'The Fabric of Love: a Semiotic Analysis of the Suspender Belt', in Backett-Milburn, K. and McKie, L. (eds) *Constructing Gendered Bodies*, Palgrave, Basingstoke.

Wittig, M. (1992a) 'One Is Not Born a Woman', in *The Straight Mind and Other Essays*, Harvester Wheatsheaf, New York.

Wittig, M. (1992b) *The Straight Mind and Other Essays*, Harvester Wheatsheaf, New York.

Wolf, N. (1990) *The Beauty Myth: How Images of Beauty are Used against Women*, Vintage, London.

Wollstonecraft, M. [1792] (1986) *A Vindication of the Rights of Woman*, ed. J.S. Mill, Dent, London.

Five

Chapter Outline

By the end of this chapter you should have a critical understanding of:

- The role of governance in the processes of social division
- Ideal state personhood and Judith Butler's analysis of subjection
- Medical policing and notifiable diseases
- State-sponsored treatment of the mentally ill
- Globalisation and its impact on citizenship governance
- Why legislating for rights and legal protection for groups has proved to be problematical for nation states
- Citizenship rights in relation to issues of asylum, migration and forced migration
- Seeking asylum on grounds of sexuality
- Restrictions on the movement of people – politicisation of migration and asylum issues
- Disetatisation: the end of sovereignty
- The state's regulation of sexuality
- Blairism as a site of sexual politics, abolishing Section 28
- Age-based categories and social divisions: is there a 'normal' childhood or a 'normal' old age?
- Sociological theories of the social position of old people and children within the wider society
- Medicalisation of unacceptable behaviour in old age
- Childhood individualisation
- The child and the emergence of the postmodern family
- Deleuze and Guattari on *becoming*
- Communitarianism and the 'new' politics of self-actualisation.

State-Sponsored Social Divisions

Introduction

The state has a clear idea of its ideal person and the processes of socialisation that all individuals should go though on the road to becoming that ideal person. Moreover, there has always been a politics of self-actualisation in which the state has played an active role. Traditionally, the ways in which the state placed individuals into categories was often assumed to be biological in nature rather than a social division. Alternatively, the state could draw upon deeply held religious convictions, traditions or widely shared common-sense beliefs. In the contemporary world, there still exist deeply held religious convictions, traditions or widely shared common-sense beliefs, however, most of us do not accept such views without question: convictions, traditions and beliefs now have to be justified.

All this has made the state's interest in the processes of self-actualisation more visible. At a time when processes of globalisation have severely restricted the power of the nation state in areas of economic policy, human rights and environmental protection, questions such as. 'Is there a 'normal' sexuality, childhood or old age?' have become politicised. Do the rationalities and technologies of governance underpin the social divisions and give rise to the discourses that allow the state to identify 'the Other'?

There is a clear conception of the ideal state personhood. Children are potentially dangerous without the moulding of adult supervision and the imposition of constraints. In addition, children need our protection from dangerous adults who *pass* as normal, in an effort to corrupt our children and make them into something undesirable. Individuals who deviate from that ideal state personhood are in any number of ways seen as a potential threat to the normal citizen. These individual thoughts and actions are believed to be self-directed, or alternatively they are unknowingly a threat, and have to have action taken against them because they lack the basic element of personhood: control of their own human agency. Such deviants need to be identified, scientifically and morally defined, classified, organised on the basis of the threat to the wider society.

Boundaries are established around such individuals, so that they become 'populations' or groups differentiated from the rest of society and clearly divided. Understanding state-sponsored social division involves looking at the role of the state relationship between agency and structure; in the processes of *subjectification* that we looked at in the chapter on gender and sexuality. As you may recall, the argument in the chapter on gender and sexuality was that the purpose of processes of *subjectification* is to restrict the process of *becoming* within the parameters of becoming. Social division is about the creation and maintenance of sites within a structure, inhabited by individuals who *become* agents and who exercise their agency in appropriate ways. Social division is about shaping who we are as individuals, what is appropriate for us, from the clothes we wear, the music we enjoy, the food we eat, to the thoughts we have. In Judith Butler's analysis, subjectification involves:

- Regulatory power that sustains subjects in a position of subordination
- The subject is located within a structure that sets limits to its subjectification
- The agency of the subject is formed in opposition to the power that maintains the site – or place in the structure – for the subject.

State-sponsored social divisions are maintained by criminalising the boundary between categories of people whom the state believes to be potential threats to the wider society. Any attempt to surmount the boundary is classed as a crime. In other words, surmounting the boundary is a prohibited act – defined by the state either by statute or by common law. Crime is unwanted conduct that breaks a range of often internalised moral precepts; moreover such actions are believed to be based upon personal responsibility or moral blameworthiness of the individual – *Mens rea* ('a guilty mind') – an antisocial or 'evil' intent that requires punishment.

Foucault attempts to explain how the state in modern societies controls the behaviour of people through knowledge-power by transforming people into subjects of the state. His central unit of analysis is *discourse* – a set of rules that set boundaries on how to think and speak about categories of people. The regimen universalises the problem of crime and individualises its causes. Foucault does not make a judgment about the underlying validity of criminological theories; he is primarily concerned with the central role of the regimen of legal discourses that are central in maintaining power relationships.

Medical Police and the Organisation of the Body

The body is a historical object and should not be viewed as a universal thing that is essentially the same at all times and in all places; the body is a constructed phenomenon, developed within a given historical and cultural context. However, the body has to be *policed* as it is a potential threat to the wider society. The most widely known form of medical policing is the *notifiable disease*; a disease specified by the state as being such a serious threat to public health that doctors are legally obliged to report any instance to the relevant government agency. In 1878 the United States Congress gave the US Marine Hospital Service a central role in information gathering on infectious diseases such as cholera, smallpox, plague and yellow fever, from US embassies overseas. These data formed the basis of decision-making in relation to appropriate quarantine measures. Moreover, since 1879 Congress has collected data from states and municipal authorities on a range of notifiable diseases. The service has expanded ever since and post September 11, the health care system in the United States has a central role to play in homeland defence.

Patrick Carroll (2002) looks at the role of the medical police in the history of Britain, and contrary to many accounts, he demonstrates that medical policing is not a phenomenon unique to continental Europe, but has a long history in Britain. From the mid-seventeenth century the notion of policing became associated with conceptions of centralised governance and the need for security: inspection, surveillance, and intelligence gathering were central to medical police practice. The police had a role to play in the realisation of public health. Plague laws, such as household segregation of the sick, were closely policed, as were concerns about sexually transmitted diseases. Under such legislation as The Contagious Diseases Acts (1866, 1869), unaccompanied women on the streets in the nineteenth century could be detained and involuntarily subjected to intrusive physical examinations for evidence of sexually transmitted diseases. Carroll identifies several areas of police practice:

- The policing of the community, notably prostitutes and the poor were singled out as potential threats to public health
- The policing of 'nuisance', which included anything that might compromise health and safety
- Inspecting the effectiveness of sanitary engineering
- Policing what could be ingested; food, drugs, water
- Policing of occupational hazards
- Policing and inspection of medical practitioners, doctors, witches, quacks. In the United Kingdom, the 1815 Apothecaries Act established minimum standards of medical practice and introduced licensing; in 1858 the Medical Act established the Medical Register and the General Medical Council.

As Carroll explains: 'medical police was designedly a "science" though one regularly expressed in a discourse of moral imperative' (Carroll 2002: 465).

Similar concerns underpin aspects of medical policing today; in the United States there are moral fears about carriers of AIDS and a witch hunt for 'patient zero', widely believed to be Gaetan Dugas, a flight attendant who was accused of spreading AIDS across North America in the 1980s. SARS also has a potential patient zero commonly believed to be Esther Mok, who is a 26-year-old Singaporean woman who was widely reported to have transmitted the SARS virus to over 100 people. Although the term patient zero emerged with the AIDS epidemic in the 1980s, the idea that police action should be taken to identify and punish particular individuals who are believed to be superspreaders of epidemics has a long history.

One of the first recorded examples of a patient zero was Mary Mallon, who became known as Typhoid Mary. Mallon was a carrier of *Salmonella typhi*, a bacillus found in human urine and faeces. From 1900 to 1904 she worked as a cook in the New York area, moving from Mamaroneck to Manhattan and then to Long Island. Her employment coincided with numerous outbreaks of typhoid fever amongst affluent New Yorkers, which is unusual given that typhoid fever is commonly associated with poverty and poor living conditions. In 1906 she was traced to Park Avenue, a penthouse apartment where the New York Health Commissioner arrested her. Whilst in custody, cultures were involuntarily taken from her which revealed that her gall bladder was seriously infected with typhoid salmonella. She refused to have her gall bladder removed, but promised never to work as a cook again. However, over the coming years she had several jobs as a cook, including a post at New York's Sloan Hospital for Women in 1915, where a serious outbreak caused deaths amongst both staff and patients. She was quarantined for life on North Brother Island.

Sexuality has long been a concern for the medical police. Henry VIII issued a decree in 1533 that made what were described as the 'unnatural practices' of same sex relationships between men punishable by death. Moreover, it was only in 1967, following the Wolfenden Report, that sexual acts between men in private were decriminalised. A case in point is that of Ernest Boulton and Frederick Park – known widely as Fanny and Stella – who in 1870 were arrested under suspicion of soliciting gay sex. The pair were seen regularly in London's theatres and markets in women's clothes and were often mistaken for good-looking female prostitutes. The jury in the trial viewed the two men as harmless, well-known and high-spirited cross-dressers. During the hearing at Bow Street Magistrates' court in London, Boulton and Park were also charged with 'conspiring to commit sodomy' – a crime that until 1862 was a capital offence in England and still carried a long prison sentence. Medical discourses were used in the trial of Boulton and Park to identify signs of sodomy that would allow the Director of Public Prosecutions to gain a conviction.

Several doctors, who were assumed to be experts in the field, conducted intrusive physical examinations on Boulton and Park to discover if the men had engaged in anal sex. The doctors were unable to agree on the significance of the physical evidence. Dalley and Crozier (2001) explore the investigations in some detail.

Also in the nineteenth century, William Acton invented a range of new medical procedures to discover whether anal sex had been practised. However, well into the twentieth century, medical discourses were drawn upon to establish the nature of homosexuality. In particular, Alfred Taylor's textbook *Manual of Medical Jurisprudence* (1864) which was updated regularly well into the twentieth century, proved highly influential. Taylor's book describes anal sex as 'the unnatural connection of a man with man' (cited in Dalley and Crozier 2001: 67).

In 1885 the House of Commons debated a Bill to raise the age of consent for girls from 13 years of age to 16, in an effort to eliminate child prostitution. However, during the debate Henry Labouchere tabled an amendment that significantly expanded the Bill's reach. Labouchere argued that any sexual touching between men should be added to the Bill and should become illegal under the phrase 'gross indecency'.

In more recent times, the threat of terrorism has become a central concern for the medical police. September 11 had a significant impact upon the medical policing of public health in the United States. Christopher Sellers (2003) looked at the environmental impact on lower Manhattan of the collapse of the twin towers. Sellers argues that we have had to change our assumptions about the character of environmental hazards. Since the 1970s, environmental protection, for example under the Clean Air Act, has assumed that risks were minimal, ever present and at a low level. September 11 made people realise that there had been no environmental risk assessment of the collapse of the twin towers and that toxins that were released in the cloud of dust and smoke contained such elements as ash from burning flesh, asbestos and ultra-fine dust from concrete containing dioxins. The smoke and dust inhalation saw an outbreak of what became known as World Trade Center cough.

Nicholas King (2003) argues that fears of bioterrorism, particularly the use of anthrax and smallpox, have led directly to increased federal funding on medical policing, especially by the Environmental Protection Agency (EPA) and the Occupational Safety and Health Administration (OSHA), in relation to the international misuse of scientific knowledge to create new environmental risks. King discusses the medical policing model prepared by the Johns Hopkins University in Baltimore and The Center for Law and Public Health at Georgetown University, Washington DC. In their proposed 'State Emergency Health Powers Act' the Universities suggested that President Bush should give himself powers to take over medical and other facilities, introduce compulsory vaccination, treatment and quarantine for individuals believed to be at risk.

State-sponsored Treatment of the Mentally III

In the sixteenth and seventeenth centuries, witchcraft and demonic possession were common explanations for mental illness. Moreover, as the Salem witchcraft trials demonstrated when 19 people were sentenced to hang for their 'crimes', the state has had a keen interest the social control of the demonically possessed, establishing a clear social division and dealing with the 'problem' in the strongest possible way. Laffey explains that:

> in Augustan and Georgian England it was widely understood that madness could have two more-or-less distinct meanings. 'Moral' madness was the subject's own fault, and he/she remained accountable for actions commissioned under its effects. The 'morally' mad individual's thoughts and actions were understood to be self-directed; at base, in moral madness, delusional ideas arose in the mind, and by definition remained within the moral province of the individual. By contrast, in 'real' madness, the sufferer was the passive recipient of body-based sickness. Correspondingly, he/she was understood to be innocent, but paid for this exculpation of moral accountability by surrendering full personhood. (Laffey 2003: 63)

In January 1763 a Select Committee was established in the United Kingdom to investigate and report on the condition of the private 'madhouses'. Their report recommended the state regulation of private madhouses. This recommendation formed the basis of the 1774 Madhouses Act. However, how did modern psychiatric practice develop in the nineteenth century?

Lengwiler (2003) argues that cooperation between psychiatry and the army from the end of the nineteenth century was central to the emergence of modern psychiatry. He argues that the Confederate Army had established military hospitals for psychiatric patients during the American Civil War (1861–5), although they were closed at the end of the war. But it was in Wilhelmine Germany between 1870 and 1914, that military psychiatry emerged as an independent discipline. Military psychiatry had a central role in the history of modern clinical psychiatry as military psychiatrists, such as Emil Kraepelin, Richard von Krafft-Ebing, Carl Westphal, Friedrich Jolly, Theodor Ziehen and Robert Sommer, developed innovative diagnostic technologies and in the case of Hermann Ebbinghaus (1850–1910) developed the gap test method of intelligence testing. These military and later governmental links were the most important in securing funding for research and helped establish important institutional links with the wider authorities, the judiciary and both local and national government. At the end of this process, psychiatry emerged as a 'social technology' used in the assessment of people believed to be on the borderline between normality and abnormality in a wide range of social contexts.

As Lengwiler points out, the first generation of intelligence tests designed for school children was invented at this time and on the basis of psychiatric recommendations:

In 1906 the War Ministry ruled that all psychiatric institutions, public or private, including the specialized institutions for epileptics and idiots, would have to report all their male and still-unrecruited patients to the military authorities, including ambulant patients. The same decision was made for schools for retarded children. Thus, the recruitment authorities had a complete list of conscripts with a suspected psychiatric condition. (Lengwiler 2003: 52)

Moreover, through the new discipline of *Kriminalpsychologie*, psychiatrists had a significant impact upon criminal law reform. They argued that it was possible to devise and administer a range of tests that could identify the criminals who could be reintegrated back into society and those who could not. As Lengwiler (2003) argues, criminal law reform successfully led to a 'medicalisation' of the judicature in Wilhelmine Germany.

In summary, whatever was believed to be the origin of mental illness, the condition was assumed to have a moral dimension to it that was a potential and serious threat to the community. Not only were the mad dangerous, but they were also unable to play a full and active role in society, they could never be classed as full citizens. Consequently, clear and easily definable state-sponsored social divisions had to be put in place to separate them from the rest of the society.

Citizenship, Globalisation and Governability

'Government' usually refers to the activity of the supreme authority within a state. However, the term 'governance' covers all aspects of the management of people's behaviour, including the influence of non-governmental organisations (NGOs), such as families, employers and friendship networks, on our behaviour. The ways in which individuals control and regulate their own behaviour is central to any understanding of governance. In addition, the ability of the state to generate, reinforce and police social division is a central element of governance. Michael Coppedge argues that governability is best understood by analysing the relationships among a number of strategic actors: 'Governability is the degree to which relations among these strategic actors observe arrangements that are stable and mutually acceptable' (Coppedge 1994: 45). The actors in question are:

- The government
- The permanent bureaucracy
- The military (and police).

In a number of societies other groups can have an impact upon governance: opposition political parties, the media, indigenous movements, trade unions, the Church, private-sector associations, peasant organisations and (post September 11) guerrillas and terrorists. These groups, argues Coppedge, have a high degree of organised control over some power resource, such as: the means of production, mass membership, public office, armed force, moral authority, or ideas and information. These groups have the ability or perceived potential to disturb public order or economic development.

In many cases the volitions, rules or conventions of governance are formalised into law; examples would include written constitutions, legal codes or provisions for formal representation. In addition, there are a range of informal arrangements that help to stabilise governance. Coppedge suggests: coalitions, party pacts and the inclination of policy-makers to sound out the private sector in an effort to avoid confrontation.

In their brief article on 'good' governance, Tandon and Kumi list the following characteristics:

- Universal protection of human rights
- Laws that are implemented in a non-discriminatory manner
- An efficient, impartial, and quick judicial system
- Transparent public agencies and official decision-making
- Accountability for decisions made about public issues and resources by public officials
- Devolution of resources and decision-making power to local levels and bodies in rural and urban areas
- Participation and inclusion of all citizens in debating public policies and choices. (Tandon and Kumi 1999: 16)

However, the central weakness of such approaches to governance is that they are built upon the pluralistic assumption that the state is rule-maker and umpire. In addition, mainstream theories of citizenship that went with such theories of governance also relied upon the now obsolete premise of the closed nation state, with rigid and well-policed borders, as Rawls made clear:

> The first is that we have assumed that a democratic society, like any political society, is to be viewed as a complete and closed social system. It is complete in that it is self-sufficient and has a place for all the main purposes of human life. It is also closed, in that entry into it is only by birth and exit from it is only by death ... For the moment we leave aside entirely relations with other societies and postpone all questions of justice between peoples until a conception of justice for a well-ordered society is on hand. Thus, we are not seen as joining society at the age of reason, as we might join an association, but as being born into a society where we will lead a complete life. (Rawls 1993: 41)

The impact of globalisation on governance was largely ignored. Globalisation is the basis of a crisis of both governability and mainstream conceptions of citizenship. As Delanty explains, 'Citizenship refers to the internal relationship between individuals and the state: its external face is nationality, which defines the rights of citizenship with respect to other states' (Delanty 2000: 72).

The modern state is based on a combination of the principles of territoriality and administrative control, supported by a monopoly of the legitimate use of violence. As Max Weber's modernist definition of the state makes clear: 'the legitimate monopoly over the use of violence within a recognized and bounded territory' (Weber 1978: 904–5). With the processes of globalisation, the power of the state can decay and dissolve. There is a great deal of debate as to the extent to which the nation state is drained of power and influence. However, there is general agreement that nation states are less powerful then they were in the past. For Delanty, the relative decline of the modern nation state has serious implications for our conceptions of citizenship and the relationship between self and other:

> Modernity was a discourse of the emancipation of the self, but the question of the other is being asked only now. The problem with 'self-determination' in postmodern times is that there is no one single self but a plurality of selves. In this move beyond the contours of the modern age we have to ask the question of the responsibility of the self for the other. The rethinking of democracy – which is a discourse of self-determination – that this entails will force us to re-establish a link with citizenship – where self and other find a point of reconciliation. (Delanty 2000: 3)

The modern citizen was a member of a nation state that was both a geographical location, political community and civil society that guaranteed a set of civil, political and social rights, allowed participation, secured a person's identity and expected the individual to fulfil a number of duties. The processes of globalisation have opened up cosmopolitan public spheres; nation states have to come to terms with greater numbers of stateless people, asylum seekers, people with dual citizenship, economic migrants, etc. However, beyond the nation state there is still little that civil society can do to uphold the rights of a citizen.

The modernist conception of citizenship is about the significance of group membership, rights, duties, participation and identity. The debate within social science on the nature of citizenship has been dominated by T.H. Marshall, who built upon the observations that Émile Durkheim made about the relationship between civic morals and social division.

The debate about the social liberal conception of citizenship usually takes its starting point from the sociologist T.H. Marshall (1964). For Marshall there are three types of citizenship rights:

- **Civil rights or our legal citizenship**: rights associated with individual freedom, such as the right to free speech, to own property, equality before the law
- **Political rights**: rights associated with democracy, such as the right to vote
- **Social rights**: mainly our welfare rights, such as the right to education, health care and social security. The philosophy that underpinned the welfare state.

> citizenship is a status bestowed on those who are full members of a community. All who possess the status are equal with respect to the rights and duties with which the status is endowed. (Marshall 1964: 84)

Critiques of Marshall

- First, Marshall's notion of citizenship is 'incomplete' in that he did not regard control over the workplace by the citizen as significant. In other words, Marshall had no conception of 'economic citizenship' based upon industrial democracy
- Second, Marshall did not take into account 'cultural rights'. In the early part of the twentieth century many governments attempted to suppress minority languages and force people to speak the majority language
- In the latter part of the century, there was a rise in the notion of multiculturalism and a growing recognition that people should not be restricted in their choice of language, religion or other cultural practices
- Marshall's work has been criticised by feminists on the grounds that it is built upon assumptions that men go out to work and women stay at home doing domestic work
- Marshall also naively assumed that the citizenship rights that we enjoy are both evolutionary and cumulative; that once an individual had won a civil or political right it could not be taken away
- Marshall had a one-dimensional view of citizenship; he made no distinction between an active citizen and a passive citizen
- Some forms of citizenship, such as emerged from the French Revolution, were based upon active involvement in social and political struggle, Marshall's conception of citizenship is passive. The citizen is a passive person who receives a range of benefits from the state.

Turner (1999) argues that an adequate understanding of the problems surrounding issues of citizenship in contemporary societies must go well beyond Marshall's framework. T.H. Marshall attempted to create a form of citizenship that took into account the two contradictory principles of *scarcity* and the *need for solidarity*.

- He defined citizenship as a collection of rights that provided the individual with a formal legal identity
- However, at the same time 'citizenship' institutions control the access of individuals to scarce resources – who gets social security, health care, housing etc.
- Citizenship not only provides criteria for inclusion and exclusion of people from the wider society but also provides the foundation for a cultural and political identity.

The issue of the citizen's duties is unexplored in Marshall's work. Marshall defines duties in terms of the duty to work, pay taxes and perform military service in times of war. Marshall has little to say about the motives and intentions of the citizen in relation to duties. In addition, he gives little attention to the issue of *voice* within his conception. People who for whatever reason choose to reject the duties, or who, through issues of *difference*, feel excluded or oppressed by the rules of poliarchy or do not share its volitions, all point to the largely 'passive' nature of citizenship for Marshall. Citizenship is not about the articulation of issues or problems for Marshall's state-led conception. In addition, argues Delanty, much of the mainstream discussion of citizenship is based upon the assumption that each citizen is a fully formed individual with the opportunities and capabilities of having their voice heard in the public domain.

In contrast to the mainstream liberal view of citizenship, cosmopolitanism could be seen as a form of inclusion that is based upon the interconnectedness of cultures; an international order based upon an expanded form of civil society that stresses a commitment to humanity rather than the nation state. Although this idea was first suggested by Kant in 1784, with the emergence of the internet and the network society such issues of global governance and global participation have become a reality. Information has become the basis for effective participation and is increasingly becoming the foundation for citizenship. Central to this argument is the status of human rights, which Delanty defines as: 'basic rights that all individuals enjoy by virtue of their humanity, whereas citizenship rights are specific to a particular community' (Delanty 2000: 69). However, Delanty also explains that 'Human rights do not refer to something that is self-evident or guaranteed by nature' (ibid.: 75). This point raises serious issues about the nature of global governance; at the moment the nation state remains the basis for the political community. Although the Maastricht Treaty does lay down some rights for all European Union citizens, most EU rights are still derivative of its nation states. We also have to take into account that 'human rights' can become a vehicle for the imposition of Western values across the world and the destruction of traditional and non-Western cultural traditions.

We need to re-evaluate political identity in a global postmodern society that stresses difference and diversity. The impact of racial diversity, multiculturalism and their relationship to citizenship and democracy were ignored by Marshall. Gorjanicyn (2000) argues that 'culture' as a shared set of meanings that groups can attach to, should form the basis of 'citizenship', rather than Marshall's idea of citizenship as a passive, formal and legalistic entitlement to civil, political and social rights. In other words, the traditional hostility between democracy within the political community of a nation state and the external and excluded 'other' that we find in mainstream citizenship analysis needs to be addressed. Cosmopolitan theorists, such as Joe Carens (1995), for example, have a commitment to citizenship in the face of a fragmented society and have argued for the global expansion of democracy. In particular there is a global duty to protect the victims of humanitarian or human rights abuse, irrespective of their place of birth or residence and irrespective of the wishes of the government of the country where the abuse is taking place. Cosmopolitan theorists have argued for the removal of institutional barriers, such as the United Nations' refusal to involve themselves in the internal affairs of a nation state, so that we have a global democratic framework of citizenship rights and governmental accountability.

Opposed to Carens's view are a number of communitarian and civic-republican positions, such as that of Honig (1998), who argues that there are real social divisions between the citizen and the Other. Honig contends that only those immigrants who share the central characteristics of the model citizen should be made welcome; others should be rejected.

ACTIVITY

Does Globalisation Create New 'Duties' in Respect of the 'Other'?

Do we have a duty to take responsibility for issues and problems that affect citizens in any country in the world?

Is citizenship associated with race, religion, language, psycho-sexual characteristics, virtues of mind, body, or character? Such ideas as a 'natural' substance that the citizen should possess as qualification for full citizenship are not so easily pushed aside. As Seyla Benhabib argues:

> Struggles over whether women should have the vote, whether non-White and colonial peoples are capable of self-rule or whether a gay person can hold certain kinds of public office are illustrations of the tension between the social and the naturalistic dimensions of citizenship. (Benhabib 1999: 719)

Questions:

➤ Are national borders arbitrary?

➤ Is there any justification for immigration policies and restricting the rights of immigrants and aliens? Give reasons for your answers.

It is important to note that even within the political community of the nation state, not all people who were born within that state enjoyed full citizenship rights, as Joydeep Sengupta explains:

> Citizenship is the legal expression of membership in the national family, carrying with it the obligation for its defence and welfare. Exclusions from the rights and duties of citizenship – such as banning homosexuals from the military or denying them the right to marry and create a family – are a symbolic ostracism from the national family. Attempts to redress the systematic exclusion of gays from full citizenship in Europe must reconcile a reprehensible history of injustice rooted in prohibitions on homosexuality in the Judeo-Christian religious traditions, and (with a few exceptions) in the criminalization, pathologization, or mere omission of homosexuality in the legal code until the 20th century. (Sengupta 2002: 28)

Legislating for rights and legal protection for groups has always proved problematic for nation states. Pluralistic/polyarchic liberal democracies have an individual rights culture. Legal protection of minority groups who share collective identities is seen as divisive, because such protection is viewed as providing additional individual liberties for minorities that are not available to the majority of citizens in the wider society.

Asylum, Migration and Forced Migration

The global refugee population grew from 2.4 million in 1975 to 10.5 million in 1985 and 14.9 million in 1990. A peak was reached after the end of the Cold War with 18.2 million in 1993. By 2000, the global refugee population had declined to 12.1 million (UNHCR, 1995, 2000). However, this includes only officially recognized refugees under the fairly narrow definition of the 1951 UN Refugee Convention, which refers only to people forced to leave their countries due to individual persecution on specific grounds. (Castles 2003: 15)

The key question is why do people want to move? Until fairly recently there were very few restrictions upon the movement of people. Many people were forcibly taken from their homes and transported over great distances to work as slaves. Between 1450 and 1900, it is estimated that almost 12 million people were forcibly exported from Africa as slaves. Slavery is the ownership of human beings who are stripped of their human rights and used in forced and unpaid labour. Such forced and unpaid labour had many benefits for the slave owners, not least of which was that it increased the monetary value of property. Land owners could see the financial benefit of creating plantations on their land. Slavery was a central element in a global economic network that linked financial institutions such as banks and insurance companies, manufacturing, processing, shipping and the development of large city ports. Even after the industrial revolution, industrialists could see the financial benefit of immigrants taking up posts in a range of occupations.

For most of Western Europe immigration restrictions were only introduced in the mid-1970s. Restrictions to the movement of people were more often than not imposed on grounds of racial prejudice, although such prejudice was rationalised in terms of national security, limited resources or public health grounds. In the latter years of the twentieth century the conflicts in former Yugoslavia, Afghanistan, Sri Lanka and Kurdistan have significantly increased the numbers of people on the move.

Even before the events of 11 September 2001, there had been a politicisation of migration and asylum issues, with the difference between forced migration and economic migration becoming distorted. In the United Kingdom popular newspapers have argued that asylum seekers are 'polluted with terrorism and disease' and are 'doubling the rate of HIV and increasing the risk of Hepatitis B twentyfold.' However, no evidence has ever been presented to support such claims. Such journalistic accounts are *discourses* that simplify complex realities and organise how we perceive the world, at the expense of alternative definitions. Discourses help individuals organise their perception of the world through a series of unacknowledged assumptions that shape our relationships with others. So asylum seekers are seen as:

- Potential terrorists
- Spreading disease
- More likely to commit crime.

Entry to many Western countries, even for short periods is becoming increasingly restricted by immigration and asylum legislation. Asylum seekers and migrant labourers have come to be regarded as a transnational threat to national security, associated with terrorism, Islamic fundamentalism, international crime, the drugs trade, and the trafficking of people – even though none of the terrorists associated with the destruction of the twin towers was a refugee or asylum seeker. Slobodan Djajic (2001) outlines the various ways in which Western governments have attempted to restrict the entry of people on the move:

- Internal measures to restrict employment opportunities
- Restricting access to public services
- Increasing resources on border controls
- Tighter rules on asylum claims
- More effective deportation procedures
- Tougher penalties on smuggling people.

International treaties and conventions that the British Government signs up to do not automatically become part of British law; for example, Britain is party to the European Convention on Human Rights (1950) and the Convention Relating to the Status of Refugees (1951). However, it was only with the passage of the Asylum and Immigration Appeal Act (1993) and the Human Rights Act (1998), that the Conventions became part of British law. In addition, the 1951 Geneva Convention and the European Convention on Human Rights only became part of British law in 2000. As Schuster and Solomos (2001) explain, until 1993 the British Government were completely free to choose who would be admitted and who would be refused entry into the United Kingdom, leaving room for a high degree of discretion and flexibility.

Kenyan and Ugandan Asians in the late 1960s are a case in point, not only did they hold British passports, they also met a number of the criteria of the Convention Relating to the Status of Refugees (1951), notably (i) a well-founded fear of persecution on the grounds of their nationality and race and (ii) the fact that they had been forced to cross international borders. However, the persecution was not instigated by Britain, the state whose passports they held. The British Government chose not to honour its international obligations under the 1951 Convention but instead introduced the 1968 Commonwealth Immigrants Act which redefined British citizenship by introducing the concept of 'patriality' and withdrew the right of entry and settlement to the Kenyan and Ugandan Asians:

> The main distinction between refugees and asylum seekers at that time was in terms of security of residence – once accepted as a refugee, one was generally free from the threat of removal; travel documents – with the issue of a refugee passport by the Home Office, one could leave and return to Britain; and the right to have their family come and join them. In terms of welfare, both refugees and asylum seekers were entitled to social security benefits at the same level as British citizens and others with Leave to Remain. They had access to local authority housing, income support, education and healthcare. (Schuster and Solomos 2001: 35)

The Asylum and Immigration Appeal Act (1993) introduced a right of appeal for asylum seekers. However, later legislation, notably the Asylum and Immigration Act (1996), undermined the appeals system by introducing a 'white list' of countries where, in the opinion of the British Government, there was no 'serious' risk of persecution.

As Cohen (2002) explains, the 1996 Act linked virtually all non-contributory benefits, including child benefit, to a person's immigration status. Asylum seekers remained eligible only for income support, housing benefit and council tax benefit, and only if their asylum claim was lodged in the United Kingdom. In the UK the National Asylum Support Service (NASS) contracts to provide housing for asylum seekers. However, Cohen identifies the following problems with the contracts that NASS has made with the private sector:

- Properties not meeting housing regulations
- Asylum seekers arriving with no vouchers and no food
- Asylum seekers arriving at properties with no hot water
- Asylum seekers not allocated to GPs
- Asylum seekers not having sufficient information to access schools
- Asylum seekers being placed in areas where there is racial tension. (Cohen 2002: 537)

As Slobodan Djajic (2001) explains, in most OECD countries only people seeking asylum from countries that have not signed the UN Convention on Human Rights and the UN Convention on Refugees and who have not passed through a country that has signed both conventions are likely to have their applications for asylum granted.

ACTIVITY

Immigration Restriction into the United States

Read the following accounts as to why immigration should be restricted.

> There are many rational reasons for restricting immigration to well below the present legal rate. First, most immigrants are transformed sooner or later into U.S. super-consumers, furthering both local and global environmental deterioration. Second, immigrants often bring with them cultural preferences for large families, which take a generation or more to fade away, meanwhile adding to our nation's gross over-population. A third, sad cost may be political fractionation as an ever larger and more diverse set of pressure groups oppose one another and all manner of legislative proposals. We have long been fans of diversity (e.g., Ehrlich, 1980), but wonder whether the American political system can stand much more without grinding to a halt. (Daily et al. 1995)

Reasons for restricting immigration into the United States

These include:

- Racism
- Influence of racist groups
- Economic threat to jobs from a source of cheap labour
- Opposition of the unions, who believe that immigrants might be used as strike-breakers
- Fear of political extremism
- Fear of terrorism
- US policy of isolationism.

> The reasons for reducing immigration from its current high level (over 800,000 last year – not counting additional hundreds of thousands of illegal immigrants) relate primarily to our nation's current rapid population growth, and the need to harness our workforce to a high-wage, high-skill economy that is internationally competitive. (Martin 1993)

Question:

> ➢ Do you find any of the justifications for restricting immigration cited above convincing? Give reasons for your answer.

UK Asylum System

According to The Immigration and Nationality Directorate, the main features of the UK asylum system are:

- All claims receive a fair hearing
- Fast-track processes mean that some claims (and subsequent appeals) are dealt with in about four weeks. Claimants may be detained for all or part of that time
- All claimants have a responsibility to cooperate with the authorities considering their claim. They must:

  — Tell the truth about their circumstances
  — Obey the law. It is a criminal offence to submit a claim involving deception, the maximum penalty for this is two years' imprisonment
  — Keep in regular contact with the authorities considering their claim
  — Leave the country if their claim is ultimately rejected

- Support is provided to asylum seekers who are destitute whilst their claims for asylum are being considered. Accommodation is provided on a 'no choice' basis in parts of the UK where there is less pressure on accommodation than in London and other parts of the South East. Asylum seekers are given subsistence payments in order that they may purchase food and other goods. This 'dispersal' of asylum seekers and their support is provided by the National Asylum Support Service (NASS)
- Some claimants are removed to another EU member state in order to pursue their claim there, if that member state is responsible for the claim under the terms of the Dublin Convention. Some other claimants are removed in order to pursue their claim in a safe country outside the European Union
- Asylum seekers can appeal against refusal of their application or for the grant of exceptional Leave to Remain rather than on the basis of refugee status. There is now a single 'one stop' right of appeal
- The Government is also introducing a scheme to regulate immigration advisers to prevent asylum seekers being exploited by unscrupulous or incompetent advisers
- Those who are unsuccessful on appeal will be required to leave the UK. If necessary, they will be removed
- Those who are recognised as refugees will be granted immediate settlement in the UK and will be helped to build a new life. (Source: The Immigration and Nationality Directorate)

Canadian Immigration

According to Don DeVoretz (2001), between 1967 and 1996 almost 5 million immigrants settled in Canada. Immigrants now make up 17 percent of the

Canadian population. The 1951 Immigration Act laid the foundation of Canada's immigration policy because it identified the characteristics, in terms of the human capital characteristics, of the people who were believed to make a significant contribution to the economy. This became codified in the 1960s when Canada introduced a 'points system' to decide who should be allowed into the country. For a person to be allowed into Canada, that person had to demonstrate that they would fully integrate into the labour market.

Other Commonwealth countries had much more explicitly racist policies in place. Rainer Winkelmann (2001) explains how both Australia and New Zealand had explicit racial discrimination in the area of immigration until 1987 in the case of New Zealand and 1966 in the case of Australia. Commonwealth citizens with white European heritage and Irish citizens were allowed unrestricted access into New Zealand until 1974, but it was not until 1987 that New Zealand dropped its policy of 'ethnic preference' in immigration and effectively brought to an end its 'White New Zealand' policy. Australia maintained a 'traditional source' preference list for immigrant origins until 1991, when their 'White Australia' policy finally came to an end. Both countries introduced a points system which, like the Canadian system, attempts to maintain a high degree of labour market compatibility. Immigration policies in Australia, New Zealand and Canada are based upon the assumption that immigrants are potentially harmful to the nation's economy and as such, entry must be carefully policed with harsh punishments for unwanted people who attempt to cross the border. In Canada under the Immigration and Refugee Protection Act (2002) courts can impose a fine of C$1 million or life in prison for smuggling people into the country.

However, the power of the nation state has started to diminish because the processes of globalisation of politics, and *disetatisation* – the possible end of effective sovereignty of the nation state – have had a significant impact upon on the politics of asylum.

Disetatisation: the End of Sovereignty

The nation state was once believed to be the primary unit of power. As Crook and Pakulski (1992) explains, the modernisation of politics concerned four interrelated processes:

1 The detachment of political action from other forms of activity
2 The incorporation of almost all power within the executive mechanisms of the state
3 An expansion of political participation
4 The rise of largely class-based 'power politics'.

However, all four of these processes are now in decline, as societies in the contemporary world are going through important transformations, which Crook and

Pakulski refer to as 'postmodern' in nature. This transformation is taking place because the processes which brought about the modern world, both for functionalists and for Marxists – rationalisation, commodification and differentiation – are becoming 'hyperdifferentiated'. In other words, the processes of modernisation became so exaggerated as to become free of all constraint. This gave the world an unpredictable, contradictory and fragmented feel to it.

We are moving from a situation within modernity of:

- **Commodification:** a process whereby business overrules notions of aesthetic value, a view taken up by both Marxists and mass culture theorists. In other words, any physical item or service can be bought or sold
- **Rationalisation:** the process whereby life in the modern world becomes highly consistent, calculable and predictable, as in the case of Weber's conception of bureaucracy
- **Differentiation:** the process whereby subsystems within the social system become functionally interdependent.

This move is to a situation within the postmodern condition of:

- **Hyper-commodification:** the spread of the commodity form into all areas of social and personal life
- **Hyper-rationalisation:** creates a series of tensions that become self-limiting to the point of irrationality
- **Hyper-differentiation:** an inexhaustible number of divisions emerge which effectively wear down the meaningfulness of distinctions between independent areas of social life.

Modern culture was built upon the idea of aesthetic 'progress' or the development of a cultural tradition. However, within the postmodern condition, such traditions and ideas of cultural development are fragmented. In the postmodern condition individuals are faced with an 'archive of styles', 'pastiche' and 'parody'. In addition, these cultural transactions have a global nature. Culture is a product of supranational bodies, outside of the control of a nation state. A most important part of this movement is the decreasing relevance of the state. As Crook explains, there are four elements to this process:

1 A horizontal redistribution of power and responsibility to autonomous corporate bodies; private companies control people's lives in ways which only nation states did in the past.
2 A vertical redistribution of power and responsibility to local councils, civic initiatives and extra-state self-governing bodies; the nation state loses power to quasi non-state bodies, for example, 'agencies' like the UK Child Support Agency.
3 The marketisation and privatisation of previously state-run enterprises.
4 An externalisation of responsibility by shifting it to supra-state bodies such as the European Union and the United Nations.

The nation state is dissolving and both its economic significance, political and military power are becoming assimilated into global networks. As Crook explains:

[T]he 'Gulf War' of 1990–1 might be seen as the first postmodernized war. It could not be fought in terms of the interests of a particular state but was legitimated in terms of the interests of the entire global community of states, with openly a few minor ones standing against it, that is, by claims to be a 'new world order'. The majority commitment of the US forces could only be accomplished under UN sponsorship and if bankrolled by the Arab oil-states and Japan – that is, only if detached from their own nation-state. Moreover, the war was a live-to-air mass-mediated event in which much of the entire global community participated vicariously. It was therefore immediate, brief and available in every home with a TV set, a prime example of the reduction of time-space distances. (Crook 1992: 45–6)

The state then has started to diminish because of the globalisation of politics which has had a significant effect on the politics of asylum. Saskia Sassen (1996) argues that the exclusive territoriality of the nation state has been destabilised by the processes of economic globalisation, with sovereignty being partly redistributed to other organisations. However, nation states still maintain the right to decide which non-nationals will be allowed to cross their borders. States still retain the sole right to grant entry into a country, under conditions and restrictions of their own choosing. A case in point is the decision of the British Government in 2003 to make successful completion of a 'citizenship test' a condition of entry for people who wish to live and work in the United Kingdom.

In addition, states view immigration and some forms of asylum claims – such as economic migrants and 'bogus' asylum claims – as a relation between the individual seeking entry and the potential host nation state. Immigration and asylum claims are seen as the product of individual choices – the rational choices of individuals acting as rational utility maximisers, attempting to get maximum benefit for minimum cost by migrating to a place where economic opportunities are assumed to be better. The larger geo-political aspects of migration, including the possibility of 'forced migration' are largely ignored. However, Sassen argues that 'Large-scale international migrations are embedded in rather complex economic, social, and ethnic networks. They are highly conditioned and structural flows' (Sassen 1996: 14).

Sassen goes on to explain that when a state wants to exercise its power over immigration, it has to engage with other 'interested social forces' who are concerned with 'the furthering of economic globalisation' (ibid.: 16). The significance of Sassen's argument is that she points out that in the current phase of globalisation, a process that is taking place within a given nation state may not have its origins within that nation state. A case in point is the delinking of central banks from the executive branch of government. The relationship between the nation state and the global community is not zero-sum; under the banner headline of 'deregulation' many nation states – most notably with 'New Right' dominated governments, such as the Thatcher–Reagan Administrations – withdrew the nation state from exercising its sovereignty over a wide range of areas and replaced it with a complex set of global arrangements. As Sassen explains:

Economic globalisation has also been accompanied by the creation of new legal regimes and legal practices and the expansion and renovation of some older forms that have the effect of replacing public regulation and law with private mechanisms and sometimes even by-pass national legal systems. (Sassen 2001: 193)

ACTIVITY

Citizenship Classes for British Nationality

In 1981 the British Government passed the British Nationality Act which provided a legal definition of who was entitled to be classed as a British Citizen. The Act established three separate forms of citizenship:

1 **British Citizenship**: people who were born in the United Kingdom or who had a parent born in the UK
2 **British Dependent Territories Citizen**: people who were born or resident in a British dependent territory.
3 **British Overseas Citizenship**: people who were born or resident in one of the following British Overseas Territories:

- Anguilla
- Bermuda
- British Antarctic Territory
- The British Indian Ocean Territory
- British Virgin Islands
- Cayman Islands
- Falkland Islands
- Gibraltar
- Montserrat
- Pitcairn Islands
- St Helena
- Ascension Island
- Tristan Da Cunha
- South Georgia and the South
- Sandwich Islands
- Turks and Caicos Islands

In September 2003 the British Government announced that any immigrant wishing to become a British citizen would be expected to swear allegiance to the Crown and to successfully complete language and citizenship classes, which would stress the duties and responsibilities of a British citizen. A failure to take the Pledge of Allegiance or to pass the tests would not end their residency status, but would prevent them from gaining a British passport and from voting in UK elections.

Immigrants would be given a handbook for living in Britain, and would formally learn about important elements of British life including:

- Everyday needs such as gas and electricity companies
- Education and the National Health Service
- How British democracy works

(Continued)

(Continued)

- How to buy a National Lottery ticket
- Institutions from Parliament to local councils.

'We are not trying to define Britishness, we are trying to define what people need to settle in effectively.' (Professor Sir Bernard Crick)

The Pledge:

"I will give my loyalty to the United Kingdom and respect its rights and freedoms. I will uphold its democratic values.
I will observe its laws faithfully and fulfil my duties and obligations as a British citizen."

Concluding the Citizenship Ceremony

"May you find your lives enriched, and in turn, may you enrich the lives of others and your community.
Ladies and gentlemen, will you all please stand and give a round of applause to welcome our fellow British citizens."

(Source: http://news.bbc.co.uk/1/hi/uk_politics/3202901.stm)

Question:

➢ What do you believe is the purpose of introducing the above measures?

The British Government argues that the citizenship tests are an attempt to generate a more 'active' form of citizenship. However, the discussion of active citizenship in the work of Bruce Ackerman raises important issues about asylum.

Bruce Ackerman: The Dialogic Theory of Liberal Legitimacy

Bruce Ackerman (1980) in his book *Social Justice in the Liberal State* argues that we live in a world of scarce resources and struggle in which we have to constantly justify our claims for resources. Ackerman rejects the central assumptions of social contract theorists; rather he assumes that people have no rights except for the ones that they acquire through their constant interaction with others who may be making claims for our resources:

> Rather than linking liberalism to ideas of natural right or imaginary contract, *we must learn to think of liberalism as a way of talking about power, a form of political culture.* ... If there is anything distinctive about liberalism, it must be in the *kinds of reasons* liberals rely on to legitimate their claims to scarce resources. Nazis are not liberals because there is *something* about the reasons they give in support of their claims that is inconsistent with the organizing principles of liberal power talk. (Ackerman 1980: 6–7; italics in original)

Ackerman proposes a number of conditions. Firstly, for the justification of power to be legitimate, it must be intelligible and consistent. Secondly, claims to power must be neutral; power claims that depend upon one person claiming to be a moral authority are illegitimate in a liberal society. In other words, any claim to legitimacy which depends upon one person claiming to be intrinsically superior to fellow citizens should be rejected.

Ackerman makes a distinction between *manna* – imaginary resources which can be transformed into any material object in the world – and the citizen. A stone can be manna but cannot be a citizen, although we might give stones some rights and protection, as we do with the Grand Canyon. Areas of natural beauty can be given the right to our protection but this does not make them citizens. A lion is manna but not a citizen, even though it has some communicative competence and can roar its dissatisfaction. Manna does not pass what Ackerman calls the *dialogic test for citizenship*: 'a liberal relationship is defined as a social condition in which power wielders ask and answer each others' questions of legitimacy' (Ackerman 1980: 71).

The liberal state as a political system, according to Ackerman, is nothing more than a collection of individuals who can participate in a dialogue in which all aspects of their power position may be justified in a certain way. The political system is constituted by this process of dialogic interchange. Moreover, any individual who wishes to be classed as a citizen must be able to fulfil a minimum dialogic competence. This minimum dialogic competence for citizenship involves firstly the ability to pass the *defensive test*, which is the ability to say 'because I am at least as good as you are'. And secondly a person must pass the *inquiry test* which is the ability to say 'why should you get it rather than I?'

Finally, Ackerman argues that there is a *behavioural condition for citizenship* which is broken if you attempt to deprive a person of their rights to material subsistence if that person has done nothing to deprive you of yours.

For Ackerman, active participation in dialogue is central to the notion of citizenship. It is by such exchanges of dialogue that power and legitimacy are established, the rules of the political system are established and maintained, and by which our freedom and vision of the good life are established and maintained.

ACTIVITY

Questions:

➤ Does the British Government's plan for the introduction of citizenship classes enhance the possibility of an active citizenship?

➤ Are there any reasons for the refusal of a state to grant access on grounds of asylum contained within Ackerman's argument?

Asylum and Sexuality

A number of people seek asylum on grounds of their sexuality because they are lesbians, gay men and bisexuals. Amnesty International estimates that as many as 70 countries still have laws banning same-sex relationships. According to the UK Lesbian & Gay Immigration Group (before April 2003, known as the Stonewall Immigration Group), for a long time, the British Government refused to accept that people who face persecution because of sexual orientation should be recognised as refugees or be considered for asylum. However, in March 1999, the House of Lords decided that lesbians and gay men who face persecution constitute a 'social group' under the 1951 Convention. The Home Office has also interpreted the Lords' ruling to include individuals who face persecution because of their HIV status. Any individual seeking asylum on grounds of their sexual orientation or HIV status needs to demonstrate that they face serious harm such as execution, physical violence, torture from the Government (or that the Government is unwilling or unable to protect them from such harm). However, facing prosecution for consensual same-sex acts does not in itself constitute persecution.

Jenni Millbank (2002) argues that persecution on the basis of sexuality is fairly common in many countries and for gay men has become an accepted basis for a refugee claim on the ground of being a member of a 'particular social group'. There is an argument within feminist refugee literature that women (whether lesbian or heterosexual) are less likely to have their asylum claims accepted. A great deal of the maltreatment of women, including the use of sexual assault as a method of persecution, takes place in private. Lesbians are also much less likely to be granted refugee status on grounds of sexual persecution. Whereas gay men cases are more likely to face persecution from a state employee, such as a police officer, the harassment of lesbians is often classed as 'domestic' in the sense that it is more likely to be carried out by former male partners, family members, or current female partners' families.

THE STONEWALL GROUP'S 'EQUALITY 2000' CAMPAIGN

This campaign targeted five areas of discrimination against lesbian and gay people on which it hoped to influence change by the year 2000: it demanded equality at school, in love, at work, as parents and as partners. Successes were achieved in the removal of the ban on lesbians and gay men in the armed forces, and changes in immigration rights for same-sex partners, while the continuing defeat of attempts to reduce the legal age of consent to one of parity with that for heterosexual sexual activity were yet to reach a conclusion. (Wise 2000: 3)

Taking its starting point from John Locke's *Treatises of Government* (1690), which argued that men had a natural right to life, liberty and property, citizenship is seen to be both universal and equal. Social liberalism is the most influential theory of citizenship in Europe and North America. This perspective assumes a rather passive form of citizenship in which all people born within a given nation state are citizens of that nation state and as such are given a number of formal legal and political rights, duties and responsibilities. Other assumptions include:

- All men can think, therefore all men are equal
- Individualism – if individuals make a mistake this is unfortunate for that individual and their immediate family or friends. However if a strong and powerful government makes a mistake, then many people suffer.

John Rawls

Rawls discusses the notion of citizenship within the context of a wider discussion of justice. He makes a distinction between the public sphere and the private sphere. In the public sphere, social and political institutions should be based upon principles of justice:

- All people should have equal rights guaranteed by a system of basic liberties
- The system of equal rights helps to secure self respect
- People are free from coercion
- Participation in politics is a right, not an obligation
- Social and economic inequality should emerge from an open competition between people, based upon equality of opportunity.

However, in contrast to the arguments of Rawls and the social liberals, the state has historically demonstrated a keen interest in a number of areas of the citizen's private life, in particular the area of sexuality.

The State's Regulation of Sexuality

Nazi Persecution of Homosexuals

The most stringent form of state regulation of sexuality was by the Nazis. In particular, the Nazi regime had a long history of persecuting homosexuals. In 1928 the party officially condemned homosexuality on the grounds that it encouraged 'womanish emotionalism' amongst men which could make the German people the plaything of their enemies. The Nazis introduced Paragraph 175 of the German Legal Code, that involved a programme to 'clean up' Germany of homosexuality, including the forced closure of gay bars in 1933 and the Rohm purge of June 1934. The latter was based upon the assumption that homosexuals were responsible for spreading disease amongst the German people and that homosexuals were suspected of involvement in treasonable conspiracies. Dr Carl Vaernet conducted detailed medical experiments on homosexual inmates at Buchenwald up until the very end of the war. Himmler, in his role of the head of the German police, ordered the surveillance of suspected homosexuals, and authorised the arrest of homosexual actors and artists in 1937. In 1941 any police officer or SS member found guilty of homosexuality would be sentenced to death. In 1943 the Central Office for Combating Homosexuality introduced compulsory castration for homosexuals. In addition, many thousands of gay men were killed in concentration camps. Surprisingly, Paragraph 175 remained on the statute books until 1994.

Recent UK Legislation on Homosexuality

Although one would not automatically think of Blairism as a site of sexual politics, the Labour Government was elected on a platform of abolishing Section 28 and reducing the age of consent for sexual acts between men from 18 to 16 years of age. However, Wise (2000) argues that the lesbian and gay movements in the UK have been two of the least successful 'new social movements' when it comes to bringing about legislative change in the interests of their activists. Up until 2003, Section 28 of the Local Government Act (1988) remained on the statute books and although the Labour Government did seem to accept much of Stonewall's 'Equality 2000' campaign, the attempt to repeal Section 28 was treated with derision by some sections of the popular press even though Section 28 contravened the Human Rights Act. As Stuart Hall explained with his conception of Thatcherism as a hegemonic authoritarian populist formation, derived from the work of Antonio Gramsci (Hall 1988), the 'New Right' sexual hegemony of the moral wrongness of homosexuality is still firmly entrenched in the popular psyche. In addition Wise (2000) argued that:

- Britain still has an unequal age of consent for gay men
- Same-sex partnerships are not recognised in law
- Lesbian and gay parents and their children have cause to feel insecure
- There persists anti-gay discrimination in the labour market.

ACTIVITY

Section 28 of the UK Local Government Act (1988)

According to Section 28, a local authority should not:

- Intentionally promote homosexuality or publish material with the intention of promoting homosexuality
- Promote the teaching in any maintained school of the acceptability of homosexuality as a pretended family relationship.

The Conservative UK Government introduced Section 28 as a measure against so-called 'loony left councils', i.e. Labour-controlled councils who used their position of influence to present positive images of lesbian and gay people, and who provided services to cater for their needs. Baroness Young argued that Section 28 was needed to 'protect' vulnerable young men from making the 'wrong' 'lifestyle choice'. In other words, there is a commonly held belief amongst the 'New Right' in the deviant status of homosexuality.

Cardinal Thomas Winning, head of the Roman Catholic Church in Scotland, in a speech made in Malta on 21 January 2000, referred to homosexuality as a 'perversion' and the Anglican Bishop of Liverpool was the first non-Catholic clergyman in England to support Cardinal Winning. In doing so he posed the disarmingly honest question, 'is there a moral difference between gay and straight relationships?' No reference was made to the needs or feelings of young gay people or to tolerance for what adults choose to do, and instead he argued that there *are* moral differences and that straight is best, citing the extinction of the species, the design of genitals and the transmission of disease in homosexual but not heterosexual sexual activity (by implication, and of course erroneously, he seems to be referring to HIV/AIDS here) as his evidence. (Wise 2000: 9)

Questions:

➤ Is there a need for Section 28? State the reasons for your answer.

➤ Is there 'a moral difference between gay and straight relationships'? Again state the reasons for your answer.

➤ Should any Government attempt to regulate the sexuality of the adult population? Again state the reasons for your answer.

Old Age

Our approach, then, is an attempt to meet the question of the social production of old age. It is less concerned with studying the characteristics of old age than with examining the production of these characteristics by the social system. (Guillemard 1991: 2–3)

Age-based categories are often assumed to be biological divisions rather than social divisions. However, is there a 'normal' childhood or a 'normal' old age? The rationalities and technologies of governmentality underpin the social division and give rise to the discourses that support age identities.

In the latter half of the twentieth century many countries experienced an increase in the number of old people within the population. The old are regarded as a distinct grouping within the population, and in a similar fashion to race, sex, sexuality and childhood, this distinction is believed to be biological in nature. The term *ageism* was coined by Robert Butler in 1969. Looking at data on labour market trends in the United Kingdom, Loretto et al. (2000) demonstrate the extent of ageism. From the early 1970s onwards there has been an accelerating trend to 'early exit' from the labour market, especially amongst men during periods of recession. There are a number of different routes out of employment for the older person: early retirement; redundancy; dismissal and ill-health but very few of these individuals return to full-time employment. Loretto et al. argue that such discrimination is irrational and based upon negative stereotypes of older people rather than on sound commercial grounds. Older people are believed to be 'less productive, have less relevant skills, are resistant to change and new technology, are less trainable, leave employment sooner so that training has a lower rate of return and are more prone to absenteeism and ill-health' (Loretto et al. 2000: 283). The old are believed to be different because they are beyond maturity.

From the fifteenth to the eighteenth centuries, many Europeans developed a heightened concern with the phenomenon of witchcraft, seeing a new sect hostile to humanity. Thus, governments and society organised 'hunts' for these alleged witches: accusing, torturing and executing thousands of people. The intensity and viciousness of these hunts varied from place to place, as did their focus on particular targets such as women.

Alan Macfarlane (1970) argues that in Tudor and Stuart England the old were targeted for witchcraft allegations more often than the young. During this period class divisions expanded and there was growing pressure on economic resources. Class tensions led to an increase in hatred towards individuals who were believed to be an economic burden upon their communities such as the old and the poor, who perhaps unintentionally were much more likely to be the victims of witchcraft allegations. Such accusations of witchcraft were a response to communities having to justify breaking this obligation to elderly members. It is worth quoting Macfarlane at length on this issue:

[P]opulation growth and changes in ownership created a group of poorer villagers whose ties to their slightly wealthier neighbours became more tenuous. People increasingly had to decide whether to invest their wealth in maintaining the old at a decent standard of living or in improvements which would keep them abreast of their yeoman neighbours … During the period between 1560 and 1650 the internal institutions which had dealt with the old and poor, church relief, the manorial organisation and neighbourly and kinship ties were strained. People still felt enforced to help and support each other, while also feeling the necessity to invest their capital in buying land and providing for their children. The very poor were not the problem. They could be whipped and sent on their way, or hired as labourers. It was the slightly less affluent neighbours or kin who only demanded a little help who became an increasing source of anxiety. To refuse them was to break a web of long-held values. (Macfarlane 1970: 205–6)

PERSISTENCE OF WITCHCRAFT ALLEGATIONS IN AFRICA

Nation Correspondent Nairobi:

The increasing number of murders of elderly people on allegation that they are practising witchcraft is causing concern in Malindi.

'Cases of lynching of those suspected to be witches have been on the increase and we are worried that unless there is intervention from the social organisations, the situation could worsen,' said Mr Charles Ontita, the local police boss.

He said two to four cases were being reported every month, mainly in the rural parts of the district. 'The elderly people are just attacked and killed in cold blood and the killers are never reported. This makes it difficult for the police to make any arrests.'

Mr Ontita added that the residents were not cooperating with police investigations and had refused to volunteer any information. He said relatives and neighbours were uncooperative.

Only one suspect had been arrested in the past three months although 10 people had been killed. A man was arrested last week over the killing of Kahindi John Katana, a 56-year-old traditional medicineman. The suspect had sought treatment from Mr Katana, then later turned on him and hacked him to death using an axe.

'It seems elderly people are especially at risk. … We need to ascertain what is causing these murders,' said Mr Ontita.

(Source: *The Nation*, posted on allafrica.com; 28 October 2003)

Tim Judah (2002) reported on the BBC website that there has been a startling increase in accusations of witchcraft against elderly women in Mozambique. Frequently such accusations have led to murder and violent attacks or at least to the women being disowned by their families. Judah suggests that the increase in accusations is related to high rates of HIV and AIDS.

Theorising about old age is diverse. The old experience bodily changes, and the changes are universally greeted with fear and repulsion. The beauty system applies to older women in no uncertain terms, advertisements for beauty products warn individuals to constantly be on the look-out for signs of ageing and to deal with them quickly and efficiently. Carrigan and Szmigin (2000) argue that the advertising industry either ignores older people or presents them via a set of negative stereotypes or caricatures: decrepitude; imbecility and physical repugnance. Dementia, for example, is the name given to a behavioural syndrome that involves individuals involving themselves in a range of unacceptable behaviours:

- Loss of intellectual capacity
- Loss of memory
- Difficulty in retaining information
- Difficulty in decision-making
- Difficulty in thinking through complex ideas
- Difficulty in carrying out practical tasks, notably in acquiring new skills and competencies.

From a biomedical/clinical perspective, dementia is a personal tragedy, the condition is a disease that involves the inevitable decline in cognitive function and eventually the loss of self. However, the imposition of a set of medical categories can be viewed as a medicalisation of unacceptable behaviour. In other words, dementia is a discursive formation, based upon a dementia-as-disease episteme, that transforms unacceptable behaviour into a biomedical disease. As Daniel Davies explains: 'As discourse creates the *effects of the will to know*, the disease-category now authorises socio-cultural norms' (Davies 2004: 4). The central question is, can personhood be maintained if that individual is without effective memory or without what is believed to be adequate awareness? The medical category does little to explain what aspects – if any – of a person's being are changed by the behavioural syndrome.

Advertisers fail to reflect the 'real life' of older people. Even in advertisements for products that are aimed at older people, advertisers still make use of younger models. Carrigan and Szmigin conclude that advertisers 'fail in their duties of beneficence, non-maleficence, non-deception and non-discrimination towards older people' (Carrigan and Szmigin 2000: 229).

Growing old is a sign of increasing constraints upon the good life. Minichiello et al. (2000) found that words used to describe and explain aspects of the old person's life were not words used by older people to describe their own experiences. Older people are aware that they are seen as being 'old', and many old people attempt to distance themselves from the wider group of 'old' people. Betty Friedan describes an interview she conducted with a lady from Palm Springs. She quotes that the lady:

> with flaming red hair who was clearly older than I, said, 'Oh how nice, I hear you're writing a book about those poor old people.' And I heard myself say. 'No, I'm not writing a book about them. I'm writing a book about us.' And she said, 'Oh no, not me! I'm never going to be old.' (Friedan 1993: 53)

Such ideas can be reinterpreted as forms of oppression against older people. Biggs and Powell draw upon Foucault's analysis of 'technologies of self' to argue that the identities of older people are 'kept in place through the deployment of integrated systems of power and knowledge and a routine operation of surveillance and assessment' (Biggs and Powell 2001: 93). Foucault attempts to explain how the state in modern societies controls the behaviour of people through knowledge-power by transforming people into subjects of the state. His central unit of analysis is *discourse* – a set of rules that set boundaries on how to think and speak about categories of people. Foucault does not make a judgment about the underlying validity of theories such as Alzheimer's disease or senile dementia, he is primarily concerned with the central role such medical discourses have in maintaining power relationships.

Everingham (2003) argues that Giddens's notion of the individualisation of the 'life trajectory', in which the individual has no one form of being because we are what we make of ourselves if only we can hold tradition at arm's length – is an effective account of leading a life within late modernity – provided that the individual concerned has many years of life before them. However, Giddens's account is highly individual and cannot give an adequate account of the inter-connectedness of generations. Self-actualisation amongst older people needs to have a greater emphasis upon the 'communitarian turn' – on the 'self within the community' that places a greater emphasis on the moral conduct of helping others to achieve personal growth. The same points would also apply to Ulrich Beck's conception of individualisation.

A number of authors have explored the argument that old age should be examined by use of the social model of disability to understand the position of old people in society. Discourses of later life form the basis for forms of discrimination and allow professional carers to control key aspects of the older person's life. Oldham (2002) argues that the social model of disability can apply to later life in terms of:

- The political argument, notably the emphasis on self-advocacy
- The distinction between impairment and disability – individuals are prevented from participating because of discourses of disability. Old age is seen in medical terms, as a personal tragedy, a form of chronic illness and as dysfunctional, irrespective of the abilities of the individual.

Zarb argues that 'statutory services that are available mostly create and reinforce older disabled people's dependency and frustrate their attempts to maintain control over their lives' (Zarb 1993: 66). However, in contrast, Heywood et al. (2002) argue that many disabled people have criticised the concept of 'independent living' as a form of privatisation that involves state withdrawal from care and the unpaid use of relatives as primary carers for people with impairments. Similar arguments apply to the care of older people.

SOCIOLOGICAL THEORIES OF THE OLD IN SOCIETY

Disengagement Theory: This approach is described as broadly functionalist in nature. Disengagement Theory is primarily concerned with the role of old age within the social system, its focus is on the functioning of the social system rather than on individual adjustment or attitudes. All individuals are conscious of their own death and functionalists assume that there should be a mutual severing of ties in society. This is an inevitable process in which the most important social roles are abandoned by the old order to maintain social order. The process might be initiated by the aging person or by other elements within the social system, and the withdrawal may be partial or total. As Cummings and Henry explain, ageing is: 'an inevitable process in which many of the relationships between a person and other members of society are severed, and those remaining are altered in quality' (Cummings and Henry 1961: 210). Old people are phased out of the most important social roles as their competence diminishes and are replaced by younger people. The assumption here is that this replacement will reduce potential disruption to the social system.

Activity Theory: Although still broadly functionalist in nature, this approach is basically the opposite of Disengagement Theory. Old people have a need to maintain their middle age for as long as possible, so as to avoid a drop in life satisfaction. Activity theory makes the assumption that old age has a sharp division from other age groups and that ongoing social activity, within recognised social roles, is important for the maintenance of a person's self-concept. Havighurst and Albrecht (1953) argue that old people need to address the following issues if they are to maintain activity:

* Adjust to declining health and physical strength
* Adjust to retirement and reduced income
* Adjust to the death of a spouse or other family members
* Adjust to living arrangements different from what they are accustomed
* Adjust to pleasures of aging, i.e. increased leisure and playing with grandchildren.

Subculture Theory: Old people have a set of shared values and beliefs that are not widely shared within the population; an 'age consciousness'. In addition, the old are separated from the wider society because of retirement.

Personality Theory: Old people can be one of two personality types: *reorganisers* who replace work and the middle age lifestyle with an alternative set of arrangements; and *the disengaged*, who withdraw from a whole range of activities.

Labelling Theory: This approach is derived from the work of Erving Goffman and suggests that individuals who are perceived as *old* are likely to have a range of stereotypical constructions imposed upon them such as being 'senile'.

Chris Phillipson presents 'a critical account of the position of elderly people in a capitalist society' (Phillipson 1982: 1). Phillipson argues that the logic of capitalism as a system of accumulation and exploitation is incompatible with the needs of older people. Capitalism put profits before the needs of individuals – and old people have more needs than most and less ability to pay. Hence older people are more likely to be in poverty and poor health.

Childhood

Childhood is the most extensively governed sector of personal existence. In different ways, at different times, and by many different routes varying from one section of society to another, the health, welfare and rearing of children has been linked in thought and practice to the destiny of the nation and the responsibilities of the State. The modern child has become the focus of innumerable projects that purport to safeguard it from physical, sexual and moral danger, to ensure its normal development, to actively promote certain capacities of attributes such as intelligence, reducibility and emotional stability. (Rose 1989: 121)

The processes of rationalisation that underpin modernisation, as outlined by Weber (1922), were applied by the state to child development. But why did the modern state become increasingly involved in the regulation of childhood? The concept of *socialisation*, which outlines the processes by which children learn the shared norms, values and discourses that allow each of us to become a normal functioning person within a society, suggests that pre-socialised children are essentially savages. If children are not given effective moral guidance at an early phase in their lives, this could pose a serious threat to the social order. Parents had to be moral exemplars, provide guidance, support and impose a strict moral code on their children. Effective, rational and well-ordered socialisation of children was seen as a key element in the management of its citizens by the state.

Socialisation

From very early on in life we are socialised, for example, into appropriate gender roles. Through their discursive positioning, parents are in a position to shape the vision of the world for the immature child and are also in a position, through controlling the way young children dress, their forms of talk, behaviour and manners, of shaping the perception that people have of the child. Institutional forces impose upon us appropriate ways of behaving for boys and girls. Behaviour is interpreted as normal or abnormal, and such behaviours are prescribed as gender specific.

Children's literature is especially useful for studying the discourses that make up everyday life. It is widely accepted that children's literature contains both explicit and implicit messages about the workings of power in society. Pescosolido et al. (1997) argue that 'the intended clarity and moral certainty with which adults provide children with tales of their world offer a fortuitous opportunity to examine social relations and belief systems' (Pescosolido et al., 1997: 444). Through their focus on the United States, they also argue that during periods of deep racial conflict, African American characters virtually disappeared from children's books. A number of researchers in the field of gender division have described such institutional forces, and the discourses that go with them, as a form of *hegemonic masculinity*.

Baker-Sperry and Grauerholz's (2003) analysis of Grimm fairy tales is relevant here; they draw upon the work of Lorber (1994) who argues that gender imagery plays a central role in the persistence of gender division: 'the cultural representations of gender and embodiment of gender in symbolic language and artistic productions that reproduce and legitimate gender statuses' (Lorber 1994: 30–1). Children's fairy tales that emphasise such things as women's passivity and beauty, are *gendered scripts* that help to legitimise and support the dominant gender divisions. The feminine beauty ideal, by which they mean the socially constructed notion of female physical attractiveness, is represented in many children's fairy tales. The feminine beauty ideal is one of a woman's most important assets and something all women should strive to achieve and maintain. Moreover, as we saw in the chapter on gender and sexuality, many feminists acknowledge that many women willingly engage in 'beauty rituals'.

The search for beauty, and the effort to maintain what beauty a woman may have, are central in many women's lives. European and North American women spend a great deal of time, energy and money on beauty. Beauty regimes have become central organising principles in the everyday lives of many women. The feminine beauty ideal can be seen as a normative means whereby social control is accomplished through the internalisation of values and norms that serve to restrict women's lives. Drawing upon the work of Fox (1977), Baker-Sperry and Grauerholz argue that in the process of female socialisation, women internalise norms and adopt ways of behaving that reflect and reinforce their relative powerlessness, making external forces less necessary.

To explore cultural associations with beauty, Baker-Sperry and Grauerholz asked several general questions, such as:

- Is there a clear link between beauty and goodness? (yes/no)
- Are there instances where danger or harm is associated with beauty or desirability? (yes/no), and, if so
- Is beauty or desirability the cause? (yes/no).

Such questions, however, cannot tap the subtle but powerful messages surrounding beauty.

In Baker-Sperry and Grauerholz's analysis, several patterns emerged, including the associations between beauty and economic privilege, beauty and race, beauty and goodness, and beauty and danger. The discourse analyses of the Grimm stories revealed several themes in relation to beauty; often there is a clear link between beauty and goodness, most often in reference to younger women, and between ugliness and evil. Moreover, whilst beauty is often rewarded, lack of beauty is punished. Finally, a significant number of the Grimm stories link beauty and jealousy. Female characters such as the stepmother in *Snow White* show the importance of beauty for women and the symbolic lengths to which some women are believed to go to maintain or acquire beauty.

Re-workings of the Grimm stories in Disney films such as *Cinderella* and *Snow White* tend to increase the references to women 's beauty and men's handsomeness.

> This finding suggests that both men and women are being increasingly manipulated by media messages concerning attractiveness, a trend that is undoubtedly linked to efforts to boost consumerism. This trend does not necessarily contradict a social control perspective. (Baker-Sperry and Grauerholz 2003: 722)

However, Baker-Sperry and Grauerholz conclude that:

> The recent film *Shrek*, whose main woman character is ultimately transformed into an ogre rather than the beautiful maiden she was believed to be, may begin to challenge the value and meaning of women's beauty. But such retellings of fairy tales are rare, and the cumulative effect of the more traditional tales, in conjunction with the unidirectional nature of media, makes such agency difficult. Indeed, the 'beauty' of messages that may serve as normative controls is that so few question or challenge their legitimacy. (Ibid.: 725)

To break with the beauty system or any other central element of *hegemonic masculinity* is to run the risk of being labelled. In relation to wider issues of sexuality, this raises the important question that underpinned the debate about Section 28: At what age could a child be said to be gay? Because children are denied citizenship rights and are assumed to be unable to make decisions about their sexuality, the state has been used to protect the child from the gay propaganda of lesbian and gay new social movements who might attempt to encourage children into a gay or lesbian lifestyle.

Unlike many of the social divisions that we have explored, nothing could appear more normal than childhood. Childhood is different from adulthood for several reasons:

- Children are in full-time compulsory education
- Children are not allowed to do full-time paid adult work
- Children are the economic and moral responsibility of their parents
- Children are protected by a state-sponsored protective framework of regulation.

It is commonly assumed that the experiences we have in the early phase of our lives are biologically determined and that this developmental phase is a common experience for all people, irrespective of the social divisions they may encounter in later life. However, childhood has a history. Childhood is a distinctly 'modernist' conception that has its origins in the manifesto of childhood, *Emile* (1762) by Jean-Jacques Rousseau. In his book *Centuries of Childhood*, Phillip Aries argued that childhood did not exist in medieval society:

> In medieval society the idea of childhood did not exist; this is not to suggest that children were neglected, forsaken or despised. The idea of childhood is not to be confused with affection for children: it corresponds to an awareness of the particular nature of child-hood, that particular nature which distinguishes the child from the adult, even the young adult. In medieval society, this awareness was lacking. That is why, as soon as the child could live without the constant solicitude (care) of his mother, his nanny or his cradle-rocker, he belonged to adult society. That adult society now strikes us as rather puerile (childish): no doubt this is largely a matter of its mental age, but it is also due to its phys-ical age, because it was partly made up of children and youths. (Aries 1962: 125)

Similarly, argues Aries, the fundamental concept of education was alien to the medieval world view:

> Medieval civilization ... knew nothing as yet of modern education. That is the main point: it had no idea of education. Nowadays our society depends, and knows that it depends, on the success of its educational system. It has a system of education, a con-cept of education, an awareness of its importance. New sciences such as psycho-analysis, pediatrics (a branch of medicine which specialises in children) and psychology devote themselves to the problems of childhood, and their findings are transmitted to parents by way of a mass of popular literature. Our world is obsessed by the physical, moral and sexual problems of childhood. This preoccupation was unknown to medieval civilization, because there was no problem for the Middle Ages: as soon as he had been weaned, or soon after, the child became the natural companion of the adult. (Ibid.: 395)

This is not to say that human infants did not exist, or that such infants were not biologically immature. However, what the statement means is that the dis-courses that allow us to understand the biological immaturity of the infant as a 'child' did not develop until into the nineteenth century. The biological immatu-rity of the human infant is a phase of our development, but the notion of this phase of our lives as *childhood* as the 'Other' to the adult, is a social construction.

Jenks on Childhood

According to Chris Jenks, we cannot understand the identity of the child except in relation to our understanding of the adult; the relationship is locked within a binary reasoning, unlike many other forms of identity. For Jenks, 'The child ... has not escaped or deconstructed into the post-structuralist space of multiple and self-presentational identity sets' (Jenks 1999: 3). In other words, within the study of childhood, most conceptions of what it means to be a child are expressed in essentialist and biologically determined terms. However, argues Jenks, the boundaries of childhood are maintained by a number of discourses found with institutions such as the family, nursery, school and the clinic; institutions established to process immature individuals, by standardisation and normalisation, into the uniform thing, 'the child'.

Many theorists and researchers in the area, such as Parsons (1951) and a whole range of functionalists who adopted the concept of socialisation to postmodernists such as Deleuze (1989) with his concept of becoming along the line of organisation, have described how the state has taken a keen interest and active involvement in child development on the grounds that children are potentially dangerous without the moulding of adult supervision and the imposition of constraints. The state attempts to impose constraint upon the child because children without compliance are a threat to the public order. Jenks continues:

> These boundaries do not simply delineate the extent and compass of the child in society but they do proscribe a social space which in turn, and at a different level, express the control component exercised in the framework of that social system and the control variant which reveals the interests that sustain its functioning. (Jenks 1999: 12)

The notion of childhood is also a *gendered* conception:

> The concept of childhood developed as an adjunct to the modern family ... 'childrenese' became fashionable during the seventeenth century. ... Children's toys did not appear until 1600 and even then were not used beyond the age of three or four ... But by the late seventeenth century, special artefacts for children were common. Also in the late seventeenth century we find the introduction of special childhood games ... *childhood did not apply to women.* The female child went from swaddling clothes right into adult female dress. She did not go to school, which, as we shall see, was the institution that structured childhood. At the age of nine or ten she acted, literally, like a 'little adult'; her activity did not differ from that of an adult woman. As soon as she reached puberty, as early as ten or twelve, she was married off to a much older male. (Jenks 1999: 48).

For Jenks:

- Childhood is a social construction, distinct from biological immaturity
- Childhood is not a natural or a universal aspect of the human life cycle
- Childhood is a socio-political concept, in a similar fashion to race, gender and sexuality, it is a variable of social analysis
- Children do not passively accept the imposition of childhood definitions upon their behaviour, they actively interact with and rebel against adults' conceptions.

Other Social Constructions of Childhood

The notion of what constitutes a 'child' varies over time but also from place to place and differs within discourses of race, class, gender and sexuality. Stuart

Hanson (2000) identifies the following themes within the dominant construction of childhood:

- The notion of the child is rooted in nature
- The child as *en route* to adulthood – the 'incomplete adult'
- The child is vulnerable and in need of the protection of adults.

A number of contributions to the sociology of childhood have investigated the positioning of children in relation to adults. Are adults and children ontologically different? In terms of status, and in terms of the opportunity of children to participate in the wider society, children have far fewer opportunities to act as citizens.

Childhood is positioned as subordinate within society. Moreover, the status of 'child' and the associated notion of 'generation' come to form a legally legitimate reason for excluding children from the enjoyment of citizenship rights. Many adults assume that children have a limited capacity to be active citizens. By excluding children from exercising citizenship rights, adulthood becomes a privileged status. Discourses of childhood are built upon concepts of dependence, deviance, deficiency, innocence and vulnerability. Such discourses restrict children's ability to become independent actors.

Hanson (2000) quotes several researchers who argue that we need to recognise that the separation between childhood and adulthood is a false one to make. Adulthood is not a fixed state that can be used to make judgements about the physical, moral, sexual or intellectual development of an infant. In addition there is what Chris Jenks (1996) refers to as the 'forced commonality of an ideological discourse of childhood' (Jenks 1996: 122). There is a series of state-sponsored institutions that regulate the discourse and construction of childhood, such as: families, local authorities, schools, commercial and not-for-profit child care organisations, board of film classification regulators, television watchdogs.

Drawing upon the work of Giddens, Devine argues that:

> Children's social positioning is … an active process as they continually evaluate and monitor their behaviour (both practically and discursively), in light of the expectations and evaluations of others … The transformative potential, for both adults and children, within such a context is immense, as practice becomes shaped through a process of reflection, critical engagement and negotiation. (Devine 2002: 307)

Ideas of childhood innocence, purity and the need for protection also have histories. When children are described and discussed in terms of exercising their own agency in defiance of adult social constructions of everyday life, it is often cauched in terms of *deviancy*. This is true of Paul Willis's book *Learning to Labour* (1977), where a group of working-class 'lads' attempt to import masculine shopfloor culture into the classroom in an effort to reject the dominant ideas that the teaching staff attempt to impose in the school.

Although Devine (2002) is writing about Ireland, her comments would probably be accepted in most parts of the affluent world:

[A]dult discourse on children has been framed primarily in paternalistic terms, children's rights defined negatively in terms of protection from abuse and inadequate care, rather than in terms of empowerment or the questioning of their status in relation to the adult group as a whole. (Devine 2002: 316)

The Protection of Children and the Concept of Incest

Childhood is a social construction, created by adults and imposed upon biologically immature individuals in an effort to marginalise them in the wider society and exercise control over them. This can be seen most clearly in the way in which the state attempts to 'protect' children from sexuality. The problem here is that if we empower children and define them in adult terms, as we have done in previous centuries, the notion of 'abuse' disappears. In a discussion of incest Foucault explains that:

Incest was a popular practice, and I mean this, widely practised among the populace, for a long time. It was towards the end of the 19th century that various social pressures were directed against it. And it is clear that the great interdiction against incest is an invention of the intellectuals ... If you look for studies by sociologists or anthropologists of the 19th century on incest you won't find any. (Foucault quoted in Jenks 1999: 94)

There is no specific definition of incest in England before the nineteenth century. It was not until the Punishment of Incest Act (1908) that incest was regarded a criminal matter; up until then incest was regarded an ecclesiastical matter and although condemned by Canon Law, the criminal and civil courts had no jurisdiction. However, the Matrimonial Causes Act (1857) did make incestuous adultery one of the grounds that a wife could cite to divorce her husband. In Scotland, under the Criminal Procedure (Scotland) Act 1887, incest became punishable by death. However, in many countries such as the United States, incest was not an indictable offence and was punished by the imposition of a fine and/or a period of imprisonment only if state legislation permitted. Similar punishments were applied in a number of European countries such as Italy, Germany and Austria.

CHILD PROTECTION LEGISLATION IN ENGLAND AND WALES, 1833–2002

Batty (2002) and Moore (1993) provide us with a comprehensive outline of the child protection legislation and initiatives in England and Wales, which include the following land marks:

1833 The first Factory Act attempted to regulate the working conditions of children and young people in factories

(Continued)

(Continued)

1870 Education Act passed, introducing a national system of elementary education

1889 After a campaign by the National Society for the Prevention of Cruelty to Children (NSPCC) that was established in 1884, the following initiatives were taken:

- The state took powers to intervene directly in the relationship between parents and children; the ill-treatment of a child became illegal
- Police had the power to enter any premises if a child was believed to be in danger
- Guidelines on the employment of children were issued
- Begging by children was criminalised.

1894 State powers were extended to include the following measures:

- Children were allowed to give evidence in court
- The mental cruelty of adults against a child was criminalised
- Denying a child medical attention was criminalised.

1906 The establishment of school dinners in the UK

1908 The Children's Act was passed: children were no longer treated as adults in the criminal justice system

1932 The Children and Young Persons Act 1932 was introduced which extended the powers of juvenile courts under the 1908 Act. Supervision orders were introduced for children believed to be at risk

1948 Following a number of well-publicised cases of cruelty by foster parents, the Children Act 1948 placed a legal obligation on all local authorities to appoint a Children's Officer and to establish a Children's Department that would oversee the problems faced by children who did not have a normal home life

1952 Local authorities given powers to investigate cases of child neglect

1963 Children's Act passed which placed an obligation upon local authorities to prevent families from becoming problem families

1970 Under the Local Authority Social Services Act 1970, Children's Officers and local authority Children's Departments were unified in new family-centred social services departments

1974 Following the conviction of a man for the murder of his stepdaughter, child protection services were reorganised. Child Protection Committees were established independently of local authority social services departments to coordinate the agencies involved with the safety of children believed to be at risk

1989 The Children Act 1989 became law with the following provisions:

- Children are the responsibility of their parents, the local authority should be helpful and supportive of parents
- The legal duties and responsibilities of the parent can only be transferred to the local authority after a court hearing

(Continued)

(Continued)

- Children had the right to protection from abuse and exploitation
- The state had the right to make inquiries to safeguard the welfare of children.

1991 The government report *Working Together Under the Children's Act* explains that when abuse is suspected to be the cause of a child's death, the relevant Child Protection Committee will conduct an investigation

1998 The Government introduced *Quality Protects*, a programme that set targets for local authorities. Local authorities have to demonstrate by 2004 that they are fulfilling their statutory obligations regarding children at risk of abuse

1999 The Protection of Children Act 1999:

- The Act aims to prevent paedophiles from working with children and young people
- All child care organisations have to make available to the Government details of anyone suspected of putting children at risk.

2000 The Children and Young People's Unit was established to:

- Coordinate all the strands of government policy in relation to children and young people
- Establish partnerships between charities and community organisations
- Establish a children's fund to provide services to 'at risk' children.

2002 Following the death of child abuse victim Victoria Climbié, the Government announced the establishment of the first *children's trusts*, bodies that bring together all the relevant professionals that deal with the needs of the child under the control of the local authority.

In summary, dominant discourses of childhood are based upon assumptions of innocence and vulnerability that constrain the capability of the child to construct or define themselves as capable or independent human agents. What children do and say is not interpreted in relation to the child's understanding of the world, but in relation to the discourses of childhood that the state uses to manage its citizens effectively. In the United Kingdom, the 1989 Children's Act was based upon the *paramountcy principle* – that the needs of the child came first. However, as Michael Wyness explains, the Children's Act.

> extends the role of the guardian *ad litem* in mediating between children and the institutional adult world. Young children's voices and opinions are heard through an adult whose role is to convey the child's interest to an adult audience of social workers and court officials.

Child-centredness is largely rhetorical.

ACTIVITY

Risk, Childhood Individualisation and Zombie Categories

As we have seen in earlier chapters, Ulrich Beck argues that modernity is breaking free from the contours of classical industrial society and that we are in the midst of a transition from an industrial society to a risk society. A central feature of the risk society is the process of *individualisation*, individual design at the centre of our life narrative, whereby individual people are cut loose from previously supportive social forms, for example family, social class, neighbourhood or fixed gender roles. Individuals now compose their own life narrative, in other words they create the biography that they want. Our individual biography becomes an 'elective biography' or 'risk biography' (Beck and Beck-Gernsheim 2002: 3), our biographies become *self-reflexive* as the given determinations over our future paths or life narratives that dominated industrial society are dissolved and our destiny is placed in our own hands: 'the nationally fixed social categories of industrial society are culturally dissolved or transformed. They become "zombie categories" which have died yet live on' (ibid.: 27).

A *post-familial family* has emerged which allows individuals greater opportunity to make lifestyle choices. However, consider the following quote from Beck, and address the question that follows:

> The child is the source of the last remaining, irrevocable, unexchangeable primary relationship. Partners come and go. The child stays. Everything that is desired, but not realizable in the relationship, is directed to the child. With the increasing fragility of the relationship between the sexes the child acquires a monopoly on practical companionship, on an expression of feelings in a biological give and take that otherwise is becoming increasingly uncommon and doubtful. Here an anachronistic social experience is celebrated and cultivated which has become improbable and longed for precisely because of the individualization process. The excessive affection for children, the 'staging of childhood' which is granted to them – the poor overloved creatures – and the nasty struggle for the children during and after divorce are some symptoms of this. The child becomes the final alternative to loneliness that can be built up against the vanishing possibilities of love. It is the private type of re-enchantment, which arises with, and derives its meaning from, disenchantment. (Beck 1992)

Clearly from the above quote 'childhood' is not a zombie category, as gender, class and race have become for Beck. According to Chris Jenks, in Beck's analysis of the risk society: 'children are seen as dependable and permanent, in a manner to which no other person or persons can possibly aspire' (Jenks 1996: 107).

Question:

➢ How and why do children come to have such a special place within the risk society?

The Child and the Emergence of the Postmodern Family

As we have seen in previous chapters, in the past few decades there has been a series of demographic shifts that significantly impacted upon family patterns:

- A rising divorce rate
- A growth in the illegitimacy rate especially amongst young mothers who are still children themselves
- A significant increase in lone parenting, surrogate mothers, and gay and lesbian families
- An increasing number of women in the workforce and the consequent decline in the financial need for women to marry
- And with the greater liberation of women, the knocking down of what Shorter (1975) refers to as the 'nest' conception of nuclear family life.

These changes highlighted the arbitrary nature of family roles and undermined the assumed biological nature of motherhood. In contrast to the Marxian and functionalist view of motherhood as the product of biologically determined differences, postmodern perspectives view motherhood as a patriarchal and heterosexual construct. In the postmodern world, motherhood is a contested social category that can only be understood within the given gender regimes of modernity. Family relationships and other living arrangements within a range of households, not traditionally classed as families, have become more ambivalent, diverse, contested, fluid and undecided in nature.

Households now reflect a multiplicity of relationships that people find themselves in and household structures reflect the values, attitudes, opinions, lifestyles and personalities of the household members/participants. In the late twentieth century there was a lesbian baby boom in the industrialised countries. Lesbian households with children, either via donor insemination, adoption, or fostering can be variously named: the reinvented family, dual-orientation households, lesbian-led families, planned lesbian mother families, etc. However, there remain both legal obstacles and prejudice against lesbians and gay men adopting children. Charlotte J. Patterson found that lesbian and gay parents and their children are a diverse group. However, courts in the United States have expressed a number of concerns about the possible effects on children of having gay or lesbian parents.

- The development of sexual identity may be impaired among children of lesbian or gay parents for instance, that children themselves are more likely to become gay or lesbian
- Children's personal development may be impaired; children may be less psychologically healthy.

ACTIVITY

UN Convention on the Rights of the Child, 1989

The convention is organised around four core principles:

1   Non-discrimination
2   The best interests of the child.
3   Rights to survival and development.
4   Giving attention to the views of the child – including rights in relation to cultural identity, language and values.

Look at the United Nations web pages on the 'Rights of the Child' at: www.unicef. org/crc/

Questions:

➤   In the light of the discussion above on the emergence of the postmodern family: Does the UN Convention empower the child?

➤   Do you believe that the UN Convention will have a significant impact on the lives of children? Give the reasons for your answer.

Becoming: the Role of the State beyond the Fixed Conception of 'Being'

State-sponsored divisions and the categories that they give rise to are often assumed to be biological in nature rather than social divisions. However, is there a 'normal' sexuality, childhood or old age? Are citizens of other countries potential threats? The rationalities and technologies of governmentality underpin social divisions and give rise to the discourses that support these individuals' *given* identities. Each and every one of us is involved in a process of becoming. In theory we can become whatever we desire but in practice we do not, because the powerful forces of the state are at work, restricting our processes of becoming.

In his text *What Children Say* (1998) Deleuze explains that children never stop talking about what they are doing or trying to do. Children do this by means of dynamic trajectories and drawing mental maps of those trajectories. This map is essential to our psychic activity. These maps form lines, such as the line of immanence, which are constantly referred to in Deleuze's work.

For Deleuze, there is no fixed conception of 'being'; instead he looks at the self in terms of an imminent or emerging 'becoming' which has no established elements that define or constrain our identity. The emergent becoming is built upon a practical ontology. Becoming is 'molecular' in nature and is described in terms of emitting particles which enter into proximity with particles of the thing which the self wishes to become: woman, child, animal, dog, vegetable, minor, imperceptible, etc. Becoming is a tension between modes of desire plotting a vector of transformation between molar coordinates. Becoming is then directional; 'becoming' allows the self to emerge into anything it chooses, a process in which the body is involved in leaving its normal habitat. This process is not simply a matter of imitating or metamorphosis as imitation involves respect for boundaries that constrain the self. All forms of becoming are said to be 'minoritarian' in nature, in that all forms of becoming involve movement away from the 'standard man' that is firmly rooted on the plane of organisation. This movement away from the plane of organisation can be taken to the point whereby identity is destroyed in any conventional sense. Immanence is immanent only to itself. This is what Deleuze and Guattari refer to as 'becoming-imperceptible' which sweeps away the majority.

The state has an image of how the individual should behave and think in every situation and circumstance. This self-evident system of thought is what Deleuze terms *the abstract machine*. Today it is the human sciences that have taken on this role of the abstract machine for the modern apparatuses of power.

One of the central themes in Deleuze is the relationship between power and desire.

In his discussion of the process of becoming, Deleuze describes two types of 'plane': the plane of organisation and the plane of consistence/immanence.

The Plane of Organisation

This plane is concerned with the formation of subjects and attempts to crush desire by use of things like the law. This plane is said to be made up of molar lines with segments; both individuals and groups are made up of 'lines'. This molar line with segments includes such things as the family, the school, the factory and retirement. This line is one of 'rigid segmentarity' in which individuals are moulded to behave and think in appropriate ways. Deleuze gives us the examples of people in the family telling others, 'Now you're not a baby any more', and at school, 'You're not at home now'. Segments are then devices of power in that they fix a code of behaviour within a defined territory. In the last analysis, the state 'overcodes' all the segments. This overcoding 'ensures the homogenisation of different segments' (Deleuze and Guattari, 1988: 129). This is achieved by the use of 'the abstract machine' which imposes the normal/usual ways of thinking and behaving from the point of view of the state.

The Plane of Consistence/The Plane of Immanence

In contrast to the molar line with segments, the plane of consistence is concerned with molecular fluxes with thresholds or quanta. These are lines of segmentarity that are molecular or supple. These lines are detours and modifications; they are lines of becoming. On the plane of organisation, the segments depend upon 'binary machines'; you are one case or its logical alternative. For example, you are one class or another; one sex or the other; one race or the other. These classifications appear to be dichotomic but operate diachronically. If you are not a man or a woman then you are a transvestite. To move along this plane one must first construct it; the plane does not pre-exist desire. As we move along this plane that we have constructed, we become a 'body without organs'. By this term Deleuze means a body without organisation; one who fulfils their desires by attempting liberation from the plane of organisation. Desire only exists when it is assembled or machined. The plane of consistence is concerned with movement, and it deals with 'hecceities' rather than subjects. Hecceities are degrees of power. The plane of consistence is described as:

> successions of catatonic states and periods of extreme haste, of suspensions and shootings, coexistences of variable speeds, blocks of becoming, leaps across voids, displacements of a centre of gravity on an abstract line, conjunction of lines on a plane of immanence, a 'stationary process' at dizzying speed which sets free particles and affects. (Deleuze and Parnet 1987: 95)

Every person or group can construct a plane of immanence on which to lead his or her life.

Territorialisation/Deterritorialisation

The issue of territorialisation is about the problem of holding together heterogeneous elements (Deleuze and Guattari 1988: 323). Not to follow the line of organisation is referred to as 'deterritorialisation'. In this process 'knots of arborescence' – by which Deleuze means thinking hierarchies – become 'resumptions and upsurges in a rhizome' (ibid.: 134). Territory for Deleuze is an assemblage; it is a environment experienced in harmony, with a distance between people marked by 'indexes' which form the basis of 'territoralising expressions' and 'territorialised functions'. The basis of territory is aggressiveness. However, territory regulates the coexistence of individuals of the same species by keeping them separated. The effect of territory is to allow different people to coexist by specialising in different activities.

The direction of the process of 'territorialisation' is referred to by Deleuze as a 'refrain' – which is an aggregate of expressions and territorial motifs. The refrain acts upon whatever surrounds it and forms an organised mass. As Deleuze and

Guattari explain, within a territory, 'Every consciousness pursues its own death, every love-passion its own end, attracted by a blackhole, and all the blackholes resonate together' (1988: 133).

This is the operation of the line of organisation and it is about killing desire by preventing 'the absolute deterritorialisation of the cogito' (ibid.: 133). It is within deterritorialisation that we construct the field of immanence or the plane of consistency – a very different assemblage from the line of organisation. The assemblage that makes up the field of immanence is constructed piece by piece in which a person 'takes and makes what she or he can, according to taste' (ibid.: 157). This is the 'body without organs', the 'connection of desires, conjunction of flows, continuum of intensities' (ibid.: 161). The body without organs may not be easy to compose and there is no guarantee that it will be understood.

The person is made up of bundles of lines, such as lines of flight, lines of drift, and customary lines. Some of these lines are imported from the outside, some emerge by chance, and some are invented. The lines have singularities, segments and quanta and they are not easily differentiated, notably because the lines themselves are an invention of cartography.

In the case of becoming-dog, a person does not literally become a dog in the way that Kafka's character Gregor Samsa becomes an insect. Rather, when a person is involved in becoming-dog this means becoming a body without organs, escaping Oedipality and leading a life which is entirely immanent in nature. Becoming is the process of individuation, free from organisation: 'Becoming produces nothing other than itself' (ibid.: 238).

Becoming is about the process of desire, by liberating the body from the line of organisation. If we take the example of 'becoming-woman', the line of organisation imposes a universal woman upon some bodies. Young women will be told, 'stop behaving like that, you are not a little girl anymore', 'you're not a tomboy', etc. This is what Deleuze refers to as *aborescence*, which is the submission of a person to the line of organisation, the installation of a semiotic and subjectification onto the body. Psychoanalysis is one technique used for doing this imposition, and hence for repressing desire. The body without organs is what is left when you take away all organisation and aborescence, allowing becoming to happen.

The human being is often seen to be a segmentary animal and is segmented in a binary fashion: male–female, adult–child, etc.

Becoming-animal

Becoming-animal is absolute 'deterritoralisation' (Deleuze 1975: 13). It is the schizo escape from the Oedipus Complex. However, for Deleuze, in the case of Gregor Samsa, this ends in failure as he attempts to re-Oedipalize himself, as the transformation is incomplete. Becoming-animal was explored by Kafka in a number of stories; the story of Samsa in *The Metamorphosis*, in which Samsa becomes-insect, which involves the deterritorialisation of his family relationships and his bureaucratic and commercial relationships from his working life. Other stories include: 'Investigations of a Dog'; 'Report to the Academy' and 'Josephine the Singer'.

When faced with a simulacrum, animals, children and the ignorant, who do not possess the antidote of reason and knowledge, lose the distinction between truth and illusion. The animal could never have a real thought because it would simultaneously forget what it was on the verge of thinking. To become-animal is to make use of a machine of expression that expresses itself first and conceptualises later. Pure content is not separate from its expression.

Back to Modernity: the Blair Project as the Moral Turn in British Politics

'What was strong then is fragile now' Tony Blair, Labour Party Conference 1996

The social construction of alterity through a state-sponsored management of becoming is directly related to both order within the community and social division. Seeking to establish and maintain an effective social division between individuals who have a lifestyle that the Blair Government approves of and those who do not, is one of the central tasks of the 'abstract machine' of the state in the United Kingdom.

Citizenship describes both the relationship between the state and the individual and at the same time political relationships between individuals. Whatever you feel should be included within a citizenship education curriculum and whatever competencies and outcomes you feel such a curriculum should address, citizenship education inevitably brings together political and educational ideologies in an effort to redefine the relationship between the state and the individual. These relationships are never static; at present the relationships between the state and young people and young people and the community are becoming increasingly problematic. The idea that 'something needs to be done about out-of-control young people' underpins much Government policy and in particular the policy of introducing citizenship education. In the early 1990s, an image of young people emerged in popular film and television which Henry Giroux has referred to as 'Border Youth'. The characteristics of border youth were that they had few secure psychological, economic or intellectual markers. As Giroux explains, such youths were condemned 'to wander across, within, and between multiple borders and spaces marked by excess, otherness, difference, and a dislocating notion of meaning and attention' (Giroux 1999: 103). Young people, argues Giroux, randomly move from one place to the next with no sense of where they have come from or where they are going. Alienation is driven inward and emerges in comments like 'I feel stuck'. Irony slightly overshadows a refusal to imagine any kind of collective struggle. Reality seems too desperate to care about.

In Giroux's opinion, this vision of youth was seen in such films as *River's Edge* (1986), *My Own Private Idaho* (1991) and *Slackers* (1991). We could add to this list films such as *Bill and Ted's Excellent Adventure* (1992) and the popular television programme and film *Wayne's World*.

In a similar fashion, David Blunkett was reported in *The Guardian* as saying:

> This week's reports show that too many of our towns and cities lack any sense of civic identity or shared values. The tradition of political citizenship in the UK is so weak that to raise the issue of what unites us is deemed marginal at best, dishonest at worst. (*The Guardian*, 14 December 2001)

In other words, something needs to be done about the young people because they are out of control. Many older people's opinions of the young today are that they are lacking in morality and ambition, they are lazy, work-shy, rude, have poor manners, and are dangerous. Citizenship education is about the *remoralisation* of young people in Britain. The state has its preferred lifestyle for young people, a lifestyle that values paid employment over all alternative ways of financing lifestyles.

The *Daily Mail* has described young people today as 'a terrifying generation of murderous, morally blank wolf-children, fatherless, undisciplined, indulged one minute then brutalized the next' (28 April 2002). Furthermore, 'As we go around the country and talk to people, there seems no issue that matters more to people than anti-social behaviour and street crime' (*Daily Mail*, 30 April 2002).

Lynda Lee-Porter also writing in The *Daily Mail* argued that 'Too many children have no education, discipline, supportive families, a structure to their lives and future.' These factors all lead to trouble, which results in children 'knowing about their rights but not their responsibilities.' Lynda Lee-Potter concludes by saying that 'unless we face the truth, increasing generations of no-hopers will be born and they too will be victims destined for brutal lives' (*Daily Mail*, 1 May 2002).

The Blair Government sees citizenship education as one of the central ways of ensuring that young people can be taught duties and responsibilities – in other words, of socialising young people into the state's preferred lifestyle choices for young people. In 2002 the Government published a Green Paper on 14–19 Education in which it said:

> Post-16 Citizenship should enable young adults to exercise social responsibility and extend their potential effectiveness by active participation in their education and training and their communities. (Green Paper, *14–19: Extending Opportunities, Raising Standards*)

Citizenship classes should include instruction on how to take part in democracy; how to express themselves; make young people aware of current events and ready to debate issues, including some basics of how laws are made and who declares war. As Sir Bernard Crick argued, 'Citizenship is a necessary condition for a more participatory society' (Crick 1999: 337).

Moreover as *The Guardian* argued, 'it is vital that we develop a stronger understanding of what our collective citizenship means, and how we can build that shared commitment into our social and political institutions' (*The Guardian*, 14 December 2001). However, the original report on *Education for Citizenship and the Teaching of Democracy in Schools* warned that:

> Schools can only do so much. We must not ask too little of teachers but equally we must not ask too much. Pupils' attitudes to active citizenship are influenced quite as much by ... many factors other than schooling: by family, the immediate environment, the media and the examples of those in public life. Sometimes these are positive factors, sometimes not.

As *The Guardian* argued, 'Citizenship means finding a common place for diverse cultures and beliefs, consistent with our core values' (14 December 2001). Different cultures have their beliefs but they still need to meet the needs of common values in the British society. In the Thatcher years, trade unions were seen as 'the enemy within'. In the Blair years, Asylum seekers have become the enemy from without and young people have taken on the 'role of enemy within'; both groups can be made safe by citizenship education. As David Blunkett suggested, asylum seekers should take a form of citizenship test, together with an English test and swear an oath of allegiance to Britain. These measures should enhance our sense of citizenship, which the Government appears to believe, will bring together society.

Within the Blair project, the notion of communitarianism can be seen as an attempt to rebuild the idea of 'the community' within an uncertain/postmodern world where cultures and morality appear to be fragmented; individuals can select any identities they wish: lesbian, gay, green, vegan, etc. Most importantly, belonging to a neighbourhood with a sense of 'community' appears to have become a thing of the past. In Blair's view, our most cherished institutions, such as marriage, the family and even friendship, have become fragile.

Blair would appear to accept Giddens's argument that *life politics* emerges from *emancipatory politics* and is a politics of self-actualisation, in other words, life politics 'concerns debates and contestations deriving from the reflexive project of the self' (Giddens 1992: 215). This means that life politics is about the unhindered creation of a self that you are happy with. If you wish to be gay, straight, a new age traveller or an office worker, you should be free to do so without others making judgements about you.

The Blair Government has used communitarian ideas to significantly change our conception of citizenship. Before Blair became Prime Minister, citizenship was something that was given to all people who were born in Britain, or who could otherwise make a legitimate claim for a British passport. As a British citizen, an individual could draw upon the resources of the welfare state, the social security system, the education service, local authority housing, etc. Blair has taken the *given* element out of British citizenship; now citizenship has to be earned through making a contribution to the community. As the new Clause 4 makes clear, if people do not make a contribution to the community, then they cannot expect the community to provide them with resources. Blair believes that paid work is morally superior to all the alternatives. This is fully and clearly reflected in our programmes of citizenship education, which clearly outlines the lifestyles or forms of becoming which the state is willing to sponsor. Individuals are free to choose any lifestyle that they wish, and people should respect people for what they choose to be. However, people who choose a lifestyle that does not have paid work as a central element will feel the full force of the abstract machine of the state, as they will run the risk of having citizenship rights taken away.

Blair makes it clear that certain lifestyle choices, notably lone parenting without paid work, will not be funded by the community because is not an acceptable form of *becoming*. That person becomes the Other in Blair's Britain, abstracted from relations with others and identified as a moral and financial drain upon the community. The Blair project is authoritarian because under the guise of citizenship with its Citizenship Curriculum and language of exercising choice, autonomy, political literacy, duties and rights, the Blair Government imposes conditions upon choice and reinterprets acquiescence as a democratically derived choice. Blair has criminalised the lifestyles of poorer people; people who choose not to work and to live on benefits have been made to feel morally inferior to the rest of the community and for them citizenship is denied.

In other words, as was argued above, the social construction of alterity is directly related to both order within the community and social division. Seeking to establish and maintain an effective social division between individuals who have a lifestyle that the Blair Government approves of and those who do not, is one of the central tasks of the 'abstract machine' of the state in the United Kingdom.

Conclusion

Although the work of Deleuze and Guattari is difficult to follow, they give a clear account of how and why the state is involved in the processes of becoming. The state has a preferred personality and form of being for the individual. To depart from the state's preferred personality and form of being is to run the risk of becoming viewed as a criminal, a deviant or having a number of labels attached to your self. Families, schools, colleges, the media and a whole range of other institutions put pressure on the individual self not only to behave in particular ways but also to internalise thoughts, feelings and values and allow them to become part of the self. Those who refuse to accept the homogenising and coercive impact of the state and its abstract machine will be classified into different types of persons and clear social divisions are imposed.

References

Ackerman, B. (1980) *Social Justice in the Liberal State*, Yale University Press, New Haven, Com.

Aries, P. (1962) *Centuries of Childhood*, Penguin, Harmondsworth.

Baker-Sperr, L. and Grauerholz, L. (2003) 'The Pervasiveness and Persistence of the Feminine Beauty Ideal in Children's Fairy Tales', *Gender and Society* 15(5): 711–26.

Batty, D. (2002) 'Timeline: the History of Child Protection', *The Guardian*, October 10

Beck, U. (1992) *The Risk Society*, Sage, London.

Beck, U. and Beck-Gernsheim, E. (1995) *The Normal Chaos of Love*, trans. Mark Ritter and Jane Wiebel, Polity Press, Cambridge.

Beck, U. and Beck-Gernsheim, E. (2002) *Individualization: Institutional Individualism and its Social and Political Consequences*, Sage, London.

Beetham, D. (1999) *Democracy and Human Rights*, Polity, Cambridge.

Benhabib, S. (1999) 'Citizens, Residents, and Aliens in a Changing World: Political Membership in the Global Era', *Social Research*, 66(3): 709–29.

Biggs, S. and Powell, J.L. (2001) 'A Foucauldian Analysis of Old Age and the Power of Social Welfare', *Journal of Aging & Social Policy*, 12(2): 93–111.

Bogue, R. (1989) *Deleuze and Guattari*, Routledge, London.

Butler, Judith (1990) *Gender Trouble: Feminism and the Subversion of Identity*, Routledge, London.

Butler, Judith (1993) *Bodies That Matter: On the Discursive Limits of 'Sex'*, Routledge, London.

Butler, Judith (1997) *The Psychic Life of Power: Theories in Subjection*, Stanford University Press Stanford, Cal.

Carens, Joe (1995) 'Aliens and Citizens: The Case for Open Borders', in Beiner, R. (ed.), *Theorizing Citizenship*, SUNY Press, New York.

Carrigan, M. and Szmigin, I. (2000) 'Advertising in an Ageing Society', *Age and Society* 20(2): 217–33.

Carroll, P.E. (2002) 'Medical Police and the History of Public Health', *Medical History* 46(4): 461–94.

Castles, S. (2003) 'Towards a Sociology of Forced Migration and Social Transformation. (Global Refugees)', *Sociology* 37(1): 13–22.

Chandler, D. (2003) 'New Rights for Old? Cosmopolitan Citizenship and the Critique of State Sovereignty', *Political Studies* 51(2): 332–49.

Cohen, S. (2002) 'The local state of immigration controls', *Critical Social Policy* 22: 518–43.

Coppedge, M. (1994) 'Prospects for Democratic Governability in Venezuela', *Journal of Interamerican Studies and World Affairs* 36(2): 39–65.

Crick, B. (1999) 'The presuppositions of citizenship education', *Journal of Philosophy of Education* 33: 337–52.

Crook, S. and Pakulski, J. (1992) *Postmodernization: Change in Advanced Society*, Sage, London.

Cumming, E. and Henry, W.E. (1961) *Growing Old: The Process of Disengagement*, New York: Basic Books.

Daily, C., Ehrlich, A. and Ehrlich, P. (1995) 'Response to Bartlett and Lytwak', *Population and Immigration Policy in the United States*. http://dieoff.org/page98.htm

Dalley, I. and Crozier, B. (2001) 'The Medical Construction of Homosexuality and its Relation to the Law in Nineteenth Century England', *Medical History* 45(1): 61–82.

Delanty, G. (2000) *Citizenship in a Global Age: Society, Culture, Politics*, Open University Press, Buckingham.

Deleuze, G. (1975) *Kafka: Towards a Minor Literature*, University of Minnesota Press, Minneapolis.

Deleuze, G. (1989) *Masochism*, Zone Books, New York.

Deleuze, G. (1989) *Cinema 2: The time-image*, trans. H. Tomlinson and R. Galeta, University of Minnesota Press, Minneapolis.

Deleuze, G. (1990) *The Logic of Sense*, Columbia University Press, Columbia, NY.

Deleuze, G. (1994) *What Is Philosophy?* trans. Hugh Tomlinson and Graham Burchell, Columbia University Press, Columbia, NY.

Deleuze, G. (1997) *Difference and Repetition*, trans. Paul Patton, Athlone Press, London.

Deleuze, G. (1998) *Essays Critical and Clinical*, trans. D.W. Smith and M.A. Greco, Columbia University Press, Columbia, NY.

Deleuze, G. and Guattari, F. (1983) *Anti-Oedipus: Capitalism and Schizophrenia*, University of Minnesota Press, Minneapolis.

Deleuze, G. and Guattari, F. (1988) *A Thousand Plateaus: Capitalism and Schizophrenia*, Athlone Press, London.

Deleuze, G. and Parnet, C. (1987) *Dialogues*, Columbia University Press, NY.

Devine, D. (2002) 'Children's Citizenship and the Structuring of adult–child Relations in the Primary School', *Childhood: A Global Journal of Child Research* 9(3): 303–20.

DeVoretz, D. (2001) 'Canadian Immigration: Economic Winners and Losers', in Djajic, S. (ed.) *International Migration: Trends, Policies and Economic Impact*, Routledge, London.

Djajic, S. (ed.) (2001) *International Migration: Trends, Policies and Economic Impact*, Routledge, London.

Everingham, C. (2003) 'Self-actualisation and the Ageing Process from an Inter-generational Life-course Perspective', *Ageing and Society* 23: 243–53.

Foucault, M. (1969) *The Order of Things: An Archaeology of the Human Sciences*, trans. Alan Sheridan-Smith, Tavistock Publications, London.

Foucault, Michel (1977) *Discipline and Punish: The Birth of the Prison*, trans. Alan Sheridan-Smith, Penguin, London.

Foucault, Michel (1990a) *The History of Sexuality Vol. 1*, trans. Robert Hurley, Penguin, London.

Foucault, Michel (1990b) *The Care of the Self: Vol. 3 of The History of Sexuality*, trans. Robert Hurley, Penguin, London.

Foucault, Michel (1992) *The Use of Pleasure: The History of Sexuality Vol. 2*, trans. Robert Hurley, Penguin, London.

Fox, G.L. (1977) 'Nice Girl: Social Control of Women through a Value Construct', *Signs: Journal of Women in Culture and Society* 2: 805–17.

Friedan, B. (1993) 'Betty Friedan: Now She's Making Waves in the "Fountain of Age"', interview with Alice V. Luddington, *Geriatrics* 48(12): 52–55.

Giddens, A. (1992) *The Transformation of Intimacy: Sexuality, Love, and Eroticism in Modern Societies*, Polity Press, Cambridge.

Giroux, Henry, A. (1999) 'Public Intellectuals and the challenge of children's culture: Youth and the politics of Innocence', *The Review of Education, Pedagogy and Cultural Studies* 21(3): 193–225.

Gorjanicyn, K. (2000a) *Citizenship and Democracy in a Global Era*, Chapter: 'Citizenship and Culture in Contemporary France: Extreme Right Interventions', Macmillan, Basingstoke.

Gorjanicyn, K. (2000b) *Labor Essays 2001 For the people: Reclaiming our Government*, Chapter: 'Redefining Citizenship and Public Interest: Feminist Perspectives', Pluto Press in association with the Australian Fabian Society, Annandale, NSW.

Guillemard, R.A., Kohli, M. and van Gunsteren, H. (1991) *Time for Retirement. Comparative Studies of Early Exit from the Labour Force*, Cambridge, University Press, Cambridge.

Hall, S. (1997) *Representations: Cultural Representations and Signifying Practices*, Sage Publications, London.

Hanson, R.K. (1997) 'Predictors of sex offense recidivism', in *Research Summary: Corrections, Research and Development* 2(1).

Havighurst, R.J. and Albrecht, R. (1953) *Older People*, Longmans, New York.

Heywood, F., Oldham, C. and Means, R. (2002) *Housing and Home in Later Life*, Open University Press, Buckingham.

Honig, B. (1998) 'Immigrant America? How "Foreignness" Solves Democracy's Problems', *Social Text* 3: 1–27.

Jenks, C. (1999) *Childhood*, Routledge, London.

Judah, T. (2002) Elderly 'Witches' Persecuted in Mozambique: bbc.co.uk posted Wednesday, 3 July.

Kaldor, M. (1999b) 'Transnational Civil Society', in Dunne, T. and Wheeler, N.J. (eds) *Human Rights in Global Politics*, Cambridge University Press, Cambridge.

King, N. (2003) 'The Influence of Anxiety: September 11, Bioterrorism and American Public Health', *Journal of the History of Medicine*, 58(4): 433–41.

Laffey, P. (2003) 'Two Registers of Madness in Enlightenment Britain. Part 2', *History of Psychiatry*, 14(1): 63–81.

Lengwiler, M. (2003) 'Psychiatry beyond the Asylum: the Origins of German Military Psychiatry before World War I', *History of Psychiatry*, 14(1): 41–62.

Lorber, J. (1994) *Paradoxes of Gender*, Yale University Press, New Haven, Com.

Loretto, W., Duncan, C. and White, P. (2000) 'Ageism and Employment: Controversies, Ambiguities and Younger People's Perceptions', *Age and Society* 20(3): 279–302.

Macfarlane, A. (1970) *Witchcraft in Tudor and Stuart England*, Macmillan, Basingstoke.

McNeil, P. (1981) 'Old Age in Society Today', *New Society*, 19 November.

Martin, J. (1993) 'Reducing Illegal Immigration: The Options', The Centre for Immigration Studies website http://www.cis.org/articles/1993/back893.html

Marshall, T.H. (1950) *Citizenship and Social Class and Other Essays*, Cambridge University Press, London.

Mayall, B. (2000) 'Research with Children: Working with Generational Issues', in Christensen, P. and James, A. (eds) *Research with Children: Perspectives and Practices*, Falmer Press, London, pp. 120–35.

Millbank, J. (2002) 'Imagining Otherness: Refugee Claims on the Basis of Sexuality in Canada and Australia. (lesbian and gay asylum-seekers)', *Melbourne University Law Review*, 26(1): 144–78.

Mills, J. and Mills, R. (eds) (2000) *Childhood Studies: A Reader in Perspectives of Childhood*, Routledge, London.

Minichiello, V., Browne, J. and Kendig, H. (2000) 'Perceptions and Consequences of Ageism: Views of Older People', *Ageing and Society*, 20(3): 253–79.

Moore, S. (1993) *Social Welfare Alive!*, Stanley Thornes, Cheltenham.

Norris, C. (1992) *Uncritical Theory: Postmodernism, Intellectuals, and the Gulf War*, University of Massachusetts Press, Amherst, Mass.

Oldham, C. (2002) 'Later Life and the Social Model of Disability: a Comfortable Partnership?', *Ageing and Society* 22: 791–806.

Pescosolido, B., Grauerholz, E. and Milkie, M. (1997) 'Culture and Conflict: The portrayal of Blacks in U.S. Children's Picture Books through the Mid- and Late-Twentieth Century', *American Sociological Review* 62: 443–64.

Phillipson, C. (1982) *Capitalism and the Construction of Old Age*, Macmillan, Basingstoke.

Pilloud, S. and Louis-Courvoisier, M. (2003) 'The Intimate Experience of the Body in the Eighteenth Century: between Interiority and Exteriority', *Medical History* 47(4): 451–72.

Punch, S. (2002) 'Research with Children: The Same or Different from Research with Adults?', *Childhood: A Global Journal of Child Research* 9(3): 321–41.

Rose, Nikolas (1989) *Governing the Soul*, Routledge, London.

Sassen, S. (1996) 'Whose city is it? Globalization and the formation of new claims', *Public Culture* 8, 205–23.

Schuster, D. and Solomos, A. (2001) 'Race, immigration and asylum: New Labour's agenda', *Ethnicities*, 4(2): 267–300.

Sellers, C. (2003) 'September 11 and the History of Hazard', *Journal of the History of Medicine*, 58(4): 449–58.

Sengupta, J. (2002) 'Gay Rights and European Citizenship', *The Gay & Lesbian Review Worldwide*, 9(6): 28–31.

Shorter, E. (1975) *The Making of the Modern Family*, Basic Books, New York.

Tandon, R. and Kumi, N. (1999) 'What Is Good Governance?', *Foreign Policy*, Fall: 16.

Turner, B. (1999) 'McCitizens: risk, coolness and irony in contemporary politics', in B. Smart (ed.) *Resisting McDonaldisation*, Sage, London.

Waites, M. (2000) 'Homosexuality and the New Right: The Legacy of the 1980s for New Delineations of Homophobia', *Sociological Research Online* 5(1), http://www.socresonline.org.uk/5/1/waites.html

Waters, M. (1995) *Globalisation*, Routledge, London.

Waters, M.J. (1997) 'Inequality after Class', in Owen, D. *Sociology after Postmodernism*, Sage, London.

Willis, P. (1977) *Learning to Labour: How Working-Class Kids Get Working-Class Jobs*, Saxon House, Farnborough.

Winkelmann, R. (2001) 'Immigration policies and their impact: the case of New Zealand and Australia', in Djajic, S. (ed.) *International Migration: Trends, Policy, and Economic Impact,* Routledge, London.

Wise, S. (2000) ' "New Right" or "Backlash"? Section 28, Moral Panic and "Promoting Homosexuality" ', *Sociological Research Online,* 5(1), http://www.socresonline.org.uk/5/1/wise.html

Wolf, N. (1990) *The Beauty Myth: How Images of Beauty are Used against Women*, Vintage, London.

Wyness, M. (1999) 'Childhood, agency and education reform', *Childhood*, 6(3): 353–68.

Zarb, G. (1993) 'Ageing with a Disability', in Johnson, J. and Slater, P., *Ageing and Later Life*, Sage, London.

Conclusions

This book is about attempting to understand and explain social divisions. Modernity is driven by a striving for stable classifactory systems and for order, in addition modernity has an uneasiness with ambiguities and ambivalence which disturbs and destabilises neat boundaries and borders. Modern people do not respond to each other as individuals but have a tendency to view others in terms of a category. These modern classifications are essential in character, we assume that a surface difference reflects a deeper understanding of the nature of a person.

Social divisions are sets of categories. Social categories are not simply given, they have to be established and maintained and the process through which they appear is known as *social division*. Foucault attempts to explain how the state in modern societies controls behaviour of people through knowledge-power by transforming people into subjects of the state. His central unit of analysis is *discourse* – a set of rules that set boundaries on how to think and speak about categories of people. Foucault does not make a judgment about the underlying validity of theories; he is for the most part concerned with the central role such discourses have in maintaining power relationships. The most effective, durable and enduring social divisions are the ones that we believe are rooted in nature. Such divisions are believed to be based upon categories that are beyond the control, or choice, of the individual human agent. However, as we have seen in each chapter, 'the body' is not simply a biologically given thing, nor is the body a universal thing that is *essentially* the same at all times and in all places. The body is a constructed phenomenon, and historical object developed within a given historical and cultural context of social division, understood by reference to discourses of the body.

ACTIVITY

What Is Identity?

Identity is about belonging, about what you have in common with some people and what differentiates you from others. At its most basic it gives you a sense of personal location, the stable core to your individuality. But it is also about your social relationships, your complex involvement with others. (Jeffrey Weeks quoted in Bradley 1996: 24)

Identity is a point of *suture*: 'between the social and the psychic. Identity is the sum of the (temporary) positions offered by a social discourse in which you are willing for the moment to invest.' (Hall 1997: 401)

Harriet Bradley (1996) looks at gender, race and class as 'discursive categories' and argues that social identities can be analysed on three levels:

- **Passive identities:** people may recognise class inequality, but may not think of themselves as having a class identity
- **Active identities:** when people act because they have an identity forced upon them or are discriminated against because of some aspect of themselves such as race
- **Politicised identities:** identities that are formed through political involvement in groups such as Outrage.

Question:

➤ Is your identity formed in relation to social divisions? State the reasons for your answer.

Ideas about the nature of social division are used as resources in a process of self-definition that has come to be known as *subjectification*. One important element of social division is how individual people as agents within a social structure attempt to define themselves in relation to a range of powerful discourses. However, this concept of subjectification is not solely about self-definition; subjectification is only possible in relation to social division. The social construction of alterity is directly related to both order and social division. In summary, the processes of alterity/subjectification are the essence of social division and the purpose of these processes is to restrict the individual agency from fully *becoming*. Social division gives the processes of subjectification a degree of objectivity it may otherwise lack and links subjectification to alterity. The individual has the restriction of social division placed upon them, which they experience directly through the processes of subjectification.

The impact of globalisation on social division has been less well investigated. Globalisation has demonstrated the arbitrary nature of social division. Many feminists would argue that global capitalism is a socially constructed process that relies upon conventional patriarchal meanings.

All of us have some link to a nation state, a class, a sexuality, a race, an ethnicity and any number of other categories. Some social divisions are formal, often legally defined and policed, others are informal and blurred. For a long time I assumed that social divisions apply to *other* people and not to me. We only accept the notion of a plurality of human beings and the differences between people when we accept that social division is morally and politically valid. In this book I have attempted to undermine the notion of 'natural' and 'invisible' or 'non-problematic' categories of people and the social division that such categorisation gives rise to. I have attempted to demonstrate that all of us are involved in a process of social division. In Giddens's terminology, the process of social division is *instantiated* in people's life histories, social division is both a *medium* and an *outcome* of processes we all participate in everyday. We live in a world with social division because people like you and me invent, impose and regulate such divisions; people like you and me create the category of the *Other* – people who often, with the guidance of the state, we may learn to fear, despise, patronise or criminalise. I have attempted to identify the categorising processes that underpin social division.

As we have seen in each chapter, people differ in many ways; many differences take on a *relational form* where we differentiate *ourselves* from *others* who are thought to share a common feature that makes them superior or inferior. Differences of this kind are *social divisions* and they share a number of common features:

- They are found in all social, historical and cultural setting
- They are significant for the lives of individuals
- They can be institutionalised and well-established by legal codes
- They are connected with inequality and injustice
- They are connected with processes of social change
- They can be material, cultural and social in nature
- They form the basis for the allocation of *resource* in its widest sense of the term, including the scarce resources of prestige, admiration and respect.

In sharp contrast to the argument that the origin of social division is found in discourse, Maxine Sheets-Johnstone is highly critical of the 'linguistic turn'. She argues that we need to develop a corporeal analysis of the tactile-kinesthetic nature of the body; the living body is a *semantic template* of bodily logos:

> [T]here is an indissoluble bond between hominid thinking and hominid evolution, a bond cemented by the living body ... The *tactile-kinesthetic body* is the sentiently felt body, the body that knows the world through touch and movement. (Sheets-Johnstone 1990: 4–5; italics in original)

She argues that analogical thinking is basically corporeal; tool-making developed from our experience of the hardness of the teeth compared with the softness of the tongue, and enumeration takes place only on and with the tactile-kinesthetic body: 'One-to-one corporeal ratios were the conceptual ground of numerical thinking' (ibid.: 85–6). Drawing upon Piaget's example of a young child opening its mouth in harmony with its opening of a matchbox, Sheets-Johnstone similarly argues that the ability of paleolithic people to create cave drawings and other pictorial art forms also develops from corporeal meanings derived from the tactile-kinesthetic body. On the important question of how people get from corporeal experiences to concepts, Maxine Sheets-Johnstone argues that iconic spatio-kinetic corporeal representation is thus evident all the way from mimicry through display and gestural language to hominid primordial language.

Subjective reality has an impact upon individuals' perception of their own body. Sheets-Johnstone assumes that she can view the body in the same manner as the first hominids and that there was one valid and commonly accepted hominid vision of the body. There is no reason to accept this assumption. In addition, are our ideas of racism, sexism, homophobia, ageism and such like, concepts or 'iconic spatio-kinetic corporeal representations'? Do such discriminatory ideas have their origins within the human body? Or are there forces at work from within institutions such as the family, the state, the criminal justice system, the education system, and the 'caring' professions, that are attempting to mould our subjective reality?

Deleuze and Guattari criticise the discourses and institutions that repress desire and proliferate fascist subjectivies. The state attempts to control and limits becoming or the processes of self-production, by the use of what Deleuze terms the 'abstract machine'. The state involves itself in such processes of subjectification because of the fear that we may become nomads. The state attempts to place each and every one of us upon the 'line of organisation', killing our desire and attempting to make us internalise the state's preferred way of living a life. So that *becoming* becomes socialisation into accepted forms of organisation and not a free process of individuation. Social division is a central element of the 'abstract machine'. The process of social division involves placing both ourselves and others into appropriate categories that restrict our subjective reality, behaviour and our becoming.

The conclusion to this book is that social divisions are *sets of categories*. The social construction of alterity is directly related to both order and social division. Social division is a central element of the 'abstract machine'. Our individual life histories which are linked to social division, our participation in discourses of appropriate ways of behaving for people within a division, and the resources that we draw upon to make our discourses appear and feel valid and reliable, are both a *medium* and an *outcome* of dividing processes.

References

Bradley, H. (1996) *Fractured Identities: Changing Patterns of Inequality*, Polity Press, Cambridge.
Pilloud, S. and Louis-Courvoisier, M. (2003) 'The Intimate Experience of the Body in the Eighteenth Century: between Interiority and Exteriority', *Medical History* 47(4): 451–72.
Sheets-Johnstone, M. (1990) *The Roots of Thinking*, Temple University Press, Philadelphia.

Index